MANAGING EMERGENCIES AND CRISES

Naim Kapucu, PhD

Founding Director, Center for Public and Nonprofit Management
University of Central Florida
Orlando, Florida

Alpaslan Özerdem, PhD

Professor of Peacebuilding, Centre for Peace and Reconciliation Studies
Coventry University
Coventry, United Kingdom

JONES & BARTLETT
LEARNING

World Headquarters
Jones & Bartlett Learning
5 Wall Street
Burlington, MA 01803
978-443-5000
info@jblearning.com
www.jblearning.com

Jones & Bartlett Learning books and products are available through most bookstores and online booksellers. To contact Jones & Bartlett Learning directly, call 800-832-0034, fax 978-443-8000, or visit our website, www.jblearning.com.

Substantial discounts on bulk quantities of Jones & Bartlett Learning publications are available to corporations, professional associations, and other qualified organizations. For details and specific discount information, contact the special sales department at Jones & Bartlett Learning via the above contact information or send an email to specialsales@jblearning.com.

This publication is designed to provide accurate and authoritative information in regard to the Subject Matter covered. It is sold with the understanding that the publisher is not engaged in rendering legal, accounting, or other professional service. If legal advice or other expert assistance is required, the service of a competent professional person should be sought.

Production Credits
Publisher: Michael Brown
Managing Editor: Maro Gartside
Editorial Assistant: Chloe Falivene
Production Assistant: Rebekah Linga
Marketing Manager: Grace Richards
Manufacturing and Inventory Control Supervisor: Amy Bacus
Artist: diacriTech
Composition: Cenveo Publisher Services
Cover Design: Kristin E. Parker
Permissions and Photo Researchers: Amy Mendosa and Lian Bruno
Cover Image: Man cleaning oil spill: Courtesy of Leif Skoogfors/FEMA; Wildfire: © Peter Weber/ShutterStock, Inc.; Flooding/Florida Ave: © Caitlin Mirra/ShutterStock, Inc.; Tornado: © lafoto/ShutterStock, Inc.; Fema sign: © Robert A. Mansker/ShutterStock, Inc.
Printing and Binding: Malloy, Inc.
Cover Printing: Malloy, Inc.

Library of Congress Cataloging-in-Publication Data

Kapucu, Naim.
  Managing emergencies and crises / Naim Kapucu and Alpaslan Ozerdem.
     p. ; cm.
  Includes bibliographical references and index.
  ISBN 978-0-7637-8155-2 (paper)
  1. Emergency management. 2. Crisis management. 3. Disasters I. Ozerdem, Alpaslan. II. Title.
  [DNLM: 1. Disasters. 2. Civil Defense—organization & administration. 3. Disaster Planning—organization & administration. 4. Emergencies. 5. Relief Work—organization & administration. WA 295]
  HV551.2.K384 2012
  363.34'8—dc23

                    2011027797

6048

Printed in the United States of America
15   10 9 8 7 6 5 4 3 2

Dedicated to

Ayşegül Kapucu
and
Mahmure Özerdem

Contents

Acknowledgments

We acknowledge the assistance of our graduate students, Erlan Bakiev, Fatih Demiröz, Vener Garayev, Sana Khosa, and Samuel Turner in undertaking research for this book. Their diligent work played a critical role in its preparation, and they carried out their role with a high level of enthusiasm and academic excellence. We acknowledge Professor Richard T. Sylves's contribution of reviewing questions in the book. We'd also like to thank the six reviewers whose comments have strengthened the manuscript. Finally, we would like to express our gratitude to the team at Jones & Bartlett Learning: Catie Heverling, Chloe Falivene, Teresa Reilly, and Rebekah Linga, for their excellent support throughout this project.

Reviewers

Evan D. Duff, EdD
Dean of Extended Education, Assistant Professor
School of Business
Mount Olive College

Richard W. Hally, MS
Professor
Department of Fire Science
Manchester Community College

Olurominiyi Ibitayo, PhD
Professor
School of Public Affairs
Texas Southern University

Paulette Laubsch, DPA
Director, MSHS
School of Administrative Science
Fairleigh Dickinson University

Joseph D. Macri, PhD
Professor
Online Learning
DeVry University

John P. Tiefenbacher, PhD
Professor, Director
Department of Geography
Texas State University

This book is structured and written in such a way that each chapter can be read separately, which we think is essential to respond to the needs of busy professionals and academics. Reading all chapters consecutively is our recommendation, but if you prefer to go directly to the topics and issues that are most relevant to you, such a targeted study will still provide a picture of the wider emergency management issues covered in other chapters. This broader scope is essential to provide a level of general contextualization in each chapter. Although focusing on only certain areas of the book offers a faster and more effective way of reaching the information you find most relevant to your circumstances, this strategy has the inevitable consequence of repetition of some key issues, processes, and phases between chapters.

Chapter 1

Introduction

A wide range of natural hazards, of both sudden onset (earthquakes, tornados, tsunamis, and floods) and slow onset (global climate change, environmental degradation, and deforestation), continue to pose a major risk to the lives and livelihoods of large populations around the world. Coupled with human-made disasters that are caused by technological failures (industrial accidents, spillages, explosions, and fires), the new security phenomenon of the post–September 11, 2001 context has extended the scope of emergencies, such as those based on violence (terrorism, insurgency, and civil strife). Consequently, the scale, frequency, and intensity of crises faced by the world have dramatically increased over the last decade, and there is a critical need for a careful stock-taking on disaster-management knowledge. With this purpose in mind, the aim of this book is to present the experience of emergency management from a continental perspective by focusing on the emergency response systems, processes, and actors primarily in the context of the United States, with additional examples from Europe and other continents.

In the face of these geological, climatic, environmental, and security hazards, policy makers and practitioners on both sides of the Atlantic need to revisit the understanding of hazard, vulnerability, risk, and disaster management. Owing to its collateral and indirect effects, a seemingly rapid-onset disaster can easily turn into a protracted emergency situation, as disasters can exacerbate the physical, sociopolitical, economic, and environmental vulnerabilities of societies, making them prone to other types of hazards. For example, an earthquake may propagate other hazards, some of which may occur immediately (such as a tsunami), and others that will arise over the medium to long term (such as landslides and political unrest). If disaster mitigation, preparedness, response, and recovery are undertaken in an ad hoc and inappropriate way, it can do more harm than good. Consequently, populations could be trapped in highly vulnerable living conditions.

This book approaches the subject from a "social" rather than a "natural" phenomenon perception, putting the main emphasis on the "vulnerability" aspect of disasters instead of concentrating on "hazards" as the term is conventionally applied. Consequently, the exploration of institutional, sociocultural, and political characteristics of responding to crises more effectively forms the main thrust of discussions in this book.

Before understanding crisis or disaster management, we must define crisis and disaster. Coombs (1999) suggests that crises are perceptual; thus industrial or natural disasters are not accepted as crises by some. "A crisis is the perception of an unpredictable event that threatens important expectancies of stakeholders and can seriously impact an organization's performance and generate negative outcomes" (Coombs, 1999, p. 2). Crises are unpredicted, but they must also be expected. In differentiating between a crisis and an incident, the latter is defined as a minor, localized disruption (Bazerman & Watkins, 2004; Coombs, 1999). Time pressures and limited control are the prevailing barriers to crisis resolution (Burnett, 1998). Parsons (1996) divides crises into three types: immediate, emerging, and sustained. Immediate crises occur when we are unable to research the problem and certainly will not have a detailed plan prepared, well rehearsed, and ready to snap into action. Emerging crises occur slowly but are no more predictable than immediate crises, which makes response activities difficult. Sustained crises can last weeks, months, or even years.

In contrast, Faulkner (2001) compares crises and disasters by their nature. As shown in **Figure 1-1**, Faulkner defines a crisis as a situation where the cause is self-inflicted, a result of incompetence in management structures. In contrast, disasters refer to such situations where an enterprise is confronted with sudden and uncontrollable catastrophic changes.

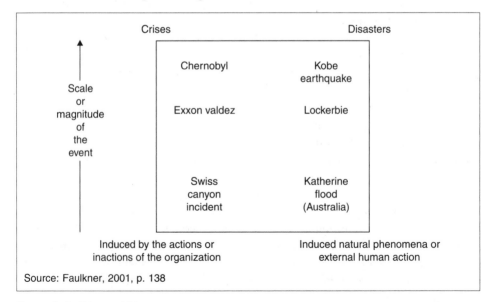

Figure 1-1 *Crises and Disasters*

In disaster response, each activity is supposed to be governed by a set of policies and procedures under the auspices of a lead agency. A myriad of governmental, international, and local organizations take part, each with its own specific roles and responsibilities. Who is responsible for which activity, with which means, and what are some of the key considerations to be borne in mind in the planning and implementation of disaster response? In the emergency phase, ensuring the survival of the maximum number of "victims," resuming the provision of basic services and infrastructure, protecting and assisting vulnerable groups, and paving the way for a speedy and effective reconstruction are some of the primary objectives.

This book demonstrates how practice fares against the theory of emergency management, utilizing wide experiences from the United States, Europe, and some select international cases. In these analyses, the discussion explores state–civil society cooperation and the effectiveness of existing prevention and preparedness mechanisms. As such, the specific roles attributed to governmental, international, and private-sector participants at a legislative level and the activities by which actors conduct their work together are explored.

Experience shows that the successful management of routine and catastrophic disasters is closely linked to the way leadership and decision making is structured and communicated. It is often the case that from mitigation to response, a wide range of myths exist among civil society and disaster management organizations about each other's roles, capacities, and capabilities. Therefore, this book deals with a series of misconceptions about how different stakeholders could and should take part in crisis and emergency management through a number of case studies.

Finally, having reviewed the experience of responding to disasters in varying contexts, this book addresses the ethical concerns of contemporary disaster response in terms of accountability, politicization, corruption, and humanitarian imperative. These areas are the sources of some of the most common criticisms in emergency response around the world; consequently, it is necessary to set the framework for an effective emergency management organization after investigating the possible methods to avoid such shortcomings. In terms of ways to improve current practice, the book takes an agency-centric perspective and elaborates on recommendations related to contingency planning, training, decision making, and coordination. Furthermore, future directions for development are considered by focusing on the crisis management systems in the United States and in Europe.

To lay the foundations for future discussions, Chapter 2 presents an overview of the principal hazards, vulnerabilities, and risks in the United States and Europe, elaborating on key terminology and concepts. To elucidate how to deal with emergencies more effectively and link response with recovery, it is imperative that the book explores the concept of vulnerability and investigates the role it plays in the creation of disasters. More importantly, how vulnerability could be tackled in the response and recovery phases, so that disaster-affected societies can have a real hope for an effective, relevant, and sustainable rebuilding, is the main question that Chapter 2 seeks to answer (Alexander, 1997). This general review of principal hazards that affect the United States and European countries also includes the increased focus on terrorism as the most high-profile hazard in modern society.

Chapter 3 focuses on the mitigation and preparedness phases of emergencies and crises. In general, mitigation is the initial phase of all-hazards emergency management, although it may be a component in the other phases as well, and should be considered long before an emergency occurs so as to eliminate or reduce the probability of the occurrence of an emergency or disaster. Mitigation includes activities designed to postpone, dissipate, or lessen the effects of a disaster or emergency. Preventing the development of hazardous areas, such as homes built on floodplains, or adjusting the use of these areas, such as by elevating structures, can reduce the incidence of flood damage. Meanwhile, preparedness focuses on planning how to respond in case of an emergency or disaster, and developing capabilities and programs that contribute to a more effective response. Preparedness offers insurance against emergencies, as mitigation activities cannot always prevent emergencies from happening (Quarantelli, 1998; Waugh, 1994). Thus the objective in Chapter 3 is to explore these two key phases of disaster management by investigating the issues of cooperation, collaboration, and communications in a national response framework. How emergency operations are activated and run and which roles can be designated at intergovernmental and interorganizational levels are also covered in this chapter.

Chapter 4 elaborates on the context of activities in disaster response and recovery. Response is the first phase and occurs when the disaster is imminent or soon after its onset. The typical activities in this phase are intended to minimize the risks created in an emergency by protecting the people, environment, and property, and to provide emergency assistance for disaster victims. The response phase also includes efforts to reduce the probability or extent of secondary damage through such measures as security patrols to prevent looting, and to reduce damage with efforts such as sandbagging against impending floodwaters or remedial movement of shelters in heavily contaminated fallout areas, or other measures that will enhance future recovery operations, such as damage assessment. Recovery activities continue beyond the emergency period immediately following a disaster. Their purpose is to return all systems—informal and formal—to as near their normal state as possible. They can be broken down into short-term and long-term activities. Short-term activities attempt to return vital human systems to minimal operating standards and usually encompass approximately a two-week period. With specific reference to the state–civil society relationship in the context of the relief-to-reconstruction continuum, Chapter 4 incorporates response and recovery experiences from a number of post-disaster environments.

The first section of this book concludes with Chapter 5, which focuses on myths and demands within emergency preparedness and response so as to present a holistic picture of a wide range of responsibilities and roles by different actors, putting emphasis on the neglected yet critical involvement of affected communities themselves. Overall, the public in the developed world increasingly expects better public-sector leadership before, during, and after emergencies (Kapucu & Van Wart, 2006). Public participation in all phases of disaster management represents an important step toward more effective and collaborative disaster response (Col, 2007). As leaders of first-response activities, local administrators should have basic scientific knowledge of possible disasters that might happen in their region. In the United States, homeland security is now considered a national responsibility, and is "about the integration of a nation and a world—driven by a philosophy of shared responsibility, shared leadership, and shared accountability—in essence, a renewed commitment to the federalism upon which our nation was founded" (Ridge, 2004). What such integration means to different societies is explained by exploring the concept of community resilience. The discussions in Chapter 5 show that efforts to create disaster-resilient communities have not always been successful because of government neglect of three important facts about people: 1. often people do not act rationally; 2. people are not completely obedient; and 3. people are culturally, socioeconomically, and intellectually very diverse. At the same time, as argued in this chapter, it is not solely the government's responsibility to perform emergency management functions, and society as a whole should be engaged in all phases of emergency management, necessitating education on the prevention of potential environmental hazards (Özerdem & Jacoby, 2006).

The second section of this book addresses issues related to decision-making processes with specific reference to leadership and challenges faced in the interaction between individual and institutional levels of emergency management stakeholders. Chapter 6 presents an overview of such stakeholders at local, state, federal, and private-sector levels and their responsibilities, as well as investigating the role of the local emergency program manager. The task for leaders of agencies is to respond to a disaster in ways that protect and preserve lives and properties. Local authorities and disaster-affected people are often the first responders. In the United States, for example, if the mission is largely federal in nature, the response operations can be federalized. In European countries, the main response would be national, but supranational structures for major disasters could be activated, if required. In most U.S. states, county governments are responsible for coordinating emergency response operations, and some major cities have their own emergency operations centers. Unfortunately, disasters tend to easily overwhelm the resources and capabilities of local governments, so they rely on assistance from state governments, with some emergencies requiring federal government intervention as well. High standards of responsiveness and the ubiquitous media compel political leaders and administrative heads to coordinate resources effectively. Thousands of organizations are currently engaged in monitoring known and suspected hazards, and encouraging hazard reduction. Nonprofit voluntary groups range from large environmental groups to small church or community organizations. Some offer highly specialized disaster-related skills, such as search and rescue, amateur radio communications, and emergency feeding or shelter, whereas others are much broader in scope (Comfort, 2006).

Chapter 6 explores how coordination of the massive number of public, nonprofit, and private organizations involved in catastrophic disasters requires both horizontal and vertical communication and decision making (Christoplos, 2003).

The nature of disasters necessitates the involvement of various sectors, organizations, and stakeholders; thus collaboration plays an important role in achieving success. With this point in mind, Chapter 7 unpacks the process of decision making in managing disasters and crises. The chapter investigates the main decision-making styles and attributes of an effective decision maker, and explores the challenges of ethical decision making and problem solving.

Chapter 8 builds upon this discussion by focusing on the main styles of decision making in emergencies: transformational leadership; the ability to inspire a sense of common vision and mission; a decentralized approach that engages organizational members; and charisma. During this coverage, it is asked whether the U.S. military's leadership approach might be effective in disasters due to its centralized command and control structure and its emphasis on training and leadership at all levels. Conversely, a flexible leadership approach is vital for understanding the varying leadership roles across the four intertwined phases of emergency management (Derthick, 2007; Waugh & Streib, 2006). Using a number of case studies, the importance of "executive powers" for timely and effective decisions in response to disasters is explored in depth in Chapter 8.

A key task of emergency management is to ensure that the public is adequately prepared for impending disasters so that loss of life and property is minimized. Governments have an important role to fulfill in collecting and disseminating this kind of information (Boin, Hart, Sterm, & Sundelius, 2005). A recurring theme in many analyses, such as those undertaken in the wake of Hurricane Andrew in 1992 and the September 11, 2001 terrorist attacks, is that information collection and sharing were deficient. Indeed, the inability to obtain and disseminate accurate rescue and recovery information is partly to blame for the slow governmental rescue and recovery response during Hurricane Katrina in 2005. Chapter 9 argues that a governance approach should be adopted in both building infrastructure and sharing the disaster risk (Comfort, 2006). A shared vision should be built among public, nonprofit, and private organizations to ensure a sustainable civil infrastructure and reduce the risk of disasters. Furthermore, Chapter 9 examines how the relationship between people and sources of information can influence hazard preparedness. Because trust in civic emergency planning agencies influences preparedness, the relationships among people, civic agencies, and the information provided must be considered when planning communication. Familiarity with information about hazards underlines the relative importance of trust; moreover, levels of trust are influenced by community characteristics (Paton, 2007).

The third and final section of this book focuses on institutional aspects of emergency and crisis management in terms of team building, accountability, evaluation, collaboration at the international level, and future challenges. Effective disaster management requires an ability to assess and adapt capacity rapidly, restore or enhance disrupted or inadequate communications, utilize flexible decision-making processes, and expand coordination and trust of emergency response agencies. These requirements are imposed upon conventional bureaucratic systems that rely on relatively rigid plans, exact decision-making protocols, and formal relationships that assume uninterrupted communications. Yet, "in crises circumstances the disparities between demand and supply of public resources are much bigger, the situation remains unclear and volatile, and the time to think, consult, and gain acceptance for decisions is highly restricted" (Boin et al., 2005, p. 11).

Chapter 10 examines the U.S. National Response Plan (NRP), which establishes a comprehensive, all-hazards approach to enhance the United States' ability to manage domestic incidents. This plan places a strong emphasis on the coordination and integration of capabilities at all levels of government, private organizations, nonprofit organizations, and individual citizens. Local governments play an important role, as the plan calls for handling all incidents at the lowest possible organizational and jurisdictional level. To support this strategy, a variety of coordination mechanisms link local responses to federal capabilities for intelligence gathering and incidence response National Academy of Public Administration (NAPA, 2004). The NRP encompasses several key concepts: threat assessment strategies; incident reporting; vertical and horizontal communication and information sharing; training and exercising; mitigation strategies; organization and planning to mobilize resources at different levels; response and recovery activities; safety of personnel and the population; and hazard-specific components of the preceding elements.

Response to disasters is not a simple task that any single organization could handle alone, but rather requires the involvement of a network of well-coordinated organizations. Chapter 11 argues that this interaction often brings a clash between bureaucratic and collaborative cultures. In a bureaucratic culture, performance is measured based on the expectations of the supervisor. In contrast, in a collaborative network, performance is measured based on the collective mission and goal. The status is not important in networks; instead, the contribution to attaining collective goals is seen as essential. Thus accountability in a network organization is a matter of contributions. Chapter 11 explains the complexity of ethical concerns in the context of disaster management. For example, in public–public partnerships, hierarchical and professional accountability obstructs partnership development, whereas political accountability facilitates partnership development. In public–private partnerships, legal, professional, and political accountability promotes partnership development, whereas hierarchical accountability impedes it. In private–private partnerships, which are characterized by an absence of hierarchical accountability, legal and political accountability works toward partnership development. Moreover, from the collection of funding to its delivery, the assistance of relief and reconstruction is often open to manipulation and corruption. Using a number of different

examples, Chapter 11 focuses on the issues of accountability, professional misconduct, and ethical dilemmas.

Disaster management has become increasingly international in scope. Disaster-
affected countries typically require international coordination and collaboration to
ensure effective mitigation and response operations. In an attempt to contribute to
the knowledge in international emergency management and improve governance of
response operations, Chapter 12 identifies current systems of international disaster
management with regard to coordination, collaboration, and networking capacities.
It closely examines the major actors and the activities of international organizations
such as the United Nations (UN), North Atlantic Treaty Organization (NATO), World
Bank, International Federation of Red Cross and Red Crescent Societies (IFRC),
and World Health Organization (WHO) in managing international disasters and coordinating initiatives to do so. This study then identifies problems in the system in
terms of coordination and collaboration, and proposes ways of effectively resolving
them. This chapter benefits significantly from an article in the *International Journal
of Emergency Management* (Kapucu, 2011).

Finally, Chapter 13 discusses future directions in emergency and crisis management based on the coverage in this book. These considerations can be classified as
challenges and opportunities at the global, national, and professional levels. Many
of the trends identified by emergency management scholars in the early 1990s continue to dominate emergency management today, including increased exposure to
environmental hazards, increased capabilities offered by advanced emergency management information technology, increased recognition of the need for pre-impact
action in the face of inertia or outright resistance, and the increased professionalization of the emergency management field. Nonetheless, some new issues have
emerged that must be addressed, including the potential for changes in the nature
of environmental hazards and the increased salience of terrorism as a threat to communities throughout the United States and Europe and in other regions.

References

Alexander, D. (1997). The study of natural disasters, 1977–1997: Some reflections on a changing
field of knowledge. *Disasters, 21*(4), 284–304.

Bazerman, M. H. and M.D. Watkins. (2004). *Predictable Surprises: The Disaster you should have
Seen Coming and How To Prevent Them.* Boston: Harvard Business School Press.

Boin, A., Hart, P., Sterm, E., & Sundelius, B. (2005). *The politics of crisis management: Public
leadership under pressure.* New York: Cambridge University Press.

Burnett, J. J. (1998). A Strategic Approach to Managing Crises. *Public Relations Review, 24*(4),
475–488.

Christoplos, I. (2003). Actors in risk. In M. Pelling (Ed.), *Natural disasters and development in a
globalizing world* pp. 95–109. London: Routledge.

Col, J. M. (2007). Managing disasters: The role of local government. *Public Administration Review, 67*(suppl), 114–124.

Comfort, L. K. (2006). Cities at risk: Hurrican Katrina and the drowning of New Orleans. *Urban Affairs Review, 41*(4), 501–516.

Coombs, T. (1999). *Ongoing crisis communication: Planning, managing and responding.* Thousand Oakes, CA: Sage.

Derthick, M. (2007). Where federalism didn't fail. *Public Administration Review, 67*(suppl), 36–47.

Faulkner, B. (2001). Towards a framework for tourism disaster management. *Tourism Management, 22*(2), 135–147.

Kapucu, N. (2011). Collaborative governance in international disasters: Nargis cyclone in Myanmar and Sichuan earthquake in China cases. *International Journal of Emergency Management. 8*(1): 1-25.

Kapucu, N., & Van Wart, M. (2006). The emerging role of the public sector in managing extreme events: Lessons learned. *Administration & Society, 38*(3), 279–308.

National Academy of Public Administration (NAPA). (2004). *Advancing management of homeland security: Managing intergovernmental relations for homeland security.* Washington, DC: Author.

Özerdem, A., & Jacoby, T. (2006). *Disaster management and civil society: Earthquake relief in Japan, Turkey and India.* London: I. B. Tauris.

Parsons, W. (1996). *Crisis management. Career Development International.* 1, 5, 26–28.

Paton, D. (2007). Preparing for natural hazards: The role of community trust. *Disaster Prevention and Management, 16*(3), 370–379.

Quarantelli, E. L. (1998). *What is a disaster? Perspectives on the question.* London: Routledge.

Ridge, T. 2004. *Remarks by Secretary of Homeland Security Tom Ridge at the American Association of Port Authorities Spring Conference.* Retrieved May 19, 2011 from http://www.dhs.gov/xnews/releases/press_release_0379.shtm.

Waugh, W. L., & Streib, G. (2006). Collaboration and leadership for effective emergency management. *Public Administration Review, Special Issue,* 131–140.

Chapter 2

Hazards, Vulnerability, and Disaster Risk

Chapter Objectives

- Analyze hazards, vulnerabilities, and risks.
- Understand hydrologic, geophysical, biological, and technological hazards.
- Identify causes and effects of different types of hazards, including floods, earthquakes, tsunamis, hurricanes, tornados, and wildfires.
- Understand and contrast physical, structural, and social vulnerabilities.
- Discuss how community hazards and vulnerability analyses are conducted and identify emergency management interventions.

Introduction

This chapter describes the principal environmental, technological, and human-made hazards that are of greatest concern to emergency managers in communities throughout the United States and Europe. Each of these hazards is described in terms of the physical processes that generate it, the geographical areas that are most commonly at risk, the types of impacts and typical magnitude of hazard events, and hazard-specific issues of emergency response. The chapter also describes how pre-impact conditions act together with event-specific conditions to produce a disaster's physical and social consequences, which ideally can be mitigated by emergency management interventions. In addition, this chapter discusses how emergency managers can assess the pre-impact conditions that produce disaster vulnerabilities within their communities, before concluding with a discussion of vulnerability dynamics and methods for disseminating hazard/vulnerability information.

Hazards

Hazards are potentially damaging physical events, phenomena, or human activities that cause loss of life, injury, property damage, social and economic disruption, or environmental degradation (Makoka & Kaplan, 2005). They are external factors that affect the society or elements at risk, whereas vulnerabilities are the internal factors that affect the transformation of hazards into disasters. In other words, vulnerabilities determine a hazard's impact on the society or element at risk (Birkman, 2007; Lauire, 2003). Although communities might experience any of numerous hazards, it is important for a region to be aware of those threats that are most likely to affect the community most severely. Ordinarily, a differentiation will be made between "natural" and "human-made" hazards. Hazards that fall within the natural classification are those that occur as part of our environment; human-made hazards are those that arise directly from human activity.

The term "natural disaster" is widely described by scholars as a misnomer, as it can confuse perceptions and divert courses of action (Alexander, 1997; Apthorpe, 1998). This potential is due to the necessity to discriminate between a hazard and a disaster; whereas a hazard can be an environmental event, a disaster is the culmination of a hazard and the existing human vulnerabilities. Thus the categorization here refers explicitly to natural hazards rather than disasters to avoid conflicting understandings.

Natural hazards—floods, earthquakes, tsunamis, volcanic hazards, hurricanes, tornados, and wildfires—can have varying levels of predictability that some human-made disasters lack. For example, modern technology has allowed us to know when hurricanes have formed in the open ocean and the general direction in which these hurricanes are heading. Although predicting these paths can be difficult, residents can nevertheless be alerted ahead of time to start preparations. Furthermore, other naturally occurring phenomena such as floods and volcanic eruptions can be anticipated on some level. In contrast, just like many terrorist incidents, natural hazards can strike with very little or no warning. Examples include earthquakes, tornados, and flash floods.

Natural hazards are impossible to prevent. Human control over the occurrence of natural events is very limited, necessitating a focus on the mitigation, preparedness, response, and recovery actions for natural hazards rather than prevention. Prevention is possible for human-made hazards, as they include an inherent human factor. Technological threats are not as frequent as natural ones, but it is still vitally important that communities be prepared for them. Even though these threats come to fruition less frequently, they often result in higher casualties and greater fallout due to the high danger to individuals' lives that they pose (Bullock, Haddow, Coppola, Ergin, Westerman, & Yeletaysi, 2006; Lauire, 2003).

Finally, human-made disasters, in general, can be categorized as either technological or sociological. Technological disasters are the results of failure of technology, such as engineering or structural failures, transport disasters, nuclear accidents, or environmental disasters. Sociological disasters have a strong human motive, such as workforce violence, criminal acts, stampedes, riots, and war (Alexander, 1997, 2002; Waugh, 2000).

Principal Hazards in the United States and Europe

Hazards vary in every region in the world, depending on geographical characteristics. Due to the vast areas they cover, the diversity in their climates, and political issues, the United States and Europe are subject to several different types of hazards. It is vitally important for both the public sector and the private sector in all areas to be aware of the kinds of threats that are most common in their geographic region and to prepare for the occurrence of such hazards. This awareness allows a community to be fully engaged and educated as to how its members might be affected by an emergency. Otherwise, the human, physical, and financial capital of emergency management authorities may prove inadequate for effective emergency management. This section highlights the predominant hazards that threaten the United States and Europe.

Earthquakes

Earthquakes are inevitable, unstoppable, and unpredictable geophysical natural events that occur on the earth's surface. They have devastating effects and cause remarkable impact on the lives of people. An earthquake may inflict high costs in the form of casualties, injuries, and enormous physical damage if it occurs in close proximity to an urban area. The primary threats from an earthquake are ground shaking, surface faulting, and ground failure (Lindell, Prater, & Perry, 2007). Ground shaking can cause a building to collapse if it is not built to withstand the motion of a quake. Surface faulting is the appearance of cracks on the earth's surface, which is a relatively less dangerous and largely avoidable threat. If buildings, utilities, and other facilities are built away from fault lines, the risk associated with surface faulting will be minimized; however, it is not always possible to predict the location of a surface fault. Ground failures entail the subsidence of tracts of land due to plate movement; they can cause buildings to collapse or tilt, as well as provoke landslides. Note that an earthquake itself causes relatively low numbers of casualties, if any; rather, the environment, buildings, and other vulnerabilities exacerbate the consequences of an earthquake.

Tsunamis, landslides, dam failures, hazardous material spills, and fires are secondary hazards that can result from an earthquake. These kinds of disasters can lead to more casualties than the initial earthquakes themselves (Lindell et al., 2007). The destruction of infrastructure as a result of an earthquake can constrain the activities of first responders, whose effectiveness relies upon rapid action, as the majority of the injured people trapped under collapsed buildings will lose their lives if they do not receive aid within 24 hours.

Earthquakes affect both the United States and Europe to a significant extent. Approximately 75 million people living in 39 U.S. states are considered "at risk" from moderate to great earthquakes. In Europe, Greece, Italy, and Turkey are particularly prone to this hazard.

In 1964, the United States experienced the strongest earthquake in its history in Alaska, with 128 people losing their lives as a result of this disaster. The 9.2-magnitude quake initiated a tsunami, taking 15 and 113 lives, respectively (U.S. Geological Survey [USGS], 2009b). The deadliest earthquake, however, was in 1906 in San Francisco, California; it caused the loss of approximately 3000 lives and $524 million in property damage (USGS, 2009a). The most recent fatal earthquakes occurred in California in 1989 and 1994. In 1989, a quake in California's Santa Cruz Mountains in 1989 resulted in 63 deaths, 3757 injuries, and $6 billion in property damage (USGS, 2009c). The 1994 Northridge earthquake in California caused 60 deaths and more than 7000 injuries, left 20,000 people homeless, and cost $20 billion, making the incident the most expensive seismic disaster in U.S. history (FEMA, 2009a; Pacific Earthquake Engineering Research Center [PEER], 2005).

The European continent has records of earthquakes dating back to ancient history, and it continues to suffer their effects to this day. Most recently, in 2009 a 6.3-magnitude quake in L'Aquila, Italy, killed 308, injured 1000, and left 40,000 homeless (USGS, 2009d). The most devastating earthquake in recent years was the 1999 earthquake in Marmara, Turkey. In a country where 65% of the population lives in high-earthquake-risk areas, the Marmara earthquake was the most powerful of the 20th century, killing 17,127, injuring 43,000, and destroying 75,000 buildings (Özerdem & Jacoby, 2006). Other significant events include the earthquake in southern Italy in 1980, which produced 4689 casualties and 7700 injured persons, and that in Bucharest, Romania, in 1977, in which 1581 people were killed and 10,500 were injured (National Geophysical Data Center [NGDC], 2010).

In recent years, some countries have experienced a great deal of destruction and damage due to earthquakes. **Table 2-1** provides a snapshot of the five most destructive earthquakes in terms of fatalities from 2001 until 2011.

Table 2-1 *Five Most Destructive Earthquakes from 2000-2010*

Year	Magnitude	Fatalities	Region
2004	9.1	227,898	Off west coast of northern Sumatra
2010	7.0	222,570	Haiti
2008	7.9	87,587	Eastern Sichuan, China
2005	7.6	80,361	Pakistan
2003	6.6	31,000	Southern Iran

Credit: U.S. Geological Survey Department of the Interior/USGS

Hurricanes

Hurricanes are some of the most dangerous, destructive, and deadly meteorological events. The most severe type of tropical storm, they occur due to a marked temperature increase on the ocean surface. Depending on the category of the hurricane (**Table 2-2**), the wind speed may range from 74 miles/hour to 150 miles/hour or more. Hurricanes are also called cyclones or typhoons in other parts of the world; specifically, Atlantic or Eastern Pacific storms are referred to as hurricanes, Western Pacific storms are called typhoons, and Southern Pacific storms are called cyclones.

A hurricane can cause secondary hazards such as tornadoes, storm surges, flooding, and local ponding (Lindell et al., 2007). Every year, on average, of 10 tropical storms occurring, 6 of them turn into hurricanes. Every three years, 5 hurricanes hit the U.S. coast (Atlantic), and 2 of these 5 hurricanes are classified in Category 3 or higher. These storms can result in millions or even billions of dollars of damage (Federal Emergency Management Agency [FEMA], 2009b). Hurricanes, which are well understood in terms of their occurrence and movement, caused relatively fewer casualties in the 20th century than in previous centuries, but the physical damage attributable to them has increased dramatically in recent decades (Lindell et al., 2007). The development of hurricane modeling and the relatively slow speed at which these storms travel also provide more opportunities for citizens and authorities to prepare for this hazard. Technology assists emergency managers in monitoring potential hurricane activity and issuing warnings, if necessary, although the storms may sometimes develop rapidly. Despite the greater advance warning of their impending arrival, increases in population and urbanization in

Table 2-2 *Categories of Hurricanes*

Category	Speed Range		Description
	Mi/Hr	Km/Hr	
1	74–95	119–153	Very dangerous, some damage
2	96–110	154–177	Extremely dangerous, extensive damage
3	111–130	178–209	Devastating damage
4	131–155	210–249	Catastrophic damage
5	>155	>249	Catastrophic damage

Courtesy of NOAA

hurricane-prone coastal areas have augmented the property damage caused by hurricanes (Lindell et al., 2007).

In the United States, the hurricane with the most disastrous consequences in terms of human fatalities occurred in 1900 in Galveston, Texas, when 6000 persons lost their lives out of a community of 18,000. Hurricane Katrina in 2005, however, was the single most catastrophic natural disaster in U.S. history. More than $6 billion has been provided directly to victims of Hurricane Katrina for housing and other needs through the Individuals and Households Assistance Program. The U.S. Small Business Administration provided $10.4 billion in disaster loans, and the National Flood Insurance Program paid more than $15.3 billion to policy holders in the wake of Katrina (FEMA, 2006). More significantly, the impotence of the authorities in the face of disaster led to criticism that the U.S. response to Katrina was more akin to that of a developing country than the world's foremost superpower (Brodie, Weltzien, Altman, Blendon, & Benson, 2006).

Tornadoes

According to FEMA (2010), tornadoes are the most violent type of storm seen in nature. Tornadoes form through the replacement of descending cold air with rising warm air. Approximately 900 tornadoes occur in the United States annually (Lindell et al., 2007). Texas, Kansas, Arkansas, Oklahoma, Missouri, Florida, and Louisiana are the most tornado-prone U.S. states. Five metropolitan areas in Florida alone are in the top 10 tornado-prone areas ("Colo., Texas Lead the Top 10 Most Tornado Prone Areas," 2009). Tornadoes are frequently reported in the Rocky Mountains as well. In general, the tornado season starts in spring and lasts until summer. Tornadoes may also occur along with hurricanes, but their prediction is not possible. A tornado can form within a few hours without any warning or sign and can cause significant damage within a short period of time. The majority of deaths from these storms occur in mobile homes and poorly constructed buildings (Kusenbach, Simms, & Tobin, 2009).

The deadliest tornado in the U.S. occurred in 1925, impacting three towns in the states of Missouri, Illinois, and Indiana, killing 695 people, and injuring 2027. In 2007, a mile-wide tornado struck Greensburg, Kansas, killing at least 10 people and devastating 95% of the town (Tornado Project, 1999). The number of observed tornadoes throughout the United States has increased in recent years as the midsection and southern parts of the country, commonly referred to as Tornado Alley, have experienced an increase in population (Johnson, April 28, 2011). Six southern states in the United States were impacted by the April 26-28 Tornado outbreak in 2011, making it the biggest natural disaster in the United States since Hurricane Katrina. More than 300 people died across six states (Alabama, Tennessee, Mississippi, Georgia, Virginia and Kentucky) with the highest death toll in Alabama, and thousands were left injured and homeless (Bacon & O'Keefe, 2011). Not all deaths and injuries were caused directly by the tornadoes but were a result of the straight-line winds, hail, flash-floods, and thunderstorms that accompanied the tornadoes. The devastation of these tornadoes is being compared to that caused by Hurricane Katrina, and more than 1,680 people spent April 27, 2011 in Red Cross shelters (Robertson & Severson, April 28, 2011).

Floods

Several different types of floods are distinguished. Riverside flooding occurs when surface runoff rises to flood level, while flash flooding happens when surface runoff becomes a flood in less than 6 hours. Alluvial fan flooding, in contrast, occurs at the foot of steep valleys where deposits of alluvium accumulate. Dam failures are the consequence of accumulated downstream water rising the stream bank. Surface ponding occurs when surface waters cannot drain away, so that they accumulate in a limited area. Fluctuating lake levels can result in seasonal short-term flooding. Lastly, control structure (dams or levees) failures can lead to flooding (Lindell et al., 2007).

Flood risk is assessed based on the number of floods expected every 100 years, based on their incidence over the last century (Lindell et al., 2007). Note that this index does not actively predict flood incidence, but rather acts as a guide to identify flood-prone areas.

Floods are the most common natural hazards in the United States, with 75% of Presidential Disaster Declarations being ordered for such incidents (Lindell et al., 2007). Every year, 100 motorists die in the United States because of floods (Frech, 2005). Figures from the last 30 years indicate that, on average, 127 people lose their lives every year due to flooding in the United States. When compared to the last 30 years' average number of deaths caused by lightning (73 deaths), tornadoes (65 deaths), and hurricane (16 deaths) hazards, the severity of flooding becomes evident (National Oceanic and Atmospheric Administration [NOAA], 2009). Overall, more than 10,000 people have lost their lives in the United States because of floods since 1900. On average, floods cause $2 billion of property damage every year (NOAA, 2009). More than $100 billion damage after Hurricane Katrina was a result of hurricane and flood damage caused by the storm in New Orleans (NOAA, 2009).

The FEMA Mitigation Directorate manages the national Flood Insurance Program (NFIP) to address preparation for and the consequences of flood hazards in the United States. Approximately 20,000 communities participate in this voluntary program by implementing floodplain management. An estimated $1 billion in flood damage has been prevented as a result of NFIP projects and property owners' flood insurance purchases (FEMA, 2009c).

In the period from the 1950s to the 1990s, the number of floods in European river basins dramatically increased, from 11 per decade to 64 per decade (van Alphen, Martini, Loat, Slomp, & Passchier, 2009). During this period and into the early

2000s, there was growing concern about the threat of flooding, as the incidence of such events continued to rise. In August 2002, Europe witnessed its most devastating flooding in recent history, affecting both the Elbe and Danube river basins and resulting in an estimated $16.5 billion of damage. These particular floods were caused by a "Genoa cyclone"—a familiar low-pressure weather system known to have precipitated severe flooding over the last centuries (Becker & Grünewald, 2003). However, similar levels of flooding had been recorded in the past to much less effect, with the difference in damage experienced being attributed to recent settlement development on floodplains. In response to these widespread floods and more recent incidents, the European Commission and national governments have consolidated their approach to mitigating and preparing for floods, including the development of a European Flood Alert System (Elliott & Macpherson, 2010; European Commission, 2008).

Wildfires

Wildfires pose a significant risk to people living close to or using facilities in the wilderness. Wildfires can be classified into three groups: (1) Wildland fires burn nothing except vegetation as fuel; (2) interface fires influence both natural life and built structures; and (3) firestorms are distinguished from other fires by the severity at which they burn, which makes them almost impossible to extinguish (Lindell et al., 2007).

Wildland fires can be further parsed in three groups. First, surface fires are low-intensity hazards, usually burning light fuels with little damage. Second, crown fires usually occur as a result of surface fires and burn down the upper branches of trees, which may fall and cause the fire to spread. Third, ground fires are the least common, yet most dangerous type of fire; they destroy all living creatures on the surface of the ground (U.S. Fire Administration, 2001).

Equally importantly, secondary hazards following wildfires include landslides, erosion, flooding, debris flow, deterioration in water quality, and the introduction of invasive species. These developments exacerbate the consequences of wildfires and hinder recovery actions. In the long term, wildfires' effects include reduced access to recreational areas, damage to community infrastructures, and diminished cultural and economic resources (USGS, 2006).

National forests and grasslands in the United States constitute 193 million acres, an area equivalent to state of Texas (U.S. Forest Service, 2008). From 1960 to 2008, more than 5.3 million wildfires burned through more than 190 million acres. Thus an average of 108,000 wildfires burned approximately 4 million acres every year (National Interagency Fire Center, n.d.). These fires tend to take place in the arid West and Southeast regions. In the western United States, wildland–urban interface (WUI) areas have expanded significantly in the last few decades, as 38% of new home construction has occurred close to WUI areas (U.S. Fire Administration, 2002).

As more people build housing in WUI areas, the job of fire fighters becomes more complex and difficult.

Wildfires are also a common summer threat in southern Europe, predominantly affecting the Iberian peninsula, Italy, and the Balkans (European Commission, 2010). For example, in 2009, bush fires in Greece destroyed 12,000 hectares of forest and a large number of properties. The average area burned every year in Europe is 500,000 hectares (1.2 million acres), by 50,000 fires (European Commission, 2001). Recognizing the dangers and disruption caused by these fires, the European Commission (2000) funds a number of projects to identify high-risk areas, develop accurate systems for fire detection, and coordinate solutions for the control and reduction of fires and restoration of the affected areas.

Human-Made Hazards

Human-made hazards can be the result of an accident, such as an industrial chemical leak or oil spill, or an intentional act. In general, these threats have an element of human intent, negligence, or error, or involve a failure of a human-made system (which is usually a complex one). Such disasters can affect the safety, health, and welfare of people, and cause damage or destruction to property. Overall, they are classified into four groups summarized by the acronym CBRNE: chemical, biological, radioactive/nuclear, and explosive. These hazards include terrorist attacks, which usually have political purposes and target civilians and critical infrastructures. Human-made disasters are the least frequent types of disasters, but can have the most traumatic and remarkable impact on peoples' lives.

Chemical weapons are produced for the purpose of killing, injuring, and incapacitating people. First utilized during World War I, they are relatively easy to produce with readily available chemicals. These substances can be used along with explosives and aerosol devices, and can affect targeted individuals through inhalation, drinking, eating, or direct contact (Bullock et al., 2006; Department of Homeland Security, 2002).

Biological weapons are living organisms that are targeted at humans, crops, and livestock, and cause disease. They not only inflict casualties, but can also result in a large amount of economic damage. The effects of biological weapons may not become evident until a long time after their use, which makes this kind of hazard especially dangerous. Such weapons may also use readily available chemicals, and can be used alongside explosives. To disperse a biological agent effectively through explosives, it is important that a low-order explosive be used so that the biological agent is not completely consumed within the explosion. When an individual is infected by a biological agent, that person may then become contagious to others, multiplying the effect of the initial biological attack (Bullock et al., 2006).

Nuclear and radiological weapons are the most destructive and most difficult to acquire of the CBRNE categories. A nuclear weapon devastates living creatures, infrastructure, and buildings, and it contaminates natural sources such as water and soil. The initial loss of life and enduring effects on victims may be dramatic, and the economy of the affected area may be severely damaged. Radioactive weapons are explosives that emit dangerous radioactive materials, commonly known as dirty bombs. Their impact is directly related to the proximity of the victims to the source of the radioactive contamination (Bullock et al., 2006; Department of Homeland Security, 2002).

Another type of human-made hazard stems from political tensions, when combatants use readily available chemicals to construct CBRNE weapons that can be used alongside explosives. Terror incidents usually target humans, infrastructure, or symbols that are important for people. Terrorist events also occur less frequently than natural hazards, but in some cases their political, economic, and human consequences might be much more devastating than those attributable to any other type of hazard. For example, sabotage to nuclear facilities is a potential nuclear/radioactive hazard that requires relatively little technical expertise, but can inflict remarkable damage to people and economy. Thus the security of these facilities has great importance. Conventional armaments and explosives remain the most commonly used means of terrorist attack.

Although human-made hazards occur relatively infrequently in the United States and Europe, they carry significant impact because of their political nature. People may eventually get used to living with natural disasters, so that a natural event might not attract notable attention. In contrast, even an unsuccessful attempt at a terrorist attack can alter the focus of a population and political circles to a different point. Hence, it appears likely that human-made disasters will remain at the top of the emergency management agenda. Additionally, technological advancements have led to the emergence of cyberthreats and other issues that raise concerns about countries' ability to maintain their national security. For example, today it is possible for someone to break into air traffic control systems or banking systems electronically, thereby causing a lot of harm and mayhem in a country.

Perceptions of the threat from human-made disasters have shifted rapidly in recent decades. After World War II, the main focus of emergency management in the United States was civil defense. In the 1960s, concerns about natural disasters outweighed civil defense needs, and emergency preparedness shifted from nuclear war to natural hazards. During the 1970s, disaster management was introduced to the national political agenda, as FEMA was established by the Carter administration in 1979. Priorities were heavily dominated by Cold War fears under Reagan during the 1980s, which were characterized by an emphasis on nuclear attack preparation. When James Lee Witt took control of FEMA during the Clinton administration, however, the vision and direction of the organization changed again. Witt was the first director of FEMA who had emergency management experience; with him at the helm of FEMA, the focus of national emergency management shifted to natural disasters once more.

The September 11, 2001 terrorist attacks were a milestone for emergency management systems in the United States and the world. The attention of the global community turned to terrorism-related hazards, and human-made disasters moved to the top of the agenda again, as President George W. Bush established the Department of Homeland Security (DHS) following the attacks. It was declared that "to ensure security of our people and preserve our democratic way of life" was the top priority of this new Cabinet-level department (Department of Homeland Security, 2002, p. 7). The 1993 World Trade Center attack in New York, the 1995 Murrah Federal Building bombing in Oklahoma City, and the September 11, 2001 attacks are the most infamous human-made attacks that the United States has experienced.

The heightened threat of terrorism has not only been significant for the United States, but also for several other countries that have dealt with attacks. The 2003 Istanbul bombings, 2004 Madrid bombing, 2005 London bombings, and 2008 Mumbai bombing have all contributed to growing concerns about global terrorism since September 11, 2001.

In addition to terrorist threats, political violence in the form of civil strife or armed conflicts is another human-made hazard that needs to be considered, particularly in the context of Europe. In the mid-1990s, the bloody disintegration of Yugoslavia and the ethno-religious wars in Bosnia-Herzegovina and Croatia showed that war as human-made disaster is never far from Western civilization. The North Atlantic Treaty Organization (NATO) intervention in Kosovo in 1999 was undertaken to protect against mass human right abuses and to alleviate security concerns of the ethnic Albanian population. As recently as 2008, Russia intervened militarily in South Ossetia, an autonomous region in Georgia. The frozen armed conflict in Nagorno-Karabakh (an area between Azerbaijan and Armenia), the Transnistria-Moldova territorial dispute, the Kurdish separatism movement in Turkey, and the ongoing division of Turkish and Greek sides of Cyprus are other examples of political violence as human-made hazards that continue to have considerable socioeconomic and political impacts in Europe. Since early 2011, a number of countries in the Middle East and North Africa (MENA), such as Bahrain, Egypt, Libya, Syria, Tunisia, and Yemen have experienced a wave of political transformation that is often referred as the 'Arab Spring.' It has already resulted in deathly political violence, mass displacement, and widespread socio-economic and physical destruction in many of these countries. While Saudi Arabia has assisted the Sunni-led government of Bahrain to quash its Shia rebellion by deploying its troops in the country, NATO has undertaken an extensive military intervention against Muammar Gaddafi's regime in order to support the national insurgency movement. As of June 2011, the MENA region was still experiencing a high level of political turmoil, insurgency, and external military interventions.

Impacts

A disaster's impact can be interpreted in six different spheres: physical, social, psychological, demographic, economic, and political (Lindell, 2002, as cited in Lindell et al., 2007). The physical impacts of a disaster are the primary forms of destruction—casualties and damage—and are clearly visible in comparison to other types of impact. They are the sole determinant of a disaster: Without any actual or potential physical impact, there is no disaster. All other impacts are possibilities, but are by no means necessary for the classification of a disaster. Put simply, a disaster is a "situation or event, which overwhelms local capacity, necessitating a request to national or international level for external assistance . . . that causes great damage, destruction and human suffering" (EM-DAT, 2007). Different people or groups may cite a variety of combinations of effects in categorizing an event as a disaster, but they predominantly refer directly to physical impact as the essential criterion.

Alexander (1997) identifies four commonly used elements in the definition of a disaster to be the number of deaths, the value of damage and losses, the impact on the social system, and geophysical definitions. Some sources go as far as relying on quantifiable damage to declare a disaster. For example, the Centre for Research on the Epidemiology of Disasters will term an event a "disaster" only if it results in 10 or more deaths, 100 people affected, a declaration of a state emergency, and a call for international assistance (United Nations International Strategy for Disaster Reduction [UNISDR], 2006). Different hazards may have a range of physical impacts, which can be divided into human and nonhuman categories. For instance, a biological disaster will affect only people, leaving the inanimate infrastructure unscathed. Similarly, an oil spill may destroy marine life, yet not physically affect the nearby human population. The majority of disasters, however, involve a conjunction of these impacts, whereby loss of human life is often inseparable from destruction of the built and natural environments.

A population can be affected socially by disasters, which can act to aggravate or create tensions between different social groups or, conversely, to bridge former divisions. As discussed throughout this book, Hurricane Katrina is known to have affected poor, black residents proportionally more severely than it did the affluent, white subset of the population. This is no surprise; the disparity between global disaster deaths is split by the north/south division of development and prosperity, such that the less fortunate fare worse, with an average fatality count of 1000 compared to the north's meager 10 deaths (Pelling, Özerdem, & Barakat, 2002). The intriguing aspect of Hurricane Katrina, however, was that it occurred in a large city in a developed country, and the racial divergence reignited entrenched divisions in United States society.

Just as a disaster can have positive and negative effects upon development, as explored by Özerdem (2003), disasters are not entirely destructive in their social impacts. Conflict in Aceh ended with unexpected rapidity in the eight months following the 2004 Indian Ocean tsunami, and similar effects have been experienced internationally in the past, albeit on a varying scale (Le Billon & Waizenegger, 2007).

The existing demography can be drastically altered through the displacement of populations from an affected area or from deaths. Lindell et al. (2007) provide a formula to assess the demographic change following a disaster:

$$Pa - Pb = B - D + IM - OM$$

In this equation, "Pa is the population size after the disaster, Pb is the population size before the disaster, B is the number of births, D is the number of deaths, IM is the number of immigrants, and OM is the number of emigrants" (Lindell et al., 2007, p. 160). Smith and McCarty (1996) demonstrate the demographic change due to Hurricane Andrew in Dade County, Florida. They note that of the 353,000 people who were forced to leave their residences, more than 40,000 did not return to Dade County. Similarly, Stivers (2007) has investigated the demographic impact of Hurricane Katrina, stating that more white residents than black residents have returned to New Orleans. Preceding the hurricane, African Americans constituted two-thirds of the city's population, but their share dropped to 46% following the disaster (Nossiter, 2006, as cited in Stivers, 2007).

A popular measure of a disaster is its economic impact—that is, the significant costs associated with repairing damaged property and reestablishing commerce. Rebuilding homes, replacing property, resuming employment, restoring businesses, and rebuilding infrastructure constitute the economic impact (Bullock et al., 2006). According to Bullock et al. (2006), FEMA spent more than $25.4 billion on declared disasters and emergencies between 1990 and 1999. This figure was estimated at $3.9 billion for the 1980–1989 period, although Lindell et al. (2007) point out that there is no organization that calculates total spending on this activity. If critical infrastructure such as a power plant or communications center were to be damaged in a disaster, the economic consequences would be catastrophic. However, the economic impacts of disasters are not limited to property damage, as disasters may also alter people's spending patterns and decrease consumption (Lindell et al., 2007).

In terms of political impacts, catastrophic disasters in the United States have influenced and resulted in federal-level policy and program changes in managing emergencies. For example, the September 11, 2001 attacks led to revisions and improvements in the Federal Response Plan, which in turn prompted the development of a National Response Plan and the creation of the Department of Homeland Security (Kapucu, 2006). Federal-level changes in disaster management programs and policies are also greatly influenced by the role of presidential emergency management. According to Kapucu (2009), the role of presidential management of disasters has often been important in the United States because the strengths and weaknesses in disaster management and response "often [determine] the political future of presidents and their administrations" (p. 768). President George W. Bush was greatly criticized for the weak and slow federal response to Hurricanes Katrina and Rita. Currently, in the wake of the BP oil spill crisis in the Gulf of Mexico, prospective changes and reviews are being considered in the National Response Framework and the National Incident Management System (NIMS) under President Barack Obama's administration.

Thus disasters are becoming increasingly politicized, and as such can unite individuals who share a common grievance in a challenge against their government due to poor handling of a recovery or the lack of mitigating action prior to a disaster. Lindell et al. (2007) emphasize that the recovery period can trigger many political tensions.

For example, re-zoning attempts in disaster-stricken areas may irritate property owners because their property values could decline and they might not be able to reconstruct their property to pre-disaster conditions. With growing awareness of the potential political cost of disasters, there is an intensified pressure for leaders to appear to be in control during an emergency. In this respect, President Obama has been keen to avoid the BP oil spill disaster being portrayed as equivalent to President Bush's Hurricane Katrina failures.

Vulnerability

As indicated previously, natural hazards are affected by regional variations in environment, but all areas are vulnerable to human-made hazards. Emergency managers tend to specialize in mitigating the risks associated with the particular hazards they are most likely to encounter, but must also prepare for an unlikely occurrence. For instance, a region prone to hurricanes should also have plans in place for radioactive spills and biological hazards, as the high winds associated with a hurricane may damage industrial assets within the community. In some instances, hazards can create secondary ones. Lightning spawned by a run-of-the-mill thunderstorm in Florida's summer months may set fire to wooded areas and endanger homes. Drought-like conditions present another factor for emergency managers to deal with, so they must work together with forestry departments to ensure that the loss of woodlands and property is minimized.

Lindell et al. (2007) have investigated the effects of pre-disaster conditions in conjunction with existing conditions on disasters. A disaster can be analyzed by determining the three pre-impact conditions: hazard exposure, physical vulnerability, and social vulnerability.

A community's hazard exposure is determined by the geographical location of its people and the events that threaten their lives.

Vulnerability can generally be described as the potential for loss, although consensus is lacking on a more detailed definition (Cutter, 1996; Cutter, Boruff, & Shirley, 2003). In the past, vulnerability has been limited to physical susceptibility; however, understanding of this concept is now becoming more comprehensive, to include susceptibility, exposure, coping capacity, adaptive capacity, social inequalities, and physical, institutional, and economic weaknesses (Bender, 2002; Birkman, 2007). Different scholars typically add different phenomena to the definition of vulnerability based on their own perspectives, making the concept rather indistinct. Nevertheless, if vulnerability is considered from hazards perspective, it is possible to define it as "the likelihood that an individual or group will be exposed to and adversely affected by a hazard . . . the indication of hazards of place (risk and mitigation) with the social profile of communities" (Cutter, 1993, as cited in Cutter, 1996, p. 532).

Physical vulnerability is defined as "the properties of physical structures that determine their potential damage in case of a disaster (e.g., material type and construction quality)" (Ebert, Kerle, & Stein, 2008, p. 277). Physical vulnerability represents the culmination of human vulnerability, agricultural vulnerability, and structural vulnerability. In essence, humans are vulnerable to events that threaten their physical body, food source, and surrounding environment.

Social vulnerability is defined by Wisner et al. (2004, p. 11, as cited in Lindell et al., 2007) "as people's capacity to anticipate, cope with, resist and recover from the impacts of a natural hazard." Cutter et al. (2000) identify the factors influencing social vulnerability to natural hazards as lack of access to resources, including information and knowledge; limited access to political power and representation; certain beliefs and customs; weak buildings or individuals; and infrastructure and lifelines.

Hurricane Katrina drew attention to the political choices that were made in response to the disaster without focusing on the long-term vulnerability of the city and their people. While the idea of social vulnerability is not new to emergency management, the U.S. population has experienced an awakening concerning their social vulnerability to disasters. Given the greater focus on reducing communities' social vulnerability, emergency managers will have greater success in preventing disasters (Enarson, 2007). Of course, social vulnerability is not the only facet of a community's composition to be considered when planning for disasters.

Some social scientists have argued that Hurricane Katrina was not a "natural disaster," but rather a social catastrophe in which some of society's groups suffered disproportionately (Sylves, 2008). While many may debate the accuracy of this statement, Hurricane Katrina did shine a spotlight on the wide range of vulnerabilities that exist within a community.

Assessment of Vulnerability and Disaster Risk

Vulnerability assessment is a broad concept that can be discussed in several different contexts. Vulnerabilities vary according to the hazards, human ecology, and social changes involved. The International Federation of Red Cross and Red Crescent Societies (IFRC) underlines the importance of answering the question, "Vulnerabilities to what?" (IFRC, n.d., p. 12). Every disaster and every geographical location have unique circumstances; as a consequence, it is not possible to propose a single vulnerability assessment methodology. Each hazard poses different risks to communities at different levels. Nevertheless, a general idea of vulnerability assessment can be formulated as an equation of physical and social vulnerabilities. This section discusses a number of important vulnerable groups that must be addressed by emergency managers: the elderly, the poor, and ethnic minorities.

Elderly people are one of the most vulnerable social groups in the society. Gibson and Hayunga (2006) underline that the majority of the 1330 people who lost their lives in Hurricane Katrina were elderly people. In Louisiana, 71% of all victims were older than age 60, and 47% were older than age 75 . Sixty-eight people were found dead in nursing homes after the hurricane. Also, many of the elderly people evacuated were taken to inappropriate places without considering their special needs (Gibson & Hayunga, 2006).

Elderly people are considered vulnerable because many of them have physical disabilities, chronic illnesses, personal sensitivities, and functional limitations. Aldrich and Benson (2008) note that approximately 80% of U.S. adults aged 65 or older have at least one chronic health condition. Nearly half of the adults at the age of 65 or older have hypertension, 20% have coronary heart disease and 9% have experienced a stroke. It is important to consider effective planning and communication, identify who will need help and what kind of need, and develop evacuation practices for the elderly people to mitigate their vulnerabilities in the setting of a disaster (Bender, 2002; Gibson & Hayunga, 2006).

Poverty remains an intimidating obstacle for a resilient community in terms of effective emergency preparedness and mitigation. Poverty-stricken people more likely focus on their daily survival; preparing for potential disasters remains a distant idea for them. McMahon (2007) notes that one reason why some people did not evacuate New Orleans before Hurricane Katrina came ashore was a lack of proper means of transportation. McMahon (2007) adds that 50% of the poor households in New Orleans did not have sufficient transportation to exit the city.

Poor communities are also more prone to the effects of disasters. They cannot afford to build strong infrastructures that would not be destroyed by a disaster. As noted earlier, the majority of the life losses during tornadoes occur in mobile houses. Simmons and Sutter (2008) underline this point by noting that, between 1985 and 2006, 42% of tornado fatalities occurred in mobile homes. These houses are preferred by poor people because they are more affordable, but offer unreliable protection against disasters.

Minority-dominated and ethnically diverse communities are also more vulnerable to disasters. Kemp (2007) emphasizes that marginalization of groups in a society is a result of classification in social structure. According to Cutter and Emrich (2006), a community's demographic characteristics, social capital, and access to lifelines are factors that can either increase or decrease the susceptibility of people to disasters. Due to their lack of political representation, minorities' conditions and cultural differences might not be stressed in the local emergency management plans. Moreover, lack of political empowerment and discrimination can exacerbate the conditions for minorities and widen the gap between these groups and the majority population (Lemyre, Gibson, Zlepnig, Meyer-Macleod, & Boutette, 2009).

Stivers (2007) underlines the racial issues that became evident in the wake of the Hurricane Katrina disaster. Pre-Katrina New Orleans was dominated by African American people. According to Stivers (2007), discrimination by public officials against this population exacerbated the impacts of Hurricane Katrina, in part as a result of the racial difference between the victims and the responders. Elliot and Pais (2006) mention race issues along with economic status and poverty as factors determining the severity of Katrina's effect. According to these authors, the average black worker in New Orleans was four times more likely to lose his or her job after the storm than the average white worker. As a result of these complex factors and racial concerns, African American people were less inclined to evacuate the city than white people (Elliot & Pais, 2006). As Kemp (2007) notes, when the humane aspect of disaster responses and recovery is ignored, minorities and ethically diverse groups tend to become more vulnerable to the hazards and in return this would have the potential to trigger future disasters.

To prepare for and mitigate disasters, measuring community vulnerabilities and assessing the risks to which communities are exposed is vital. In the United States, FEMA has mandated implementation of risk and vulnerability assessment in state mitigation plans for state governments. Money, through grants, is used as the primary motivator by FEMA to encourage states to implement mitigation strategies including vulnerability assessments. Cutter et al. (2000) list characteristics of vulnerabilities as population and structure (measured, for example, as total population or total housing units), differential access to resources or greater susceptibility to disasters due to physical weaknesses (e.g., number of females, minorities, people younger than age 18, and people older than age 65), wealth and poverty (e.g., mean house values), and level of physical and structural vulnerability (e.g., number of mobile homes).

Chakraborty et al. (2005) developed a formula for assessing the social vulnerability in an evacuation context, particularly for hurricane-prone regions such as Florida. In their research, these authors identified variables indicating social vulnerabilities related to population and structure, differential access to resources, and populations with special evacuation needs. They developed a Social Vulnerability for Evacuation Assistance Index (SVEAI) and formulated it as follows:

$$\text{SVEAI} = \sum \text{SVEAI}i/n$$

In this equation, SVEAIi stands for the social vulnerability for evacuation assistance index of each variable and n stands for the number of vulnerabilities (Chakraborty et al., 2005).

Moreover, the impact of a disaster is directly related to the risk that a community faces. Birkman (2007) has adopted four parameters from Davidson (1997) and Bollin et al. (2003) to determine the level of risk that a community faces: exposure, hazard frequency or severity, local capacity, and vulnerability. Communities' physical planning, social capacity, economic capacity, and management potential also influence the risks that they face and the way they respond to those risks (Bollin & Hidajat, 2006).

Calculating the risks that communities face is possible by measuring each individual factor; overall risk can be reduced by acting upon these results. The prevention/mitigation phase of emergency management deals with hazards before they present themselves. These efforts aim to stop the hazards from emerging or reduce their impact via the application of certain methods, so that exposure to disaster will be reduced. Unfortunately, some disasters are inevitable and unstoppable, such as hurricanes and earthquakes. In these cases, reduction of vulnerabilities can help to significantly decrease the risks that communities are exposed to in the case of a disaster.

Vulnerabilities differ depending on geographical location, population characteristics, and the types of hazards to which an area may or may not be subject to (e.g., a house in Florida may not have to withstand a snowstorm, but it needs to withstand hurricane-force winds). Population characteristics usually become a factor when an area has a sizable population of one of the preidentified most vulnerable groups (e.g., elderly, children, lower-income population). Structural vulnerabilities can usually be easily foreseen and prevented (such as building homes outside of floodplains). In other instances, the risks cannot be easily determined (e.g., a levee system built using substandard materials, such as poor soil). Most of these risks can be mitigated by passing and enforcing strict building codes (which would include government oversight at every level) and following zoning laws. This, however, is not where mitigation should end.

Because individual preparedness has long been seen as a major cornerstone of pre-impact planning, emergency managers should address what they can do to help households prepare for such events. Localities should focus on helping prepare their residents for the types of disasters that their area might face. For example, if an area has a nuclear facility nearby, it must prepare its residents for a potential meltdown. Likewise, if an area could be considered a target for terrorists, community leaders must train the residents about what to do in case of an attack. Oftentimes, many emergency managers focus on the type of disaster most likely to occur, while neglecting others that might potentially occur (e.g., gearing responses toward natural threats, instead of adopting an all-hazards approach to planning), which can leave them exposed to unexpected threats. One of the best ways for emergency managers to help their communities, including their most vulnerable residents, is to get a better understanding of their needs and the needs of the individual situations that they may face. A number of ways to do so have been proposed (Enarson, 2007):

1. Build on local community knowledge of disasters.
2. Prepare and deliver effective warning messages (news that will reach all diverse populations, including blind, deaf, and minority individuals).
3. Develop shelters.
4. Anticipate the need for translators, child care, medical equipment, and other resources.
5. Avoid wasting resources on unnecessary supplies due to bias.

Assessing risk, training staff, and facilitating coordination will enable managers to handle the particular hazards to which their regions are prone. Technology can aid in mitigation, of course, but in some cases is not adequate. Not all hazards are known in advance, yet must still be anticipated. Lindell et al. (2007) emphasize that the variables in the risk assessment equation are quite weak in power (there are few historical data) and uncertain (a changing environment and habitats will influence the hazard's impact). Further, it is not possible to predict the physical impact and the magnitude of a hazard before it occurs. Citizens should be prepared to heed warnings when at all possible and should take measures to protect property and family members from danger. All parties should be aware that principal hazards can create other dangerous circumstances, as seen with the New Orleans levees.

Lindell et al. (2007) identify intervention measures as including hazard mitigation, emergency preparedness, and recovery preparedness; these practices are intended to reduce the physical and social effects of a disaster by limiting casualties and damage, and by providing financial and material resources as emergency relief and to support recovery. In addition, these authors recommend a Hazard/Vulnerability Assessment (HVA) to increase understanding of how hazard characteristics produce physical and social impacts. The knowledge gained through an HVA can be then utilized in developing emergency management interventions. While they demonstrate that public resources are under-utilized, Lindell et al. conclude that federal and state agencies need to put more data on their websites and make them more accessible to the public in the United States.

Likewise, advances in technological tools are giving emergency managers an ever-increasing ability to foresee the effects of a natural hazard, and in some cases to foresee the disaster itself. This increased knowledge can greatly improve the way a community mitigates disaster during calm periods as well as improve the recovery efforts after a disaster has occurred. Sylves (2008) describes how science plays a role in the formation of disaster policy and politics. Science and technology can be used in all phases of disaster management, including modeling to assist in the development of mitigation and preparedness procedures. For example, flood models can be created using elevation data to predict storm surge and inland flooding scenarios.

Geographical Information Systems (GIS) are widely used tools for mapping and visualizing the vulnerabilities of disaster-prone areas. Flax, Jackson, and Stein (2002) explain how the Community Vulnerability Assessment Tool (CVAT) can be used to assess vulnerabilities via GIS systems. In their case study, Hannover County, North Carolina, used GIS systems to identify the spatial relationships between critical resources and hazards. As part of the CVAT analysis, GIS applications enabled county officials to identify critical facilities located in high-risk areas. Furthermore, with the help of GIS, the officials realized that some critical services such as fire and police would be unable to respond to certain locations in an emergency due to the effects of certain hazards such as floods (Flax et al., 2002).

One of the most interesting components of the science and technology role in emergency management can be found by reviewing the Department of Homeland Security organizational chart. While Department of Homeland Security itself has an Under Secretary of Science and Technology, most of the governmental agencies that have a role in disaster research are found outside of this department. Examples include the U.S. Geological Service, the Army Corps of Engineers, and the National Oceanic and Atmospheric Administration. Thus, regardless of the amount of technology used in disaster research, relationship building will play a key role in ensuring effective disaster management at the federal level. These agencies must learn to work together to be effective. Essentially, emergency management depends on a blend of different disciplines to be successful in identifying and mitigating hazards as well as preventing disasters. As McEntire (2004) emphasizes, vulnerabilities are the only variable in the disaster equation that can be controlled by humans.

Furthermore, assessment of vulnerabilities can be made at the national level as well as at the local level. Birkman (2007) discusses the vulnerability index developed by United Nations as an example (UNDP, 2004, as cited in Birkman, 2007). United Nations (UN) efforts to assess vulnerability and risk focus on this issue from both the national and international perspectives. The organization's own studies use mortality data as the basis for risk analysis. This analysis equalizes hazards based on the number of casualties they might potentially inflict and tries to understand why societies with similar levels of exposure to natural hazards can be more or less at risk, or experience a higher or lower level of fatalities (Birkman, 2007). By using the local-level perspective, vulnerabilities assessment can achieve success with the participation of all stakeholders to the process. Participation of business owners, public agencies, nonprofit organizations, and civil society organizations is necessary for better assessment of vulnerabilities and development of mitigation strategies (Flax et al., 2002; Wood, Good, & Goodwin, 2002).

Although abundant research was available to New Orleans' government prior to August 2005, there was a sense of complacency and lack of urgency among local government officials concerning the threat posed by a large hurricane. Both local and Louisiana state authorities also failed to act on the data provided by the Army Corps of Engineers (Daniels, Kettl, & Kunreuther, 2006). It is clear that politics played a pivotal role in the failures in response to Hurricane Katrina. In 2004, the Weather Research Center predicted that in 2005 the Louisiana–Alabama coast had a 40% chance of experiencing a land-falling tropical storm or hurricane based on its Orbital Cyclone Strike Index (OCSI). Moreover, in 2001, the Center predicted that the chance of a landfall event within the next year in the same area was 70%. Reasonable actions in response to this information would have included strengthening the levees or better planning the mass evacuation of the city. Thus, while science and technology can be very accurate in predicting different disaster scenarios and the situation in which a structural asset fails, it still takes politicians and emergency managers to act on these predictions to mitigate any one of many potential disasters.

Conclusion

On many levels, emergency managers are the soothsayers of disaster planning. They must predict what their vulnerabilities are, which hazards will affect them (some being obvious, others less so), and which decisions can be made to decrease the impact of disaster on their community. They must remember to use every tool available, including technology and the social sciences, to make the best, most well-educated decisions under the most immense pressure. In the end, the fate of the community rests on the decisions they make, and they must be prepared to make decisions for the entire community. One of the most delicate balances they will have to face is making sure that they apply equal time to all hazards and do not focus entirely on the single risk they believe will affect them most. Likewise, they must understand that one plan will not work for everyone in the community. In this regard, emergency managers can rely on past experiences, technological advances, social science studies, and community involvement to develop the "best practices" approach for their locality.

Review Questions

1. If you were asked to improve and redesign the U.S. hurricane response in terms of evacuation housing efforts and short-term housing in the wake of Hurricane Katrina, what would you propose be done? Your answer here requires that you review and discuss the flaws of the current U.S. hurricane disaster response and evacuation policy. You also need to consider how the governmental response to Hurricane Katrina proceeded. Are the reforms currently taking place in the Department of Homeland Security and FEMA enough to correct the problems with the Katrina response? If a Katrina-scale disaster were to hit New Orleans next year, what has been done since 2005 to provide for the needs of those who are unable to evacuate the city? Has the United States learned its lesson from its mistakes in the original Katrina disaster?

2. You are the emergency manager for a coastal town that has seen hurricane activity in the past. You have been asked to prepare a presentation on flooding. What would you include in your plan? Which types of flooding are important to discuss? Discuss the presentation you would put together.

3. This is a flood disaster assignment; you are asked to select your hometown if it has experienced a flood or, if it has not, to select the city of your choice that has experienced a flood disaster. Flood disasters are not new. Why has flood vulnerability been so long tolerated in the United States and Europe? Was flood vulnerability tolerated in your municipality of interest before it was flooded? Are local governments in flood-prone areas fundamentally responsible for their own protection, or are they conditioned to entrust higher-level governments with that authority? Levee construction and maintenance have been alleged to be weak, and some claim that

incompetent jurisdictions have been left with responsibility for floodworks that are capable, if they fail, of devastating their own communities and communities outside their own jurisdictions. What should be done about this issue?

4. Who is responsible in the municipal flood disaster you are addressing (see Question 3)? What is the role of the National Flood Insurance Program in this municipality? Was the program in effect well before the municipal flood disaster? Has it failed in abating flood disasters? Explain.

5. The U.S. Army Corps of Engineers (USACE) is an agency with a very long history of work in construction, operation, and maintenance of infrastructural works (e.g., dams, levees, revetments) and nonstructural, disaster mitigation works. The USACE also owns, operates, and maintains other massive infrastructure systems (e.g., lock systems, navigable waterways, bridges, ports). Consequently, USACE became an important player in the U.S. system of emergency management, particularly in the 1980s and 1990s. Explain the role of the USACE in disaster management. Does this agency occupy an influential organizational position in the Pentagon? Is the USACE politically important or powerful? Is it effective as a flood-fighting organization? Is it culpable in any way for the levee failures around New Orleans during and after Hurricane Katrina? Is structural mitigation of the type advanced by the USACE outmoded given the U.S. societal emphasis on nonstructural mitigation? Should all U.S. floodworks be nationalized and made the responsibility of the USACE?

6. Think about engineering in the context of disaster policy. Are U.S. disasters often a manifestation of failed infrastructure that is poorly engineered, poorly maintained, and poorly designed for the hazards the structures are likely to face over their operating lives? Has the federal disaster infrastructure rebuilding policy been hijacked by state and local officials, as well as by the building trades and contractors, in such a way that subnational governments engage in moral hazard to exploit federal reconstruction relief? How has engineering helped mitigate disasters, and how have engineers pressed the public and their elected officials to act on their mitigation recommendations? How do environmental and structural engineers engage the political process, and do disasters give them any advantage in this engagement?

7. How might the information you gained from this chapter affect you personally and professionally?

References

Aldrich, N., & Benson, W. F. (2008). Disaster preparedness and the chronic disease needs of vulnerable older adults. *Preventing Chronic Disease, 5*(1), 1–7.

Alexander, D. (1997). The study of natural disasters, 1977–1997: Some reflections on a changing field of knowledge. *Disasters, 21*(4), 284–304.

Alexander, D. (2002). *Principles of emergency planning and management.* Harpenden, UK: Terra Publishing.

Apthorpe, R. (1998). *Towards emergency humanitarian aid evaluation*. Canberra: NCDS Asia Pacific Press, Australian National University.

Bacon, P. & O'Keefe, E. (2011). Tornadoes kill 300 across South. Retrieved from The Washington Post on May 20, 2011, from http://www.washingtonpost.com/national/tornadoes-carve-path-of-death-destruction-across-south-with-at-least-250-dead/2011/04/28/AFJ1os7E_story_3.html.

Becker, A., & Grünewald, U. (2003). Disaster Management Policy Forum: Flood risk in Central Europe. *Science, 300*, 1099. Retrieved form http://www.pik-potsdam.de/glowa/pdf/presse/becker_science.pdf.

Bender, S. (2002). Development and use of natural hazard vulnerability: Assessment techniques in the Americas. *Natural Hazards Review, 3*(4), 136–138.

Birkman, J. (2007). Risk and vulnerability indicators at different scales: Applicability, usefulness and policy implications. *Environmental Hazards, 7*, 20–31.

Bollin, C., Cárdenas, C., Hahn, H., Vatsa, K.S., 2003. Natural Disasters Network: Comprehensive Risk Management by Communities and Local Governments. Inter-American Development Bank. Available at http://www.gtz.de/en/themen/uebergreifende-themen/nothilfe/1817.htm.

Bollin, C., & Hidajat, R. (2006). Community-based disaster risk index: Pilot implementation in Indonesia. In J. Birkmann (Ed.), Measuring vulnerability to natural hazards: Towards disaster resilient societies (pp. 271–289). Tokyo/New York/Paris: UNU-Press.

Brodie, M, Weltzien, E., Altman, D., Blendon, R., & Benson, J. (2006). Experiences of Hurricane Katrina evacuees in Houston shelters: Implications for future planning. *American Journal of Public Health, 96*(6), 1402–1408.

Bullock, J. A., Haddow, G. D., Coppola, D., Ergin, E., Westerman, L., & Yeletaysi, S. (2006). *Introduction to homeland security*. China: Butterworth-Heinemann.

Chakraborty, J., Tobin, G. A., & Montz, B. E. (2005). Population evacuation: Assessing spatial variability in geophysical risk and social vulnerability to natural hazards. *Natural Hazards Review, 6*(1), 23–33.

Colo., Texas lead the top 10 most tornado prone area. (2009). *Insurance Journal*. Retrieved November 16, 2009, from http://www.insurancejournal.com/news/national/2008/07/09/91746.htm.

Cutter, S. L. (1996). Vulnerability to environmental hazards. *Progress in Human Geography, 20*(4), 529–539.

Cutter, S. L., Boruff, B. J., & Shirley, W. L. (2003). Social vulnerability to environmental hazards. *Social Science Quarterly, 84*(2), 242–261.

Cutter, S. L., & Emrich, C. T. (2006). Moral hazard, social catastrophe: the changing face of vulnerability along the hurricane coasts. *Annals of the American Academy of Political and Social Science, 604*, 102.

Cutter, S. L., Mitchell, J. T., & Scott, M. S. (2000). Revealing vulnerability of people and places: A case study of Georgetown County, South Caroline. *Annals of the Association of American Geographers, 90*(4), 713–737.

Daniels, R. J., Kettl, D. F., & Kunreuther, H. (Eds.). (2006). *On risk and disaster: Lessons from Hurricane Katrina*. Philadelphia: University of Pennsylvania Press.

Davidson, R., 1997. An urban earthquake disaster risk index. Report No.121, The John A. Blume Earthquake Engineering Center, Stanford.

Department of Homeland Security. (2002). National strategy for homeland security. Retrieved November 26, 2009, from http://www.dhs.gov/xlibrary/assets/nat_strat_hls.pdf.

Ebert, A., Kerle, N., & Stein, A. (2009). Urban social vulnerability assessment with physical proxies and spatial metrics derived from air- and spaceborne imagery and GIS data. *Natural Hazards, 48*(2), 275–294.

Elliott, D., & Macpherson, A. (2010). Policy practice: Recursive learning from crisis. *Group and Organization Management, 35*(5), 572–675.

Elliot, J. R., & Pais, J. (2006). Race, class, and Hurricane Katrina: Social differences in human responses to disaster. *Social Science Research, 35*(2), 295–321.

EM-DAT. (2007). EM-DAT glossary. Centre for Research on the Epidemiology of Disasters. Retrieved July 15, 2010, from http://www.emdat.be/glossary/9.

Enarson, E. (2007). Identifying and addressing social vulnerabilities. In W. L. Waugh, Jr., & K. Tierney (Eds.), Emergency management: Principles and practice for local government (2nd ed., pp. 257–278). Washington, DC: ICMA.

European Commission. (2000). What is Europe doing? Forest fires. Retrieved April 8, 2010, from http://ec.europa.eu/research/leaflets/disasters/en/forest.html.

European Commission. (2001, July). Forest fires in southern Europe, Report No. 1. Retrieved April 8, 2010, from http://ec.europa.eu/echo/civil_protection/civil/pdfdocs/forestfiresreportfinal.pdf.

European Commission. (2009). JRC Scientific and Technical Reports, Report No. 9: Forest fires in Europe 2008. Retrieved April 8, 2010, from http://effis.jrc.ec.europa.eu/download/forest-fires-in-europe-2008.pdf.

European Commission. (2010). The Welcome to EFAS_IS Portal. Retrieved May 19, 2011, from http://efas-is.jrc.ec.europa.eu/.

Federal Emergency Management Agency (FEMA). (2006). By the numbers: One year later. Retrieved November 25, 2009, from http://www.fema.gov/news/newsrelease.fema?id=29109.

Federal Emergency Management Agency (FEMA). (2009a). Earthquakes in the United States. Retrieved November 24, 2009, from http://www.fema.gov/hazard/earthquake/usquakes.shtm.

Federal Emergency Management Agency (FEMA). (2009b). Hurricane hazards. Retrieved November 25, 2009, from http://www.fema.gov/hazard/hurricane/hu_hazard.shtm

Federal Emergency Management Agency (FEMA). (2009c). The National Flood Insurance Program. Retrieved November 25, 2009, from http://www.fema.gov/about/programs/nfip/index.shtm.

Federal Emergency Management Agency (FEMA). (2010). Tornado. [Retrieved May 19, 2011 from] http://www.fema.gov/hazard/tornado/index.shtm.

Flax, L. K., Jackson, R. W., & Stein, D. N. (2002). Community Vulnerability Assessment Tool methodology. *Natural Hazards Review, 3*(4), 163–176.

Frech, M. (2005). Flood risk outreach and public's need to know. *Journal of Contemporary Water Research & Education, 130*, 61–69.

Gibson, M. J., & Hayunga, M. (2006). *We can do better: Lessons learned for protecting older persons in disasters.* Washington D.C.: AARP.

International Federation of Red Cross and Red Crescent Societies (IFRC). (n.d.). The importance of vulnerability and capacity assessment. Retrieved November 26, 2009, from http://www.ifrc.org/docs/pubs/disasters/Vca_part1.pdf.

Johnson, K. (April 28, 2011). Predicting tornadoes: It's still a guessing game. Retrieved from The New York Times on May 20, 2011, from http://www.nytimes.com/2011/04/29/us/29tornadoes.html?scp=1&sq=Predicting%20Tornadoes:%20It%E2%80%99s%20Still%20a%20Guessing%20Game&st=cse.

Kapucu, N. (2006). Examining the National Response Plan in response to a catastrophic disaster: Hurricane Katrina in 2005. *International Journal of Mass Emergencies and Disasters,* *24*(2), 271–299.

Kapucu, N. (2009). Leadership under stress: Presidential roles in emergency and crisis management in the United States. *International Journal of Public Administration, 32,* 767–772.

Kemp, R. B. (2007). Classifying marginalized people, focusing on natural disaster survivors. *Proceedings of the North American Symposium on Knowledge Organization, 1.* Retrieved from http://dlist.sir.arizona.edu/1908.

Kusenbach, M., Simms, J. L., & Tobin, G. A. (2009). Disaster vulnerability and evacuation readiness: Coastal mobile home residents in Florida. *Natural Hazards.* doi: 10.1007/s11069-009-9358-3.

Laurie, P. (2003). Disaster development and community planning, and public participation: How to achieve sustainable hazard mitigation. *Natural Hazards, 28*(2–3), 211–228.

Le Billon, P., & Waizenegger, A. (2007). Peace in the wake of disaster? Secessionist conflicts and the 2004 Indian Ocean tsunami. *Transactions of the Institute of British Geographers, 32*(3), 411–427.

Lemyre, L., Gibson, S., Zlepnig, J., Meyer-Macleod, R., & Boutette, P. (2009). Emergency preparedness for higher risk populations: Psychosocial considerations. *Radiation Protection Dosimetry,* 1–8.

Lindell, M. K., Prater, C., & Perry, R. W. (2007). *Introduction to emergency management.* Hoboken, NJ: Wiley.

Makoka, D., & Kaplan, M. (2005). *Poverty and vulnerability: An interdisciplinary approach.* Universitat Bonn.

McEntire, D. (2004). *The status of emergency management theory: Issues, barriers, and recommendations for improved scholarship.* Paper presented at the FEMA Higher Education Conference, June 8, 2004, Emmitsburg, MD.

McMahon, M. (2007). Disasters and poverty. *Disaster Management and Response, 4,* 95–97.

National Geophysical Data Center (NGDC). (2010). Significant earthquake database. Retrieved April 6, 2010, from http://www.ngdc.noaa.gov/nndc/struts/form?t=101650&s=1&d=1.

National Interagency Fire Center. (n.d.). Fire information: Wildland fire statistics. Retrieved November 25, 2009, from http://www.nifc.gov/fire_info/fires_acres.htm.

National Oceanic and Atmospheric Administration (NOAA). (2009). Understanding damage and impacts: Why does flood cause so many deaths? Retrieved November 25, 2009, from http://www.nssl.noaa.gov/primer/flood/fld_damage.html.

National Weather Service. (2010). National Hurricane Center: The Saffir-Simpson Hurricane Wind Scale summary table. Retrieved April 6, 2010, from http://www.nhc.noaa.gov/sshws_table.shtml?large.

Özerdem, A. 2003. Disaster as Manifestation of Unresolved Development Challenges: The Marmara Earthquake, Turkey. In Pelling, M. (ed.) *Natural Disasters and Development in a Globalizing World* pp. 199-213. London, Routledge.

Özerdem, A., & Jacoby, T. (2006). *Disaster management and civil society: Earthquake relief in Japan, Turkey and India.* London: I. B. Tauris.

Pacific Earthquake Engineering Research Center (PEER). (2005). Northridge earthquake. Retrieved November 24, 2009, from http://nisee.berkeley.edu/northridge/.

Pelling, M., Özerdem, A., & Barakat, S. (2002). The macro-economic impact of disasters. *Progress in Development Studies, 2,* 283–305.

Robertson, C. & Severson, K. (April 28, 2011). South assesses the toll after a deadly barrage of tornadoes. Retrieved from The New York Times on May 20, 2011, from http://www.nytimes .com/2011/04/29/us/29storm.html?scp=9&sq=tornado%20outbreak&st=cse.

Simmons, K. M., & Sutter, D. (2008). Manufactured home building regulations and the February 2, 2007 Florida tornadoes. *Natural Hazards, 46,* 415–425.

Smith, S. K., & McCarty, C. (1996). Demographic effects of natural disasters: A case study of Hurricane Andrew. *Demography, 33*(2), 265–275.

Stivers, C. (2007). "So poor and so black": Hurricane Katrina, public administration, and the issue of race. *Public Administration Review.* 67, Supplement s1, 48-56.

Sylves, R. (2008). *Disaster policy and politics.* Washington, DC: C.Q. Press.

Tornado Project. (1999). Tornadoes in the past: 2007. Retrieved November 25, 2009, from http:// www.tornadoproject.com/past/pastts07.htm.

United Nations International Strategy for Disaster Reduction (UNISDR). (2006). Disaster statistics 1991–2005: Introduction. Retrieved March 22, 2008, from http://www.unisdr.org/ disaster-statistics/introduction.htm.

U.S. Fire Administration. (2001). Wildland fires: A historical perspective. *U.S. Fire Administration Topical Fire Research Series, 1,* 3. Retrieved November 26, 2009, form http://www.usfa .dhs.gov/downloads/pdf/tfrs/v1i3-508.pdf.

U.S. Fire Administration. (2002). Fires in the wildland/urban interface. *U.S. Fire Administration Topical Fire Research Series, 2,* 16. Retrieved November 26, 2009, from http://www.usfa .dhs.gov/downloads/pdf/tfrs/v2i16-508.pdf.

U.S. Forest Service. (2008). About us. Retrieved November 25, 2009, from http://www.fs.fed.us/ aboutus/.

U.S. Geological Survey (USGS). (2006). Wildfire hazards: A natural threat. Retrieved November 26, 2009, from http://pubs.usgs.gov/fs/2006/3015/2006-3015.pdf.

U.S. Geological Survey (USGS). (2009a). Deaths from U.S. earthquakes. Retrieved November 24, 2009, from http://earthquake.usgs.gov/earthquakes/states/us_deaths_sort.php.

U.S. Geological Survey (USGS). (2009b). Historic earthquakes. Retrieved November 24, 2009, from http://earthquake.usgs.gov/earthquakes/states/events/1964_03_28.php.

U.S. Geological Survey (USGS). (2009c). Historic earthquakes: Santa Cruz Mountains (Loma Prieta), California. Retrieved November 24, 2009, from http://earthquake.usgs.gov/ earthquakes/states/events/1989_10_18.php.

U.S. Geological Survey (USGS). (2009d). Significant earthquakes: L'Aquila, Italy 2009. Retrieved April 6, 2010, from http://earthquake.usgs.gov/earthquakes/eqinthenews/2009/us2009fcaf/.

U.S. Geological Survey (USGS). (2011). Largest and deadliest earthquakes by year. Retrieved January 27, 2011, from http://earthquake.usgs.gov/earthquakes/eqarchives/year/byyear.php.

van Alphen, J. Martini, F., Loat, R., Slomp, R., & Passchier, R. (2009). Flood risk mapping in Europe, experiences and best practices. *Journal of Flood Risk Management. 2,* 285–292.

Waugh, W. L. Jr. (2000). *Living with hazards, dealing with disasters: An introduction to emergency management.* Armonk, NY: M. E. Sharpe.

Weather Research Center. (2004, December). *The WRC Newsletter.*

Wood, N. J., Good, J. W., & Goodwin, R. F. (2002). Vulnerability assessment of a port and harbor community to earthquake and tsunami hazards: Integrating technical expert and stakeholder input. *Natural Hazards Review, 3*(4), 148–157.

Chapter 3

Prevention/Mitigation and Preparedness for Emergencies and Crises

Chapter Objectives

- Identify guiding principles of emergency mitigation and preparedness as two key phases of emergency and crisis management.
- Explore the emergency management frameworks in the United States and United Kingdom.
- Identify ways to apply the frameworks in mitigation and preparedness.
- Describe the relationship between disaster mitigation and sustainability.

Introduction

This chapter provides an introduction to hazard mitigation and preparation, describing their differences, their benefits, and their integration into the later phases of emergency management. In this discussion, problems in the adoption and implementation of mitigation policies are described and some methods of addressing them are presented, emphasizing the relationship between households and the community emergency response, especially warnings and the implementation of protective actions such as evacuation and sheltering-in-place (Fuld, 2003). The chapter continues with the presentation of the legislative basis for disaster management in both the United States and the United Kingdom. Basic principles of emergency planning and the process of assessing the emergency response organization's ability to perform four basic functions—emergency assessment, hazard operations, population protection, and incident management—are also outlined (Fowler, Kling, & Larson, 2007). Communities are most effective in preparing to implement these functions if they follow fundamental principles of emergency planning, as presented in this chapter. The chapter concludes with discussion of the relationship between hazard mitigation and sustainability.

Initial Phases of Emergency Management: Mitigation and Preparation

This section focuses on the initial two phases in emergency management: mitigation and preparation. Mitigation is the primary step toward emergency management in all situations. It should be considered long before a hazard occurs, with a view toward reducing the probability of a disaster. Consequently, preparation is understood as planning how to respond in the case of an emergency or disaster, and developing capabilities and programs that contribute to a more effective response. Preparedness, by comparison, is a sort of "insurance against emergencies," as mitigation activities alone do not fully protect against hazards (Coleman, 2006; Quarantelli, 1998).

This section explores these two key phases of disaster management by expanding on the preceding definitions with examples, and by discussing their benefits and limitations. It also offers a brief comparative study of experiences in New Orleans and Qinglong County, raising a number of issues that will continue to be addressed in the remainder of the chapter.

Mitigation

Perhaps one of the most valuable aspects of emergency management, mitigation involves taking preventive measures so as to diminish the effect a hazard inflicts upon a community. The potential for damage can be substantially reduced through the identification of vulnerabilities and the implementation of systems to minimize or eliminate these. Cuny (1983) advocates mitigation as a two-way process, acting to reduce physical and economic vulnerability and to strengthen social structure. In contrast, Blaikie et al. (1994) consider vulnerabilities to be a result of root causes and dynamic pressures, a view that lends credence to a more holistic approach in tackling communities' vulnerabilities.

Despite the progressive extent of mitigation as a concept, efforts to address it in practice are largely based on immediate and direct policy implementation, the reasons for which will be explored in future discussion on limitations. While Godschalk (2007) recognizes the importance of the role played by national agencies in mitigation planning, including necessary legislative requirements, he emphasizes the importance of local government in developing viable community mitigation plans and overall community sustainability. Community-level mitigation practices include both social and technical approaches. Although imposing building codes and reducing structural vulnerability are clearly important, however, these efforts are not sufficient for a comprehensive mitigation program. For example, the United Kingdom has implemented policy initiatives to mitigate the consequences of floods in the country, as approximately 12,000 km² is at risk of flooding (Schneider, 2002; Tunstall, Johnson, & Penning Rowsell, 2004). The government has provided guidance (Planning Policy Guidance, 25) for mitigation activities including structural defense, public awareness, land-use planning, and addresses social, economic, and environmental issues (Coleman, 2006; Tunstall et al., 2004). To establish the social aspect of mitigation, awareness, understanding (Comfort, 2007; Paton, 2003), and community adaptability (Godschalk, 2003) should be considered, along with the other aspects of the mitigation practices. Individuals should be aware of their own responsibility for mitigating hazards, rather than simply delegating their responsibilities to public officials.

A successful mitigation plan requires the utilization of stakeholder and community resources to address the needs and sustainability of a community as a whole. Attention must be paid not only to current hazards, but also to the prevention of future hazards that could stem from unwise development choices. The United States has undertaken measures to develop such a plan, through the Disaster Mitigation Act of 2000. This legislation provides funds to states that identify risk areas, plan accordingly, and take measures to avoid catastrophic damage to lives and property. In addition, the National Flood Insurance Plan (NFIP) sets standards for newly constructed buildings that aim to make them less vulnerable to hazards (Federal Emergency Management Agency [FEMA], 2009).

The act of reducing potential damage can be effective when weaknesses are identified and measures are implemented. Floods, earthquakes, coastal storms, tornadoes, wildfires, landslides, and human-made hazards can all cause significant damage to a community. Planning for these disasters and building, preparing, and planning accordingly can greatly reduce the losses suffered. No matter how straightforward the principles of mitigation sound, the logistics of mitigating hazards are, by and large, a group effort. Politicians, emergency managers and first responders, nonprofit organizations, private industry, local government, and community members must all be involved and committed to effectively implement a mitigation effort. Resources must be organized, the communities risks assessed, and a mitigation plan developed and implemented. The mitigation efforts should be assessed for effectiveness once in place and revisions made as needed.

There is practically universal acceptance that reducing communities' risks is highly advantageous. Unfortunately, mitigation processes are typically laden with political issues, financial constraints, bureaucratic red tape, and participant resistance. Consequently, it can be difficult for authorities to justify investment in indirect mitigative measures, like those mentioned previously. The political, financial, and bureaucratic issues are inherently related, as funding is crucial to the success of these strategies, yet the crucial aspect of mitigation is that it addresses hazards before their onset. In the political sphere, it can be extremely difficult to justify adequate financial commitment for such schemes, especially when the potential for disaster is considered low and, therefore, spending in this area has low priority. For this reason, it is important to ask whether complacency stems from the political challenges inherent in mitigation strategies or from a wider lack of comprehension regarding vulnerabilities.

Local emergency managers are tasked with educating government officials on both apparent and potential risks within the community. To further this cause, it is advantageous to highlight the savings that can be realized through successful mitigation measures as well as the potential cost to infrastructure and the safety of citizens should mitigation be ignored. It has been calculated that "on average, each dollar spent on mitigation avoids $4 in future losses" (Godschalk, 2007, p. 90). Furthermore, the interaction between parties should recognize the importance of the four phases of the emergency planning process so that officials can gain a comprehensive understanding of the endeavor. An informed policy group is more equipped to make effective, financially sound decisions.

Mitigation commonly demands a collaborative effort involving different actors, whose coordination creates a logistical challenge. Politicians, emergency managers and first responders, nonprofit organizations, private industry, local government, and the community must all be engaged to effectively implement a mitigation effort. These parties must work together to mobilize resources, assess the level of risk, and develop and implement a mitigation plan. In most cases, executive support is essential to secure funding to support hazard mitigation, and to lend a degree of authority to the implementing agency.

Funding is a crucial issue to successful mitigation strategies. Even the best-drafted plan remains merely a plan without the proper funding to back its implementation. Complacency among elected officials and their constituents can prove to be a dangerous and costly situation. Does such complacency stem from a refusal to recognize vulnerability within the community or a failure to realize the existence of such vulnerability? Emergency managers must ensure that government officials receive up-to-date information on both apparent and potential risks within the community, the cost savings that can be realized through successful mitigation measures, and the potential savings to infrastructure and the safety of the citizenry that can accrue from such efforts. Nothing speaks more directly to elected officials than highlighting of an opportunity to realize cost savings while securing agency assets and increasing the protection of the residents. Furthermore, this discussion should involve detailed communication of the four phases of the planning process so that officials gain a complete understanding of the thoroughness of the endeavor.

Executive support for allocation of funding toward hazard mitigation is likely to be achieved with the realization of vertical partnerships. The federal government can become a strong ally to local and state agencies through numerous grant opportunities created to supplement local and state efforts to identify hazards, assess the risk, and create a viable mitigation plan.

Stakeholders should approach hazard mitigation planning from a broad perspective—that is, from an all-hazards approach to potential threats incorporating both natural and technological hazards into the analysis process. Flexibility is a necessity, as social and economic factors can lead to the need for plan revision. Periodic review of established performance indicators can lead to reassessment of plan direction and determination of whether the objectives have been met. If the answer is no, then plan revision is necessary to achieve long-term sustainability.

Preparation

Following mitigation in the succession of emergency management phases is preparation—that is, those actions taken to organize for the realization of a disaster, rather than to prevent one. This phase inevitably acts much like a bridge between mitigation and response. Similar to its predecessor, it is required to be carried out before a hazard arises, yet focuses on planning and equipping for the response when the emergency happens.

When a hazard evolves into a disaster, it is imperative for a system to be in place to most efficiently and effectively handle the disaster. Thus communities need to have in place a system of responses triggered by different scenarios (Godschalk, 2007). Emergency operation centers (EOCs) are increasingly common internationally as the primary actors in disaster situations. An EOC is a designated center for both events and non-events. In the event of a disaster, the EOC serves to coordinate all activities of local, national, private, and nonprofit organizations during the response. Militello et al.'s (2007) study focuses on EOCs serving as centers for training and exercises for potential disasters that bring stakeholders from different backgrounds and show them possible challenges during an incident. In addition, an EOC typically houses the Emergency Response Organization Network (ERON), which is a collection of representatives from all sectors that are responsible for maintaining the continuity of critical social services and expediting recovery (Godschalk, 2007). A local EOC will be established to work in partnership with other EOCs throughout the governmental hierarchy, providing an indispensable direct channel for information and resources (Militello et al., 2007).

Training can take the form of exercises and drills in organizations and EOCs. The three most common types of exercises are tabletop, functional, and full-scale (Perry, 2004; Peterson & Perry, 1999). Tabletop exercises, the simplest type, involve scenario-based narratives that help to define the role and tasks of participants. Functional training and exercises test specific functions and their operational abilities, whereas full-scale exercises aim to test all the functions involved in responding to an emergency. Moreover, apart from the steps included in planning and preparedness, the training and exercising of emergency plans is integral for the successful implementation and workability of plans. By engaging in training and exercising plans, improvements can be made and weaknesses can be highlighted and addressed. The plans developed in the mitigation phase should be exercised in the preparedness phase to ensure their survivability and effectiveness. Chapter 10 discusses the types of training and exercises in more detail.

Establishing the EOC and drilling its personnel through training exercises is only one example of preparative measures taken; a number of other efforts will also take place. On the one hand, at the upper level of the emergency management hierarchy, the national government can be strongly allied to local and state agencies through grant provisions to supplement their efforts to identify hazards, assess risks, and undertake viable preparative activities. In the United States, this relationship is exemplified by the National Flood Insurance Program (NFIP): In the event of damage, this insurance plan will cover financial loss (Government Accounting Office [GAO], 2009). Following the 2005 hurricanes, for example, more than 200,000 Gulf Coast residents received more than $23 billion in payments from the NFIP (FEMA, 2009). On the other hand, as with all stages of emergency management, the individual has a very important role to play. Some preparatory measures require collective action, such as the clearing of combustible materials from the streets of the neighborhood. Others require individual or family efforts, such as storing food for emergencies, elevating electronic devices from the floor, and anchoring cupboards to the wall so as to reduce personal losses.

It is reasonable to expect that preparedness efforts might be more intense after a disaster, because each disaster leaves lessons learned in its aftermath about vulnerabilities. Light's (2005) findings, however, indicate that Hurricane Katrina did not serve as a "wake-up call" for individuals regarding disaster planning. Light conducted research into the pre- and post-Katrina situations, and the results of the survey were not promising. The research revealed that more than half of the respondents who witnessed the disaster via their televisions were not better prepared after Katrina than before the hurricane struck. People also lost their confidence in their local governments, local businesses, and police services as a result of the disaster. Before Katrina, among low-income and low-education survey participants, 57% of the respondents stated that they did not know what to expect in case of a disaster; this figure did not change significantly after the hurricane, when 65% of the respondents stated they did not know what to expect in case of a disaster. Furthermore, the majority of the respondents believed that it was not possible to be very prepared for hurricanes, terrorist attacks, or pandemics, so blaming government for a lack of planning was considered unreasonable.

Case Study

Jeanne-Marie Col (2007) compared the experiences of local governments in New Orleans, Louisiana, and Qinglong County, China, related to Hurricane Katrina (2005) and the Tangshan earthquake (1976), respectively. In exploring the processes and government structures involved in these incidents, it became apparent that although some similarities existed, the overall decision-making authorities were very different in the two cases. Thus it is interesting to raise the question of whether the administrative success in Qinglong County's response was comparable to the failure of response to Hurricane Katrina.

The predominant difference identified was in the two emergency management plans. Although local officials in New Orleans were aware of the potential threat of an approaching hurricane, they lacked a clear plan for mitigation and preparation. Qinglong County, in contrast, took pre-disaster steps by providing intensified public education, hiring mitigation officers, increasing monitoring, involving citizens in exercises, and establishing a quick decision for declaring an emergency alert and mandatory evacuation. "Document 69" of Qinglong County frames the scope of activities and suggestions for both the mitigation and the preparedness phases. This comparison is remarkable, as there was no loss of life in Qinglong County despite the destruction of 180,000 buildings in the earthquake—an outcome demonstrating the clear advantages of well-structured mitigation and preparation efforts. The experience of Qinlong County supports the value of investment in comprehensive pre-disaster planning that embraces a collaborative approach and encourages involvement on all levels, from individuals to the national government.

If a comprehensive emergency plan already exists, it is vital to acknowledge that new physical and social vulnerabilities and different hazard types may emerge as a threat to communities. In some cases, disasters can reveal hidden weaknesses, which require communities to maintain an adaptive capacity to mitigate potential hazards (Godschalk, 2003; Tobin, 1999). Prater and Lindell (2000) note that each disaster is an opportunity to attract people's attention to mitigation practices and include them in the individual or political agenda. Stakeholders should approach hazard mitigation planning from a broad perspective. Flexibility is a necessity to account for inevitable fluctuations in social, political, and socioeconomic factors (Basolo, Steinberg, Burby, Levine, Cruz, & Hang, 2009). Subsequently, periodic review of established performance indicators can lead to a revision of direction. According to Lindell and Perry (2007), planning should be seen as a continuing process of analysis, plan development, and the acquisition by individuals of performance skills through training, drills, exercises, and critiques.

Emergency planning may face challenges such as a passive citizenry or encounter opposition because "it consumes resources that could be allocated to more immediate needs—police, patrols, road repairs, and the like" (Lindell & Perry, 2007, p. 166). Nevertheless, Pearce (2003) emphasizes the importance of citizen participation in emergency planning processes, which can bolster the mitigation efforts. The primary benefits of such engagement include identifying those most in need, informing people about potential hazards, and increasing trust between people and government officials. Furthermore, citizen participation can help the emergency management community identify the best ways to recover from the effects of a hazard while maintaining the best interests of the citizens.

Many local elected and appointed officials think of emergency management as a low priority because the public judges them on current performance and not on disaster planning. Given that disasters are low-probability events and are much less common than crime, emergency managers often find it difficult to substantiate the benefits of concentrating on mitigation and preparedness rather than on other areas (Godschalk, Brody, & Burby, 2003; National Institute of Building Sciences [NIBS], 2005). To face these challenges and increase communities' levels of preparedness, the following guiding principles should be used in emergency planning:

- Develop and implement an effective risk communication program.
- Manage resistance to the planning process.
- Address all hazards to which the community is exposed.
- Promote multi-organizational participation.
- Rely on accurate knowledge of the threat, likely human responses, and external resources.
- Identify the types of emergency response actions that are most appropriate, but also encourage improvisation based on continuing emergency assessment.
- Provide training and evaluation of the emergency response organization at all levels.
- Adopt a process of continuous planning and auditing.

Emergency and Crisis Management Frameworks

It is vital for countries to adopt a national approach to disasters, reframing crisis management into an auto-adaptive system that address four key points:

1. Detection of risk
2. Recognition and interpretation of risk
3. Communication of risk
4. Organization and mobilization of the community response system to reduce and respond to the risk or danger

When crises or disasters strike, the amount of damage incurred can be astronomical. This damage can be minimized, however, if a plan is constructed that addresses the possible crisis or disaster. Emergency planning is vital to ensure that the best outcome is achieved during bad times. Coordination and collaboration are important to ensure that all possible resources are being utilized during a crisis or disaster. Commonly referred to as emergency management frameworks, plans that address these issues provide a comprehensive guide for relevant agencies during a crisis, describe the command structure in such a scenario, and identify individual responsibilities. This section outlines the emergency management frameworks of the United States and the United Kingdom.

U.S. Frameworks

In the United States, preparedness is supported by three recently developed organizational structures: the Urban Areas Security Initiative, the Metropolitan Medical Response System, and the National Incident Management System (NIMS). The last of these structures is implemented through the Incident Command System and the affected jurisdiction's EOC. An important part of the emergency preparedness process is the development of emergency operations plans (EOPs), which provide responders with clear guidance and an effective framework. Any EOP encompasses four basic functions: emergency assessment, hazard operations, population protection, and incident management (Lindell & Perry, 2007). The goal of local emergency management committees (LEMCs) is to strengthen interorganizational linkages by promoting additional informal contracts—that is, verbal and written agreements among government agencies, nongovernmental organizations (NGOs), and local business.

The National Response Framework (NRF) in the United States is a comprehensive guideline that outlines key principles, roles, and structures for all actors in emergency response. "It describes how communities, tribes, States, the Federal Government, and private-sector and nongovernmental partners apply these principles for a coordinated, effective national response" (Department of Homeland Security [DHS], 2008a, p. 2). The NRF document paints a picture of response activities for local government agencies and defines situations when the federal government will become involved in disasters, such as in incidents that involve a threat to federal interests or when states cannot handle disaster situations (DHS, 2008a).

The NRF is the latest entry in a series of documents focusing on response activities for domestic incidents in the United States. It is the last step for unification, organization, and standardization of national homeland security efforts (DHS, 2008a). The initial document was the Federal Response Plan (FRP), which FEMA prepared in 1992, and which was designed to coordinate the federal agencies involved in emergency response activities (McEntire & Dawson, 2007). During the 1990s, the FRP worked without major debate. The September 11, 2001 terrorist attacks, however, changed the perspective of the federal government. Along with the establishment of the DHS, several other changes occurred in the national emergency management system. Presidential Directive Number 5 (HSPD 5) directed DHS to create the National Response Plan (NRP), which, unlike FRP, enforced a truly national approach by extending across a multitude of existing measures. The NRP merged the FRP, Federal Radiological Response Plan, Domestic Terrorism Concept of Operations Plan, Mass Mitigation Emergency Plan (Distant Shore), and National Oil Spill and Hazardous Substances Pollution Contingency Plan (Bullock, Haddow, Coppola, Ergin, Westerman, & Yeletaysi, 2006).

In 2008, NRP was replaced by the National Response Framework. Stakeholders of the plan had emphasized that NRP was bureaucratic and repetitive. Further discussions underlined complaints that NRP was insufficiently national, and all stakeholders involved in emergency management were not fully able to understand the document

(DHS, 2008a). The NRF, in contrast, includes members of the private sector, NGOs, and federal, state, local, and tribal governments in disaster planning, and is written clearly to ensure a universal understanding. The document addresses the participants in all levels of governments, the private sector, and the nonprofit sector. It further underscores how to respond to incidents, how to organize for implementing successful response, and what the critical elements of a successful response are. Lastly, NRF includes "content and plan for [an] online Resource Center" (DHS, 2008a, p. 3).

The September 11, 2001 terrorist attacks and the 2004 and 2005 hurricanes revealed many deficiencies in the U.S. emergency management system and spurred several developments in the legislative field. A comprehensive system called the National Incident Management System (NIMS) that brought a standard to emergency management activities was subsequently developed by the U.S. government and enacted with DHS HSPD 5. The DHS directive requires all federal agencies to adopt the NIMS plan, and state and local organizations to use it in their operations if they want to be eligible for federal homeland security funding (Perry & Lindell, 2007).

NIMS components include, but are not limited to, response and planning aspects of the emergency management. In the NIMS document, the system is described as follows:

> [It] provides a systematic, proactive approach to guide departments and agencies at all levels of government, nongovernmental organizations, and private sector to work seamlessly to prevent, protect against, respond to, recover from, and mitigate the effects of incidents regardless of cause size, location, or complexity, in order to reduce the loss of life and property and harm to the environment. (DHS, 2008b, p. 1)

The system is intended to serve as a tool to ensure interoperability, a set of preparedness concepts for all hazards, and standardized procedures in a dynamic system (DHS, 2008b). Flexibility and standardization are the two main concepts embedded within the NIMS documents. Because NIMS is applicable to all types of hazards and threats, without any constraints in the size and scope of the event, flexibility is inevitable and, in fact, essential. Meanwhile, standardization allows organizations from different sectors and specialties to function together with minimal (if not zero) deficiencies.

NIMS includes five components:

- Preparedness
- Communications and information management
- Resource management
- Command and management
- Ongoing management and maintenance

NIMS requires emergency management personnel and organizations to work together to enhance preparedness. Necessary mechanisms and tools are included in the system, which ensures preparedness with "planning; procedures and protocols; training and exercises; personnel qualifications; licensure and certification; and equipment certification" (DHS, 2008b, p. 9).

The communication and information management component of NIMS maintains interoperability, access to information, appropriate cooperation, and coordination of emergency agencies. Having a common operating picture is necessary for both on-scene and off-scene personnel to have a sense of the scope and conditions of an incident. Ensuring interoperability with reliable, portable, scalable, resilient, and redundant communication tools reinforces the actions of the emergency managers and helps them work together with minimal difficulties (DHS, 2008b).

The resource management component deals with the deployment of necessary resources to the incident scene. Pre-incident resource management is quite important, as are incident-moment resource deployment and post-incident resource management. Resource management becomes integral in incidents that might require different levels (local or federal) of government involvement, coordination, oversight, and processing of timely and appropriate resource delivery. Consistency, standardization, coordination, use, information management, and credentialing are the components of resource management (DHS, 2008b).

The command and management component of NIMS focuses the incident response and management. The Incident Command System (ICS), Multiagency Coordination System (MACS), and public information constitute the backbone of this component of NIMS (DHS, 2008b). Because of its inclusion of the ICS, NIMS is often perceived as a response system. ICS was developed in California in 1970s after a significant wildfire led to recognition of the importance of a structure for coordinating disparate responders. It was later adopted by the federal government and eventually became a standard for emergency responders.

Lastly, ongoing management and maintenance "establishes strategic directions for and oversight of NIMS" (Perry & Lindell, 2007, p. 178). There are two subsections within this component: National Integration Center (NIC) and Supporting Technologies. The NIC section identifies the responsibilities of NIC, while the Supporting Technologies section identifies the necessary principles to utilize technologies and science to lower the cost and improve capacity (DHS, 2008b).

Although NIMS is a comprehensive document it has limitations and requires improvements. The recent BP oil spill crisis in the Gulf of Mexico has shown us how political agendas can influence the implementation of NIMS and has highlighted some failures and shortcomings of this system that remain to be addressed.

U.K. Framework

Efforts to outline a national structure for emergencies had been under way in the United Kingdom prior to 2001 in response to a number of incidents such as severe flooding, fuel protests, and an outbreak of foot-and-mouth disease (Coaffee & Wood, 2006). In light of the September 11, 2001 terrorist attacks, however, there was increased pressure for the rapid development of an integrated system of preparedness and response, resulting in the Civil Contingencies Act (CCA) of 2004 (Smith, 2003). Efforts supported by this act are united underneath the umbrella term of "resilience"—a term that is increasingly being used in disaster management and development to describe a holistic approach to reducing communities' vulnerabilities (O'Brien & Read, 2005).

The CCA is seen as a comprehensive overhaul of British emergency protocols, and includes the creation of a Civil Contingencies Secretariat in the Cabinet Office at the apex of the expansive organizational framework. Separated into two parts, the CCA addresses local arrangements for civil protection in the first part and emergency powers in the second. In terms of disaster management, the act specifies the actions required of authorities and other parties in preparing for, and in the event of, an emergency. Plans need to cover efforts toward preventing emergencies, reducing or controlling their effects, and undertaking any other efforts necessary to protect three main groups: the vulnerable, the victims, and the responders (Cabinet Office, 2009).

Responding actors are split into either Category 1, "core responders" (emergency services, principal local authorities, and health bodies), or Category 2, "cooperating responders" (utility and transport providers, additional health bodies, and government agencies). Complete lists of these actors can be found in Schedule 1 of the CCA Office of Public Sector Information [(OPSI], 2004, p. 23). To create a platform for collaboration and communication between responders, the U.K. framework provides for Local Resilience Forums (LRFs) based on police force areas and Regional Resilience Forums (RRFs) that provide coordination between LRFs and a channel to central government.

Planning at the local level is the responsibility of Category 1 responders and must include rules for emergency identification, training and exercises, and periodic review and update procedures. At the regional level, RRFs ensure that generic response plans are in place across the region, oversee "Government Office Business Continuity Plans" to ensure the sustainability of the functions of local government, and maintain coordination for the support of local planning. Central government still has the task of preparing for mass-casualty or chemical, biological, or radioactive/nuclear (CBRN) incidents, cross-governmental efforts, and the designation of roles to departments and tiers of the command structure.

The CCA provides vital legislative support on a number of issues discussed in previous sections, which had been observed to be shortcomings in past U.K. experiences. Category 1 responders are now responsible for carrying out risk assessments for national publication; the results of these assessments are made available via the National Risk Register. The method of assessment involves the contextualization, evaluation, and treatment of risks to provide a clear and constructive measure for organizations' planning (Cabinet Office, 2010). To facilitate information exchange between actors, the CCA places a statutory duty upon both Category 1 and Category 2 responders to share their relevant information, and demands the development of resilient telecommunications that would be able to withstand emergency-related disruption.

As indicated in the earlier discussion of EOCs, a crucial part of an emergency manager's role is informing and, if necessary, warning the public of hazards. The CCA reiterates this point, emphasizing the need for existing Regional Media Emergency Forums (RMEFs) to communicate both the risk and plans preceding an emergency as well as to continue to update the public during a crisis.

The CCA marks a considerable development in British emergency preparation:

> The changes to the legislative base underpinning civil protection are wholesale. The Civil Contingencies Act, 2004 . . . clears outdated legislation, re-defines emergencies, clearly identifies the roles and responsibilities of all participatory organizations, introduces a mandatory regime for responders and replaces the previous outdated system for emergency powers. (O'Brien & Read, 2005, p. 356)

The act is not without its critics, however, who have raised questions about issues ranging from the real level of readiness in hospitals (Wong et al., 2006) to the fairly top-down method of development and application of the framework itself (Coaffee & Wood, 2006). Despite these concerns, there is widespread acknowledgment of the degree of care and the vast improvement that the CCA represents and has engendered in terms of the United Kingdom's emergency management capabilities.

Although the existing U.K. emergency management framework emphasizes resiliency through the CCA, according to O'Brien (2008) the country's existing approach is limited to the continuity of emergency operations and commercial activities in the aftermath of a disaster. That is, it fails to constructively involve communities and the public in planning for prevention of emergencies and in identifying vulnerabilities and risks (Elliott & Macpherson, 2010). O'Brien (2008) suggests that the vision of community resilience will be achieved when emergency management is expanded to involve communities on a proactive basis.

Disaster Mitigation and Sustainability

In his exploration of mitigation, Godschalk (2007) comes to the topic from a broader perspective by focusing on preparedness and the enhanced significance of mitigation in the modern age, and by exploring the cause-and-effect relationship of mitigation with community sustainability and resiliency and many other aspects of emergency management. "Decisions made about mitigation will determine the safety of the region in the face of inevitable future storms" (Godschalk, 2007, p. 90). A successful mitigation plan requires the utilization of social capital resources to address the needs and sustainability of a community as a whole. Attention must be paid not only to current hazards, but also to prevention of future hazards that could stem from unwise development choices.

Sustainability encompasses the planning of future actions that comprise multiple aspects and related goals. Mitigation in a sustainability context refers to precautions taken to decrease—if not eliminate—the risks stemming from hazards to property and to meet the needs of contemporary and future generations (El Masri & Tipple, 2002; Godschalk, 2003). Tobin (1999) defines sustainable and resilient communities as "societies which are structurally organized to minimize the effects of disasters, and, at the same time, have the ability to recover quickly by restoring the socio-economic vitality of the community" (p. 13). Based on the earlier discussions of mitigation, sustainability, and resiliency, it should be apparent that mitigation and sustainability are interdependent actions. In other words, mitigation activities are affected by sustainability plans, while sustainability efforts cannot be considered without addressing the mitigation impacts of potential hazards. Despite this interdependence, putting mitigation and sustainability efforts side by side in a framework is more challenging than expected (Schneider, 2002). When mitigation is mentioned in the same breath with sustainability, the scope of the term becomes broader and goes beyond the borders of emergency management. Planning, economic activities, and mitigation activities need to go hand in hand, which requires close relationships to be forged between the professionals who work in these different realms. Planners, emergency managers, elected and appointed officials, economic professionals, and community representatives all need to understand the importance of collective action if emergency management is to be successful.

Chakos, Schulz, and Tobin (2002) discuss the city of Berkeley, California, as representing a notable success story in terms of its mitigation actions after the 1990s. The city experienced the ravages of the Loma Prieta earthquake in 1989, which was followed by the devastating East Bay Hills fire in 1991. These two disasters triggered a series of mitigation efforts in the city covering public schools, the University of California in Berkeley (UC-Berkeley), and numerous households (Chakos et al., 2002). Public officials, community advocates, and UC-Berkeley personnel have made remarkable strides in enhancing the sustainability of the city by implementing mitigation precautions. Public schools in the city, the UC-Berkeley campus, and weak buildings were reinforced and prepared for potential disasters. The professionals and UC-Berkeley's experts kept the issue warm by making sure it stayed at the forefront of the local political agenda and pushed for results constantly. To date, the city has invested $390 million in local taxes and bonds in this effort, along with $2 million for seismic subsidies and safety programs. Chakos et al. (2002) note that after these efforts Berkeley may have the top per capita mitigation spending in the state of California, and perhaps in the United States as well.

Conclusion

Disaster planning and preparation entails more than simply guidance for those who respond to calls for assistance in the midst of an emergency; it is also an important component in connecting emergency management teams to communities. It is necessary to view mitigation and preparation as unique phases dedicated to reducing the probability of a disaster and planning how to respond to a disaster. Through mitigation efforts, it becomes possible to reduce communities' vulnerabilities through a variety of social and technical approaches that will permeate organizational structures and involve the population at the individual level. There is a clear need to plan in advance for crises, and to designate an EOC to manage stakeholders in the event that an emergency comes to pass. Although there can be difficulties in securing funding for these preliminary activities, they commonly have a favorable cost–benefit ratio and can save countless lives.

Moreover, adopting a framework and utilizing an EOP not only expands an emergency managers' knowledge of what they are seeking to find out about disasters, but also positions them to take a proactive role in the fight against delayed communication and poor teamwork among local agencies and government officials at large. Collaboration is an effective means of preparing for disastrous events. All communities should work on developing an effective emergency management plan that integrates the activities of all necessary entities that will respond to a disaster ahead of time. Doing so will ensure that more lives are saved, decrease confusion at the time of an incident, and make emergency response efforts more efficient.

Review Questions

1. A group of community leaders has asked you to describe the mitigation strategies that a local government could implement without any outside assistance. What would you recommend to your audience?

2. Why do collaboration and coordination have significance in managing crises and disasters? What are some challenges related to these aspects of emergency management?

3. How can we overcome the potential for barriers to prevent multisector and multijurisdiction agencies from working together effectively in disaster response and in recovery from disasters?

4. How can the frameworks introduced in this chapter be applied in dealing with disasters? Why are they called frameworks rather than plans?

5. How do preparedness and mitigation strategies determine disaster resiliency and sustainability of communities?

6. How might the information you gained from this chapter affect you personally and professionally?

References

Basolo, V., Steinberg, L. J., Burby, R. J., Levine, J. Cruz, A. M., & Hang, C. (2009). The effects of confidence in government and information on perceived and actual preparedness for disasters. *Environment and Behavior, 41*(3), 338–364.

Blaikie, P., Cannon, T., Davis, I., & Wisner, B. (Eds.). (1994). *At risk: Natural hazards, people's vulnerability and disasters.* London: Routledge.

Bullock, J. A., Haddow, G. D., Coppola, D., Ergin, E., Westerman, L., & Yeletaysi, S. (2006). *Introduction to homeland security.* China: Butterworth-Heinemann.

Cabinet Office. (2009). Emergency planning. Retrieved March 24, 2010, from http://www.cabinetoffice.gov.uk/ukresilience/preparedness/emergencyplanning.aspx.

Cabinet Office. (2010). Risk. Retrieved March 24, 2010, from http://www.cabinetoffice.gov.uk/ukresilience/preparedness/risk.aspx.

Chakos, A., Schulz, P., & Tobin, L. T. (2002). Making it work in Berkeley: Investing in community sustainability. *Natural Hazards Review, 3*(2), 55–67.

Coaffee, J., & Wood, D. M. (2006). Security is coming home: Rethinking scale and constructing resilience in the global urban response to terrorist risk. *International Relations, 20*(4), 503–517.

Col, J. M. (2007). Managing disasters: The role of local government. *Public Administration Review, Special Issue, 67,* 114–124.

Coleman, L. (2006). Frequency of manmade disasters in the 20th century. *Journal of Contingencies and Crisis Management, 14*(1), 3–11.

Comfort, L. K. (2007). Crisis management in hindsight: Cognition, communication, coordination, and control. *Public Administration Review, Special Issue, 67,* 189–197.

Cuny, F. C. (1983). *Disasters and development.* New York: Oxford University Press.

Department of Homeland Security (DHS). (2008a). Introducing National Response Framework. Retrieved January 15, 2010, from http://www.fema.gov/pdf/emergency/nrf/about_nrf.pdf.

Department of Homeland Security (DHS). (2008b). National Incident Management System. Retrieved January 13, 2010, from http://www.fema.gov/pdf/emergency/nims/NIMS_core.pdf.

El Masri, S., & Tipple, G. (2002). Natural disaster, mitigation and sustainability: The case of developing countries. *International Planning Studies, 7*(2), 157–175.

Elliott, D., & Macpherson, A. (2010). Policy practice: Recursive learning from crisis. *Group and Organization Management, 35*(5), 572–675.

Federal Emergency Management Agency (FEMA). (2009). Mitigation. Retrieved December 18, 2009, from http://www.fema.gov/government/mitigation.shtm.

Fowler, K., Kling, N .D., & Larson, M. D. (2007). Organizational preparedness for coping with major crisis or disaster. *Business and Society, 46*(1), 88–103.

Fuld, L. (2003). Be prepared: The future looks a lot less uncertain with the right early warning system. *Harvard Business Review, 81*(11), 20–21.

General Accounting Office (GAO). (2009, October 1). Emergency management: Preliminary observations on FEMA's community preparedness programs related to the national preparedness system. GAO-10-105T. Retrieved October 1, 2009, from http://www.gao.gov/new.items/d10105t.pdf.

Godschalk, D. R. (2003). Urban hazard mitigation: Creating resilient cities. *Natural Hazards Review, 4*(3), 136–143.

Godschalk, D. R. (2007). Mitigation. In W. L. Waugh, Jr., & K. Tierney (Eds.), *Emergency management: Principles and practice for local government* (2nd ed., pp. 89–112). Washington, DC: ICMA.

Godschalk, D. R., Brody, S., & Burby, R. (2003). Public participation in natural hazard mitigation policy formation: Challenges for comprehensive planning. *Journal of Environmental Planning and Management, 46*(5), 733–754.

Kapucu, N. (2009). Interorganizational coordination in complex environments of disasters: The evolution of intergovernmental disaster response systems. *Journal of Homeland Security and Emergency Management, 6*, 1.

Light, P. C. (2005). *Katrina effect on American preparedness.* PERI. Retrieved from https://www.riskinstitute.org/peri/images/file/postkatrina_preparedness.pdf.

Lindell, K. M., & Perry, W. R. (2007). Planning for preparedness. In W. L. Waugh, Jr., & K. Tierney (Eds.), *Emergency management: Principles and practice for local government* (2nd ed., pp. 113–142). Washington, DC: ICMA.

London Regional Resilience Forum. (2006, September). *Looking back moving forward: Lessons identified and progress since the terrorist events of 7 July 2005.* London: Government Office for London. Retrieved March 20, 2010, from http://www.londonprepared.gov.uk/downloads/lookingbackmovingforward.pdf.

McEntire, D. A., & Dawson, G. (2007). The intergovernmental context. In W. L. Waugh, Jr., & K. Tierney (Eds.), *Emergency management: Principles and practice for local government* (2nd ed., pp. 57–70). Washington, DC: ICMA.

Militello, L. G., Patterson, E. S., Bowman, L., & Wears, R. (2007). Information flow during crisis management: Challenges to coordination in the emergency operations center. *Cognition, Technology and Work, 9*(1), 25–31.

National Institute of Building Sciences (NIBS). (2005). *Multihazard Mitigation Council, Natural Hazard Mitigation Saves: An independent study to assess the future savings from mitigation activities. Vol. 1: Findings, conclusions, and recommendations.* Washington, DC: National Institute of Building Sciences. Retrieved October 7, 2009, from http://floods.org/PDF/MMC_Volume1_FindingsConclusionsRecommendations.pdf.

O'Brien, G. (2008). UK emergency preparedness: A holistic response? *Disaster Prevention and Management, 17*(2), 232–243.

O'Brien, G., & Read, P. (2005). Future UK emergency management: New wine, old skin? *Disaster Prevention and Management, 14*(3), 353–361.

Office of Public Sector Information (OPSI). (2004). Civil Contingencies Act 2004. Retrieved March 24, 2010, from http://www.opsi.gov.uk/acts/acts2004/pdf/ukpga_20040036_en.pdf.

Paton, D. (2003). Disaster preparedness: A social cognitive perspective. *Disaster Prevention and Management, 12*(3), 210–216.

Pearce. L. (2003). Disaster management and community planning, and public participation: How to achieve sustainable hazard mitigation. *Natural Hazards, 28*, 211–228.

Perry, R. W. (2004). Disaster Exercise Outcomes for Professional Emergency Personnel and Citizen Volunteers. *Journal of Contingencies and Crises Management.* 12, 2, 64–75.

Perry, R. W., & Lindell, M. K. (2007). Disaster response. In W. L. Waugh, Jr., & K. Tierney (Eds.), *Emergency management: Principles and practice for local government* (2nd ed., pp. 159–182). Washington, DC: ICMA.

Peterson, D. M. and R. W. Perry. (1999). The Impacts of Disaster Exercises on Participants. *Disaster Prevention and Management.* 8, 4, 251–255.

Prater, C. S., & Lindell, M. K. (2000). Politics of hazard mitigation. *Natural Hazards Review, 1*(2), 73–82.

Public Safety Wireless Network Program (PSWN). (2002). Answering the call: Communications Lessons learned from the Pentagon attack. Retrieved January 13, 2010, from http://www.safecomprogram.gov/NR/rdonlyres/8839D9BA-9104-4EE1-BC43-E8431C500F95/0/AnsweringCallLessonsPentagonAttack.pdf.

Quarantelli, E. L. (1998). *What is a disaster? Perspectives on the question.* London: Routledge.

Rotanz, A. R. (2007). Applied response strategies. In W. L. Waugh, Jr., & K. Tierney (Eds.), *Emergency management: Principles and practice for local government* (2nd ed.). Washington, DC: ICMA.

SAFECOM. (n.d.), Interoperability. Retrieved January 13, 2010, from http://www.safecomprogram.gov/SAFECOM/interoperability/default.htm.

Schneider, R. O. (2002). Hazard mitigation and sustainable community development. *Disaster Prevention and Management, 11*(2), 141–147.

Smith, J. (2003). Civil contingency planning in government. *Parliamentary Affairs, 56,* 410–422.

Strom, K. J., & Eyerman, J. (2008). Interagency coordination: A case study of the 2005 London grain bombings. *National Institute of Justice, 260,* 8–12.

Tobin, G. (1999). Sustainability and community resilience: The Holy Grail of hazards planning. *Environmental Hazards, 1*(1), 13–25.

Tunstall, S. M., Johnson, C. L., & Penning Rowsell, E. C. (2004). *Flood hazard management in England and Wales: From land drainage to flood risk management.* World Congress on Natural Disaster Mitigation. Retrieved January 12, 2010, from http://www.fhrc.mdx.ac.uk/resources/docs_pdfs/India%20paper%20final%20version.pdf.

Wong, K., Turner, P. S., Boppana, A., Nugent, Z., Coltman, T., Cosker, T. D. A., & Blagg, S. E. (2006). Preparation for the next major incident: Are we ready? *Emergency Medical Journal, 23,* 709–712.

Chapter 4

Disaster Response and Recovery

Chapter Objectives

- Identify guiding principles of emergency response and recovery as two key phases of emergency and crisis management.
- Analyze disaster response and recovery operational challenges.
- Explore the concepts of comprehension, communication, coordination and collaboration in disaster response and recovery.
- Understand the relief-to-reconstruction continuum.
- Review the disaster responses in case studies of the Marmara earthquake, the Hull floods, the Southeast Asia tsunami, the Haiti earthquake, and the BP oil spill disaster.

Introduction

This chapter defines disaster response and recovery in terms of their distinctive activities, and explains how they differ from activities that take place during other phases of the emergency management cycle. Beginning with a discussion of the major themes found in the literature and their application to the broader context of emergency management, the chapter explores these themes as they are applied to disaster response and recovery among all levels of a community. Many of the lessons learned from previous disasters mentioned in the discussions, such as Hurricane Katrina and past California wildfires and earthquakes, recognize the importance of preplanning in emergency management. Notably, the failures in the response and recovery related to Hurricane Katrina prompted the creation of the National Response Framework (NRF) as a measure to help governments undertake the difficult task of planning (Department of Homeland Security [DHS], 2008), the proper implementation of which relies on collaboration and communication—two aspects of emergency management that are evaluated in this chapter in regard to response and recovery planning.

It is with specific reference to the state–civil society relationship in the context of the relief-to-reconstruction continuum that this chapter examines the response and recovery experiences from a number of post-disaster environments. The major part of these discussions is dedicated to the housing, economic, and psychological recovery of households and the operational recovery of businesses, before turning to the recovery assistance that can be expected from state and federal government and from insurance.

Disaster Response

The response phase occurs when a disaster is imminent or soon after its onset. Response activities are intended to minimize the risks associated with an emergency by protecting people, the environment, property, and to provide emergency assistance to disaster victims. They also include efforts to reduce the probability or extent of secondary damage through such measures as security patrols to prevent looting; attempts to reduce damage through means such as sandbagging against impending floodwaters or remedial movement of shelters in heavily contaminated fallout areas; and other measures that will enhance future recovery operations, such as damage assessment.

In contrast to response activities, recovery activities continue beyond the emergency period immediately following a disaster. Their purpose is to return all systems— informal and formal—to as near their normal state as possible. Recovery can be broken down into short-term and long-term activities. Short-term activities attempt to return vital human systems to minimal operating standards and usually encompass approximately a 2-week period.

Predominantly reliant upon the successes of mitigation and preparation, the response phase represents the culmination of these efforts, and demonstrates their strengths and weaknesses. Rotanz (2007) focuses on applied response strategies and the act of transitioning from the preparedness phase into the response phase. When an event occurs, response strategies will need to be implemented based on the plans adopted by the relevant agencies. Large portions of the strategy may be contingent on the event itself, and plans must remain fluid to accommodate revision as the need for tweaking them becomes apparent. There are no clear lines that demarcate the transition from one phase to another. Pre-impact activities such as opening shelters, implementing evacuation plans, and ensuring communication with regional partners can be considered a function of the preparedness phase as well as the response phase. Likewise, while response activities are under way, the initiation of the recovery phase can simultaneously take place.

This section explores the response as it relates to the previous two phases of the emergency management cycle—namely, mitigation and preparation. Militello et al. (2007) highlight four challenges that undermine the effective functioning of an emergency operations center (EOC): asymmetrical knowledge and experience, barriers to maintaining mutual awareness, uneven workload distribution, and disrupted communication. With these potential obstacles in mind, the following discussion is divided into two subsections. The first deals with the issue of comprehension, and the second focuses on difficulties with collaboration and communication.

Comprehension

In the context of emergency management, comprehension refers to the understanding, knowledge, and experience of public officials and emergency response actors. In Paton's (2003) view, social understanding plays a remarkable role in disaster prevention and mitigation, with this author arguing that "public hazard education may reduce perceived risk and levels of preparedness" (p. 210). Both Paton (2003) and Light (2005) highlight individuals' tendency to transfer their responsibility for preparedness to local emergency agencies and personnel such as police and fire fighters as a justification for lack of preparedness. Developing social cognition in individuals' minds could trigger a change in their behaviors, however. Anxiety, critical awareness, and an improved risk perception of hazards are all factors that motivate individuals to prepare. Self-efficacy, outcome expectancy, response efficacy, and problem-focused coping are other components of the intention to preparation.

Comfort (2007) emphasizes the importance of knowledge and experience in a disaster response team, stating that "cognition is central to performance in emergency management" (p. 189). Noting that the disaster that followed on the heels of Hurricane Katrina was due to a collapse in mitigation and preparedness efforts, this author argues that the failure of response was due to the low perception of risk. In other words, an effective emergency response depends on insight that "enables experienced managers to lessen the contrast between planning and practice, a gap that theorists in emergency management have long sought to close" (p. 189).

Unless there is a clear recognition of risk, decision makers and policy makers at all jurisdictional levels may experience challenges in communication, coordination, and control within their respective agencies during a disaster. Thus the clear recognition of risk at the local level by first responders and emergency managers must be complemented by the clear understanding of risk by the upper management that provides resources and mutual aid for response.

It is possible to frame the emergency response to the 2005 London bombings as being in part due to the widespread comprehension of crisis management held by local and national authorities. Strom and Eyerman (2008) recognize London's history of disaster management, from the blitz bombings during World War II to the more recent acts of terrorism associated with Northern Ireland, as having necessitated widespread awareness and interagency planning. In 2002, the London Regional Resilience Forum was created as an umbrella group that integrated the government and other authorities, emergency services, private industry, and national nonprofit groups as part of the city's emergency management team. The forum was crucial in preparing for exactly such a scenario, and demonstrated the benefit of four years of planning and exercises prior to the bombing: "Familiarity with roles and partners was evident. This was greatly helped by a long series of exercises and most recently Exercise Atlantic Blue in April 2005 (which included multiple attacks on the Underground)" (London Regional Resilience Forum, 2006, p. 3).

With regard to EOCs, it is common for them to hire very few full-time personnel (Kendra & Wachtendorf, 2003; Militello et al., 2007). As a consequence, people who work within EOCs in the case of a disaster often have a lack of experience and knowledge about emergencies. Participants who take on a role in collaborative networks usually work in differing professions and may not have the skills and abilities necessary to cope with the unexpected events in the case of a hazard. Furthermore, skilled and experienced participants such as police, the Red Cross, and fire departments have to coordinate people through EOCs, making the interaction all the more complicated. This divergent level of knowledge and experience among different emergency situation participants can hinder effective coordination.

Collaboration and Communication

Given that preparing for emergencies is a multiorganizational process extending from micro-level to macro-level authorities, effective coordination is crucial for effectively assisting affected communities. Many of the challenges stem from communication issues related to working with different agencies that have unique roles, responsibilities, and plans, and to acquiring the necessary resources needed to properly prepare for disaster. However, if agencies are able to overcome these challenges and fully coordinate their functions, they will be efficient responders to disasters. As Kapucu (2009) discusses, successful emergency management involves varying levels of authority, from national down to local government. Previous experience has shown that while authority over decision making should be allocated to organizations close to the incident site, greater technical knowledge and resources are available at higher levels in the emergency management hierarchy (Lindell & Perry, 2007). Building interorganizational linkages, sharing knowledge and resources with other jurisdictions and agencies, and handling hazards in a collaborative manner is vital. The disaster itself may dictate the approach for responders and the time frame for executing coordinated activities.

One of the main challenges faced by emergency planners is that many people are not willing to financially support emergency planning. In emergency planning, it can be difficult to measure the amount of money that can be saved by placing such disaster management systems and mechanisms. Coordination and collaboration allow for a vast number of ideas and solutions to be found, and allow emergency planners to determine which ideas would be the most cost-efficient. To cope effectively with the broad scope of potential disasters, recent technological advances are indispensable.

As mentioned in previous chapters, a number of technological tools are applied in emergency management, such as geographic information systems (GIS), wireless communication systems, and the Internet (Cutter, Emrich, Adams, Huyck, & Eguchi, 2007). GIS technologies are widely used by emergency managers not only in the planning phase, but also in response actions. GIS enhances collaborative decision making in both phases. Wireless systems enhance communication between emergency management personnel and agencies. The Internet allows emergency managers to share information, knowledge, and resources instantaneously. It also makes other critical emergency management technologies such as GIS easy to use and share with other stakeholders.

Successful emergency management requires the inclusion of different stakeholders in the process. Given their varying backgrounds, technological interoperability is key to achieving success in modern-day emergency management. It can be defined loosely as the ability to operate with other agencies and share information with them in real-time actions. The U.S. Department of Homeland Security's (DHS) SAFECOM program regards technology as a key component of interoperability, along with governance, standard operating procedures, training and exercises, and usage protocols (SAFECOM, n.d.).

On the one hand, technology can bolster interoperability in all phases of emergency management, allowing actors to gather more data in a shorter time frame, make faster and more accurate decisions, and communicate with one another easily. On the other hand, interoperability requires a standardization of technology. For instance, the September 11, 2001 Pentagon attacks revealed that the majority of the fire departments that responded to the incident had compatible (800 MHz) radio equipment, while few of them were using different hardware. Jurisdictions that had compatible radio systems were able to maintain interoperability at the incident scene immediately (Public Safety Wireless Network Program [PSWN], 2002).

Organizations also use technology applications such as common databases to share information, knowledge, resources, workforces, and ideas, and to synchronize their policies. Information technologies are important for effective response and recovery in large-scale events, but the key to communication is having close working relationships with those who are involved in disaster operation and with others who might help (Fischer, 1998; Rotanz, 2007; Tobin, 1999).

Returning once again to EOCs, it is widely accepted that two of their most important functions are public information and coordination. To fulfill the public information function, the EOC gathers information from all participating organizations and is responsible for ensuring that a single credible message is distributed to the public. This use of "one voice" helps to avoid confusion and ensure that citizens are informed of protective measures, traffic conditions, evacuation recommendations, and other matters pertaining to the disaster. The messages put forth by EOCs should be easily and clearly understandable for every level of people at risk and the community as whole.

In terms of coordination, making sure that all participating agencies work together seamlessly poses a major challenge for an EOC. When dealing with several different agencies and jurisdictions, an EOC will inevitably have to negotiate with diverse personalities, roles, and responsibilities. Having an effective EOC can make a considerable difference in the quality and professionalism of a response effort. All too often, however, EOCs may suffer from communication breakdowns, an overwhelming flood of information, and unfamiliarity with software and tools that can lead to differing perspectives of the situation.

To overcome issues of inexperienced staff in the EOC, Militello et al. (2007) note that the work burden should be distributed to people based on their expertise and knowledge. Unfortunately, this situation may lead to an asymmetrical distribution of information within the EOC, meaning core personnel in the center are overloaded with work and information while other personnel have relatively few tasks. As pointed out by Lindell and Perry (2007, p. 137): "Interorganizational linkages can be impeded by geographical distance, lack of funds, lack of staff, incompatible professional perspective and terminology, lack of trust in an organization, overconfidence in one's own capability, and inequality of rewards and costs of participation of those different organizations." Through efficient mitigation and preparation, these challenges can be minimized, if not overcome entirely.

Role of Communities and Organizational Typology in Disaster Response

Perry and Lindell (2007) address disaster response and the challenges that emergency managers must plan for prior to a disaster or catastrophe. Positive aspects of a community disaster response often include unrequested citizen and organizational participation as well as emergent groups that fill service delivery gaps. At the same time, these resource opportunities present challenges in that "the arrival of people and organizations with unknown capabilities, together with poor communication among organizations, creates ambiguity about who is in charge . . . duplication of some tasks, neglect of others, underuse of resources, and tardy response to disaster demands" (Perry & Lindell, 2007, p. 160). Also, "[u]nder severe threat, the operational capacity of emergency organizations within a complex region suffers from spreading dysfunction that compounds failure and creates new dangers for vulnerable populations" (Comfort, Hauskrecht, & Lin, 2008, p. 577).

Emergency multiorganizational networks (EMONs) are one answer to strengthening coordination during disasters, but the best tactic to eliminate maladaptive response patterns is preplanning through an effective emergency operations plan

(EOP). To avoid inadequacies in the EOP, emergency managers should address five main challenges to the emergency response:

- Citizen behavioral response to disasters
- Resource and people convergence
- Role abandonment by emergency workers
- Disaster declarations
- Communications

One example of challenge aversion and understanding (applicable to the citizen behavioral response to disasters) is the finding that, contrary to popular belief, citizens respond rationally and constructively during a disaster, exhibiting prosocial behaviors such as caring for neighbors and searching for survivors. Emergency managers must expect this rationality and quell anxiety by providing as much information as possible, including explaining the threats, their consequences, and protective action recommendations (PARs). Citizens will act in accordance with these PARs, because "in times of extreme stress, citizens look to government for guidance" (Perry & Lindell, 2007, p. 162). In an information vacuum where no PARs are given, citizens will act in ways they think are reasonable, which ultimately leads to higher anxiety. Emergency managers must take this factor into account by having a response plan they are able to execute and by communicating frequently with their citizens on government actions and PARs.

Specific frameworks for disaster response, including the NRF and the National Incident Management System (NIMS), have been revamped since the September 11 terrorist attacks, but the emphasis on terrorism may come at a toll to other potential hazards faced in the United States. Specifically, the Government Accountability Office (GAO) is concerned with the limiting factors of DHS's all-hazards approach and its absorption of the Federal Emergency Management Agency (FEMA), including fund competition from a variety of agencies all housed in DHS and service duplication across government agencies outside of DHS. The in-house approach to the all-hazards response by DHS has changed the political environment for local administrators to a federally mandated, "top-down flow of communications and requirements" (Perry & Lindell, 2007, p. 171), even though local governments are expected to shoulder the burden of the disaster management. Contextual examples of federal programs governing local disaster response include the Urban Areas Security Initiative (UASI), Metropolitan Medical Response System (MMRS), and NIMS, whereby states are required to be compliant with these programs' policies and regulations to receive funding.

In the United States, the DHS's perspective toward managing emergencies and crises has been quite different from the approach used before this department's creation. The top-down approach, in particular, has sparked discussions about its effectiveness. In this context, Harrald (2006) emphasizes the importance of discipline and agility for emergency response, stating that "response organizations must possess agility and discipline to respond to extreme events" (p. 263). Discipline in emergency management in the United States has been cultivated through broad adoption of the Incident Command System (ICS). Nevertheless, structured response systems inevitably are characterized by some level of rigidity, which translates into limited adaptability and creativity. Harrald (2006) argues that both discipline and agility are needed in an emergency response. He notes that emergency managers might be able to adapt to unexpected conditions and be creative when developing solutions in stressful environments. Discipline and agility must go hand in hand for an optimal response; any other situation creates a somewhat weak organizational typology.

Harrald (2006) defines four organizational typologies based on these two attributes (**Figure 4-1**). The worst organizational typology is defined as low discipline and low agility, which leads to dysfunctional institutions. Ad hoc/reactive organizations are relatively unstructured, yet are creative and able to improvise. As long as organizations maintain their creativity and strong structure, they are described as balanced/adaptive, which means they will likely function properly in a disaster and respond to any possible uncertainties creatively. Leadership and employee training and development play key roles in the sustainability of a balanced/adaptive organizational structure. Harrald (2006) cites the U.S. Coast Guard's response to Hurricane Katrina as an example of this type of organizational response. Lastly, well-structured and rigid organizations adapt bureaucratic/procedural response systems that might prove helpful for mobilizing large organizations. The drawback of this type of organization is its inability to adapt to unpredictable and changing conditions of disasters.

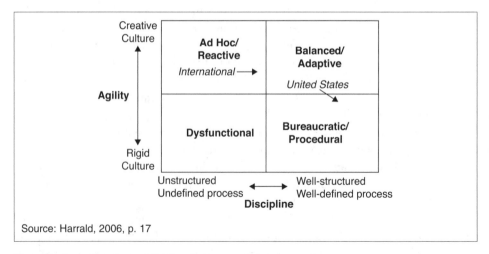

Source: Harrald, 2006, p. 17

Figure 4-1 *An Organizational Typology for Response Organizations*

Operational Challenges in Disaster Response

Challenges to emergency response start when the scope of a disaster exceeds the resources available to handle it. The majority of disasters do not cause tragic results because they are large in scope or because shortages of resources occur, but rather because a lack of coordination and cooperation among stakeholders hampers the response actions (Auf der Heide, 1996). To ensure that an emergency situation does not overwhelm the responders, planning for emergencies and mitigating potential challenges are vital. When local governments are engaged in the planning process, careful attention must be given to the potential operational challenges that can overload the emergency response operations and distract emergency personnel from their primary roles. For disaster response and recovery plans to be effective, they must adequately address how local governments will manage operational disruptions such as unanticipated resources shortfalls, destructive citizen behavior, role abandonment by emergency personnel, and the disaster declaration process. Furthermore, the challenges that emergency managers confront during the disasters can create deficiencies in the decision-making process. Without the proper measures in place, the increased risk imposed on disaster response and recovery operations can cause materialization of threats beyond the disaster occurrence itself. Local governments must be tasked with outlining how their interorganizational community-wide responses will decrease vulnerabilities to the execution of the disaster response and recovery operation (Perry & Lindell, 2007).

Destructive citizen behavior and emergency personnel role abandonment are obvious disruptions to disaster operations. Less obvious detriments are unanticipated resources shortfalls and the disaster declaration process. A lack of local government planning for resource difficulties exacerbates one of the main challenges that has long plagued disaster response operations—that of ensuring adequate availability of emergency funds, equipment, and supplies. Operational risk can be reduced with pre-disaster planning at the local level that is targeted at increasing authorities' capacity to manage resources, thereby reducing the likelihood of disruption.

Perry and Lindell (2007) also indicate that when disasters arise, citizens and communities tend to perceive all disastrous events as catastrophic and eligible for declaration. The process of declaration in different scenarios and organizations consists of varying protocols, and can be misunderstood by those who are not familiar with existing processes. Local governments should be required to plan in great detail for the declaration process and to determine how they will respond in the interim while assessments and resource allocations are pending.

McEntire (2007) emphasizes how decision-making challenges can arise during emergencies. He underlines that information during emergency situations is usually incomplete and limited. In these conditions, it is not possible for someone to take reliably informed decisions; instead, bounded rationality plays a key role in decision making in this scenario (McEntire, 2007). Yehezkel Dror (1988, as cited in McEntire, 2007) lists several sources of challenges to decision makers during disasters:

facing adversity, image production, compressed time, tragic choice, fuzzy gambling, strain and stress, and group processes. To overcome these problems, it is vital for all parties in the emergency management process to increase their situational awareness, corroborate their information with others to gauge accuracy, examine the disaster from different perspectives, meet their own and others' physical needs, and maintain an open mind (McEntire, 2007). Such decision-making related challenges are explored further in Chapter 9.

Disaster Recovery

Phillips and Neal (2007) discuss the process of recovery in its entirety, from planning to resource acquisition. A key aspect of this process is defining what the community and government envision as recovery. Emergency managers should avoid calls for a return to the pre-disaster state, as often it is latent vulnerabilities that exacerbate a hazard's effect. This definition of recovery is often developed during post-event planning, but it is important to have a recovery framework laid out prior to the onset of a disaster. Recovery is highly related to the nature and the extent of damage to the built environment. Vulnerabilities and exposure to hazards determines the level of potential damage that occurs after a hazard (Alesch, Arendt, & Holly, 2009). The recovery plan itself can either be stand-alone or included within the broader comprehensive plan (Emergency Support Function [ESF] 14 in the NRF) and will include aspects of recovery that can be anticipated (e.g., housing reconstruction/shelter, economic, environmental, debris management, infrastructure and financial resources).

FEMA puts emphasis on long-term community recovery in accordance with multiple-stakeholder decisions. Long-term community recovery is defined as "[restoring or building] a healthy, functioning community that will sustain itself over time, while taking advantage of opportunities to rebuild stronger, smarter communities and mitigate against future disasters" (FEMA, 2009, p. 2). Recovery for individuals, households, and businesses is directly related to community recovery. Establishing effective collaboration within government agencies as well as in the greater community to create such a plan normally provides the desired recovery-definition product through preparedness and advanced mitigation. For example, many government organizations already undertake comprehensive city risk analyses; thus including an agency such as a city or county planning office in the emergency planning process will offer insight into possible hazards while addressing mitigation needs.

Including business continuity in recovery plans can also present different mitigation opportunities, which will reduce the effect a crisis may have on a community's economy and infrastructure and help create a "shared vision for recovery" (Phillips & Neal, 2007, p. 213). For those businesses that are not able to create a business continuity plan and become overwhelmed by the adverse consequences of disasters, national government entities can take the initiative for providing assistance for recovery. For instance, the Small Business Administration (SBA) in the United States provides assistance to disaster-stricken businesses to facilitate their recovery. The agency has provided more than 1.8 million disaster loans to victims since 1953, representing an outlay of $47 billion (SBA, 2009). Disaster victims also have the opportunity to get technical assistance and benefit from such procurement programs.

The post-event conditions of a community after recovery may be either better or worse than the pre-event situation. Key questions to ask before starting recovery are at which level and for whom recovery is desired (Alesch et al., 2009, p. 42). Disasters have a different impact on people and businesses at different levels. These variations determine the extent, scope, and success of recovery. Damage to a number of roofs and water in the basements of a few houses is very different from damage to business centers. If damage occurs in residential areas, they can be repaired or people can move to alternative housing. If business centers are damaged, however, the recovery of the community will be significantly constrained.

The resiliency of a community has a drastic effect on recovery. A sound economic infrastructure, sufficient social and human capital, and enough knowledge and experience are all beneficial in ensuring a more rapid and less costly recovery. Conversely, if a community does not ensure readiness for a hazard and lacks commitment to resiliency efforts, achieving successful recovery and return to pre-disaster conditions would be an optimistic and inadvisable goal. Thus successful mitigation efforts and recovery plans ensure economic and residential resiliency for the community.

Emphasis throughout the recovery process focuses on citizen involvement in decision making, from planning to mitigation, to increase buy-in and provide effectively for the variety of needs present after a disaster. The opportunity to include different aspects of citizen participation presents itself in a variety of ways, including a shared vision of the rebuilt community, citizen empowerment in obtaining outside aid, provision of necessary support services, and efforts to address any housing issues that may arise. As most communities do not have in-depth recovery plans or recovery organizations that might fill the planning void, it is important for emergency managers to begin to address this gap through new partnerships and committees of community partners and citizens. Highlighting the importance of recovery planning will ultimately serve a dual purpose by preparing the entire community through a structured, well-thought-out plan while simultaneously increasing disaster awareness, mitigation, and preparedness by all segments of the population (Phillips, 2010).

The Relief-to-Reconstruction Continuum

The relief-to-reconstruction continuum has its conceptual roots in disaster relief of the 1980s, and was developed in recognition of the need to ensure a smooth transition from response to recovery activities (Macrae, Bradbury, Jaspars, Johnson, & Duffield, 1997). Prior to this period, there was "a widely-held assumption that disaster relief efforts [were] separate, even mutually exclusive, from development interventions" (Sollis, 1994, p. 451). Crucially, the continuum was intended to bridge the theoretical and practical gap in the provision of assistance following a disaster, by combining the short-term needs of victims with the long-term goals for the community (Anderson, 1994). This corresponds succinctly with the intractable disaster–development link, which views the two as existing in delicate balance, whereby failures in development may expose vulnerabilities to hazards, but disasters can in turn provide reconstruction opportunities that can develop capacities and coping strategies (Özerdem, 2003; Sollis, 1994).

The emphasis placed on the continuum derives largely from the conventional donor structures that have separated relief from reconstruction, thereby creating a division in implementing agencies to conform to funding streams (Sollis, 1994). In other words, the separation of relief and development organizations and programs is not the natural operational desire of the agencies themselves, but rather occurs largely in acquiescence to those managing the finance mechanisms. The continuum theory itself has come under criticism in more recent years, as it perseveres in distancing relief and development (placing them at opposite ends of a spectrum), thereby maintaining the structural inability to address them in unison and favoring a sequential transition, albeit with an element of cross-fading (White & Cliffe, 2000). A similar criticism may be levied against the four-stage approach to disaster management presented in this book, although emphasis is given to the significant overlap of these stages.

Disaster relief covers both response efforts and actions geared toward returning to normal conditions after a disaster. The relief-to-reconstruction process after a disaster requires the involvement of many disaster response actors. Zixing, Xifu, and Keren (2002) comprehensively explain the relief and reconstruction of Tangshan after an earthquake struck the region in 1976. As their study illuminates, disaster relief efforts consist of six parts. The first part covers the first response, rescue, and distribution of first-aid materials to disaster victims. Also, opening the vital infrastructure such as transportation, electricity, and water to service is a necessary step for reinforcing response and rescue efforts. The second part of the disaster relief effort entails the provision of living arrangements to disaster victims. The third part is prevention of epidemics, public health protection, and restoration of health institutions. The fourth part is enforcement of security and public order. The fifth part is the restoration of production, while the last part is the reconstruction of the disaster-stricken area.

The overall disaster relief process is formed by only certain aspects of response and recovery phases. The relief-to-reconstruction continuum includes provisions for planning of response and recovery together. In the United States, a series of response plans (Federal Response Plan, National Response Plan, and National Response

Framework) have been developed by the national government in an attempt to provide a well-structured disaster response. Development of recovery plans is also favored by federal and state governments, although their emphasis on recovery planning is not as strong as that on response plans. As an example of weak planning regulations, Schwab (1998) notes that most U.S. states passed planning legislation based on statutes promulgated by Department of Commerce in the late 1920s, so that these plans lack provisions for meeting the necessities of today's communities.

Response and recovery differ from each other with respect to the expected intergovernmental and interorganizational relations, participating agencies, nature of efforts, and the goal conflicts; nevertheless, some lessons learned and best practices of response could be adapted to recovery and reconstruction (Stehr, 2001). Broadly, Stehr (2001) identifies the following types of integration that are possible: horizontal integration (relationships between individuals and organizations within a community), vertical integration (relationships with extra-community systems), and centralization of a network of stakeholders as parts of the community problem-solving mechanism with respect to recovery and reconstruction. Communities without horizontal and vertical integration may experience a lack of focal organizations for recovery in the event of a disaster. In this case, nongovernmental groups may bear the burden of taking the necessary steps.

Relief efforts may continue even after the recovery phase ends. Healthcare support, including physiological, psychological, and traumatic treatments, can last longer than the reconstruction of the physical environment. Auf der Heide and Scanlon (2007) reveal a need for "community-wide emergency planning" (p. 185), and examine the role of the health sector during emergencies. Hospital personnel can better prepare to treat disaster victims if they are made aware of disasters immediately through established communication protocols, yet are more commonly made aware of a disaster by its victims. Media outlets play a key role in reporting the details of a disaster; therefore, emergency managers must develop relationships with media outlets to become familiar with the latter's continuity of operations plans.

Braun et al. (2006) underline that there is a need for collaboration and community-wide planning on behalf of medical institutions and local government; these authors' research revealed that many media outlets and volunteer organizations are not involved in the planning process and that rural communities are at greater risk of this problem. Wetter, Daniell, and Treser (2001) validate Braun et al.'s point, indicating that fewer than 20% of emergency departments in Alaska, Idaho, Oregon, and Washington have a plan in place to treat patients exposed to biological or chemicals weapons.

Studies of recent disasters reveal the importance of relief efforts for the victims of disasters. Weisler et al. (2006) provide important statistics about the mental health recovery of victims after Hurricanes Katrina and Rita. In their study, a remarkable number of cases of post-traumatic stress disorder, anxiety, and substance abuse were recorded. Furthermore, within 4 months after Hurricane Katrina, suicide rates increased almost threefold in Orleans Parish. Weisler et al. (2006) state that "the longer-term adverse health effects of the disaster can be expected to be substantial and require follow-up assessments to determine the need for mental health care services" (p. 586).

London experienced a similarly extreme event that required extensive relief efforts for the victims in the period following the initial disaster. On July 7, 2005, terrorists attacked the city's public transportations system, killing 52 individuals and injuring several hundred people. In the aftermath of the event, significant collaboration between public, nonprofit, and private sectors took place, with several entities being formed to provide relief services for the victims of the attacks. Family Assistance Center, 7 July Assistance, London Bombings Relief Charitable Fund (LBRCF), British Red Cross, and several other organizations took part in relief efforts. LBRCF gathered more than $13 million for the victims. Nevertheless, there were some challenges for relief coordination. For instance, hospitals in London were not ready to handle the high flow of wounded people, and they proved unprepared to respond to the large number of people who arrived at the hospitals through their own efforts, rather than being brought to the facilities by official emergency responders.

Case Studies

1999 Marmara Earthquake

Turkey experienced one of the most devastating disasters in its history on August 17, 1999. On that day, an earthquake with a magnitude of 7.4 on the Richter scale struck İzmit Bay, in the most developed and industrialized region of the country, for 45 seconds. The consequences of the disaster were calamitous. More than 17,000 people lost their lives, almost 44,000 were injured, 244,000 residences were damaged, and more than 500,000 people were left homeless (Çorbacıoğlu & Kapucu, 2005) (**Table 4-1**). The earthquake was one of the most destructive natural events in an industrialized area within the last century (**Figure 4-2**).

According to Çorbacıoğlu and Kapucu's study (2005), during the response to the disaster and recovery actions after the event, several difficulties were encountered. The Turkish emergency management system includes both local governments and the central government. Provinces and districts are required to form rescue and aid committees to coordinate the efforts for disaster response according to the relevant laws and regulations. Local military garrisons also prepare disaster plans in coordination with district plans. Central government agencies are responsible for preparing supplementary plans to provide aid to disaster-stricken areas and districts. The central crisis management initiatives are conducted within the Prime Ministry Crisis Management Center (PMCMC), which is supposed to coordinate allocation of resources and contributions of other organizations to response activities on a nationwide basis.

Table 4-1 *Impact of Marmara Earthquake: Summary Indicators*

Economic Indicators[1]	1999		2000		Total	
	US $ billion	Share of GNP	US $ billion	Share of GNP	US $ billion	Share of GNP
Direct Costs						
Wealth loss	3 to 6.5	1.5% to 3.3%			3 to 6.5	1.5% to –3.3%
Indirect Costs						
Impact on output	–2.0 to –1.2	–1.0% to –0.6%	1.4 to 2.4	0.6% to 1.1%		
Emergency assistance	–0.4	–0.2%	–0.2	–0.1%		
Secondary Effects						
Current account balance	–1	–0.5%	–2	–1.0%	–3	–1.5%
Fiscal impact	1.9 to 2.3	0.9% to 1.1%	1.5 to 2.3	0.8% to 1.1%	3.6 to 4.6	1.8% to 2.3%
Social Indicators for the Region Affected by the Earthquake	Midpoint		Range[2]			
Fatality rate	7.0 per 1000		2.5–14.3			
Injury rate	15 per 1000		4.6–27.7			
Homeless person			400,000–600,000			
Job losses	30.9% of labor force		20.4–48.1			

1. All estimates based on preliminary data.
2. Range across affected provinces.
Courtesy of International Bank for Reconstruction and Development/The World Bank: *Turkey: Marmara Earthquake Assessment*, 1999.

Although national disaster plans developed by both the central government and local governments outline a well-functioning disaster response, Çorbacıoğlu and Kapucu's work (2005) indicates that the response efforts did not take place as proposed in the plans. The problems with emergency management in Turkey originated in the mitigation phase, with problems in this early phase affecting the other subsequent phases. Thus lack of proper preparation hindered success in the response actions

Credit: U.S. Geological Survey Department of the Interior/USGS

Figure 4-2 *Collapsed buildings in Marmara Earthquake.*

after the disaster. Human resources in the region were curtailed and suspended for the first few days of the disaster. The central government took control of the event, and communication between local governments and the central government was very limited for the first few days.

Recovery efforts started some time after the incident took place. Responding over a wide area with dense populations and large industrial areas requires significant coordination and the cooperation of all stakeholders. An analysis of networks of organizations in the Marmara area indicated that the Prime Ministry and several regional crisis management centers served as the core of the network, and relationships between response and recovery organizations were established through them (Çorbacıoğlu & Kapucu, 2005). The Prime Ministry performed a coordinating role, while other central agencies were responsible for the transmission of aid materials and personnel to disaster-stricken areas.

Table 4-2 indicates the amount of assistance that was allocated for the death and disability compensation part of recovery efforts from the Marmara earthquake. These efforts were classified as social aid by the World Bank report published one month after the earthquake. Unlike in previous earthquake events, the Turkish government did not provide assistance to injured persons, but rather made one-time payments to permanently disabled individuals. Also, the disaster made a significant impact

Table 4-2 *Estimated Compensation for Death and Disability (in trillion TL)*

	1999	2000
Social Insurance		
Survivor benefits	10.1	1.8
• With lump-sum payment	9.5	0
• With monthly payment	0.6	1.8
Disability benefits	1.6	4.8
Social Assistance		
Lump-sum option (500 or 200 million TL)	6.6	0
Lump-sum option (US $1537 or $750)	14.4	0

Courtesy of International Bank for Reconstruction and Development/The World Bank: *Turkey: Marmara Earthquake Assessment*, 1999.

upon the industry of the country. Turkey's GDP figures went negative in 1999, and a report by the World Bank (1999) highlighted that the country needed international financial aid for economic recovery.

Hull Floods

England and Wales experienced the most serious flooding in their recent history in June and July 2007. This disaster was the most devastating event that England had experienced since World War II and the biggest civil emergency in England's history (**Figure 4-3**). The rains took the lives of 13 people, and approximately 48,000 homes and 7,300 businesses were flooded (Pitt, 2008). Hull, a town in northeastern England, was particularly hard hit and suffered more than other places. The total damage inflicted was $4.8 billion, and almost half a million people were left without electricity and water.

The intensity of rain was remarkably high and this scale of event was considered likely to happen only once every 150 years (House of Commons, 2008). The response to the 2007 floods took place at both the local level and the national level. Generally speaking, response activities did not result in failure even though there were some shortcomings. As pointed out by Pitt (2008), "The scale of the 2007 floods stretched emergency response resources to the limit and beyond, and responders in some areas were not as ready as they might have been" (p. 203). Despite the fact that heavy rain overwhelmed drainage systems and pumps remained insufficient to remove the water

© Nigel Roddis/Thomson Reuters

Figure 4-3 *The floods in 2007 damaged electricity and water infrastructure significantly*

from the area, the critical infrastructure did not fail in this extreme event (Von Meding & Oyedele, 2008). The country's Gold Command structure took control of the event and members of the armed forces were included in search and rescue activities.

Nevertheless, Pitt (2008) identifies a number of prominent challenges in the local-level response. In addition to the challenges due to the vast scope of the disaster, a lack of mutual agreement regarding protocols between different agencies occurred in some areas that floods hit. The United Kingdom's Civil Contingencies Act of 2004 requires Category 1 and 2 responders to come together in Local Resiliency Forums (LRF) based on their police force area. These responders normally have other full-time jobs, which limits their response capabilities and commitment to the LRF. Furthermore, the relatively small number of responders is inadequate for disasters that occur across wide geographical areas. Communication between agencies was also a problem in the initial phases of the floods. Some responders from different agencies received "major incident" calls from police and fire services, even though their own agency had not yet declared a major incident. The Environment Agency's flood warning system—an automated telephone-based system—did not operate in Hull because it covered only limited areas that were subject to river and coastal flooding (Coulthard, Frostick, Hardcastle, Jones, Rogers, & Scott, 2007; Von Meding & Oyedele, 2008).

The national government response to the flooding was important and helpful for the coordination of efforts. The Cabinet Office Briefing Room (COBR), which included the government's dedicated crisis management officials, was activated in the July floods and remained active for civil emergencies during the event, including during the prolonged interruption to water supplies. Department for Environment, Food, and Rural Areas (DEFRA) and the Environment Agency, as national agencies, provided ongoing oversight of the response (Pitt, 2008).

Local service interruptions that led to revenue and capital losses influenced local governments' response and recovery efforts. **Table 4-3** indicates the total costs of the floods in terms of the services of local governments. The floods influenced people's lives to a significant extent as well; Pitt's (2008) report shares the results of a survey conducted with victims of the incidents:

- Thirty-nine percent of the respondents stated that the flooding had an effect on their own or their partner's physical health.

- Thirty-one percent of people with health problems took time off work, and half of these individuals were off for more than 10 days.

- Thirty-nine percent of those who reported health problems had been to see a doctor.

The U.K. Prime Minister at the time, Gordon Brown, promised to put pressure on insurance companies to cover the expenses of the victims. The average claim for the insured homes ranged between $48,500 and $65,000. A Flood Recovery Grant (FRG) was prepared in 2007 and administered by communities and local government for

Table 4-3 *Total Flooding Costs to Local Authorities*

Local Authority Service costs	£ Million Revenue	£ Million Capital	£ Million Total
Emergency action	31.288	0	31.288
Highways	0	81.755	80.755
Schools	26.305	11.371	37.676
Housing	31.809	0	31.809
Social services	0.734	0	0.734
Other	26.621	24.134	50.754
		Total	**233.016**

Source: Pitt, 2008, p. 390.

local authorities. Local authorities used this source of funding to provide financial assistance to those parties who were affected by the flood, including victims who did not have insurance. Also, Brown's administration allocated extra resources for recovery due to the fact that the floods were considered such an exceptional incident. By June 2008, the government had made $191 million available for flood recovery.

During response and recovery, stakeholders from different backgrounds played remarkable roles. Nevertheless, according to a House of Commons report (2008), no national or regional agency has overall responsibility for surface water flooding in the United Kingdom. When the heavy rain started in 2007, no one was responsible for issuing flood warnings to those parties who were vulnerable to flooding. Both the House of Commons (2008) report and Pitt (2008) consider water-specific service agencies to be responsible for the response phase of a flooding emergency. Local authorities, water companies, internal drainage boards, asset owners, and others are the key stakeholders identified for dealing with flood hazards. **Figure 4-4** depicts the agencies that have responsibility for local drainage and flood. The stakeholder responsibilities for surface floods were determined after the summer 2007 events as part of the United Kingdom's previously started "Making Space for Water" strategy.

During the 2007 disaster, in response to the floods, volunteer organizations made notable contributions to the local public agencies in the affected areas. They

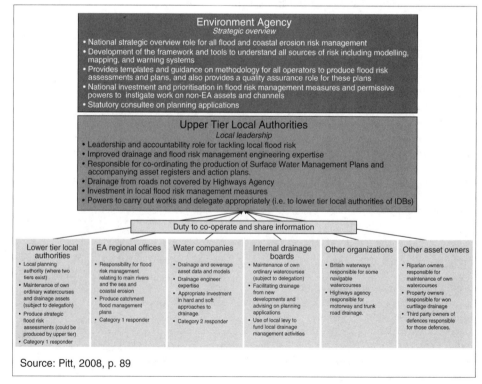

Source: Pitt, 2008, p. 89

Figure 4-4 *Stakeholders of local flood and drainage*

significantly helped in evacuation; raised funds; distributed water, food, beds, and other needed resources; and helped in the coordination of response by identifying vulnerable people (Pitt, 2008).

2004 Asian Tsunami

In 2004, one of the deadliest natural events in history occurred in South Asia. An earthquake of magnitude 9.3 on the Richter scale took place 250 kilometers southwest of Banda Aceh in northern Sumatra, Indonesia (Borrero, 2005). The earthquake was the second largest recorded in world history, and it created a massive tsunami that struck Indonesia, Sri Lanka, India, Thailand, and even Somalia. The most remarkable destruction was seen in the Banda Aceh region (**Figure 4-5**). In the wake of this event, more than 237,000 people were reported dead or missing in Indonesia (Comfort, 2006).

Louise Comfort (2006) conducted an important study on the response actions to the 2004 tsunami. In her study, she summarized the response and relief efforts in accordance with her analysis. At the time of the earthquake, Banda Aceh was a politically problematic region for the Indonesian government. Furthermore, many people who might have otherwise responded to a disaster were killed or injured in the aftermath of the tsunami, and critical infrastructures for communication were destroyed. When these factors occur simultaneously, executing a plan for coordinated response becomes very challenging, if not impossible. Distrust among the

Courtesy of Photographer's Mate 1st Class Jon Gesch/U.S. Navy

Figure 4-5 *December 26, 2004 Tsunami destroyed the Aceh province of Indonesia*

Indonesian government and army and the Aceh administration resulted in poor communication between both parties. After the tsunami, the communication infrastructure was largely destroyed, creating asymmetric information—yet another factor that can hinder trust and coordination.

Coordination becomes an unattainable goal where there is no communication between participating agencies. Unfortunately, coordination between domestic responders was not the only problem encountered following the Southeast Asia disaster. A significant number of international organizations and states sent aid to the disaster-stricken area in 2004. Comfort's research (2007) on the organizations participating in relief efforts indicates that more than half of the responding organizations (public, private, nonprofit, and special interest) were international, while national organizations accounted for only 35% of the total number of responders. Organizations at the subnational level had an even smaller role in the response actions than the national organizations, accounting for slightly more than 10% of the responding organizations. The majority of the response organizations were international agencies, including finance institutions, international humanitarian organizations, and private companies. The United Nations (UN) coordinated this international aid in cooperation with the Indonesian army.

Thus, along with public organizations, nonprofit agencies and private institutions, including international organizations, responded to the disaster. The majority of the responding agencies did not have a common communication infrastructure, so they were unable to effectively communicate with one another. For the international organizations, due to language barriers and lack of knowledge about the local culture, a necessity to conduct actions in tandem with local officers emerged. Comfort (2006) notes that two networks formed, the first operating under the UN, and the second functioning under the Indonesian government. There was remarkable disconnection between these two networks, which decreased the efficiency of the efforts to a great extent.

During the response efforts, some of the villages and households were overlooked. Inattention and delay decreased the success of response actions and created inefficiency, notwithstanding the significant endeavor spent (Comfort, 2006).

2010 Haiti Earthquake

The Haiti earthquake on January 12, 2010 was the largest earthquake (magnitude 7.0) to ever hit the region. Most parts of Haiti experienced massive destruction, including the capital city, Port-au-Prince, and smaller cities and towns around the epicenter. Initial reports indicated that one-third of Haiti's 9 million strong population was affected by this earthquake and its numerous aftershocks (Taft-Morales & Margesson, 2010). The initial death toll was reported at 230,000 fatalities, with many more people missing; a year later, Prime Minister Jean-Max Bellerive announced at a conference that the death toll had increased to 316,000 as additional bodies were found beneath the rubble (Archibold, 2011).

Haiti suffers from massive poverty, as more than 54% of its population survives on less than $1 per day, while more than 80% of its population does not receive the daily minimum ration of food standard set by the World Health Organization (Taft-Morales & Margesson, 2010). This catastrophic earthquake further hindered the country's economic development and left many more individuals homeless, without food and other resources that are essential for survival and progress.

According to a UN report, the earthquake destroyed approximately 50% of the buildings—including homes—in Port-au-Prince alone (Aon Benfield, 2010). Elements of both the physical and social infrastructure, such as schools, churches, universities, and hospitals, experienced huge blows from the earthquake (Earthquake Engineering Research Institute [EERI], 2010). Many governmental buildings collapsed or suffered major damage, such as the Parliament building; the Presidential Palace; the National Assembly; the Ministries of Finance, Public Works, Communication, and Culture; the Palace of Justice; the Tax Office; a major prison; and some foreign agencies. The UN headquarters in Haiti also collapsed and suffered huge losses, with many of the organization's workers reported missing (Aon Benfield, 2010; Taft-Morales & Margesson, 2010).

The immediate impacts of the earthquake included a major breakdown in communication lines and services, lack of water and sanitation facilities, lack of electricity and fuel to generate electricity, destruction of roads and other transportation routes such as the main port, and many collapsed buildings resulting in huge levels of homelessness (Taft-Morales & Margesson, 2010). These impacts translated into major challenges for response and relief operations. For 2 to 3 days after the earthquake struck, government officials, residents, and relief workers experienced communication and coordination challenges because the main cell phone towers and power lines had been disrupted or destroyed (Aon Benfield, 2010).

Most of the damage was attributable to poor building construction in Haiti. It is believed that the destruction could have been limited if better construction practices had been employed in the country in the past. The government of Haiti had allowed unsupervised construction in the regions despite receiving warnings by seismologists about the likelihood of earthquakes occurring in this part of the Caribbean plate boundary (Bilham, 2010). The warnings were not heeded, however, as there was no "intergenerational memory of earthquakes" in Haiti—the last earthquake there was reported in the late 1700s (Arup, 2010). Moreover, the middle class suffered the most in terms of residential area destruction and collapse, because their houses were typically built using reinforced concrete, hollow concrete, and other low-quality materials. The extremely poor, who had makeshift, basic, and light dwellings, and the wealthy class, who resided in better-constructed homes, fared better compared to the middle class (Arup, 2010).

At the time of the earthquake, the existing emergency management structure in Haiti was weak and, in fact, was in the process of being improved through the help of the World Bank and other organizations. Disaster risk management was being incorporated into improving Haiti's disaster response capabilities and into the country's overall strategy for sustainable development. However, these improvements were in their early stages and were primarily focused on mitigating the most common natural disaster in the region—namely, hurricanes (Taft-Morales & Margesson, 2010). Reports indicate that Haitians were somewhat mentally prepared for hurricanes, because they had experienced Hurricane Gustav in 2008, but were not ready for a massive earthquake (EERI, 2010). Most certainly, the country did not have the physical capacity and capabilities to deal with a disaster of this proportion.

Immediate help was sought by the President of Haiti for search and rescue missions, to develop an offshore vessel medical unit, and to help in generating electricity. Communication equipment was also requested by the government. On January 14, 2010, two days after the earthquake, the government of Haiti, the UN, and donor organizations met to coordinate their response and relief efforts and services (Taft-Morales & Margesson, 2010).

Even before the disaster, the UN had a strong presence in Haiti. After the disaster, this organization took on the crucial role of deploying various teams such as one from the UN Office for the Coordination of Humanitarian Affairs (UNOCHA), which helped to coordinate search and rescue teams. A sector or cluster approach was used by the UN to facilitate humanitarian relief efforts in the disaster-prone country. The initial relief sectors or clusters organized were Emergency Shelter and Non-food Items (led by the International Organization for Migration), Food Assistance (led by the World Food Program), Health (led by the World Health Organization), Logistics (led by the World Food Program), and Water/Sanitation (led by the UN Children's Fund [UNICEF]). Many other clusters formed as relief efforts picked up pace. The International Federation of the Red Cross and Red Crescent Societies (IFRC) also worked closely with the Haitian Red Cross Society (HRCS) and the American Red Cross to provide relief services to victims (Taft-Morales & Margesson, 2010).

The U.S. government also helped a great deal by organizing a response team led by USAID that conducted needs assessments, performed search and rescue missions, and provided logistical support. The U.S. Department of Defense deployed its military assets to aid U.S. and international relief efforts (Taft-Morales & Margesson, 2010). The search and rescue operations of USAID were complemented and joined by many other international search and rescue teams from France, Spain, Iceland, the United Kingdom, China, Chile, and some other countries. According to EERI's "Special Earthquake Report" published in April 2010, overall relief missions were very effective despite ample logistical and infrastructural challenges. It was also reported that "emergency planners and search and rescue experts have cited this event as the most successful operation in recent USAID history" (EERI, 2010, p. 6).

Overall, three factors explain the scale of destruction in the Haiti earthquake: poor-quality construction practices, a lack of building codes and regulations, and a lack of planning and awareness about earthquakes being a significant threat in the region.

Mitigation strategies to address all three concerns, such as developing policies related to construction practices, building codes, and all-hazards emergency management, should be incorporated into plans and recovery operations in any area subject to this type of disaster (Arup, 2010).

The recovery efforts in Haiti should continue to be geared toward enforcing resistant construction and building codes in place, along with developing positions for building inspectors who could help monitor the enforcement of better construction practices (Bilham, 2010). The Haiti experience also led to some recommendations about adopting building codes in other countries. Although importing building codes from other countries is a quick-fix strategy, it is considered risky because it requires a certain level of sophistication that does not exist in Haiti's construction and building industry. Importing building codes is also impractical in many cases because unique local conditions and building types need to be incorporated into the code (Arup, 2010). To mitigate future threats and develop sustainable resilience, recovery efforts are currently focusing on improvements in building construction practices. Although earthquake-proof building practices are expensive, this investment is considered integral to emergency management, as it will not only mitigate future threats but also help to employ citizens who have lost their jobs or are unemployed (Bilham, 2010).

BP Oil Spill Disaster of 2010

The BP (formerly British Petroleum) oil spill started with an explosion in BP's Macondo well in the Gulf of Mexico on April 20, 2010. The disaster was the third major oil spill that had occurred along the coast of the United States since the 1990s. The devastation and destruction caused by the BP spill surpassed the damage associated with the earlier spills, however, as the disaster threatened not only the ecosystem but also tourism, fishing businesses, and the livelihoods of many U.S. citizens that depend on coastal areas. The initial response to the spill was extremely sluggish, as it took approximately 3 months to cap the gushing oil leak in the well. Although the oil was eventually capped and leaking valves plugged, the scope of harm to the ecosystem and wildlife was inconceivable ("Gulf of Mexico Oil Spill 2010," 2011).

It is believed that the scale of the disaster could have been controlled had the liable parties acted more carefully and responsibly. Reports indicate that involved companies such as BP, Transocean, Halliburton, and other subcontractors were all guilty of not fulfilling their duties properly ("Gulf of Mexico Oil Spill 2010," 2011). An internal BP report published in September 2010 suggested that the oil spill was a result of numerous failures and shortcomings by BP and its contractors, especially Transocean and Halliburton, covering mechanical faults, human judgment errors, engineering design weaknesses, and operational shortcomings. These findings weaken the claim of sole negligence on BP's part ("Gulf of Mexico Oil Spill 2010," 2011).

Recent reports show that prior to the oil rig explosion, safety practices and company plans were not being carried out on the rig appropriately. In addition, investigations indicate that some of the main components of the well had not been monitored and inspected since 2000, implying that 3- to 5-year monitoring requirements had not been met. It was also reported that perhaps the recent substandard cementing services at the rig carried out by BP's contractor company, Halliburton, could have perpetuated the disaster ("Gulf of Mexico Oil Spill 2010," 2011). Moreover, problems in the blowout preventers were not accorded importance by the Minerals Management Service (MMS), despite warnings given by its own experts about needs to improve the existing structure ("Gulf of Mexico Oil Spill 2010," 2011).

Initially, the U.S. government underestimated the size of the disaster; as a result, the national response was highly sluggish, uncoordinated, and disorganized. There were no clear lines of authority between different levels of the government and between all liable parties. Two weeks after the onset of the disaster, the National Oceanic and Atmospheric Administration (NOAA) tried to seek the permission of the White House to utilize and publicize its worst-case models to handle the disaster, but was not granted the permission to do so ("Gulf of Mexico Oil Spill 2010," 2011).

On April 29, the government realized that the spill was worse than the initial perceptions and declared it to be an event of national significance. Decisions and plans conflicted when the White House suggested that offshore drilling should halt until a proper investigation was conducted. While the White House advised stopping any drilling operations, the Interior Department carried on issuing permits for allowing oil drilling in existing projects in the Gulf of Mexico region ("Gulf of Mexico Oil Spill 2010," 2011). Meanwhile, BP tried many methods to plug the well to stop the spill. It attempted to reactivate the seal-off valves on the blowout preventer, tried to funnel the leaking oil to a ship, and sought to pump heavy drilling fluids via lines into the preventer to cap the well. Finally, 86 days after the initial explosion, BP succeeded in applying a tight-fitting cap on the well and managed to plug the valves.

On June 15, President Barack Obama's Oval Office speech emphasized the need for improvements in the existing energy policy and the need for BP to take responsibility for the disaster and start compensating victims. A day later, BP decided to establish a $20 billion compensation fund to pay claimants ("Gulf of Mexico Oil Spill 2010," 2011). In December 2010, a civilian lawsuit asking for huge penalties to be levied was filed against BP and eight other companies in New Orleans. Moreover, many people and local businesses have filed for BP fund emergency payments as well. In fact, since the disaster, a total of 475,000 claims have been filed ("Gulf of Mexico Oil Spill 2010," 2011).

The Exxon *Valdez* oil spill in 1989 was considered an important disaster in terms of emergency management because it led to major improvements in legislation regarding oil spill disasters. Specifically, in response to this disaster, the Oil Pollution Act of 1990 (OPA)—the first legislation directly targeted at oil spills—was created. The OPA clarified the federal government's role in helping states recover from oil spills by providing funding for clean-up operations. The Oil Spill Liability Trust

Fund (OSLTF) was created under this act to provide up to $1 billion in funds for spill clean-up and recovery operations in case the responsible parties remained unknown or failed to comply (Environmental Protection Agency [EPA], 2010c). The OPA also required development of contingency plans and procedures for individual vessels and facilities to incorporate worst-case events. In addition, this law ensures that responsible entities are charged for clean-up costs. A provision was later added that requires the U.S. President to adjust and revise liability fees in accordance with the market conditions every 3 years. This added provision has not been implemented recently, however, and could not be applied to the BP oil spill crisis.

The OPA also states that oil spills within the United States will be handled by the EPA, while oil spills in offshore rigs will be managed by the U.S. Coast Guard. Furthermore, a National Contingency Plan (NCP) has been designed to manage the coordination issues between different entities working in clean-up and spill recovery activities. Although the original NCP was developed in 1968, it was improved with the establishment of OPA in 1994. The NCP is a framework or guide that seeks to mitigate threats and damages caused by spills, as it covers mandatory facility inspections and monitoring, waste removal methods, roles and responsibilities of parties responsible for recovery operations in case of a spill, regulations for reporting hazards, and environmental threat research and its funding, among other issues (EPA, 2010b). Thus OPA and NCP were the main federal-level policies and plans that were primarily available in the BP oil crisis. Along with the NCP, the NRF and NIMS are important documents and plans for response operations pertaining to an oil crisis. According to the Hazardous Materials Annex, Emergency Support Function (ESF) #10 deals with responses to actual and potential hazardous materials and the NCP's rules and ordinances serve as the basis for using federal resources when responding to oil hazards.

The EPA is an important organization that plays a key role in disasters involving hazardous materials. This agency's oil spill program helps in preparations for and responses to oil spills (EPA, 2010b). The EPA is the lead agency under ESF #10 and helps to coordinate response operations with other agencies. In the BP oil spill, it offered its assistance to the U.S. Coast Guard, which was heavily involved in efforts to control and cap the spill. The EPA also became involved in monitoring air quality near the spill, toxicity testing, and studying impacts on aquatic species or the health of coastal residents (EPA, 2010a). Other federal agencies, such as the Interior's Mineral Management Service (MMS)—since renamed the Bureau of Ocean Energy Management (BOE)—which provides information about hazardous materials and mining operations, have been sharply criticized for not carrying out complete regulatory procedures and routine assessments aboard the Deepwater Horizon station where the BP oil spill occurred.

As a result of this disaster, U.S. energy policy has been altered. The existing energy plans at the time of the disaster focused on expanding offshore oil and gas drilling. President Obama announced that the Minerals Management Service, which is responsible for overseeing offshore oil drilling, will be split into two parts: one part to carry out inspections of oil rigs and to impose safety and preventive measures, and another part to manage and oversee contracts and leases for drilling ("Gulf of Mexico Oil Spill 2010," 2011). Moreover, in August 2010, the U.S. government announced that the process for granting drilling permits will be reviewed and made more comprehensive. The White House also recommended that the use of categorical exclusions for allowing drilling permits for similar areas should be stopped, and environmental impacts assessed for each new offshore well site on an individual basis. Thus, improved regulations will be imposed that mandate stricter review of proposed deepwater drilling operations ("Gulf of Mexico Oil Spill 2010," 2011).

Along with these changes, another integral—and perhaps the most imperative—change needed is to form a single-comprehensive policy or plan that integrates piecemeal legislation and individual plans to ensure effective and timely response to a disaster of this magnitude. There are definitely good policies and plans such as the NCP, the NRF, NIMS, and OPA in place, but their coordinated implementation and understanding is important to ensure an effective response in an actual emergency. In addition, strong federal-level leadership will help in understanding the true scope of the BP oil spill disaster, in providing for the timely execution of appropriate plans and policies, and in coordinating responses between different responsible entities.

Conclusion

Several factors have the potential to create challenges to effective disaster response and recovery. Lack of communication and lack of collaboration in the planning process can be two confounding factors resulting in inadequate preparation that ultimately leads to a poor disaster response and a harder road to recovery for the affected community. "Rather than waiting for the next disaster . . . planners must . . . develop detailed operational plans that anticipate the requirements of future responses and what capabilities can be matched to them in what timeframe" (Derthick, 2007, p. 45). Thus governmental agency cooperation with citizens, private agencies, and other government agencies must take place to successfully mitigate the effects of a disaster.

A lack of a pre-disaster recovery plan puts the citizenry at undue risk from delays in critical and extended disaster relief—in effect, hamstringing a community's ability to be resilient. Local governments must plan in great detail for the disaster declaration process and determine how to respond in the interim while assessments and allocations of resources are pending. Guidelines set out by the government will not harm local communities, but rather will empower local authorities to lead response and recovery efforts. Emergency managers will need business skills and expertise to effectively coordinate and partner with public, private, and nonprofit organizations to develop a community-wide emergency plan. They must reach out to citizens, as well as local, regional, and national agencies and groups, to stimulate awareness and guarantee a safer community for all citizens.

Review Questions

1. How are intergovernmental and interorganizational response and recovery described in the National Response Framework?

2. You are the emergency manager for New Orleans. After Hurricane Katrina, many homes were severely damaged and were not safe to enter. You want to demolish these structures and remove the remaining debris. Homeowners, however, want to return to collect some of their personal effects before the structures are demolished. Would you allow homeowners to return? Why or why not?

3. Does your local government have a recovery operations plan? How are recovery issues identified and addressed in the plan? Identify the disaster recovery functions that need to be implemented if a major disaster strikes.

4. Who do you think should be involved in forming your local recovery/mitigation committee?

5. Should emergency managers include a community-wide emergency plan and federal government initiatives in their comprehensive plan to address response and recovery from a disaster for their community?

6. How might the information you gained from this chapter affect you personally and professionally?

References

Alesch, D. J., Arendt, L. A., & Holly, J. N. (2009). *Managing for long-term community recovery in the aftermath of disaster.* Fairfax, VA: PERI.

Anderson, M. B. (1994). Understanding the disaster–development continuum: Gender analysis is the essential tool. *Focus on Gender, 2*(1), 7–10.

Aon Benfield. (2010). Event recap report: 1/12/10 Haiti earthquake. Retrieved January 28, 2010, from http://www.aon.com/attachments/reinsurance/201001_ab_if_event_recap_haiti_earthquake_impact_forecasting.pdf.

Archibold, R. C. (2011, January 13). Haiti: Quake's toll rises to 316,000. *The New York Times.* Retrieved May 19, 2011 from http://www.nytimes.com/2011/01/14/world/americas/14briefs-Haiti.html?_r=1&scp=1&sq=Haiti:%20Quake%20Toll%20Rises%20to%20316,000&st=cse.

Arup. (2010). Haiti earthquake response: Arup assignment report. Retrieved January 28, 2010, from http://www.eqclearinghouse.org/20100112haiti/wpcontent/uploads/2010/07/20100522_ARUP_Haiti.pdf.

Auf der Heide, E. (1996). Disaster planning. Part II: Disaster problems, issues, and challenges identified in the research literature. *Emergency Medicines of North America, 14*(2), 453–480.

Auf der Heide, E., & Scanlon, J. (2007). The role of the health sector in planning and response. In W. L. Waugh, Jr., & K. Tierney (Eds.), *Emergency management: Principles and practice for local government* (2nd ed., pp. 183–206). Washington, DC: ICMA.

Bilham, R. (2010). Lessons from the Haiti earthquake. *Nature, 463,* 878–879.

Borrero, J. C. (2005). *Field survey: Northern Sumatra and Banda Aceh, Indonesia and after the earthquake and tsunami of 26 December 2004.* Earthquake Engineering Research Institute. Retrieved January 25, 2010, from https://www.eeri.org/lfe/clearinghouse/sumatra_tsunami/reports/EERI_report_indonesia_jcb_2-11-05.pdf.

Braun, B. I., Wineman, N. V., Finn, N. L., Barbera, J. A., Schmaltz, S. S., & Loeb, J. M. (2006). Integrating hospitals into community emergency preparedness planning. *Annals of Internal Medicine, 144*(11), 799–811.

Comfort, L. K. (2006). Asymmetrical information process in extreme events: The 26 December 2004 Sumatran earthquake and tsunami. Submitted to D. Gibbons (Ed.), *Communicable crises: Prevention, management and resolution in an era of globalization.* Monterey, CA: International Public Management Association, Naval Post Graduate School.

Comfort, L. K. (2007). Crisis management in hindsight: Cognition, communication, coordination, and control. *Public Administration Review, Special Issue, 67,* 189–197.

Comfort, L. K., Hauskrecht, M., & Lin, J. S. (2008). Dynamic networks: modeling change in environments exposed to risk. In *Proceedings of the International ISCRAM Conference* (pp. 576–585). Washington, DC.

Çorbacıoğlu, S., & Kapucu, N. (2005). Intergovernmental relations in response to the 1999 Marmara earthquake in Turkey: A network analysis. *International Journal of Mass Emergencies and Disasters, 23*(3), 73–102.

Coulthard, T., Frostick, L., Hardcastle, H., Jones, K., Rogers, D., & Scott, M. (2007). *The June 2007 floods in Hull.* Interim report by the Independent Review Body.

Cutter, S. L., Emrich, C. T., Adams, B. J., Huyck, C. K., & Eguchi, R. T. (2007). New information technologies in emergency management. In W. L. Waugh, Jr., & K. Tierney (Eds.), *Emergency management: Principles and practice for local government* (2nd ed., pp. 279–297). Washington, DC: ICMA.

Department of Homeland Security (DHS). (2008). National Response Framework. Retrieved October 11, 2009, from http://www.fema.gov/pdf/emergency/nrf/nrf-core.pdf.

Derthick, M. (2007). Where federalism didn't fail. *Public Administration Review, 67*(1), 36–47.

Earthquake Engineering Research Institute (EERI). (2010). EERI special earthquake report—April 2010. Retrieved January 28, 2010, from http://www.eeri.org/site/images/eeri_newsletter/2010_pdf/Haiti_Rpt_1.pdf.

Environmental Protection Agency (EPA). (2010a). Lisa Jackson testimony. Retrieved February 2, 2011, from http://www.epa.gov/ocir/hearings/testimony/111_2009_2010/2010_0715_lj.pdf.

Environmental Protection Agency (EPA). (2010b). National Contingency Plan (Title 42, Chapter 103, Subchapter I, § 9605). Retrieved February 2, 2011, from http://www.law.cornell.edu/uscode/html/uscode42/usc_sec_42_00009605----000-.html.

Environmental Protection Agency (EPA). (2010c). Oil Pollution Act review. *Laws and Regulations.* Retrieved February 2, 2011, from http://epa.gov/oem/content/lawsregs/opaover.htm.

Federal Emergency Management Agency (FEMA). (2009). The road to recovery 2008: Emergency Support Function # 14 Long Term Community Recovery. Retrieved February 3, 2010, from http://www.fema.gov/pdf/rebuild/ltrc/2008_report.pdf.

Fischer, H. W. (1998). The role of the new information technologies in emergency mitigation, planning, response, and recovery. *Disaster Prevention and Management, 7*(1), 28–41.

Gulf of Mexico Oil Spill 2010. (2011, February 2*). The New York Times.* Retrieved February 2, 2011, from http://topics.nytimes.com/top/reference/timestopics/subjects/o/oil_spills/gulf_of_mexico_2010/index.html.

Harrald, J. R. (2006). Agility and discipline: Critical success factors for disaster response. *Annals of the American Academy of Political and Social Science, 604,* 256–272.

House of Commons. (2008). *Flooding: Fifth report of session 2007–2008, Volume 1.*

Kapucu, N. (2009). Interorganizational coordination in complex environments of disasters: The evolution of intergovernmental disaster response systems. *Journal of Homeland Security and Emergency Management, 6,* 1.

Kendra, J. M., & Wachtendorf, T. (2003). Elements of resilience after the World Trade Center disaster: Reconstituting New York City's emergency operations centre. *Disasters, 27*(1), 37–53.

Light, P. C. (2005). *Katrina effect on American preparedness.* PERI. Retrieved from https://www.riskinstitute.org/peri/images/file/postkatrina_preparedness.pdf.

Lindell, K. M., & Perry, W. R. (2007). Planning for preparedness. In W. L. Waugh, Jr., & K. Tierney (Eds.), *Emergency management: Principles and practice for local government* (2nd ed., pp. 113–142). Washington, DC: ICMA.

London Regional Resilience Forum. (2006, September). *Looking back moving forward: Lessons identified and progress since the terrorist events of 7 July 2005.* London: Government Office for London. Retrieved March 20, 2010, from http://www.londonprepared.gov.uk/downloads/lookingbackmovingforward.pdf.

Macrae, J., Bradbury, M., Jaspars, S., Johnson, D., & Duffield, M. (1997). Conflict, the continuum and chronic emergencies: A critical analysis of the scope for linking relief, rehabilitation and development planning in Sudan. *Disasters, 21*(3), 223–243.

McEntire, D. A. (2007). *Disaster response and recovery: Strategies and tactics for resilience.* Hoboken, NJ: Wiley.

Militello, L. G., Patterson, E. S., Bowman, L., & Wears, R. (2007). Information flow during crisis management: Challenges to coordination in the emergency operations center. *Cognition, Technology and Work, 9*(1), 25–31.

National Aeronautics and Space Administration (NASA). (2007). Earthquake satellite imagery. Retrieved January 22, 2010, from http://www.nasa.gov/vision/earth/lookingatearth/indonesia_quake.html.

Özerdem, A. (2003). Disaster as manifestation of unresolved development challenges: The Marmara earthquake, Turkey. In M. Pelling (Ed.), *Natural disasters and development in a globalizing world* (pp. 199–213). London: Routledge.

Paton, D. (2003). Disaster preparedness: A social cognitive perspective. *Disaster Prevention and Management, 12*(3), 210–216.

Perry, R. W., & Lindell, M. K. (2007). Disaster response. In W. L. Waugh, Jr., & K. Tierney (Eds.), *Emergency management: Principles and practice for local government* (2nd ed., pp. 159–182). Washington, DC: ICMA

Phillips, B. D. (2010). *Disaster recovery.* New York: CRC Press.

Phillips, B. D., & Neal, D. M. (2007). Recovery. In W. L. Waugh, Jr., & K. Tierney (Eds.), *Emergency management: Principles and practice for local government* (2nd ed., pp. 207–233). Washington, DC: ICMA.

Pitt, M. (2008). Learning lessons from 2007 floods. Cabinet Office. Retrieved from http://archive
.cabinetoffice.gov.uk/pittreview/_/media/assets/www.cabinetoffice.gov.uk/flooding_review/
pitt_review_full%20pdf.pdf.

Public Safety Wireless Network Program (PSWN). (2002). Answering the call: Communications
lessons learned from the Pentagon attack. Retrieved January 13, 2010, from http://www
.safecomprogram.gov/NR/rdonlyres/8839D9BA-9104-4EE1-BC43-E8431C500F95/0/An-
sweringCallLessonsPentagonAttack.pdf.

Rotanz, A. R. (2007). Applied response strategies. In W. L. Waugh, Jr., & K. Tierney (Eds.),
Emergency management: Principles and practice for local government, pp. 143–158.
(2nd ed.). Washington, DC: ICMA.

SAFECOM. (n.d.). Interoperability. Retrieved January 13, 2010, from http://www.safecomprogram
.gov/SAFECOM/interoperability/default.htm.

Schwab, J. (1998). *Planning for post-disaster recovery and reconstruction.* Chicago: American
Planning Association.

Small Business Administration (SBA). (2009). Disaster recovery plan. Retrieved February 3,
2010, from http://www.sba.gov/idc/groups/public/documents/sba_homepage/serv_da_
disastr_revcovery_plan.pdf.

Sollis, P. (1994). The relief–development continuum: Some notes on rethinking assistance for
civilian victims of conflict. *Journal of International Affairs, 47*(2), 451–471.

Stehr, S. D. (2001). Community recovery and reconstruction following disasters. In A. Farazmand
(Ed.), *Handbook of crisis and emergency management* (pp. 419–431). New York: Marcel
Dekker.

Strom, K. J., & Eyerman, J. (2008). Interagency coordination: A case study of the 2005 London
grain bombings. *National Institute of Justice, 260,* 8–12.

Taft-Morales, M., & Margesson, R. (2010). *Haiti earthquake: Crisis and response.* CRS Report for
Congress.

Tobin, G. (1999). Sustainability and community resilience: The Holy Grail of hazards planning.
Environmental Hazards, 1(1), 13–25.

Von Meding, J. K., & Oyedele, L. O. (2008, February 20–15). Flooding in New Orleans, USA and
Hull City, UK: Comparing disaster management strategies. In R. Haigh & D. Amaratunga
(Eds.), *Building resilience: CIB W89 International Conference in Building Education and
Research (BEAR 2008)* (pp. 1482–1492). Kandalama.

Weisler, R. H., Barbie, J. G. IV, & Townsend, M. H. (2006). Mental health and recovery in the
Gulf Coast after Hurricanes Katrina and Rita. *Journal of the American Medical Association,
296*(5), 585–588.

Wetter, D. C., Daniell, W. E., & Treser, C. D. (2001). Hospital preparedness for victims of chemical or biological terrorism. *American Journal of Public Health, 91*(5), 710–716.

White, P., & Cliffe, L. (2000). matching response to context in complex political emergencies: "Relief," "development," "peace-building" or something in-between? *Disasters, 24*(4), 314–342.

World Bank. (1999). *Turkey: Marmara earthquake assessment.* Europe and Central Asia Region
of the World Bank.

Zixing, W., Xifu, C., & Keren, L. (2002). Earthquake relief and reconstruction of Tangshan.
Retrieved May 4, 2010, from http://caltecheerl.library.caltech.edu/353/01/Tangshan/
Volume3_Chapter_6.pdf.

Chapter 5

Community Resilience in Disaster Response

Chapter Objectives

- Understand the importance of community resilience in emergency planning and preparedness.
- Learn about myths and misconceptions in disaster response.
- Investigate the coordination of responsibilities by different stakeholders in disaster response.
- Discuss the importance of capacity-building efforts to improve response and recovery.
- Analyze the case studies of the Kobe earthquake, Gujarat earthquake, and Hurricane Mitch.

Introduction

The public increasingly expects better public-sector leadership before, during, and after catastrophic disasters and extreme events than it has seen in the past (Kapucu & Van Wart, 2006). However, increased public participation in all phases of disaster management is an important step toward more effective and collaborative disaster response (Col, 2007). In contrast to the widespread perception among the public, uninjured victims and bystanders of a disaster are not necessarily passive, shocked, or panicked after the event happens (Lindell, Prater, & Perry, 2007). Instead, they are the first responders to the incidents who save injured people and alert public officials.

As leaders of first response activities, local administrators should possess basic scientific knowledge about possible disasters that might happen in their region (Perry & Lindell, 2007). When it comes to mitigation/preparation and response, many myths about who does what and when have emerged. Although the theory of a planned approach is explicated in the literature, analyzing experiences reveals a different reality. The normative thinking of disaster management is valuable to only a certain extent as emergency managers develop their own assumptions to structure how programs should be planned and implemented. To a large extent, the problem comes from assuming an "institutional" attitude toward this challenge, by ignoring the role of communities in disaster management phases. In other words, communities are capable of, and do, much more than disaster management practitioners and institutions often give them credit for.

In the United States, homeland security is now considered a national responsibility, not just a federal one. The meaning of such integration in different societies is explained in this chapter through an exploration of the community resilience concept. Efforts to create disaster-resilient communities have not always been successful, however. In many cases, the reason why governments are not successful in such social marketing efforts is that they neglect three important facts about people:

- At times, people do not act rationally in pre-disaster conditions. They tend not to take necessary precautionary steps for mitigation and preparedness.
- People are not completely obedient.
- People are culturally, socioeconomically, and intellectually very diverse.

It is not solely a government's responsibility to perform emergency management functions, and the whole society should be engaged in all phases of emergency management. People should be educated about prevention of potential environmental hazards. Moreover, the government should not encourage rebuilding as a primary concern; instead, it should engage people in prevention and mitigation (Multihazard Mitigation Council, 2005; Özerdem & Jacoby, 2006).

In other words, preparing for emergencies and crises is a multiorganizational and multidistrict process; for communities to handle these events effectively, effective collaboration is essential (Perry & Lindell, 2007). Although collaboration and coordination are two of the most important functions in managing crises and disasters, they are also the most challenging. Many of the challenges in this area relate to communications, while working with different agencies that have different roles, responsibilities, and plans, and acquiring the necessary resources needed to properly prepare for disaster. However, if agencies are able to properly coordinate their functions, this capability will make them more effective responders to disasters.

The main focus of this chapter is multiagency planning and coordination in relation to a culture of preparedness and resilient communities. The discussion here outlines the process of assessing the emergency response organization's ability to perform four basic functions: emergency assessment, hazard operations, population protection, and incident management. The chapter also explores disaster response myths and misconceptions in the context of three case studies, dealing with the Kobe and Gujarat earthquakes and Hurricane Mitch.

Culture of Preparedness and Resilient Communities

Resiliency is one of other key aspects of risk management. Kunreuther and Useem (2010) define resiliency as "the adaptability of a business, household, or community to cushion potential losses through inherent or explicitly adaptive behavior in the aftermath of a disaster and through a learning process in anticipation of future one" (p. 11). In other words, resiliency is defined as how well individuals and communities can adapt to changed conditions caused by disasters (Magsino, 2009). According to the National Research Council (NRC, 2009), resilience is "a response to stress and can be considered as a theory that guides the understanding of stress response dynamics; a set of adaptive capacities that call attention to the resources that promote successful adaptation in the face of adversity; and a strategy for disaster readiness against unpredictable and difficult to prepare for dangers" (p. 23).

Given that resiliency has a dynamic nature, careful long-term planning for resiliency is imperative. Such programs embrace the adaptability of society rather than its stability. Resilient communities consist of four main constituents:

- Social capital (networks within the community)
- Community competence (flexibility and problem-solving skills)
- Information and communication (communication skills, infrastructure, trusted sources of information)
- A strong economy (diverse and evenly distributed economic resources and risk)

An optimal level of these four factors results in resiliency and helps communities to function during a disaster (Kendra & Wachtendorf, 2003; NRC, 2009; Norris, Stevens, Pfefferbaum, Wyche, & Pfefferbaum, 2008). Although the process is challenging, developing measures for these factors is essential to craft intervention programs and assess their effectiveness.

Hazard mitigation planning processes represent a set of core indicators of vulnerability that are key to community resilience. However, Mileti's (1999) review of natural hazards suggests that property and human loss from natural hazards is due in part to local governments' failure to do an adequate job of steering development away from hazardous areas and a lack of mitigation that is integrated into new development and the existing infrastructure. Planning programs that focus on the location and design of development and that guide expansion of development to areas free of hazards can reduce damage (Godschalk, Kaiser, & Berke, 1998). From a preparedness and response perspective, planning can reduce vulnerability through targeted emergency management plans or through broader comprehensive plans that incorporate disaster preparation and response. Reviews of both approaches indicate that they have a positive effect in fostering the development of more rigorous hazard programs (Burby & May, 1998). Further, land-use decision making that incorporates dependent populations requires coordinated and proactive planning processes.

Civic organizations, in partnership with planning agencies, can help mitigation and disaster resiliency (Paterson, 1998).

Although measures of vulnerability have been widely utilized in studying emergency management, resilience is far less well understood. It includes those inherent conditions that allow a local governing unit, region, or network of stakeholder groups to absorb impacts and cope with an event, helping these governing units or relations change, learn, and achieve an acceptable level of functioning (Cutter & Finch, 2008).

A balance between environmental and development issues is key to developing and fostering resilience. This balance can be achieved through hazard mitigation planning and management of land uses (Burby et al., 1999). Resilience is linked to the built environment and the location of development (i.e., homes, industry, and infrastructure). Disaster studies suggest that natural hazards result when impinging social forces render some groups more vulnerable than others. These social forces include gender, social class, ethnicity, race, seniority, and place of residence (Enarson, Fothergill, & Peek, 2006; Peacock, Morrow, & Gladwin, 1997). Past research has indicated that rural communities are particularly vulnerable to natural hazards. In fact, a recent report by Oxfam America (2009) described some of the disadvantages of the rural Southeast United States (e.g., poverty, race, ethnicity, age, and gender) that render these rural communities vulnerable to natural hazards.

Research has provided two distinctive ways to analyze the role of culture in preparing and responding to natural hazards. One set of studies has examined culture at the organizational level, focusing on how communities and organizations develop a culture that might increase vulnerability, particularly in sociotechnical disasters (Hopkins, 1999; Turner, 1978). Another set of studies has investigated culture as it relates to the processes of political, social, and cultural marginalization and their effects on disaster vulnerability and recovery (Phillips, 1993). The premise underlying this work is that culture is an important feature to address as it relates to vulnerability.

Social networks—defined as "the interactions between people and organizations, including who knows, works with, or communicated with whom, that can be mapped" (Magsino, 2009, p. 2)—are particularly affected by natural hazards. In essence, disaster situations usually disrupt social interaction networks; thus knowledge about the vulnerabilities of the social networks is intrinsically related to the resilience of the community. This process might be complicated in communities if they lack access to social capital and limited institutional and organizational assets (Green, 2008; Kendra & Wachtendorf, 2003; Ritchie, Ashleyand, & Duane, 2007). This important issue is explored further in Chapter 6.

The challenge in developing resilient communities lies in not only recognizing and anticipating the scope of damages, but also integrating multiple agencies, jurisdictions, and stakeholder groups in a response to a disaster (Comfort, 2006; Pelling, 2003; Ronan & Johnson, 2005). Coordination is particularly important across jurisdictions because disasters do not confine themselves to political and administrative boundaries. Thus regionalism and associated interorganizational cooperation represent another key component in assessing vulnerability (Kapucu, 2008). Due to the catastrophic nature of disasters and the fact that no single agency or organization has all the resources needed to fully support the response and recovery phase, creating cross-sector networks before a disaster is vital for effective and efficient preparedness and response to disasters. It is often argued that cross-sector partnerships effectively increase the amount of resources provided in response to disasters (Kapucu, 2009; Simo & Bies, 2007). Effective leadership and communication are also necessary to help increase preparedness and develop mitigation programs; hence they are essential to an effective response and recovery. Community response to a disaster or emergency can be successful if capacity building has taken place and the collaborating agencies have developed a shared vision, a common understanding of the problem, leadership skills, and sustainable community involvement (Beatley, 1998).

As explained in Chapter 3, failures in managing disasters are usually the consequence of a lack of preparedness, which is exacerbated by the scope of the incident. Additionally, challenges and shortcomings related to necessary resources are inevitable in disasters. Honore and Martz (2009) summarize this situation as follows: If telephone lines are not damaged or the communication tools are functioning, then there is only an inconvenient situation; in disasters, however, all the worst and unexpected conditions take place. Although the strength of certain natural events cannot be reduced, mitigation and preparation for potential hazards can decrease the impact of the event. Of course, these tasks are not solely the job of certain designated organizations or individuals; instead, realization of a culture of preparedness requires a sense of shared responsibility among all stakeholders in emergency management (Basolo, Steinberg, Burby, Levine, Cruz, & Hang, 2009). Hurricane Katrina, for example, brought several issues related to this subject to the surface, which were identified as missing aspects of successful management in emergency situations. The White House report on Hurricane Katrina underscores the necessity to ensure a nationwide culture of preparedness: "it must emphasize that the entire Nation—Federal, State, and local governments; the private sector; communities; and individual citizens—shares common goals and responsibilities for homeland security" (White House, 2006, p. 87).

Government's responsibility in creating a culture of preparedness focuses on technical preparedness and the political initiative. Heath (1995) recommends adopting a position of strategic preparedness for hazards to reduce damage from disasters. The core idea in strategic preparedness is the formulation of plans and spending efforts for training for pre-event management and preparedness. Environmental scanning, risk assessment, logistics, and development of contingency plans are all part of the technical aspect of preparedness. These functions have a role in developing the culture of preparedness, but to realize it they have to be connected with both individuals in the government and other stakeholders.

Honore and Matz (2009) examine the role of the government from a different perspective. In their work, they point out that government and public joint initiatives played significant roles in overcoming problems related to the HIV/AIDS pandemic and school desegregation. To achieve a culture of preparedness government, citizens, businesses, and other stakeholders need to work together, and some incentives have to be offered to foster this cooperation. For instance, the Department of Homeland Security (DHS, 2007) has established initiatives for creating a culture of preparedness among schools. Various programs, manuals, and publications are offered to schools to help them determine the optimal physical design of their facilities and enhance mitigation efforts. The Federal Emergency Management Agency (FEMA) also offers training through the Emergency Management Institute to schools. Additionally, more than 2200 Citizen Corps Councils endeavor to bring public, private, and nonprofit organizations and volunteers to the same table for planning emergency preparedness and response. Schools are also integrated into these efforts (DHS, 2007).

Of course, there are many challenges in establishing a culture of preparedness. The approach to different types of threats and the changing nature of the public administration both play roles in determining the level of preparedness within the society. Honore and Matz (2009) demonstrate this condition by comparing the Cold War era with the present day. During the 1960s, Americans maintained a culture of preparedness owing to the existing state of war with the Soviet Union, even if there was no real physical engagement between the United States and the Soviet Union.

Additionally, the outsourcing of services to the private sector brings more complexity to the system. In fact, bringing all of the various stakeholders to same table appears to be one of the most significant challenges that stands in the way of building a culture of preparedness.

Moreover, a general sense of optimism can generate complacency, undermining efforts to maintain preparedness (Wang & Kapucu, 2007; White House, 2006). Interestingly, complacency does not stem from a lack of information or poor knowledge about the potential hazards. Even a community that is well aware of hazards may still be unprepared for them, just because individuals have tendency to ignore and be unprepared for them (Wang & Kapucu, 2007). This factor is highly related with the cognition that Comfort (2007) emphasizes as a reason for failures in disasters. Shaw's et al. (2004) study on earthquake preparedness also confirms the hypothesis put forth by Comfort (2007). These authors' investigation revealed that education can provide useful information to people as well as the benefit of previous experience. Even so, neither of these factors is sufficient to make people prepared for earthquakes. Instead, self-education, family influence, and collective community education all assume more prominent roles in preparedness. Indeed, these three factors are key constituents of any culture of preparedness.

To summarize, a culture of preparedness can be achieved via self-determination. A collective mindset for readiness and a knowledge base of fundamental information both contribute to nurturing that culture. Government agencies may lead preparedness efforts and collaborate with private and nonprofit sectors for establishing a common understanding of the potential hazards, in addition to fulfilling their tasks related to the technical aspects of preparedness. To support community resilience in an effective manner so that the disaster response strategy can avoid entrapments of disaster response myths (discussed in the next section), multiagency planning and coordination are essential components of the process.

Myths and Misconceptions About Disaster Response

Any disaster response includes a variety of stakeholders, whose roles reflect their differing perspectives. Even though it is commonly believed that public agencies are the primary responders, usually uninjured victims and bystanders are the first people who engage in response activities. Other misconceptions often arise about the behaviors of disaster victims, perhaps due to media influence (Lindell et al., 2007). Wenger et al. (1975) point out that panic flight, looting, higher crime rates, and disaster shock are notable myths about individuals' behavior after a disaster. They also emphasize that calling these phenomena "myths" does not mean that they never take place, but rather emphasized the lack of evidence that they commonly occur in the aftermath of an incident (Wenger et al., 1975).

Individuals' reactions to disaster conditions will differ in accordance with their personal conditions, environment, and previous experience. As Lindell et al. (2007) note, there is no such thing as a homogeneous population or public. Rather, different segments of a population will have different degrees of special conditions, which will inevitably alter their behavior in the case of a disaster. Individuals with special needs (i.e., visually impaired, hearing-impaired, and mobility-impaired individuals; people with medical conditions; single working parents; people with intellectual disabilities), minorities, transient populations, and middle- or upper-class residents, for example, are likely to have different willingness to evacuate or participate in response actions. Their ability to receive disaster warnings will be different as well (Lindell et al., 2006, 2007).

People who are in the vicinity of a disaster or a victim are likely to demonstrate different behavioral patterns than might usually be expected. People usually seek help from friends, families, and other types of informal networks in the case of a disaster. In the aftermath of a disaster, few choose to use public shelters; instead, the majority go to their relatives, friends, or hotels (Lindell et al., 2007; Wenger et al., 1975). For medical transport, the results of research are equally surprising. According to Quarantelli (1983, as cited in Lindell at al., 2007), a large proportion of victims of a disaster (46%) are taken to the hospital by their peers, bystanders, or their own vehicles. Most victims are taken to the nearest hospital (75%) and are treated in a single facility (67%). Because this situation is likely to cause overcrowding in core facilities, careful planning of medical emergency operations is imperative to ensure successful outcomes for as many patients as possible.

Media coverage after a disaster plays an important role in the emergence and expansion of myths, and the accuracy of media reports in such scenarios is likely to be impeded. The information delivered by mass media has the potential to be biased, inaccurate, and incomplete (Fischer, 1998; Wenger et al., 1975). Reporters tend to seek out unique events in the aftermath of an incident, and they prefer to highlight incidents that correspond to their preconceived image of "a disaster" (Quarantelli & Dynes, 1972, as cited in Wenger et al., 1975). Wenger et al. (1975), Tierney et al. (2001), and Lindell et al. (2007) note that individuals' behaviors do not seem to match the prevailing myths about reactions in an emergency setting, especially in the post-disaster phase. Contrary to the general perception, people tend to react rationally with the limited information they have about the situation in the aftermath of an incident. They use informal networks and their social capital to ask for help. Crime rates do not increase—and in some contexts can even decrease—and looting rarely happens (Lindell et al., 2007).

Emergency managers need to prepare for and respond to disasters with knowledge about potential individual behavior during an incident. Predictable behavior of people during the incidences eases the response and recovery efforts to be undertaken. Leaving myths, exaggerations, and misconceptions behind and focusing on the facts facilitates better predictions and planning of individual actions.

Coordination in Disaster Response and Capacity Building

Planning and stakeholder inclusion in recovery, as discussed earlier in this chapter, has been a major issue in the switch to the National Response Framework (NRF) from the National Response Plan (NRP). The Government Accountability Office (GAO, 2008b) has addressed the transition from the NRP to the NRF, and the challenges associated with both. Originally, the NRP was created to provide a response system applicable to all levels of government and organizations in the event of a disaster. After disasters such as Hurricane Katrina, however, officials recognized the necessity to change the NRP to a more open-ended system of preparedness, which they hoped could then be applied at any level of government. The resulting system was the NRF. Unfortunately, there was a major oversight in the NRF, in that this framework omitted many stakeholders who play a major role in disaster response—for instance, citizens and the private health sector.

The GAO (2008b) has criticized the Department of Homeland Security in the past because it "did not collaborate with non-federal stakeholders as fully planned or required in developing the National Response Framework" (p. 9). As shown during Hurricane Katrina, a continued lack of collaboration among intergovernmental responders during disaster planning stages can be a fatal mistake. To rectify this problem, the GAO made recommendations for the next iteration of the NRF, including that FEMA develop policies and procedures that outline "(1) the circumstances and time frames under which the next NRF revision will occur and (2) how FEMA will conduct the next NRF revision, including how its National Advisory Council and other non-federal stakeholders—state, local, and tribal governments; the private sector; and nongovernmental organizations—will be integrated into the revision process and the methods for communicating with these stakeholders" (GAO, 2008b, p. 28). Incorporating stakeholder buy-in and recommendations will be vital in creating an NRF that is able to effectively address the preparatory needs of all communities and all organizations within those communities.

Citizen involvement in disaster response represents an alternative to civil society involvement in disaster response. Citizen Emergency Response Team (CERT) is a program that educates people about possible hazards that might occur in their area. Individuals who participate in CERT programs receive basic training about the first response to a disaster, including disaster preparedness, fire suppression, medical operations, search and rescue, and disaster psychology, and are given the basic equipment that a first responder needs (McEntire & Dawson, 2007). Particularly in communities where there is limited capacity for disaster response, CERT programs can help people organize for disaster response and meet the needs that arise in handling a potential hazard (Flint & Brennan, 2006). In this way, CERT programs help to decrease the social vulnerabilities in a community by including people from a diverse population in the process of creating a culture of preparedness.

Although such efforts are certainly laudable, the responsibility for disaster planning and creating response and recovery plans remains largely in the hands of state and local governments—despite the fact that federal agencies provide millions of dollars to help with immediate and long-term recovery efforts (Derthick, 2007; GAO, 2008a). Effective disaster response and recovery is contingent upon local governments developing community-wide emergency response plans that include strategies specific to disaster response and recovery. Local governments are best suited to respond to and recover from disasters when planning includes mitigation and recognition of the potential operational challenges that may arise during disaster response.

Derthick (2007), in the article entitled "Where Federalism Didn't Fail," illustrates the importance of communication and planning through a discussion of the successes and failures in the U.S. government's response to Hurricane Katrina. She concludes that, even though many fingers were pointed to blame various parties for the malfunction of the government response during Hurricane Katrina, the successes and failures were the collective responsibility of local, state, and federal governments. The emphasis on federal responsibility here is important because, although the burden of response is placed mostly on local and state governments because they are the first responders, "large-scale disasters usually exceed local response capabilities." Therefore, "[e]ffective preparation and response for major and catastrophic disasters require well-planned and well-coordinated actions among all those who would have a role in the response to such disasters" (GAO, 2008b, p. 27). Thus, not only does the federal government have to be prepared to act in cooperation with those already on the frontlines, but it must also be effectively prepared to deal with response as it relates to recovery. Recovery is a very expensive, complex, ongoing process that requires a long-term focus on rebuilding and restoring physical and economic infrastructures and that depends on community characteristics such as community needs, resources, and local demands (GAO, 2008a). To facilitate these efforts, local government must proactively approach response and recovery plans through partnering with local organizations and communities. It is recommended that the federal role in response and recovery plans be strengthened to satisfy this demand.

According to Rubin (2009), the NRF fails to effectively address local response so as to manage "challenges associated with the local and intergovernmental politics of disaster recovery" (p. 11). Rubin (2009) also stresses that the federal government does not accept as much responsibility in prioritizing recovery as it ought to. She argues that a National Disaster Recovery Strategy document is required by law, but has not yet been developed. After Hurricane Katrina, the Defense Authorization Act was enacted in 2007; this legislation gives the President power to call upon the military and the National Guard when a disaster or emergency situation takes place. Derthick (2007) suggests that this direct approach by the federal government damages federalism in the service of managing emergencies. She advocates instead strengthening the role of first responders and local governments via collaboration and coordination. It is also suggested that federal involvement might be increased, perhaps through creation of a national disaster recovery plan and provision of guidelines to local governments and communities, so that they can incorporate disaster plans into their own local comprehensive plans.

Moreover, while the federal government continues to provide funds to state and local governments, the U.S. government needs to ensure that these funds are apportioned and spent in the most desirable fashion. This goal is achieved when state and local governments have the capacities, such as financial and technical resources, to effectively use federal funds (GAO, 2008a).

Capacity-Building Efforts to Improve Response and Recovery

Capacity building can be defined as developing capabilities, resources, and personnel that facilitate the development of policies and procedures that proactively manage response and recovery so as to lessen the financial and emotional hardships that disasters leave in their wake. It "embraces the value of empowering communities and . . . translates this into decisions and actions that support bottom-up, community-led initiatives" (Paton, 2006, p. 310).

Phillips and Neal (2007) point out that building capacity through vertical and horizontal associations is vital to the public emergency manager. Vulnerabilities, weaknesses, and historical design and infrastructure problems and solutions can be more rationally discussed during this process. Utilizing this preparedness/mitigation stage for community "visioning" ensures a much more holistic and inclusive approach is taken toward emergency management. Addressing potential hazards, disaster response activities, and mitigation opportunities in a comprehensive plan is vital in the provision of both strategic planning and protection for the community. Successful examples of this approach include the Rebuilding Iowa Office (n.d.) and Continuity Central (2007) initiatives, in which communities with historical perspectives on repetitive disaster threats and events have committed to proactive approaches to reduce disaster effects and costs.

According to Phillips and Neal (2007), preplanning, communication, and effective intergovernmental and interorganizational relationship building are the keys to successful disaster recovery for the government manager. Furthermore, Phillips and Neal (2007) state that "few jurisdictions have the capability, resources, or staff to do this, yet, considering the immense benefits that can be achieved—it seems in a community's best interests to aggressively pursue this approach" (p. 211). Community-based efforts for disaster preparedness, response, and recovery capacity building have the "potential to make a significant and long-lasting contribution to reducing local vulnerability and strengthening adaptive capacities" (Allen, 2006, p. 97).

To successfully pursue community capacity building, the understanding of the community involved is necessary. Allen (2006, p. 86) lists four factors for ensuring capacity building:

- Technical information dissemination and training
- Raising awareness of risk and vulnerability
- Accessing local knowledge
- Mobilizing local people

These four factors not only enhance preparedness, but also spark better response and recovery in the aftermath of disasters.

Information sharing and the ability to assess transmitted information are fundamental pillars of an effective emergency response. Citizens who have the necessary tools and the training to undertake the response represent the first step to elevate a community's capacity to respond to disasters. CERT members are examples of citizens who are equipped with such basic disaster tools and knowledge.

Following the fulfillment of material needs, risk awareness might be elevated as the next step in preparation. As Paton (2003) points out, individuals' cognition for disaster preparedness and risk awareness is a necessary factor for community capacity building for coping with disasters.

Accessing local knowledge brings adaptability and flexibility to the local conditions for response and recovery actions. "Community organizing" refers to the organization of local participants for the disaster response roles and responsibilities. Allen (2006) cites local early-warning systems that are linked to regional or national information systems as examples of mobilization of local populations.

In addition to the four factors just discussed, Allen (2006) mentions social capital as another value that can ease the challenges of response and recovery. Halpern (2005) underlines the way social capital fosters effectiveness in government. Several different levels of social capital exist, including individual and organizational social capital, and each level performs different functions to bolster response and recovery actions. Social capital increases the trust among actors of the emergency management, decreases the transaction cost, and decreases the asymmetrical information flow between parties. Further, it enhances the effective and efficient use of resources in the community, identifies the vulnerable people in the community, and helps to overcome the potential tragedies among these people.

Wenger et al. (1975) and Lindell et al. (2006, 2007) point out that this type of convergence may pose a potential problem for disaster response and relief efforts after an incident. Indeed, both people and materials can undermine the success of disaster response efforts. People tend to be sympathetic to disaster victims (Ouden & Russel, 1997; Russel & Mentzel, 1990) and to support disaster relief activities as much as they can. In the aftermath of a disaster, a sufficient quantity of supplies, aid, and volunteers tend to emerge to help in response actions. In some cases, however, these resources can actually be overwhelming—far beyond sufficient—and may hinder the activities of first responders. Furthermore, convergence of humans and aid materials may cause conflict between relief organizations, produce congestion, and be disruptive to the local economy (Wenger et al., 1975). Lindell et al. (2006) state that even uninvited governmental aid, such as the arrival of extra fire teams from distant communities in the case of the Louisiana air crash, made the response more complicated, slow, and costly. The excess resources may result in more chaos and disorganization as time is wasted in trying to delineate roles for extra teams and create some work for them.

While both businesses and public organizations endeavor to manage emergencies and crises, neither of these efforts can be successful on its own (Begando, 2009). Business operations centers (BOCs) refer to a "concept to facilitate private sector communication and information sharing capabilities within existing state and metropolitan emergency operations centers" (Begando, 2009, p. 30). The integration of the private sector into emergency management programs started with supply-related operations that the public sector usually confronts. Collaboration among public and private sectors is expanding, however, and now includes planning, training activities, security, intelligence, and critical infrastructure protection. In the United

States, 85% of the country's critical infrastructure is owned by the private sector (GAO, 2006), which makes collaboration inevitable and indispensable for successful management of emergencies.

Begando (2009) notes that the U.S. states of Georgia and California have already structured the collaboration between the private sector and emergency management authorities. The State of Georgia Emergency Management Agency (GEMA) held round-table discussions with private-sector partners and local government representatives to form a framework to facilitate these relationships. The core function of the conference was to emphasize formal means of communication and cooperation between the private and public sectors in an emergency setting. In this context, the BOCs perform roles related communication and information sharing among public and private organizations, provision of technology for resource sharing, recruitment of new private partners, and coordination of common exercises and training (Begando, 2009). No standardized plan for such interactions is possible, however, because every jurisdiction is likely to adopt its own framework (Lindell & Perry, 2007), allowing each community to develop its own tailored strategy.

Case Studies

Japan Earthquake and Tsunami 2011

On March 11, 2011, a 9.0 Richter scale earthquake hit the coast of Japan and lead to a destructive tsunami. While the nation was struggling to respond to the tsunami and earthquake, a nuclear emergency broke out in three reactors at the Fukushima Daiichi Nuclear Power Station, due to leaking radioactive gas.

The damage from the earthquake alone is believed to be limited due to the country's strong building designs and strict building codes that are followed during construction. However, the tsunami that was recorded to be 33 feet high caused most of the devastation (Mahoney, 2011). According to the New York Times (2011) the official death toll has reached 14,133, while 13,346 people are reported missing. Official sources predict that the death toll is expected to reach 20,000. As of April 25, due to the widespread destruction and the nuclear crisis, internal displacement has resulted in 130,000 people living in temporary shelters as well.

Japan is currently the third largest economy in the world and contributes 8.7% to the global GDP (Nanto et al., 2011). The total damage from the disaster has been estimated around $300 billion and around $50 billion in emergency spending and reconstruction has been earmarked by the government of Japan (The New York Times, 2011). Thus it is believed that Japan's growth will stall and stagnate for a while since its foreign direct investment will be replaced with investments to re-build, restore, and reconstruct parts of the country (UNISDR, 2011). Recessionary pressures are building in Japan and their impact will be determined by how and when the nuclear plant damage can be addressed, on the timely restoration of electrical and oil refining capacity, and how soon the industrial base can recover from damage and losses. Moreover, during the reconstruction phase the Japanese government will borrow to rebuild and restore infrastructure which will further increase recessionary pressures as Japan's national debt will experience a colossal increase (Nanto et al., 2011).

The existing leadership and their response was highly criticized in the wake of the disaster due to a lack of mitigation strategies for addressing nuclear emergencies, and for the government's ineffective response and relief efforts. Recently, the Prime Minister of Japan, Naoto Kan has declared that Japan will not invest in building more nuclear reactors, but will instead develop a new energy policy which will focus on renewable energy and conservation. The government is also being criticized for acting irresponsibly towards the numerous lawsuits that were filed opposing the nuclear industry and its operations. The government is believed to be involved in collusive activities that supported the nuclear industry and protected them against the lawsuits (The New York Times, 2011). Moreover, on April 29, a senior nuclear advisor to the Prime Minister resigned as he felt that the government was not taking his advice and appropriate steps to address the nuclear crisis, but were instead relying on ad hoc measures (The New York Times, 2011). On April 12, Japanese officials declared that although the radiation being released from the Fukushima plant has reached around 10% of the amount of radioactive materials released during the 1986 Cherboyl disaster, it has potential to exceed those levels (The New York Times, 2011).

It will take years to reconstruct and redevelop areas that have been destroyed by the disaster. Sustainable development requires a more responsible and visionary government that improves Japan's energy policy. Despite the widespread destruction of houses and infrastructure, the high death toll, a large number of displacements and injuries, and difficulties faced due to the nuclear radiation crisis, Japan and its people have shown utmost resilience and strength as a nation (UNISDR, 2011).

Kobe Earthquake

On January 17, 1995, an earthquake with magnitude of 7.2 on the Richter scale hit Kobe, Japan, at 5:46 A.M. (**Figure 5-1**). The earthquake killed more than 5000 people and injured more than 25,000. Approximately 46,000 buildings were destroyed, 310,000 people (20% of the population) were left homeless, more than 1 million individuals were left without clean water, and 800,000 were without gas supplies (Heath, 1995). The economic cost of the disaster was estimated at $100 billion (Özerdem & Jacoby, 2006). Several fires took place immediately following the quake that significantly exacerbated the scope of the disaster.

As Heath (1995) notes, although Japan's disaster management system was considered one of the most effective in the world, serious shortcomings of this system

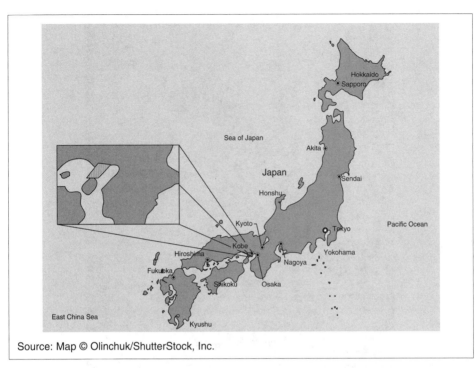

Source: Map © Olinchuk/ShutterStock, Inc.

Figure 5-1 *Impact zone of Kobe Earthquake*

were obvious in the Kobe scenario. Several problems in responding to the event were related to preparedness issues. Heath (1995) points out the slowness of the response in accordance with decision making in mobilizing resources. Decision makers were far from adaptable to the situation and looked for solutions that could "save face" and would not undermine their positions in the future. In keeping with the Japanese culture, collective action and consensus were sought in making decisions, which also slowed down the completion of steps necessary for effective response and relief actions. As Heath (1995) discusses, "the centralized nature of Japan's organizations is likely to be more routine (thus easier and faster in making decisions), but less adaptive" (p. 14). A culturally bottom-up decision-making process also impeded the coordination in the central government and corresponding actions of both Japan's Prime Minister and his Cabinet. Response agencies in the region were not sufficiently experienced in dealing with the effects of earthquakes, and consequently were not ready for the challenging conditions of a disaster.

The means of communication were heavily damaged during the earthquake (**Figure 5-2**), such that interorganizational interactions were halted and authorities were not able to gather accurate information. Consequently, many delays occurred in the coordination of organizations and calls for assistance and response actions. In one instance, a field commander drove 14 kilometers to Nishinomiya city hall to transfer information and instructions. More than 100 fires occurred in the aftermath

© STR New/Thomson Reuters

Figure 5-2 *The earthquake destroyed infrastructure significantly*

of the earthquake but it took more than 5 hours for fire services to gather 90% of their capacity (Özerdem & Jacoby, 2006).

Özerdem and Jacoby (2006) examine different disasters, including the Kobe earthquake, through a civil society lens and confirm the points made by Heath. They note that the Kobe earthquake undermined a dominant myth in Japan—that modern technology, structural mitigation, and good government have prepared the country for the severe earthquakes that have been taking place in the country for millennia. The earthquake provided an example of what would happen "when attention to integration, coordination, communication, planning and strategic planning is insufficient" (Heath, 1995, p. 23). The earthquake was a wake-up call for Japan to integrate different aspects of preparedness within its emergency management system. The Kobe experience also sensitized Japanese society to the necessity of volunteerism in disaster response and management. Public officials prepared programs to include volunteers and their organizations in the disaster preparedness and response activities. Moreover, to eliminate the shortcomings of the Kobe disaster, "better communications systems, accompanied by a number of important administrative reforms, have been developed which have improved cooperation between regional and national governments and enhanced the way that central government department co-ordinate their duties" (Özerdem & Jacoby, 2006, p. 49).

The high level of volunteerism in the aftermath of the Kobe earthquake and its invaluable contribution to the disaster response showed that the potentially effective role of communities in disaster management had been neglected in Japan, which had largely emphasized the technical aspects of mitigation strategies to that point. The myth of technological advancement as the best way of disaster preparedness was exposed by the Kobe earthquake, to such an extent that the disaster became an important turning point for state–civil society relationships in the country. With the changes in the legislation of disaster management and wider context of associational life in the aftermath of the disaster, the role of communities in disaster preparedness and response is now better integrated.

Gujarat Earthquake

Gujarat State of India experienced a devastating, magnitude-6.9 earthquake on January 26, 2001 (World Bank & Asian Development Bank, 2001). The disaster coincided with India's national Republic Day. Approximately 20,000 people lost their lives, and more than 167,000 were injured. More than 1 million homes were damaged or destroyed (**Figure 5-3**), 600,000 people were left homeless, and 910 villages were destroyed (Bremer, 2003; World Bank & Asian Development Bank, 2001).

Gujarat State is relatively successful in terms of economic activities compared to the national average for India. It has the third highest per capita income in the country. Nevertheless, a majority of the 42 million people who live in this region survive on less than $1 per day, and 70% of residents depend on the sale of cow's milk for their livelihood. Furthermore, although the caste system was made illegal in 1949, 70 to 80 million people (especially minorities) in the country remain in poverty because of the caste system (Bremer, 2003); 7% of the Gujarat population adheres to the scheduled caste system.

Common ideas, beliefs, and perceptions about disaster response and preparedness in developed countries do not match well with the facts of the Gujarat earthquake. Sharma (2001) indicates that the Civil Disaster Response System was handicapped and civil response to the disaster remained insufficient. The state response to the disaster was quite slow; indeed, without the relief efforts undertaken by local public officials, there would not have been any government response to the incident scenes within the first 24 hours after the earthquake (Özerdem & Jacoby, 2006). Lack of coordination of stakeholders of response and relief actions,

© Jason Reed/Thomson Reuters

Figure 5-3 *80-90% of the buildings near the epicenter of the Gujarat Earthquake were destroyed*

overdependence on bureaucracy, and lack of necessary skills for disaster relief resulted in an ineffective response. Over time, the sympathy of people and convergence of human and material aids exceeded the absorption capacity of affected villages. Further, due to media coverage that focused unduly on Bhuj, food aid for victims was channeled to this area, while other disaster-stricken villages did not receive any aid for days (Özerdem & Jacoby, 2006).

The response of military forces was significantly better than the civil efforts. On the one hand, remarkable coordination problems occurred after several hundreds of local nongovernmental organizations (NGOs) and international relief groups started relief efforts. On the other hand, the military could not handle the overall response and relief actions. The common problem of victim distribution to the hospitals was exacerbated by the lack of medical personnel in Bhuj. Approximately 91% of all patients used their private vehicles, trucks, or buses to travel more than 200 kilometers and reach buffer-zone hospitals (Roy, Shah, Patel, & Coughlin, 2002). Özerdem and Jacoby (2006) note that the Border Security Force carried victims to their bases after the closure of the main city hospital. Although a significant shortage of medical personnel was apparent in the region, a medical team consisting of 17 doctors returned to Mumbai because they did not do noteworthy work in Bhuj because of lack of coordination.

Comfort (2003) points out three challenges stemming from communication systems in this scenario. First, communication disparities between different levels of governments and responding organizations impeded the success of the response. At the village level, official warnings or communication was not an option; instead, people communicated with one another simply by word of mouth and through networks of families and friends. At the district level, communication was conducted via satellite phones. In the larger towns, police radios and army communications became effective. At the state level, sophisticated communication tools were used. The different means of communication between responding organizations led to problems in dissemination of information and asymmetrical transfer of information. A second challenge occurred in association with the first one, as different information technologies led to different results in information processing. Lastly, a difference in information management resulted in significant complications in effective coordination of response actions. Roy et al. (2002) also state that there were problems in coordinating local disaster relief groups, with international organizations working through local groups being more effective.

Comfort (2003) identifies five conditions that inhibited the disaster preparedness efforts in India: high exposure to seismic risk, limited organizational capacity to implement necessary mitigation and preparedness endeavors, poor economic conditions, lack of scientific knowledge, and lack of experience and practice. According to Bremer (2003), potential hazards such as earthquakes, floods, cyclones, and epidemics have forced Indian governments to improve their preparedness to the disasters. Yet, an imbalanced distribution of income, poverty, lack of necessary knowledge, and the caste system persist, impeding the diffusion of a culture of preparedness to all layers of society. McNabb and Pearson (2010) emphasize the difficulty for poor communities in preparing for low-probability risks: People cannot pay attention to disaster preparedness while primary needs such as housing, health care, education, or clean water remain unmet. In Gujarat, the government had asked people to have at least one earthquake-proof room in their homes before the earthquake, yet poorly constructed buildings and tents remained inadequate to meet the mitigation and preparedness standards necessary for protection against an earthquake.

The 2001 earthquake significantly damaged the Gujarat State. Lack of a culture of preparedness and mitigation, and lack of coordination between government agencies deterred effective disaster relief endeavors. In some cases, an overwhelming flow of aid to region exceeded the capacity of local officials to handle relief logistics, resulting in a waste of materials. The disaster in Gujarat draws attention to the necessity of improving the disaster management system in the region, especially in terms of the need for a culture of preparedness and for interagency coordination.

Hurricane Mitch

In 1998, Hurricane Mitch hit Central America with remarkably destructive power. The deadliest hurricane in the western hemisphere since 1780, it killed more than 11,000 people, left 3 million homeless, and inflicted damage exceeding $5 billion (National Oceanic and Atmospheric Administration [NOAA], 2009). The President of Honduras, Carlos Flores Facusse, emphasized the destructive nature of the hurricane, claiming that 50 years of progress in his country had been undone by the storm (Glantz & Jamieson, 2000). Most of the deaths were the result of floods and mudslides, even though many cities were evacuated before the hurricane.

Nicaragua was one of the countries affected by Hurricane Mitch. Nicaragua's history records indicate that, between 1972 and 1996, 11 disasters struck the country. "These eleven disasters have resulted in 107,118 dead, 123,071 injured or disabled, 6,533 missing, and 656,011 displaced people, have left a further 1,861,002 people without homes, and affected directly or indirectly another 3,201,737 people. That is more than 77% of the total population of the country if one uses the calculated parameters of the actual total population" (Rocha & Christoplos, 2000, p. 3). Although the damages inflicted by these disasters have dramatically affected the people of Nicaragua, disaster mitigation and preparedness are not part of the country's political agenda (Rocha & Christoplos, 2000). Instead, Nicaraguans have a cultural tendency to be short-sighted, which deters people from making long-term plans, including disaster preparedness. In essence, short-sightedness plays a greater determinant role in people's behavior than a culture of preparedness does.

Hurricane Mitch caused the most damage to Honduras (**Figure 5-4**). It hit the country as Category 5 hurricane, killing at least 10,000 people (Glantz & Jamieson, 2000). The hurricane affected 90% of the country's infrastructure and severely damaged the economy. Honduras had experienced a similar level of destruction 25 years prior, when Hurricane Fifi caused approximately 8000 deaths and $1 billion in damage in 1974. As the national government was not capable of responding to the disaster, the international community conducted response efforts.

Since Hurricane Fifi in 1974, mitigation and preparation efforts in Central America had been minimal. Most of the issues raised following the 1974 disaster remained unaddressed in 1998, when Hurricane Mitch struck (Glantz & Jamieson, 2000). Poverty, a lack of political will to conduct mitigation and preparation activities, and a lack of risk awareness hindered efforts. Disaster-prone developing countries like Honduras and Nicaragua are often struggling to maintain a minimal standard of living, so that other things remain relatively unimportant in the short term. Disasters like Hurricane Mitch, however, threaten their economic, social, and political development. In this challenging milieu, it is important to consolidate growth efforts with mitigation and preparedness to protect the progress that has already been achieved.

Courtesy of Debbie Larson, NWS, International Activities/NOAA

Figure 5-4 *Flood and debris flowing along Rio Choluteca, Tegucigalpa, Honduras*

Conclusion

Disaster planning and preparedness entail more than just guidance for those who adhere to its direction, but they can certainly help connect emergency response teams to communities, and communities to the larger society. Unfortunately, myths and distorted knowledge about the emergency response may alter the focus of these efforts and lead to ineffectiveness in actions. Lindell et al. (2007) underscore the notion that each segment of society must be treated separately. Leaving misconceptions behind and conducting a deep analysis of society and identification of potential human behavior in case of disasters are imperative for managing the first response to an emergency. Resiliency and preparedness in society play key roles in minimizing the effects of unexpected events.

The application of scientific measures to emergency planning and response would minimize misconceptions, particularly those stemming from inaccurate and incomplete media coverage. Collaboration is an effective means of preparing for disastrous events.

Ideally, communities should work on developing an effective emergency management plan that integrates all necessary entities that will respond to a disaster ahead of time. Doing so will ensure that more lives are saved, decrease confusion in the heat of the moment, and make efforts more efficient.

Review Questions

1. How can you define disaster resiliency? How can a culture of preparedness be defined? What is the relationship between the two?

2. How can you analyze the cases presented in the chapter from disaster resiliency and culture of preparedness perspectives?

3. A group of community leaders has asked you to describe the mitigation strategies that a local government could implement without any outside assistance. What would you recommend to your audience?

4. Why do collaboration and coordination have significance in managing emergencies and crises? What are some challenges in this area? How can inter-organizational, multi-jurisdiction, and cross-sector networks help create disaster resiliency?

5. How can we overcome barriers that might prevent multisector and multijurisdiction agencies from working together in response to and recovery from disasters?

6. How might the information you gained from this chapter affect you personally and professionally?

References

Allen, K. M. (2006). Community based disaster preparedness and climate adaptation: Local capacity building in the Philippines. *Disasters, 30*(1), 81–101.

Basolo, V., Steinberg, L. J., Burby, R. J. Levine, J., Cruz, A. M., & Hang, C. (2009). The effects of confidence in government and information on perceived and actual preparedness for disasters. *Environment and Behavior, 41*(3), 338–364.

Beatley, T. (1998). The vision of sustainable communities. In R. J. Burby (Ed.), Cooperating with nature: Confronting natural hazards with land-use planning for sustainable communities (pp. 233–262). Washington, DC: Joseph Henry Press.

Begando, A. D. (2009). Rethinking emergency management. *Disaster Recovery Journal, 22*(3), 30–34.

Bremer. R. (2003). Policy development in disaster preparedness and management: Lessons learned from the January 2001 earthquake in Gujarat, India. *Prehospital and Disaster Medicine, Special Report.*

Burby, R. J., Beatley, T., Berke, P. R., Deyle, R. E., French, S. P., Godschalk, D. R., et al. (1999). Unleashing the power of planning to create disaster resistant communities. *Journal of the American Planning Association, 65*(3), 247–258.

Burby, R. J., & May, P. J. (1998). Intergovernmental environmental planning: Addressing the commitment conundrum. *Journal of Environmental Planning and Management, 41*(1), 95–110.

Col, J. M. (2007). Managing disasters: The role of local government. *Public Administration Review, Special Issue,* 114–124.

Comfort, L. K. (2003). Information technology and efficiency in disaster response: The Buhj, Gujarat earthquake of 26 January 2001. In *Conference Proceedings of International Conference on Earthquake Loss Estimation and Risk Reduction,* Romania, Bucharest, October 22–24, 2002.

Comfort, L. K. (2006). Cities at risk: Hurricane Katrina and the drowning of New Orleans. *Urban Affairs Review, 41*(4), 501–516.

Comfort, L. K. (2007). Crisis management in hindsight: Cognition, communication, coordination, and control. *Public Administration Review, Special Issue,* 189–197.

Continuity Central. (2007). Disaster declarations and related information. Retrieved February 5, 2010, from http://www.continuitycentral.com/news03561.htm.

Cutter, S. L., & Finch, C. (2008). Temporal and spatial changes in social vulnerability to natural hazards. *PNAS, 105*(7), 2301–2306.

Department of Homeland Security (DHS). (2007). Facts sheet: Creating culture of preparedness among schools. Retrieved March 23, 2010, from http://www.dhs.gov/xnews/releases/pr_1193754645157.shtm.

Derthick, M. (2007). Where federalism didn't fail. *Public Administration Review, 67*(1), 36–47.

Enarson, E., Fothergill, A., & Peek, L. (2006). Gender and disaster: Foundations and directions. In H. Rodriguez, E. L. Quarantelli, & R. Dynes (Eds.), *Handbook of disaster research* (pp. 130–146). New York: Springer.

Fischer, H. W. (1998). *Response to disaster: Fact versus fiction and its perpetuation: The sociology of disaster.* Lanham, MD: University Press of America.

Flint, C., & Brennan, M. (2006). Community emergency response teams: From disaster response to community builders. *Rural Realities, 1,* 3.

Glantz, M., & Jamieson, D. (2000). Societal response to Hurricane Mitch and intra- versus intergenerational equity issues: Whose norms should apply? *Risk Analysis, 20*(6), 869–882.

Godschalk, D. R., Kaiser, E. J., & Berke, P. R. (1998). Integrating hazard mitigation and local land use planning. In R. J. Burby (Ed.), *Cooperating with nature: Confronting natural hazards with land use planning for sustainable communities* (pp. 85–118). Washington, DC: Joseph Henry/National Academy Press.

Government Accountability Office (GAO). (2006). *Critical infrastructure protection: Progress coordinating government and private sector efforts varies sectors' characteristics.* GAO-07-39.

Government Accountability Office (GAO). (2008a). *Disaster recovery: Past experiences offer insights for recovering from Hurricanes Ike and Gustav and other recent natural disasters.* GAO-08-1120.

Government Accountability Office (GAO). (2008b). *National Response Framework: FEMA needs policies and procedures to better integrate non-federal stakeholders in the revision process.* GAO-08-768.

Green, R.A., (2008). Unauthorised development and seismic hazard vulnerability: A study of squatters and engineers in Istanbul, Turkey. *Disasters, 32*(3), 358–376.

Halpern. D. (2005). *Social capital.* Malden, MA: Polity Press.

Heath, R. (1995). Kobe earthquake: Some realities of strategic management of crises and disasters. *Disaster Prevention and Management, 4*(5), 11–24.

Honore, R., & Martz, R. (2009). *Survival: How a culture of preparedness can save you and your family from disasters.* New York: Atria Books.

Hopkins, A. (1999). Counteracting the cultural causes of disaster. *Journal of Contingencies and Crisis Management, 37*(3), 141–149.

International Federation of Red Cross and Red Crescent Societies (IFRC). (n.d.). Photo galleries India Gujarat earthquake. Retrieved March 26, 2010, from http://www.ifrc.org/photo/india2/1.asp.

Kapucu, N. (2008). Collaborative emergency management: Better community organizing, better public preparedness and response. *Disasters: The Journal of Disaster Studies, Policy, and Management, 32*(2), 239–262.

Kapucu, N. (2009). Public administrators and cross-sector governance in response to and recovery from disasters. *Administration and Society, 41*(7), 910–914.

Kapucu, N., & Van Wart, M. (2006). *The emerging role of the public sector in managing extreme events: Lessons learned. Administration & Society, 38*(3), 279–308.

Kendra, J. M., & Wachtendorf, T. (2003). Elements of community resilience in the World Trade Center attack. *Disasters, 27*(1), 37–53.

Kunreuther, H., & Useem, M. (2010). Principles and challenges for reducing risks from disasters. In H. Kunreuther & M. Useem (Eds.), *Learning from catastrophes: Strategies for reaction and response* (pp. 1–13). Upper Saddle River, N.J.: Wharton School Publishing.

Lindell, K. M., & Perry, W. R. (2007). Planning for preparedness. In W. L. Waugh, Jr., & K. Tierney (Eds.), *Emergency management: Principles and practice for local government* (2nd ed., pp. 113–142). Washington, DC: ICMA.

Lindell, K. M., Prater, C., & Perry, R. W. (2006). Fundamentals of emergency management. Retrieved from http://training.fema.gov/EMIWeb/edu/fem.asp.

Lindell, K. M., Prater, C., & Perry, R. W. (2007). *Introduction to emergency management.* Hoboken, NJ: Wiley.

Magsino, S. L. (2009). *Applications of social network analysis for building community disaster resilience: Workshop summary.* Washington, DC: National Academies Press.

Mahoney, M. (2011). The Japan Earthquake and Tsunami and what they mean for the U.S. [Retrieved from the FEMA website on May 20, 2011] http://www.fema.gov/library/viewRecord.do?id=4620.

McEntire, D. A., & Dawson, G. (2007). Intergovernmental context. In W. L. Waugh, Jr., & K. Tierney (Eds.), *Emergency management: Principles and practice for local government* (2nd ed., pp. 57–85). Washington, DC: ICMA.

McNabb, M., & Pearson, K. (2010). Can poor countries afford to prepare for low-probability risks? In H. Kunreuther & M. Useem (Eds.), *Learning from catastrophes: Strategies for reaction and response* (pp. 100–120). Upper Saddle River, N.J.: Wharton School Publishing.

Mileti, D. S. (1999). *Disasters by design: A reassessment of natural hazards in the United States.* Washington, DC: Joseph Henry Press.

Multihazard Mitigation Council. (2005). *Natural hazard mitigation saves: An independent study to assess the future savings from mitigation activities. Vol. 1: Findings, conclusions, and recommendations.* Washington, DC: National Institute of Building Sciences. Retrieved from floods.org/PDF/MMC_Volume1_FindingsConclusionsRecommendations.pdf.

Nanto, D. K., Cooper, W. H., Donnelly, J. M., & Johnson, R. (2011). *Japan's 2011 earthquake and tsunami: Economic effects and implications for the United States*. Congressional Research Service (CRS) Report for Congress.

National Oceanic and Atmospheric Administration (NOAA). (2009). Mitch: The deadliest Atlantic hurricane since 1780. Retrieved March 26, 2010, from http://www.ncdc.noaa.gov/oa/reports/mitch/mitch.html.

National Research Council (NRC). (2009). *Applications of social network analysis for building community disaster resilience*. Washington, DC: National Academies Press.

Norris, F. H., Stevens, S. P., Pfefferbaum, B., Wyche, K. F., & Pfefferbaum, R. L. (2008). Community resilience as a metaphor, theory, set of capacities and strategy for disaster readiness. *American Journal of Community Psychology, 41*(1–2), 127–150.

Ofori-Amoah, A. (n.d.). Overview of the event. Retrieved February 24, 2010, from http://www.uwec.edu/jolhm/EH2/Ofori-Amoah/Kobe%20Earthquke/Overview.htm.

Ouden, D., & Russel, G. W. (1997). Sympathy and altruism in response to disasters: A Dutch and Canadian comparison. *Social Behavior and Personality, 25*(3), 241–248.

Oxfam America, (2009). *Exposed: Social vulnerability and climate change in the US Southeast*. Washington, DC: Author.

Özerdem, A., & Jacoby, T. (2006). *Disaster management and civil society: Earthquake relief in Japan, Turkey and India*. London: I. B. Tauris.

Pararas-Carayannis, G. (2000). Major earthquakes in Japan and the Southern Kuril Islands in the 20th century. Retrieved February 24, 2010, from http://www.drgeorgepc.com/EarthquakesJapan.html.

Paterson, R. G. (1998). The third sector: Evolving partnerships in hazard mitigation. In R. J. Burby (Ed.), *Cooperating with nature: Confronting natural hazards with land-use planning for sustainable communities* (pp. 203–230). Washington, DC: Joseph Henry Press.

Paton, D. (2003). Disaster preparedness: A social cognitive perspective. *Disaster Prevention and Management, 12*(3), 210–216.

Paton, D. (2006). Disaster resilience: Integration, individual, community, institutional, and environmental perspectives. In D. Paton & D. Johnson (Eds.), *Disaster resilience: An integrated approach* (pp. 305–316). Springfield, IL: Charles C. Thomas.

Peacock, W. G., Morrow, B. H., & Gladwin, H. (1997). *Hurricane Andrew: Ethnicity, gender and the sociology of disasters*. London: Routledge.

Pelling, M. (2003). *The vulnerability of cities: natural disasters and social resilience*. London: Earthscan.

Perry, R. W., & Lindell, M. K. (2007). Disaster response. In W. L. Waugh, Jr., & K. Tierney (Eds.), *Emergency management: Principles and practice for local government* (2nd ed., pp. 159–182). Washington, DC: ICMA.

Phillips, B. D. (1993). Cultural diversity in disaster: Shelter, housing, and long-term recovery. *International Journal of Mass Emergencies and Disasters, 11*(1), 99–110.

Phillips, B. D., & Neal, D. M. (2007). Recovery. In W. L. Waugh, Jr., & K. Tierney (Eds.), *Emergency management: Principles and practice for local government* (2nd ed., pp. 207–233). Washington, DC: ICMA.

Rebuilding Iowa Office (RIO). (n.d.). Welcome to the Rebuilding Iowa Office website. Retrieved February 5, 2010, from http://rio.iowa.gov/.

Ritchie, L., Ashleyand, G., & Duane A. (2007). Social capital theory as an integrating theoretical framework in technological disaster research. *Sociological Spectrum, 27,* 103–129.

Rocha, J. L., & Christoplos, I. (2000). *Disaster mitigation and preparedness in Nicaragua after Hurricane Mitch. Report for assessing "NGO natural disaster mitigation and preparedness projects: an assessment and way forward"* (ESCOR Award No. R7231).

Ronan, R. K., & Johnson, D. M. (2005). *Promoting community resiliency in disasters: The role for schools, youth, and families.* New York: Springer.

Roy, N., Shah, H., Patel, V., & Coughlin, R. R. (2002). The Gujarat earthquake (2001) experience in seismically unprepared area: Community hospital medical response. *Prehospital Disaster Medicine, 17*(4), 186–195.

Rubin, C. B. (2009). Long term recovery from disasters: The neglected component of emergency management. *Journal of Homeland Security and Emergency Management, 6(1),* 46.

Russel, G. W., & Mentzel, R. K. (1990). Sympathy and altruism in disaster response. *Journal of Social Psychology, 130*(3), 309–317.

Sharma, V. K. (2001). Gujarat earthquake: Some emerging issues. *Disaster Prevention and Management, 10*(5), 349–355.

Shaw, R., Shiwaku, K., Kobayashi, H., & Kobayashi, M. (2004). Liking experience, education, perception and earthquake preparedness. *Disaster Prevention and Management, 13*(1), 39, 49.

Simo, G., & Bies, A. L. (2007). The role of nonprofits in disaster response: An expanded model of cross-sector collaboration. *Public Administration Review, 67*(6), 1098–1111.

The New York Times. (2011). Japan — Earthquake, Tsunami and Nuclear Crisis (2011). Retrieved on May 20, 2011 from http://topics.nytimes.com/top/news/international/ countriesandterritories/japan/index.html?scp=1-spot&sq=japan%20tsunami&st=cse.

Tierney, K. J., Lindell, M. K., & Perry, R. W. (2001). *Facing the unexpected: Disaster preparedness and response in the United States.* Washington D.C.: Joseph Henry Press.

Turner, B. (1978). *Man-made disasters.* London: Wykeham.

United Nations International Strategy for Disaster Reduction [UNISDR]. (2011). The recent earthquake and tsunami in Japan: Implications for East Asia. *World Bank East Asia and Pacific Economic update, 1,* 1-2. Retrieved on May 20, 2011, from http://www.unisdr .org/we/inform/publications/18587.

U.S. Geological Survey (USGS). (2010). Hurricane Mitch Central America. Retrieved March 26, 2010, from http://landslides.usgs.gov/research/other/hurricanemitch/.

Wenger, D. E., Dykes, J. D., Sebok, T. D., & Neff, J. L. (1975). It's a matter of myths: An empirical examination of individual insight into disaster response. *Mass Emergencies, 1,* 33–46.

White House. (2006). Federal response to Hurricane Katrina: Lessons learned. [Retrieved March 20, 2010, from http://georgewbush-whitehouse.archives.gov/reports/katrina-lessons-learned.pdf.

World Bank & Asian Development Bank. (2001). Gujarat earthquake recovery program assessment report. Retrieved March 26, 2010, from http://siteresources.worldbank.org/ INDIAEXTN/Resources/Reports-Publications/gujarat-earthquake/full_report.pdf.

Chapter 6

Emergency and Crisis Management Stakeholders

Chapter Objectives

- Discuss the roles of participants in the emergency management process, including local, state, federal, private-sector, and nonprofit-sector responsibilities.
- Obtain an overview of the integrated emergency and crisis management system.
- Discuss emergency management stakeholders and their roles in disaster response and recovery networks.
- Analyze the role of the local emergency management agency in the networked environment.

Introduction

Before the 20th century, almost all nations dealt with disasters at a local level, through the work of helping communities, neighborhoods, relatives, and religious organizations. In the last century, however, nations began to deal with environmental and human-made disasters at the governmental level by forming specialized organizations to address the demands of crises (Sylves, 2008). As Waugh (2003) summarizes, today the United States has a national network of public agencies, nonprofit organizations, and private firms that provide services before, during, and after all types of disasters. These groups include the Federal Emergency Management Agency (FEMA) and its state and local counterparts, emergency response agencies, the American Red Cross (ARC), and "other general purpose nonprofit organizations, regional and local charities and civic organizations, and firms that provide services ranging from emergency planning to debris removal to psychological counseling" (Waugh, 2003, p. 376).

In most U.S. states, county governments are responsible for coordinating emergency response operations, but some major cities have their own emergency operations centers as well. However, major disasters can quickly overwhelm the resources and capabilities of local governments, so most of the time local governments rely on assistance from state governments to bolster their response and recovery efforts. Some human-made or natural disasters might require the federal government's intervention as well.

In the United Kingdom, the main response activities are conducted at the local level, yet efforts of local governments are strongly integrated with national authorities (Pitt, 2008). In addition to local and national entities, supranational structures for regional and major disasters are available, if needed. These occur in two forms: state based and independent. The former include bodies such as the United Nations (UN), European Union (EU), North Atlantic Treat Organization (NATO), and Association of Southeast Asian Nations (ASEAN), which have existing protocols and networks established for the event of a large-scale emergency affecting any member state and an ability to extend assistance to nonmembers. The latter consist of organizations such as the International Committee of the Red Cross (ICRC) and other international nongovernmental organizations (INGOs) that are able to deploy internationally upon the request of governments.

Both the high standards set for responsiveness and the ubiquitous reporting of mass media compel political leaders and administrative heads to coordinate resources effectively. Thousands of organizations are engaged in monitoring known and suspected hazards and encouraging hazard reduction efforts. Nonprofit voluntary groups may be chartered or otherwise recognized by law as tax exempt; they range from large environmental groups to small church or community organizations. Some have developed highly specialized disaster-related skills, such as search and rescue, amateur radio communications, and emergency feeding or shelter, whereas others are much broader in scope (Comfort, 2006; Crandall, Parnell, & Spillan, 2010).

Although federal guidelines and best practices in the United States (e.g., National Incident Management System [NIMS], National Response Framework [NRF]) provide a framework for the structure of emergency management departments, Edwards and Goodrich (2007) make it clear that "one size does not fit all" in this environment; instead, each emergency management department must be carefully crafted to fit the unique needs of a given locality. Emergency management and homeland security also appear to be subject to political will, even though these arenas are bipartisan in nature. What implications does the injection of politics have on emergency and crisis management? Does it impede or facilitate effective emergency management practices? In short, the answers to these questions are dependent upon a number of factors.

It is in relation to these concerns that this chapter introduces a number of actors in the field of emergency management and examines some of the problems inherent in dealing with the complex emergency management policy process. The chapter focuses on the role of stakeholders in emergency and crisis management. Significantly, networks, partnerships, and the theory of social capital are illustrated throughout the practices discussed in the literature. The emergency management field exemplifies "management by network in action" by way of collaborative emergency management. Nonhierarchical structures (in the form of networks) are becoming ever more important in all sectors, and in emergency management they are critical, and by no means optional. The cross-sectoral nature of emergency management is evident in the necessity for stakeholder involvement from all sectors to assist in all four phases of emergency management.

Stakeholders: Local, State, Federal, Private-Sector, and Nonprofit-Sector Responsibilities

A stakeholder is defined as any entity—public or private, directly or indirectly affected—that has a vested interest in the outcome of a disaster. In emergency management, there are many stakeholders to consider, ranging from governmental entities to private corporations to community-based groups. The emergency manager is a primary stakeholder in a disaster, but other parties, such as the Department of Transportation, individual volunteers, and insurance agencies, also have interests in the ongoing operations and final outcome of a disaster. Intergovernmental relations bind these entities together, creating a web of interdependency and support.

Lindell, Prater, and Perry (2006) discuss community stakeholders as falling into three categories: social groups, economic groups, and political groups. The smallest component of social groups is households, although households have a share in all phases of emergency management because they are the primary source of vulnerability for any hazard. Citizens groups, such as those that play a role in neighborhood watch programs and Community Emergency Response Teams (CERT), also have a stake in the emergency response. A CERT is a group of citizens who are trained by local emergency management authorities to provide an initial response to hazards. At the next level, nonprofit organizations and nongovernmental agencies (NGOs) play roles in different phases of emergency management. The American Red Cross, Salvation Army, and many other nonprofit organizations provide a vast array of services in emergency and crisis situations, including search and rescue, shelter, supplies, coordination, and funding (Gerber, 2007; Lindell et al., 2006).

Economic groups consist of the businesses in an area. The range of businesses varies from local stores that employ a few people to multinational corporations that have thousands of workers. The impact of a hazard on businesses may inflict irreparable damage to communities. People may become unemployed, consumers may alter their shopping and consumption patterns, and economic life might not return to pre-disaster conditions. To prevent adverse economic consequences, businesses collaborate with emergency management authorities. Another issue that makes businesses indispensable partners in emergency planning is the fact that approximately 85% of critical infrastructures are owned by the private sector in the United States (Government Accountability Office [GAO], 2006). The protection of these infrastructures is vital for both the government agencies and business sectors, and a strong collaboration is necessary for successful protection.

The final stakeholders are the political groups that are part of the governmental system. Many different stakeholders exist in various levels of governmental structures, of which agencies and political figures are the main constituents. The relationship between such organizations might be both vertical and horizontal. For instance, a local emergency manager might apply for grants from the federal government; try to meet the demands of FEMA; and work with state agencies, local fire rescue services, the local police department, the public works department, the planning department, and emergency management agencies in other jurisdictions. Each agency has its own working style, complexities, and culture, yet complements other agencies in terms of emergency and crisis management (Bashir, Lafronza, Fraser, Brown, & Cope, 2003; Lindell et al., 2006). Nevertheless, the smooth collaboration of different organizations and avoiding duplications is no easy feat. In some cases, public agencies may lobby for legislation that is appropriate for their organizational culture and goals, while simply disregarding the proposed law's effects on any collaboration with other agencies.

Overview of an Integrated Emergency and Crisis Management System

In the United States, emergency management's history started with the Cold War against the Soviets, when civil defense became the top priority. The Civil Defense Act of 1950, which was signed after the successful testing of an atomic bomb by the Soviets in 1949, was the starting point for legislation related to this field. Its passage was followed by the creation of the Federal Civil Defense Administration. Later, the United States adopted a dual-use approach to emergency management, based on preparing both for an enemy attack and for natural disasters (Sylves, 2008). Sylves (2008) gives details about the multihazard approach and changes that occurred in U.S. emergency management after the passage of the 1974 Disaster Relief Act during the Nixon administration: "The Disaster Relief Act of 1974 brought state and local governments into all-hazard preparedness activities and provided matching funds for their emergency management programs" (p. 55). Major changes in laws, programs, policies, and organizations has since followed in response to various catastrophic disasters (Rubin, 2007). For instance, FEMA was founded in 1979 as a result of the Three Mile Island nuclear accident; its emergence brought many structural changes to the emergency management system.

After the Stafford Act of 1988 was passed to revise the United States' disaster management program, there was a movement away from use of the military in disasters and toward civilizing the emergency management process. As Sylves (2008) notes, "camcorder politics" was part of the impetus for this trend, referring to the now-common ubiquitous media coverage of disaster management. News channels such as CNN started to broadcast live from disaster sites, and these reports were then used as a tool of public relations by presidents.

In the late 1990s, homeland security assumed a position of elevated importance in U.S. emergency management. The rise of terrorist attacks beginning 1995 started a new trend that evolved the perception of emergency management from a matter of civil defense to one of homeland security. The New York and Washington, D.C., terrorist attacks in 2001 consolidated this trend in emergency management policy, which led to an increased focus on security and made major changes in organizational structures (Sylves, 2008).

Of course, emergency management functions cannot operate within a vacuum; they are inextricably linked to an array of governmental, private, nonprofit, and voluntary entities. Involving stakeholders in all phases of emergency management is critical, as this discipline relies upon networks and the information, resources, and manpower of other governmental and nongovernmental organizations. As Edwards and Goodrich (2007) point out, the time scale is important when bringing stakeholders "into the fold." Emergencies and crises are nonlinear events. For this reason, emergency managers should work to bring in new stakeholders while an event is recent, before time dilutes its impact. The concepts of social capital and management by network are also evident in the current practice of fostering working relationships with stakeholders to "create and sustain disaster-resilient communities" (Edwards & Goodrich, 2007, p. 53).

The emergency management system in the U.S. consists of multiple levels of government involvement and stakeholders from various fields. The local, state, and federal government becomes involved in the system based on the scope of each disaster. Households and businesses are at the grassroots level of the system in place, and the current approach emphasizes the importance of awareness and preparedness of individuals. The social and economic capacities of individuals and businesses within their communities create associations which take role in the system at upper levels of policy making. According to Lindell et al. (2006), the social, professional, or economic associations are involved in the disaster management system at the state and federal levels.

Federalism plays a significant role in emergency management in the United States by forcing local and state governments into compliance with federal laws and regulations, for better or for worse. On the one hand, although federalism may initially be perceived as a negative concept (effectively hamstringing local governments), it may prevent fragmentation in emergency responses among the varying levels of government. On the other hand, a decentralized approach to emergency management has significant implications for practitioners, particularly the potential for what

McEntire and Dawson (2007) term "vertical strains" and "horizontal fractures" in the emergency management structure. These hazards must be contrasted with the freedom conferred by a federalist system to localities (McEntire & Dawson, 2007).

The federalist system does seem conducive to emergency management by network and coordination with stakeholders. Coordination is defined by McEntire and Dawson (2007) as the "collaborative process through which multiple organizations interact to achieve common objectives" (p. 61). Coordination with both governmental and nongovernment stakeholders not only serves to meet the goal of fostering disaster-resilient communities, but also assists with resolution of critical issues for practitioners, such as resource allocation. The process of stakeholder involvement improves the capacity of communities to deal with disasters in the future and, in addition, disaster experiences can hasten recovery and create more resilient communities for the next time a disaster strikes (Gerber, 2007; Waugh & Streib, 2006). Emergency managers must assess their stakeholder network and utilize these partnerships as well as pool resources to work on obtaining external grant funds. Comfort (2007) defines coordination as "aligning one's actions with those of other relevant actors and organizations to achieve a shared goal" (p. 194). She emphasizes that coordination strongly depends on efficient communication and that inadequate coordination among stakeholders can diminish the achievement of a common action framework.

Relationship building and collaboration are primary contributors to the management by network approach deployed in emergency situations. Patton (2007) describes collaborative emergency management as "the integration of a wide range of organizations and entities into the day-to-day work of emergency management" (p. 72). Management by network can facilitate synergy, whereby the combined efforts of members produce something more powerful than could be achieved by the various parties independently. At the same time, practitioners must deal with the drawbacks of collaborative management, which include accountability issues and higher administrative costs.

Collaboration forces emergency managers to move outside their traditional role, and into that of facilitator (Patton, 2007). In this context, the emergency manager serves as the nexus for local businesses, faith-based organizations, nonprofit organizations, and volunteers to convene and offer up their resources to assist with emergency management. Patton (2007) indicates that the following factors can facilitate successful collaborative arrangement:

- Energy
- Creativity
- Openness to change
- Cooperation on the part of disparate stakeholders to achieve common goals
- A common vision
- Shared ownership
- Leadership from all organizational partners

Because it involves some level of delegation and, therefore, loss of control, the concept of collaborative action may not be received well by all emergency managers. It is crucial for these skeptics to be convinced of the significance and empowerment gained by engaging stakeholders in this process. In the context of collaborative emergency management, it is important to investigate whether legal liability is shared evenly and what would happen if plans developed by managers are not followed. Nicholson (2007) reviews the relevant concerns.

Given the need for stakeholder involvement in the context of collaborative emergency management, laws and statutes have been implemented that limit liability but can unfortunately create a barrier to partnership. Due to the threat of lawsuits, another stakeholder has been introduced into emergency planning—the legal advisor. These individuals advise managers in the creation of plans so that a series of best practices can be established to reduce liability (Nicholson, 2007). They also have assisted in the creation of statutes at different levels of government.

At the federal level in the United States, the Robert T. Stafford Disaster Relief and Emergency Assistance Act and the Homeland Security Act of 2002 regulate the involvement of the federal government in the emergency cycle (Nicholson, 2007). The primary regulation states that the federal government will not involve itself until after the resources of the local and state level stakeholders are exceeded. The Federal Tort Claims Act gives immunity to managers for discretionary decisions made during planning and response. At the state and local levels, the executive branch can be considered the primary stakeholder in emergency management, and for this reason the highest-ranking executive officer (e.g., governor, mayor, or emergency manager) has his or her responsibilities established by laws and statutes. In many jurisdictions, these stakeholders are often granted extra powers during an emergency that allow them to give instructions without concern for potential liability (Nicholson, 2007). Practitioners must consider the ramifications associated with additional powers conferred during an emergency or crisis situation. In addition, the liability associated with an emergency response can be more severe if the stakeholders do not make, follow, and test/improve their plans.

Nonprofit organizations and volunteers assisting in the response to an emergency or crisis must also consider their own liability in this scenario. Many U.S. states have "Good Samaritan" statutes that excuse civilian responders from liability when they are assisting in medical situations; likewise, the Volunteer Protection Act of 1997 protects volunteers from liability due to acts of negligence (Nicholson, 2007). Even with this legislation in place, however, some liability has to be assumed by the authority that assigns volunteers to an action. All stakeholders must take into consideration the legal liability resulting from each action or lack of action on their part pertaining to the emergency response (Nicholson, 2007). Even with good intentions and legal processes in place, responders must be careful not to destroy the rights of those whom they are attempting to assist.

Roles of Emergency Networks and Emergency Managers

Wilson and Oyola-Yemaiel (2001) argue that we have witnessed a change in direction for emergency management since 1960. According to Rubin (2007), emergency management is now primarily practiced at the local level. Nevertheless, national organizations such as the American Red Cross and some federal and military agencies have played prominent roles in responding to disasters over the past two centuries (Rubin, 2007).

Power is not completely concentrated within the federal government, however. Emergency managers often build collaborative networks involving a multitude of agencies (Patton, 2007), although they may retain a degree of control through their central location within the network of stakeholders. Because optimally they will possess unique experience and skills, emergency managers might exert power through their expert status (Rainey, 2003). States also possess a degree of power, which sometimes prompts them to reject federal mitigation initiatives through private property rights or local land-use policies. "The different types of state–local relationships should also be investigated to determine the most effective ways that state government can assist local emergency managers in planning for and carrying out emergency operation" (Labadie, 1984, p. 494). Finally, citizens who feel strongly about government response following a disaster can exert political power in elections to support or reject officials based on their perceptions of the response (Sylves, 2008).

When a disaster strikes, it often encroaches upon more than one jurisdiction, yet local government remains the front line of official public responsibility. At the same time, state and federal agencies are likely to give their support when damage is severe and widespread. For instance, most local and state governments can deal with a Category 2 hurricane on their own, but it would be more of a challenge for them to deal with a terrorist attack without federal assistance (Sylves, 2008). Considering that local governments have primary responsibility before, during, and after disasters, they must develop and maintain a plan of emergency management to fulfill their responsibilities to provide for the protection and safety of the public. The role of the state is similar to that of the local agency—to maintain an effective organization and prepare plans, facilities, and equipment. Moreover, state organizations must manage an active program at both state and local levels. The role of the federal organization is to provide national program policy and guidance, as well as technical and financial assistance when necessary (McLoughlin, 1985).

When management networks grow larger, the complexity of the relationships increases as well (Kapucu, 2009). Federal-level organizational networks are represented by the Federal Response Plan (FRP). "The NRP/NRF is essentially a matrix organization, adapted from the FRP to represent a national network including the public, private and nonprofit sector organizations as well as individual citizens"

(Kapucu, 2009, p. 4). Some have suggested that government organizations should be managed on a less hierarchical and process-oriented basis, as the "command and control" system cannot meet the needs of today's complex environment. Local organizations have mutual agreements with other counties and jurisdictions, and likewise states have mutual agreements between one another through the Emergency Management Assistance Compact (EMAC). At the federal level, the NRP (now the NRF) assigns responsibilities to federal support agencies (Patton, 2007).

When an incident occurs, the local-level emergency operations center has the primary responsibility for addressing it. Local organizations, as part of the emergency operations plan, have a duty to provide aid to the community in times of need. They are also charged with the task of educating and informing the community about how to handle emergencies and which procedures to follow during such emergencies. The community itself is sometimes empowered through various first response programs, such as the CERT program. Both Patton (2007) and Kapucu (2008) highlight the importance of the media as essential collaborators and stakeholders in emergency management; local governments, for example, can use the media to relay important information to the community.

To be an effective emergency manager, one must be concerned with stakeholders that have something to lose or gain with their involvement in the process. Stakeholders at the local level are especially important, due to their increased role and responsibility in disastrous events. State-level stakeholders are equally important, as they typically act as "intermediaries, helping to implement federal policies, training communities in best practices, and funneling federal grant monies" (McEntire & Dawson, 2007, p. 58). Finally, federal-level stakeholders play a highly visible role through their involvement, especially since the end of the Reagan era and the beginning of the trend toward "nationalizing disaster management" (Sylves, 2008, p. 64).

The Role of Local Emergency Program Managers in the United States

Waugh and Streib (2006) argue that after the 1990s, professional emergency managers started to switch from the roles of authoritarian warden or civil defense directors, to a more collaborative leadership model practicing open communication and broad collaboration. The process of redirection highlighted the role of local government officials. "Increasingly, local government officials have recognized the need for improved co-ordination within the emergency response system" (Wilson & Oyola-Yemaiel, 2001, p. 122). Waugh and Streib (2006) state that since the terrorist attacks on September 11, 2001, and the catastrophic hurricanes of 2004 and 2005, the profession has changed, and the duties of emergency managers have become more complicated.

The role of different agencies in the United States has always been debated in terms of jurisdiction. Kapucu (2009) emphasizes that in the past many stakeholders did not know one another and that these parties should be brought together for periodic training exercises. "In network structures, the underlying assumption is that no single individual understands the whole problem, but that each member of the organization is likely to have insight and a responsibility to act on the best knowledge available" (Kapucu, 2009, p. 4).

Lindell et al. (2006) observe that a disaster creates a window of opportunity for policy change. At the local level, the local emergency manager is the political entrepreneur who will take the initiative for pushing necessary policy decisions. The window of opportunity does not last long for a local emergency manager to draw policy makers' and citizens' attention. Prater and Lindell (2000) hypothesize about changes in stakeholder opinions with respect to emergency mitigation. Six months before a disaster, stakeholders' perception of disaster mitigation appears to be equally distributed between opponent and proponent views. In contrast, 6 months following the disaster, the perception of stakeholders shifts to the proponent view. Eighteen months after the disaster ends, the perception almost returns to the same condition as 6 months prior to the disaster. There is a limited time frame for convincing stakeholders of policy decisions, so the local emergency managers ought to be aggressive policy entrepreneurs in fostering disaster awareness and better mitigation and preparedness measures.

Fowler et al. (2007) have explained the importance of managers' perceptions on crisis preparedness. In their work, they operationalized constructs that were formerly identified in the previous crisis and disaster preparedness literature, and they empirically evaluated the variables they identified that are important to crisis and disaster preparedness research. As a result of this study, Fowler et al. (2007) empirically showed the significance of managers having a higher perception of crisis preparedness than other employees, regardless of the size of the city and organization. For instance, one of the success stories mentioned by these authors is Morgan Stanley Dean Witter, the World Trade Center's largest tenant with 3700 employees. The company stayed loyal to its evacuation plan during the 2001 terrorist attack, which proved critical in saving lives.

In Florida, organizations such as Florida Power and Light (FPL) help to restore electricity from downed power lines following hurricanes and other natural disasters. The Department of Transportation coordinates evacuations, the public works department clears roadways of debris to allow first responders access to incident cites, and privately owned hotels provide shelter for evacuees. Before a disaster, engineers, scientists, and city planners assess the high-risk points in areas likely to be affected by flooding and wind damage, and construct levees and windscreens accordingly. Listing the stakeholders in a disaster situation reveals a plethora of players—federal, state, and local government officials; businesses; public, private, and nonprofit agencies; relief agencies; community-based response programs; media organizations; volunteers; and insurance agencies.

The stakeholders mentioned previously have varying degrees of power to influence how emergency management is conducted in the United States. Presidents are able to exert legitimate power, which is virtually universally accepted, based on the authority vested in the office of the presidency (Rainey, 2003). They are also able to exert their executive authority to formulate policies that affect every community in the nation (Sylves, 2008) by approving or denying requests for disaster declarations and reorganizing federal relief agencies. Examples of presidential power include the creation of FEMA during the Carter administration (Rubin, 2007, p. 33), President Reagan's somewhat frequent denial of federal disaster declarations (Sylves, 2008), and the demotion of FEMA from cabinet status to a subordinate agency of the Department of Homeland Security (Public Strategies Group, 2008).

Additionally, United States presidents are able to exert a great deal of power through the spending authority that is granted them through the Disaster Relief Fund. Federal agencies are able to exert coercive power by enticing state and local agencies to conform to federal standards. For example, state and local agencies that receive federal funding are required to adopt the National Incident Management System (Sylves, 2008), while localities that wish to be eligible for post-disaster FEMA funding must have approved mitigation programs in place (Godshalk, 2007).

The Role of Local Emergency Program Managers in the United Kingdom

In the United Kingdom, the emergency management system melds national and local organizations together. Arbuthnot (2005) explains that the duties of all "blue light" services (police, ambulance, fire, and coast guard) as Category 1 responders were addressed in the Civil Contingencies Act (CCA) of 2004. The same law also introduced a structured Incident Command System (ICS) to response agencies. The necessity of collaboration and information sharing was also addressed in the legislation, requiring the cooperation of Category 1 and Category 2 responders within the local resiliency area. The integrated emergency management mentioned in the CCA was not a new concept; indeed, a police-led hierarchy of Gold, Silver, and Bronze command structure has been in effect in the United Kingdom since the 1980s (Arbuthnot, 2005). These tiers are responsible for the strategic, tactical, and operational aspects of emergency management, respectively. When a Gold-level response is activated for strategy development for an event, however, usually a superior body such as the Cabinet Office Briefing Room (COBR) will take command.

Figure 6–1 provides a general framework for how the central response system would operate at the national level. Fundamentally, Cabinet Office Briefing Room (COBR) is activated during a major national disaster. COBR includes Civil Contingencies Committee (CCC) which is activated in all emergencies and Intelligence Cell which is activated in terrorist events. These bodies oversee the response operations (HM Government 2010). Situation Cell is a supportive element in the national response mechanism and it is ensures that there is one authoritative control of the situation. Senior management in the COBR is also supported by Operational

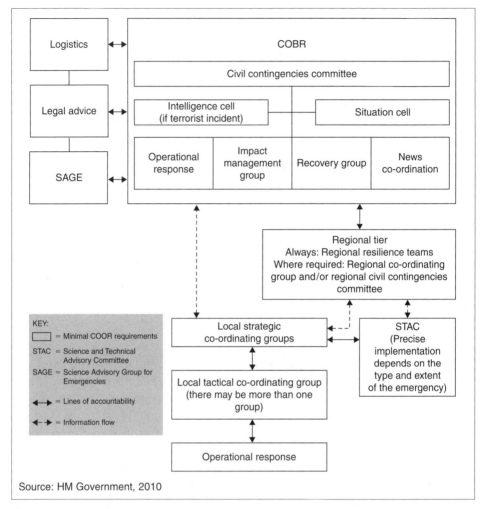

Figure 6-1 *Inter-Agency Command in UK: National Level*

Response Groups, Impact Management Group, Recovery Group, and News Coordination Group. These sub-parts of the structure are activated based on the disaster situation. If Intelligence Cell is activated, Joint Terrorism Analysis Centre (JTAC) and Defense Intelligence Staff (DIS) will be part of it (HM Government, 2010).

The logistics and legal advice teams feed COBR with necessary information if needed. Science Advisory Group for Emergencies (SAGE) provides scientific and technical advice to officials when necessary. It serves as a liaison between scientific and technical experts and the policy makers, and also ensures a timely and accurate communication between these two (HM Government 2010). Science and Technical

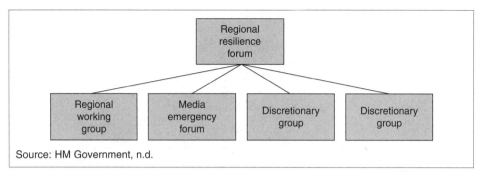

Source: HM Government, n.d.

Figure 6-2 *Inter-Agency Command: Regional Coordination*

Advisory Committee's (STAC) functions at the local level provides information on scientific and technical issues (HM Government 2010).

As can be seen in **Figure 6-2**, the regional-level agency coordination is simpler in terms of command structure. The Cabinet Office publishes an Emergency Preparedness document that sets out a generic framework for Regional Resiliency Forums (RRFs) as primary entities for coordination of stakeholders. Subgroups within the RRF include public agencies, media, and voluntary groups. Also, representatives of the Environment Agency, Maritime Coastguard, Armed Forces, and Government News Networks have a stake in this effort in their roles as national governmental organizations. The voluntary sector provides assistance at the local level, as members of the Voluntary Sector Civil Protection Forum. In addition to these core participants, Local Resiliency Forums (LRFs) might have additional members due to varying regional situations.

July 7, 2005, Bombings in London

In 2005, London experienced one of the most remarkable terror events in its history. On July 7, four suicide bombers hit London's transportation system (**Figure 6-3**). Three bombs in the Underground (subway system) and one on a bus were detonated, killing 56 and injuring several hundred people. Mayor Ken Livingstone returned from the 2012 Olympics elections (which London won), and then–Prime Minister Tony Blair cancelled his meetings at the G8 summit to attend to the response.

As indicated in **Table 6-1**, local agencies were the primary responders in coordination with national government agencies. National agencies were mainly led by the COBR, and were responsible for strategy development, monitoring intelligence flow, and coordination of national stakeholders. Nonprofit organizations were involved in relief efforts, and private companies took a role in reestablishment of damaged communication infrastructure and certain supportive functions.

© Dylan Martinez/Reuters/Landov

Figure 6-3 *July 7 attacks incident scene*

Table 6-1 *Frequency Distribution of Organizations in Response to and Recovery from the July 7, 2005 Bombings*

Type	Number of Organizations	Percentage of Total Responding Organizations
Public—national	20	34%
Public—local	24	41%
Public—total	**44**	**76%**
International	4	7%
Nonprofit	6	10%
Private	4	7%
Total	**58**	**100%**

Source: Kapucu, 2011.

Figure 6-4 illustrates the contribution of each type of agency to the response. Local agencies were most active in the initial response, while the latter phases were dominated by national organizations and nonprofits. As depicted in Figures 6-2 and 6-3, national and local stakeholders responded to the incidents in accordance with the U.K. emergency response/recovery and preparedness frameworks that are derived from Civil Contingencies Act of 2004.

Figure 6-5 depicts the response network specific to the July 7 bombings. The participating agencies were identified through the examination of reports published by the British government and content analysis of news reports between 3 weeks before and after the incidences. After the attacks, a collaborative network focused on disaster response was created based on the previously established framework. The illustration of the network of relations indicates that the Metropolitan Police Services (MPS) was the central organization in the network. COBR also coordinated with MPS regarding local-level response activities. COBR was the key organization for the coordination of upper-level organizations, including international entities (represented by circles in Figure 6-5).

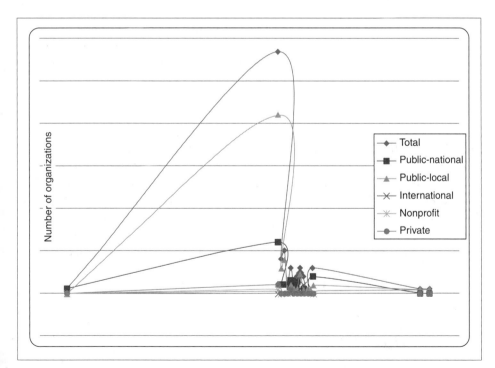

Figure 6-4 *Actors involved in response and recovery activities, July 7 Bombings, May 1-August 24, 2005*

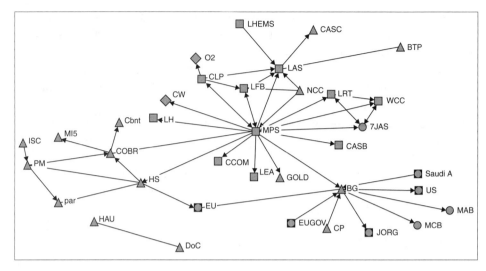

Figure 6-5 *July 7 Bombings Response Network*

Conclusion

Emergency managers should concern themselves with all stakeholders in the emergency management cycle, from the public, nonprofit, and private sectors. In previous times, these sectors were often overlooked in the four phases of emergency management, but are now recognized as critical areas of support and a necessity. This was especially true in the September 11, 2001 attacks, where Kapucu (2006) determined that out of 1530 domestic organizations involved in the response, 1176 were nonprofit organizations, 149 were private organizations, and 73 were federal or public organizations (Kapucu, 2008). Examples of nonprofit stakeholders that emergency managers can include in their consideration include the Institute for Business and Home Safety (IBHS), the International Association of Emergency Managers (IAEM), and various nonprofit organizations that fall under the umbrella of National Voluntary Organizations Active in Disaster (NVOAD). Examples of private-sector groups and organizations to include are the local chamber of commerce, private businesses that can be contracted out for recovery operations, and individuals and groups involved in business continuity planning. Finally, examples of public stakeholders to include are the Federal Emergency Management Agency, Department of Homeland Security, Transportation Security Agency, and Centers for Disease Control and Prevention.

Review Questions

1. How is a "stakeholder" defined, especially in the context of emergency management? Provide some examples from your communities.
2. Who are the stakeholders that emergency managers should be concerned about?

3. At what level in the system and by which different stakeholders are different types of emergency management decisions made?

4. How can emergency managers involve these stakeholders in the emergency management process?

5. Which types and amounts of power do different stakeholder groups have, and how do they influence the emergency management policy process?

6. Is it fair or unfair to claim that homeland security policy since the September 11, 2001 attacks has centralized control of disaster management at the federal level in the United States, weakening local control over local emergency management?

7. Many Americans support disaster relief provided by the national government, in part because they believe most or all of the federal aid goes to individuals and families who are victims of the disaster. Few average Americans understand that a huge share of federal disaster aid goes from one level of government (federal) to another (state and local governments) through "public assistance." A massive share of this aid replaces, repairs, or rebuilds local and state infrastructure (as well as facilities of nonprofit organizations that qualify for such funding). Is government-to-government disaster aid a sensible arrangement in your view? Or is it another federally supported public works endeavor that national taxpayers cannot really afford? Do state and local governments deserve public assistance money?

8. How might the information you gained from this chapter affect you personally and professionally?

References

Arbuthnot, K. 2005. *Multi-agency incident command in the UK*. International Workshop on Emergency Response and Rescue, Taipei, Republic of China.

Comfort, L. K. (2006). Cities at risk: Hurrican Katrina and the drowning of New Orleans. *Urban Affairs Review, 41*(4), 501–516.

Comfort, L. K. (2007). Crisis management in hindsight: Cognition, communication, coordination, and control. *Public Administration Review,* 67(Supplement s1), 189–197.

Crandall, W. R., Parnell, J. A., & Spillan, J. E. (2010). *Crisis management in the new strategy landscape.* Los Angeles: Sage.

Edwards, F. L., & Goodrich, D. C. (2007). Organizing for emergency management. In W. L. Waugh, Jr., & K. Tierney (Eds.), *Emergency management: Principles and practice for local government* (2nd ed., pp. 39–56). Washington, DC: ICMA.

Four years, 52 dead, £100m—no convictions. (2009, July 29). The Guardian. Retrieved February 18, 2010, from http://www.guardian.co.uk/uk/2009/apr/29/july-7-london-bomb-trial.

Fowler, K. L., Kling, N. D., & Larson, M. D. (2007). Organizational preparedness for coping with a major crisis or disaster. *Business and Society, 46*(1), 88–103.

Godschalk, D. R. (2007). Mitigation. In W. L. Waugh, Jr., & K. Tierney (Eds.), *Emergency management: Principles and practice for local government* (2nd ed., pp. 89–112). Washington, DC: ICMA.

Government Accountability Office (GAO). (2006). Critical infrastructure protection: *Progress coordinating government and private sector efforts varies sectors' characteristics.* GAO-07-39.

Her Majesty's Government. (n.d.). Emergency preparedness: Guidance on Part I of the Civil Contingencies Act 2004, its Associated regulations and non-statutory arrangements. Retrieved from http://www.cabinetoffice.gov.uk/media/131903/emergprepfinal.pdf.

Her Majesty's (HM) Government. (2010). Emergency Response and Recovery: Non Statutory Guidance Accompanying The Civil Contingencies Act 2004. Available at http://www.cabinetoffice.gov.uk/sites/default/files/resources/emergency-response-recovery_0.pdf.

Kapucu, N. (2006). Interagency communication networks during emergencies: boundary spanners in multi-agency coordination. *American Review of Public Administration, 36*(2), 207–225.

Kapucu, N. (2008). Collaborative emergency management: Better community organizing, better public preparedness and response. *Disasters, 32*(2), 239–362.

Kapucu, N. (2009). Interorganizational coordination in complex environments of disasters: The evolution of intergovernmental disaster response systems. *Journal of Homeland Security and Emergency Management, 6,* 1.

Labadie, J. R. (1984). Problems in local emergency management. *Environmental Management, 8*(6), 489–494.

Lindell, M. K., Prater, C. S., & Perry, R. W. (2006). *Fundamentals of emergency management.* Emmitsburgh, MD: Federal Emergency Management Agency.

McEntire, D. A., & Dawson, G. (2007). The intergovernmental context. In W. L. Waugh, Jr., & K. Tierney (Eds.), *Emergency management: Principles and practice for local government* (2nd ed., pp. 57–70). Washington, DC: ICMA.

McLoughlin, D. (1985). A framework for integrated emergency management. *Public Administration Review, Special Issue, 45,* 165–172.

Nicholson, W. C. (2007). Legal issues. In W. L. Waugh, Jr., & K. Tierney (Eds.), *Emergency management: Principles and practice for local government* (2nd ed., pp. 237–256). Washington, DC: ICMA.

Patton, A. (2007). Collaborative emergency management. In W. L. Waugh, Jr., & K. Tierney (Eds.), *Emergency management: Principles and practice for local government* (2nd ed., pp. 71–86). Washington, DC: ICMA.

Pitt, M. (2008). Learning lessons from 2007 floods. Cabinet Office. Retrieved from http://archive.cabinetoffice.gov.uk/pittreview/_/media/assets/www.cabinetoffice.gov.uk/flooding_review/pitt_review_full%20pdf.pdf.

Prater, C. S., & Lindell, M. K. (2000). Politics of hazard mitigation. *National Hazards Review, 1*(2), 73–82.

Public Strategies Group. (2008). Traditional consolidation and the FEMA failure. Retrieved June 20, 2009, from http://www.psgrp.com/resources/osborneletterfema.html.

Rainey, H. (2003). *Understanding and managing public organizations.* San Francisco: Jossey-Bass.

Rubin, C. B. (2007). *Emergency management: The American experience 1900–2005* (2nd ed.). Fairfax, VA: PERI.

Sylves, R. (2008). *Disaster policy and politics: Emergency management and homeland security.* Washington, DC: CQ Press.

Waugh, W. L. Jr. (2003). Terrorism, homeland security and the national emergency management network. *Public Organization Review, 3*(4), 373–385.

Waugh, W. L. Jr., & Streib, G. (2006). Collaboration and leadership for effective emergency management. *Public Administration Review, 66*(Supplement s1)131–140.

Wilson, J., & Oyola-Yemaiel, A. (2001). The evolution of emergency management and the advancement towards a profession in the United States and Florida. *Safety Science, 39,* 171–131.

Chapter 7

Decision Making in Managing Disasters and Crises

Chapter Objectives

- Understand the decision-making process and difficulties in response to disasters.
- Identify what can be done to make good decisions during disaster response operations.
- Identify ways to overcome political problems and harness increased attention on disasters to the benefit of the response and emergency management program in general.
- Analyze attributes of an effective decision maker.
- Discuss ethical decision making and problem solving.

Introduction

Due to the uncontrollable nature of disasters affecting masses of people and requiring the involvement of various sectors, organizations, and stakeholders, collaboration plays an important role in achieving successful results. This can be observed most prominently in an increase of response effectiveness and a reduction in casualties. Team or collaborative decision making in extreme and dynamic events is a process through which many actors contribute to the outcome based on their power within the group.

Emergency managers and responders are challenged with making difficult decisions whenever a disaster strikes. Largely, these decisions are made based on the foremost principle of emergency management—to save as many lives as possible. For instance, during Hurricane Katrina, the United States Coast Guard did not wait to get authorization to begin search and rescue missions, but rather set out immediately, thereby saving many lives (Cigler, 2007). Even though the Coast Guard earned the praise of the public for its efforts, its success was small in comparison to the lack of organization, communication, and other discrepancies in the response efforts following Katrina. According to Cigler (2007), responders understand that "those who respond together, should prepare together," with clearly defined roles (p. 71). Emergency responders can overcome challenges by creating proactive and well-tested plans that focus on facilitating responses to disasters. Cigler (2007) also states that, to be effective, all members of the network defined in the emergency management plan should be clear about and understand their roles, which will remove obstacles in the pathways of communication and assist in more efficient coordination.

The chapter begins with a discussion of the difficulty of making good decisions during disasters and explores ways to overcome such challenges. The political aspects of disasters are also identified in the chapter, including interorganizational conflict, blame, and disagreements about declarations and the distribution of relief. The chapter concludes by describing strategies to reduce interorganizational conflict, protect employment, and harness the increased attention paid to disasters for the benefit of the response and emergency management program in general.

Sound decision making is a linchpin when it comes to managing emergencies and crises in the most effective and efficient manner possible (Federal Emergency Management Agency Emergency Management Institute [FEMA EMI], 2005). Poor, or erroneous decisions made prior to a hurricane's landfall, for example, may actually exacerbate a crisis and spawn unintended consequences (Allison & Zelikow, 1999; Dayton, 2004). In a sense, uninformed decision making and use of a decision-making process that does not take into account environmental factors are prone to failure when it comes to providing effective emergency response. Effective decision making is a requirement of emergency managers, but the very conditions under which decisions are being made present practitioners with significant challenges that work to impede sound decision making and problem solving. The following section explores the factors preventing quality decision making during crises, and identifies the skills and tools that can be utilized to overcome these barriers.

The Decision-Making Process: Key Factors and Potential Barriers

Decision making is a process requiring input of several actors and is affected by several factors related to the disaster characteristics and environment, the decision maker, and the tools and mechanisms utilized to arrive at the ultimate decision.

Factors Affecting Decision Making

Uncertainty

According to Tierney et al. (2001), organizations face several types of operational challenges posed by the disaster. Notably, response operations as well as their coordination in response to disasters must be accomplished under conditions of uncertainty, urgency, and limited control. Uncertainty may result in increased cognitive workload, which can be reduced if the procedures and rules are fixed (Aguirre, 1988; Crichton, Flin, & McGeorge, 2005; Kapucu & Garayev, 2011).

According to Moynihan (2008), decision makers may face three types of uncertainties: (1) substantive uncertainty, which refers to a lack of knowledge about the problem; (2) strategic uncertainty, which is due to multiple actors' autonomy and independence from others in making their own decisions; and (3) institutional uncertainty, which arises from differences in norms, values, and organizational culture. Although substantive uncertainty is determined by the scope and level of the disaster, strategic and institutional uncertainties are largely dependent on the way interorganizational networks are formed. While Gist (1998) deems uncertainty avoidance to be a valid strategy to provide effective decisions, Therrien (1995) sees interorganizational networks as a tool to deal with the issue of uncertainty during emergencies.

Time Pressure

Time pressure is another factor that can negatively affect the decision-making process. According to Grabowski and Roberts (1999), time pressure produces additional burdens especially in terms of information management, which affects information flow and results in delays. While time pressure may produce better results for trained personnel because it triggers intuitive decision making based on previous experience (Dror, 1988; Lin & Su, 1998), it has mostly negative effects because of most individuals' incomplete and unsophisticated decision-making processes. Because information is limited and decisions must be made under conditions of boundedness (Forster, 1999; Kapucu, 2006), the resulting decisions can hardly hope to produce comprehensive solutions. Training, exercises, and simulation are among tools that can minimize the negative effects of time pressure characteristic of emergency and disaster situations (Lin & Su, 1998).

Risk

Risk, coming with decision-making responsibility as well as from the disaster environment, is yet another factor influencing the decision-making process. According to Perry (1985), a decision maker follows three steps: (1) risk identification, which refers to uncertainty reduction activities through active research and monitoring; (2) risk assessment, which involves determining the likely consequences of the risk assessed; and (3) risk reduction, which entails reduction—if not elimination—of the risk to the "acceptable" level. Kunreuther et al. (2004) claim that risk management can be effective only if it is based on risk assessment and risk perception. Achieving this goal requires accounting for two facts—(1) disaster risks are interdependent and (2) partnerships are an effective tool to shape risk reduction strategies. According to Sacco, Galletto, and Blanzieri (2003), risky decisions are made based on assessment of gains and losses as well as weights given to them. Vlek and Stallen (1980), in contrast, argue that uncertainty is the most important factor determining the level of risk. Overall, the level of risk must be assessed and minimized to make effective decisions during extreme events.

Stress

One of the inevitable aspects of emergency management is stress brought by the typically chaotic environment and disorderly actions. Saunders et al. (1996) define stress as a situation in which demands exceed the resources available. Although a moderate level of stress may be constructive, overwhelmingly stressful situations tend to prevent effective policy and decision making, especially as a result of participants' decreased ability to concentrate on the already available resources (Dror, 1988; Smart & Vertinsky, 1977). Keinan (1987) arrives at a similar conclusion, noting that there are three ways decision makers can and do make mistakes in stressful situations: (1) premature closure, in which the decision is made before analyzing all available alternatives; (2) nonsystematic scanning, in which there is nonsystematic, disorderly, and disorganized assessment of the available information; and, (3) temporal narrowing, in which decision makers do not have the ability to allocate sufficient time to assess each and every alternative.

Flin (2001) argues that stressors such as time pressure are more likely to influence the classical analytical decision-making style rather than the intuitive decision-making style because intuitive decision makers can quickly adapt themselves to new conditions. Danielsson and Ohlsson (1999), by comparison, argue that the main reason that stress arises is the lack of perfect and required information and knowledge in an emergency situation.

Information

Information management is another factor affecting the decision-making process. Flueler (2006) argues that because information is a type of purpose-oriented and future-based knowledge, it can serve as a tool to reduce uncertainty. According to Inzana et al. (1996), preparatory information helps reduce anxiety and increases performance accuracy in situations characterized by high stress.

Carley and Lin (1997), however, suggest that effective emergency response is possible only through minimization of information distortion, which they classify into five categories:

- Missing information (unavailability of certain required information)
- Incorrect information (the information at hand is erroneous)
- Agent unavailability (analysts or reporters who otherwise provide information are absent)
- Agent turnover (replacement of analysts and reporters with novices)
- Communication channel breakdown (reporting failure due to technological or technical problems)

These authors state that information distortion results in ambiguity, which can be eliminated through the following strategies: (1) the better technology strategy—design the procedure right; (2) the better training strategy—train people; and (3) the better design strategy—design the organization right.

Danielsson and Ohlsson (1999) suggest that emergency information management should especially focus on information reliability, information relevance, and information availability.

Previous Experience and Training

Previous experience is also a factor that might positively affect the decision-making process. Crichton, Flin, and Rattray (2000), for example, emphasize the importance of developing nontechnical skills such as enhancement of decision-making skills through simulation and training. Likewise, Flin, Slaven, and Stewart (1996) suggest that simulation and training would improve performance during emergency and disaster situations. Simulations, according to Haggerty (2007), help develop, improve, and enhance high-pressure decision making, and can be used to develop a mental model of emergencies in advance of disasters. Carley and Lin (1997) distinguish between experience-based and procedure-based decisions, asserting that organizations that focus on the former type of decision making generally exhibit higher performance than organizations that adopt the latter type. Mendonca and Fiedrich (2004), in turn, point to the importance of regular training exercises under time pressure as a means to help develop creative thinking.

Decision-Support Systems

Decision-making support systems (DSS) are an essential part of disaster management, which targets elimination of noise in terms of information and other factors essential to produce effective decisions. The main purpose of the DSS is to support intuitive thinking through the assistance of technology (both hardware and software). According to Olcer and Majumder (2006), DSSs help reduce time pressure, thereby enhancing information management. They are also helpful in adapting to idiosyncrasies of human decision making (Wallace & De Balogh, 1985). Wallace and De Balogh (1985) argue that the use of DSSs is inevitable when emergency and disaster management is considered. According to Lindell et al. (2005), such systems can also help reduce uncertainty in the environment, and provide more and better information about disaster estimates and probable costs as well as life losses to enhance decision making.

Shared Mental Models

Lastly, shared mental models play an important role in determining the decisions ultimately made. According to Fiore et al. (2003), shared mental models at the individual, team, and organizational levels can facilitate both coordination and the overall decision-making process. Construction of a shared mental picture about the emergency situation through situation assessment is vital to arrive at widely accepted decisions. In this regard, trust is one of the factors that would affect the level of cooperation among key decision makers as they seek to establish a shared mental model (Kapucu, 2006).

Stages of Decision Making

Decision making is the mental process resulting in the selection of a course of action among several alternatives during emergencies and disasters (FEMA EMI, 2005; Ritchie, 2005; Ulmer, Sellnow, & Seeger, 2007). Decision making here will be addressed at the three chronological stages of disaster management: prior to a crisis, during a crisis, and following a crisis.

Decision Making Prior to Crises

The decision-making process begins before a disaster strikes. Indeed, decision making before disasters must be a routine occurrence. "Often the number, type, and magnitude of decisions and problems that must be addressed during an emergency are a direct outgrowth of decisions that were (or weren't) made at the outset of the emergency, or even before the emergency began" (FEMA EMI, 2005, p. 22). FEMA EMI (2005) illustrates this point by describing the case of Fort Rice, North Dakota, which had been expecting flooding due to severe rain. The mayor and emergency management professionals were uncertain as whether to make evacuation mandatory, because they recognized the unwillingness of farmers to leave their properties. After long discussions, the mayor and his team decided to activate the Emergency Alert System and begin an evacuation without a mandatory order. This case illustrates how difficult it can be to make decisions given the varying interests of different stakeholder groups and under time constraints.

Decisions made under nonemergency conditions are made with deliberation and without stress, with decision makers being able to take the time to weigh the various alternatives and train for and exercise the plan. The U.S. National Incident Management System (NIMS) document proposes a structured and adaptive decision-making method for emergency managers. Standard operation procedures (SOPs) and emergency operations plans (EOPs) are drawn up in the pre-crisis period; they then provide guidance to decision makers in the case of an actual disaster (FEMA EMI, 2005). Nevertheless, the complex nature of emergencies demands flexibility in plans and procedures, which may turn out to be inadequate to effectively manage real-world incidents.

According to Ritchie (2005) "[a]t the pre-event and prodromal stage of a crisis or disaster activities can be undertaken by public and private sector organizations and managers to develop strategies and plans to stop or limit the impacts of a crisis or disaster (ranging from employee strikes, terrorist attacks, economic recessions, etc.)" (p. 674). This author suggests that the most difficult tasks in designing pre-crisis strategies are recognizing crises in an appropriate way and implementing coping strategies. To assist decision makers in handling these aspects effectively, Ritchie (2005) discusses several techniques for managers: strategic planning, contingency planning, issues analysis, scenario analysis, risk analysis and hazard mapping, and integrated emergency planning. These techniques encompass advocating a wide scope of observation of potential and past disasters, engaging in prediction, creating alternative plans, examining external environments, analyzing possible scenarios, and creating coordination centers. Brief descriptions of these strategies are provided here.

- *Strategic Planning.* This concept involves strategic analysis of the operating environment; establishment of specific direction and strategies to achieve organizational goals; development of structural, financial, capital, and human resources to implement the identified strategies; and continuous evaluation and monitoring of the end results.

- *Contingency Planning.* This concept includes utilization of alternative plans that can be implemented when and if a disaster strikes that alters the strategic direction of an organization. Contingency plans are especially useful in times of uncertainty, as they provide a direction in complex environments.

- *Issues Analysis.* Similar to contingency planning, issues analysis allows for analysis of trends in external environment with the purpose of designing appropriate strategies for possible changes in that environment.

- *Scenario Analysis.* This strategy includes developing hypothetical and detailed scenarios to identify a potential end state. Scenario analysis fosters discussion on issues that are highly likely to arise in the future, with the results of these discussions serving as contingency or emergency plans in the future.

- *Risk Analysis and Hazard Mapping.* This concept includes analysis of historical events and disasters to identify the potential risks of their reoccurrence. The overall purpose of risk analysis and hazard mapping is to minimize risk or exposure to risk.

- *Integrated Emergency Planning.* This concept entails creation of an emergency management command center and warning systems as well as a plan of coordination among organizations in charge.

Crichton et al. (2000) argue that effective preparation for disasters depends not only on appropriate planning, but also on the preparedness of personnel. Training and exercises involving both emergency management personnel and citizens play a vital role in ensuring adequate pre-crisis preparation and good decision making. In most organizations, the main focus is on increasing familiarity and experience with specific situations. Crichton et al. (2000) categorize exercises into three types: seminar, tabletop, and live exercise. Seminars and tabletop discussions have the disadvantage of not promoting the development of immediate-response skills; they also carry some costs. "These types of exercise generally test response organization effectiveness and the application of procedures, but they are limited in respect of their ability to promote the level of tactical response demanded in situations requiring immediate decisions" (Crichton et al., 2000, p. 209). Emergency management professionals need to have consistent training at all levels. Most tactical and simulation training is done at a local level, as the majority of emergency management personnel are employed by local emergency management agencies (Rubin, 2007).

Organizations in different fields also use pre-incident decision-making training programs. For example, the Tactical Decision Games (TDG) training technique is employed by the United States Marines for developing tactical skills and decision-making ability in the military (Crichton et al., 2000). The main goal of this technique is to teach personnel to handle the sometimes thorny issues in complex situations caused by disasters by exercising nontechnical decision-making and problem-solving skills based on scenarios. In addition, participants experience unfamiliar roles, which are assigned to them as part of the scenario. During the exercises or shortly thereafter, participants and the exercise facilitator exchange feedback, increasing the value of their experiences: "Participants can see how others deal with the situation, and gain insights to add to their own repertoire of patterns of accident management . . . In a group or team session, TDGs foster the development of shared or compatible mental models of the task and the roles of each participant, and, ultimately, skills such as situation awareness and leadership" (Crichton et al., 2000, p. 211).

TDG has been used in the training of Scottish Prison Service employees. When this strategy was used in combination with other techniques, high levels of learning were reported among prison staff after they participated in a field operation. Right after the beginning of TDG exercise, prison staff experienced two incidents—fire and hostage taking—and were able to achieve positive outcomes in both. After these incidents, supervisors reported that the TDG program had positively influenced the mental and tactical understanding of the Scottish Prison Service staff (Crichton et al., 2000).

Decision Making During Crises

Ulmer et al. (2007) identify three characteristics of emergencies as increasing the difficulty of decision making: surprise, threat, and short response time. They argue that an occurrence is not a crisis if it does not involve a degree of surprise. Threats are defined as events that affect the financial security of residents and others. The third most important characteristic of a crisis is the limited response time, which creates time pressure for immediate decisions. A variety of authors, in defining crises, emphasize their nature as unexpected, nonroutine, and uncertain events that threaten the high-priority goals of an organization or decision-making unit. Cosgrave (1996) references limited time, limited information, and decision load constraints as the key difficulties that emergency managers confront during emergency situations. Furthermore, this author underlines the point that dealing with the abrupt conditions of emergencies is easier when emergency managers take a systematic approach to problems, developing a decision-making system based on the quality, urgency, and acceptance of the problems being solved.

The quality of the solution required is directly related to the severity of the consequences if the problem is not addressed in the optimal manner. Trivial problems will have minimal negative consequences even if the action taken is ill advised, whereas a major decision can have wide-ranging effects if some factors influencing its outcome are neglected (Cosgrave, 1996). Acceptance of a problem grows in importance when other stakeholders are affected by the problem and the decision is being made collaboratively. Urgency is another key aspect for decision making: "deferring decisions leads to increasing the decision load of the manager where there is a constant stream of decisions to be taken" (Cosgrave, 1996, p. 30).

Cosgrave (1996) classifies decision-making styles based on three attributes. Managers may choose to act, consult, or delegate so as to resolve an issue based on its urgency and the quality of solution it requires. For example, a manager is likely to consult others for decision-making input in a situation that requires a great level of acceptance for the solution, whereas he or she may act directly when the level of acceptance needed is low. Also, when a low-quality solution is acceptable, the manager becomes more likely to delegate the decision-making process to someone else. If a high-quality solution is required in a low-acceptance incident, the manager would delegate the action with a greater care.

Good communication fosters effective decision making during emergencies and disasters. A clear and continuous flow of information removes uncertainty and helps managers to make educated decisions. Gregory (2005) emphasizes the importance of communication in response to crisis in his 2001 case study of the swine vesicular disease (SVD) epidemic in the United Kingdom, one of the largest crises in the country since World War II. "By the time the 221-day epidemic had ended, 6.5 million animals had been slaughtered and 10,157 premises had been affected. More than 1800 vets, 7000 administrative and technical support staff and 2000 troops were mobilized at its peak" (Gregory, 2005, p. 312). The main issue during this crisis in terms of communication centered on the flow of information between departments, field operational staff, and other stakeholders. The lack of information encouraged the spread of rumors on the Internet, and the situation was so uncertain that no one could verify what would happen next (Gregory, 2005). In analyzing this incident, Gregory (2005) suggests that the SVD epidemic taught emergency managers critical lessons concerning overall contingency planning, detailed communication plans, and increased preparation in general.

Rubin (2007) considers the response to the 2001 terrorist attack in New York to have largely been a success based on the protocols of the Federal Response Plan (FRP). She highlights the complication in the response spurred by the loss of the emergency operations center (EOC) in the World Trade Center. The federal response to the attack was massive; however, the coordination among federal, state, and local agencies was restricted by the communication difficulties between different agencies (Rubin, 2007). As this example demonstrates, communication is vital in decision making in immediate-response situations.

Decision Making Following Crises

Decision making after disasters is related to both relief and recovery activities. When emergency management professionals analyzed their actions following Hurricane Katrina, they produced numerous reports and lessons learned—but no changes have been made (Cigler, 2007). Recovery from Hurricane Katrina was very slow. In the first days of its aftermath, people relied on ad hoc recovery plans and had to find their own solutions to the crises at hand. "There has been no national recovery plan to comprehensively regulate issues related to individual, corporate, institutional, infrastructure, and environmental recovery (such as building codes, taxation, low-interest loans, deferments of credit payments, and debris removal and environmental cleanup)" (Rubin, 2007, p. 199). Regardless of government investment and grants for recovery, New Orleans could not replace its infrastructure completely so as to improve it.

Decisions made in times of crisis determine future recommendations for the improvement of emergency management plans. After Hurricane Katrina, many improvements were made within FEMA and in the National Response Plan (NRP), which has since been replaced with the National Response Framework (NRF). Many lessons were also learned from this incident, such as the dependence of recovery on the relationships built "among and between key decision makers" (Cigler, 2007, p. 72). Hurricane Katrina demonstrated the need for varied management approaches, flexible and hierarchical structures, and provisions to build situational awareness.

Decision-Making Styles

FEMA lists four styles of decision making: individual, group, consultation, and delegation (FEMA EMI, 2005). Group-based decision making is commonly considered to be more successful than an individual approach. According to FEMA, effective decision makers have the following attributes: knowledge, initiative, willingness to seek advice, selectivity, comprehensiveness, currency, flexibility, good judgment, calculated risk taking, and self-knowledge (FEMA EMI, 2005).

Reasoned decision making and problem solving need to be contextualized when it comes to emergency and disaster management. It may be assumed that decision making and problem solving are not any different for emergency management practitioners than they are for any other public servant engaged in serving the greater good of citizens. In reality, emergency management practitioners must be armed with specific tools and processes that enable them to cope with the unique circumstances created by emergencies. Decision making within the context of emergencies and crises takes place with limited information, in an environment where uncertainty reigns, risk abounds, and the luxury of time is noticeably absent.

Decision making within the immediate context of a crisis is informed by choices made long before such an event occurs, which affect the natural environment, human environment, and intergovernmental interactions. These decisions are outside the arena of emergency management and homeland security, yet have a direct impact on mitigation, preparation, response, and recovery efforts (Cigler, 2007). In addition to natural and human-shaped environments, the organization of and communication between governmental agencies directly impact decisions made. Problem solving focuses on the analysis of situations and the evaluation of solutions. Decision making goes a step further, to analyze each individual step within the problem-solving stage. The significance of thorough problem solving cannot be underemphasized, as poor or inaccurate problem solving can lead to erroneous decision making (FEMA EMI, 2005).

Making an accurate decision starts with the identification of the problem (FEMA EMI, 2005). Not being able to define the problem or defining it incorrectly will lead to ineffective solutions. In step 2 of the problem-solving process, managers search for available alternatives, evaluate them, and eventually choose the most appropriate (step 3). When choosing a solution, political, economic, environmental, ethical, and safety concerns will undoubtedly influence the process. Implementing a solution (step 4) will require action plans, as well as allocation of resources and personnel. In step 5, the solution is evaluated to ensure that decision makers understand their successes and shortcomings (FEMA EMI, 2005).

Political Complexities in Decision Making

Political problems can arise in nearly every phase of emergency management (Sylves, 2008). At the federal level of disaster preparedness in the United States, individuals who are appointed to highly critical positions should have emergency management decision-making expertise. Unfortunately, this is not always the case. For example, the George W. Bush administration assigned political appointees with very limited emergency management backgrounds to FEMA, resulting in a poor ability to respond during Hurricane Katrina (Cigler, 2007). Similar political issues can arise at the state level. In some instances, a gubernatorial request for a presidential disaster declaration may be made out of concerns for the governor's future "political fortunes"; by making this request, the governor appears responsive and competent in managing a disaster (McCarthy, 2009, p. 9). As a result, there is an overflow of presidential disaster declarations for relatively low-cost, small disasters—a practice that some have described as "pork barrel spending" owing to the numerous federal dollars going to local-level issues.

Other political problems can arise immediately following a disaster in the form of policy making. As Boin (2004) notes, policy making is "political in nature" and can be determined by the "framing of impacts of the crisis, processes of account-ability, and blame allocation" (p. 173). An example of a political problem arising from emergency management policy making is the authorization for use of military force and the U.S. PATRIOT Act following the September 11, 2001 terrorist attacks. Both policies were implemented hastily and led to an elaborate—and unchecked—executive power, which subsequently engendered enormous controversy during the Bush administration (Posner & Vermeule, 2009). Another politically-driven policy implemented after the September 11 attacks was the demotion of FEMA from Cabinet-level status to a subordinate agency under the Department of Homeland Security (DHS). As a result, FEMA had to focus much more on national terrorism and "lost experienced staff . . . its budget was reduced . . . [and] temporary employees became de facto permanent staff with weakened morale and diminished commit-ment" (Cigler, 2007, p. 68).

Concerns beyond political issues may also arise, such as the possibility of jeop-ardizing one's emergency management career based on the decisions made and the ways in which they are implemented. In many crisis situations, emergency managers must make decisions "without the information they require, in fluctuating organi-zational settings marked by bureau politics, and under conditions of severe stress" (Boin, 2004, p. 171). If poor consequences occur as a result of these decisions, the emergency managers in charge may appear incompetent.

Although some critics might suggest that emergency managers should stay out of politics, that it is not their job. Failure to consider politics can jeopardize the decision-making process as competing agencies fight for their share of resources or deny information to competitors (Sylves, 2008). Managing politics might be as simple as ensuring that both the Red Cross and the Salvation Army are mentioned in a press conference, or it might be as complex as making sure that fire fighters from rival Native American tribes are not deployed to the same area of a massive wildfire, which has previously been the case in the western United States.

Disasters are inevitably political events, so they affect policy choices and deci-sions to a significant extent (Selves, 2003). The ways to prepare for, mitigate, respond to, and recover from disasters are the products of political processes. Disasters also receive significant media attention, and politicians have to respond to the intense media scrutiny and make clear statements. Disasters attract attention based on the impact they have, the number of people they influence, and the policy domains they affect (Nice & Grosse, 2001). A terrorist attack would be likely to draw immediate attention from all levels of governmental bodies, whereas a natural disaster of similar scope might attract less of a spotlight. Policy makers will inevitably make faster decisions in the case of a larger or catastrophic disaster with potential political consequences. Catastrophic disasters can also be seen as a window of opportunity in which to carry out faster decision making or policy changes. The emotional impact of a crisis may lead decision makers to act rapidly and implement policies that might lack a solid basis in good decision making. As a result of these abrupt decisions, political conflicts may arise (Nice & Grosse, 2001).

To overcome these challenges, decisions should be made with the most accurate information available in a setting without emotional stress. Also, as many stakeholders as possible should be involved in the decision-making processes. Godschalk, Brody, and Burby (2003) and Pearce (2003) put emphasis on the involvement of citizens and other stakeholders in the planning efforts and mitigation practices in their local communities. Exclusion of key stakeholders (in this case, citizens) may potentially lead to failure in the application of the decisions. Godschalk et al. (2003) express their ideas on citizen participation succinctly: "without active citizen involvement in their preparation, plans for hazard mitigation can falter when efforts are made to implement recommended policies" (p. 750).

Attributes of an Effective Crisis Decision Maker

Decision making before, during, and after a disaster is probably the most difficult aspect of an emergency manager's position. Emergency managers are often burdened with making very complex decisions using scarce information in highly stressful environments. In addition to the obvious public safety ramifications, these decisions have consequences that reflect on the emergency manager's personal capabilities and competency. Additional problems can arise from the political side of emergency management, such as competition between agencies, which may result in poor decision making and policy creation. When faced with tough decisions, emergency managers would be wise to ensure that they have obtained the best situational information available and have considered, and mitigated, the potential political pitfalls involved in their decisions.

As amply demonstrated by the Hurricane Katrina scenario, practitioners must understand the multitude of factors that play a role in emergency management, and must appreciate how decisions made about matters seemingly unrelated to emergency management can affect emergencies themselves. The environmental factors that characterize the emergency management arena necessitate collection of a series of tools and processes that practitioners can use to make quality decisions.

Just as the human, natural, and political environments shape the actions in all four phases of emergency management, FEMA provides insight into how the "psychological type" of practitioners influences their decision making (FEMA EMI, 2005). Understanding the various ways in which individuals inherently approach a given problem and the resultant decision through their senses, intuition, thinking, or feelings is critical for emergency and crisis management practitioners (FEMA EMI, 2005). At the individual level, understanding one's own preferences (the dominant way one functions) helps the emergency manager better understand the strengths and weaknesses of how he or she perceives, judges, and then makes decisions (FEMA EMI, 2005).

At the group level, understanding each decision maker's preferences results in higher-quality decisions, as it allows practitioners to "flex" (i.e., assess the problem through alternative decision-making approaches) and, therefore, address a problem by adopting a variety of perspectives. In addition, understanding the various decision-making styles of others has the potential to mitigate the effects of the environmental factors that form the backdrop against which emergency managers must make critical decisions—namely, uncertainty, limited or inaccurate information, stress, and time pressure (Boin, 2004; Dayton, 2004). Given the critical nature and impact of the decisions made by emergency management practitioners, it is important for such an individual to not only "know thyself" but also to know others, so as to improve the quality of decisions made and the processes used to reach them (Dayton, 2004). This is yet another dimension of social capital within the context of emergency management.

The other factor influencing the decision-making process is stress, which makes this process especially difficult in a crisis setting. If a decision maker starts to experience a negative reaction, he or she may display physiological and psychological symptoms of anxiety and fear, to the point that the person may have a negative impact on decision making (Paton & Flin, 1999). Paton and Flin (1999) identify three styles of decision-making processes: intuitive, recognition primed (thinking for some time so as to remember the most appropriate procedure), and analytical decision making. They argue that emergency managers and those operating at a strategic level should apply the most relevant style depending upon the situation, and should know how to switch the style of decision making as necessary. In particular, it is important to know how to reduce stress in the emergency management context. "This risk, however, can be minimized by planning and establishing operational systems to support the management of the potentially high stress components of emergency response (e.g., coordination, communication, decision-making), and training for emergency and disaster work" (Paton & Flin, 1999, p. 262).

According to Crichton et al. (2000), naturalistic decision making (NDM) is an alternative to the nontechnical decision-making process. NDM can be defined as decision making by emergency professionals based on their experience and knowledge (Crichton et al., 2000). "Effective emergency management not only relies upon the knowledge and application of technical expertise and emergency operating procedures, but also depends upon the non-technical skills of the personnel involved in accident management" (p. 208). The main goal of NDM is to examine the ways professionals make decisions under conditions characterized by pressure, uncertainty, and group interactions.

In addition to implementing NIMS and maintaining situational awareness, an emergency manager facing a difficult decision must "distinguish between a problem and solution" (FEMA EMI, 2005, p. 213). An effective emergency manager should be able to communicate the problem before he or she begins to explain or define the solution. This step should occur when the manager identifies the problem and then starts to analyze the situation and figure out to what degree the problem exists. As a result of identifying the problem early in the process, the emergency management practitioner can greatly reduce the threats to effective decision making later when a disaster strikes.

The skills and tools identified within an independent study course provided by FEMA (FEMA IS-241) about decision making during disasters are valuable, but incomplete if practitioners fail to perform their duties with ethical consciousness (FEMA EMI, 2005). Ethical consciousness comprises a practitioner's demonstration of a clear understanding of the potential ethical implications surrounding his or her behavior and decision making. Practitioners must exhibit ethics in their work; moreover, citizens must also be able to perceive those ethics as being both present and appropriate.

One of the key obstacles to sound decision making in disasters is the uncertainty that can develop when emergency managers attempt to evaluate a complex, rapidly changing situation through a lens clouded by damaged infrastructure, power outages, public perceptions, observations from responders in the field, and other pressures. According to Paton and Flin (1999), environmental, organizational, and operational demands place the most intense stress upon emergency managers. Despite their training, responders and managers will inevitably encounter stressful decision-making situations, and the potential for error increases with the level of stress.

Information sharing, or a lack thereof, may also represent a major obstacle to effective decision making. A report from the Henry L. Stimson Center (2008, p. 15) noted that "information and intelligence sharing within the natural hazards community consists of a loosely defined network of national weather experts, federal, state, and local emergency management officials, and the media that work together to ensure timely dissemination of catastrophic weather information to the public when a major disaster threatens a vulnerable area." This definition suggests that a lack of effective communication remains one of the greatest hurdles to effective emergency management, even in today's information age. Ritchie (2005), however, argues that crisis communication and information sharing should be addressed carefully to avoid dissemination of disinformation in crisis situations.

The significance of effective leadership for successful emergency management has been highlighted by a number of scholars. According to Ritchie (2005), in times of crisis leadership is essential to give a clear direction to a wide range of activities "and to bring stakeholders together at an organizational and destination level for integrated crisis/disaster management" (p. 681). Ulmer et al. (2007) argue that a lack of leadership is what leads to uncertainty. During the September 11 attacks, scared employees from all around the United States were hungry for leadership (Argenti, 2002). The mayor of New York City, Rudolph Giuliani, illustrated exemplary leadership in the immediate response to the crisis, taking charge of the rescue operation and attending funerals (Ulmer et al., 2007). "His visibility, combined with his decisiveness, candor, and compassion, lifted the spirits of all New Yorkers—indeed, of all Americans" (Argenti, 2002, p. 104). During disaster and crisis situations, it is vital for managers to choose the right channel of communication to control the circumstances in which information is disseminated and to avoid chaos. Indeed, it is unacceptable not to have a strong and centralized voice during crisis; information should always be given out from a centralized source (Argenti, 2002).

To maximize the efforts of responders, emergency managers must strive to develop situational awareness regarding the state of affairs of any disaster. Situational awareness involves understanding what is currently happening and forming predictions about what is likely to happen during an event. It includes evaluating the situation, ascertaining the number of people and the material resources that are required to handle the event, and forecasting impending changes in the incident (Parker et al., 2009). A good sense of situational awareness allows the emergency management team to deploy resources where they are needed most. Accurate situational awareness occurs when decision makers' understanding of a disaster situation closely resembles the realities that are occurring on the ground. Unfortunately, emergency managers face many challenges in evaluating a disaster. Although crises demand rapid action, assessing them accurately requires time. Additionally, even though modern disasters are often accompanied by an avalanche of reports from responders and the media, obtaining truly accurate information can be challenging for emergency managers (Boin, 2004). Emergency managers can increase the accuracy of the information they receive, and thus their situational awareness, by utilizing NIMS, which standardizes information collection, sharing, dissemination, and terminology among agencies (FEMA EMI, 2005).

Ethical Decision Making in Response to Crises

To understand the role of ethics in times of crisis, it is important to define ethics and ethical perspectives in terms of emergency management. According to FEMA EMI (2005, p. 78), ethics is "a set of standards that guides our behavior, both as individuals and as members of organizations." Emergencies are ethically challenging in at least three ways: (1) the high stakes that arise because of the large number of people affected; (2) time pressure, which may complicate accurate deliberation;

and (3) incapacitated infrastructure and essential resources (Thomas, MacDonald, & Wenink, 2009). If emergency management professionals' actions and decisions disregard ethical considerations, the most common ethical implication and outcome will be disproportionate damage or harm to the people at stake. Thomas et al. (2009) consider the ability to identify and address ethical issues to be an essential skill of an emergency manager. Accordingly, an emergency manager should (1) recognize and acknowledge the existence of the ethical concept, (2) identify the specific ethical issues at hand, (3) identify basic guidelines for ethical reasoning, (4) decide who is responsible for which kinds of decisions with ethical implications, (5) prepare the respective responsible parties to make ethical decisions, (6) implement those decisions, and (7) assess whether the end result is the intended result. Following these steps will help develop ethical awareness in organizations responsible for managing emergencies.

The basic guidelines in terms of ethical decision making in response to disasters are that an emergency management professional should not exceed his or her authority, make promises that cannot be kept, or seek personal gain. Disregarding these tenets might result in ethically poor decisions whose implications include escalation of an emergency into an unmanageable case. In this regard, commitment, consciousness, and competency are the three components of ethical decision making that are directly related to the emergency manager's motivation, awareness, and skills (FEMA EMI, 2005).

Larkin and Arnold (2003) provide a more comprehensive list of ethical principles to be taken into account during emergency and disasters. These authors identify "seven cardinal virtues in times of terror": prudence (sound judgment or practical wisdom), courage (the decision to be involved with no concern about extraneous factors), justice (equitable and fair distribution of available resources according to need), stewardship (prudence in resources-wise decision making to maximize good and minimize harm), vigilance (being always able, willing, and ready), resiliency (an optimistic and sustained approach to create good despite a negative environment), and charity (self-effacing generosity and cheerfulness in caring for others). These virtue-based principles are never practiced in isolation from individual decision makers' skills and abilities; rather, emergency management professionals combine them with experience to develop competency and critical thinking (Good & Jolla, 2008). Importantly, whatever the guidelines for ethical decision making during emergency and disasters are, they should be established and accepted by responsible agencies in advance, with the primary goal being to arrive at an ethical consensus that would be applicable in various scenarios (Pesik, Keim, & Iserson, 2001).

When describing the ethical issues in relation to Hurricane Katrina in 2005, Stivers (2007) underlines the existence of an unpleasant approach in the decision-making patterns of the public officials. This author claims that "racism may have shaped policy and bureaucratic decision-making and magnified the death, destruction, and misery that storm produced" (p. 49). Accordingly, the decisions made by

FEMA and Pentagon officials, along with personnel form several other agencies, may be considered examples of biased decisions, which in turn exacerbated the disaster situation. For example, the Louisiana governor asked for 500 buses for evacuation of New Orleans; however, this number was lowered to 455 by FEMA despite the fact that even 500 buses were inadequate to evacuate the Super Dome (the primary shelter for the city of New Orleans' population). In addition, 5 helicopters that were (unwillingly) provided for the Katrina response by the Pentagon did not fly due to the fact that their permitted flight time was over.

Conclusion

Decision making under stressful conditions of crises and emergencies is naturally very different from the traditional decision making that is characterized by no environmental and contextual pressures. Uncertainty, time pressure, situation complexity, training, and previous experience are some of the factors that affect decision making in emergencies. These factors should be taken into consideration when public managers are asked to make decisions on critical issues in similar situations. The same factors should also be analyzed when accountability and performance measurement are key issues in an organization.

While decision making is generally related to individual-level analysis, group- and organizational-level decision making are also essential in emergency management situations. Generally speaking, individual decision making is the simplest and more convenient way of problem solving when the issues at hand are simple; by comparison, when one considers large-scale issues of consequential importance, it becomes imperative to involve as many actors as possible in the decision-making process.

Decision-support tools and relevant technologies are generally suggested as facilitating the decision-making process. Their main function is to minimize uncertainty, risk, and stress, and to enable users to make the most of the information and knowledge at hand. A balance should be established between the tools and techniques used and the complexity they bring to the decision-making process. While decision-support tools and technologies support analytical decision making, it is also advisable to use heuristics if and when needed. Heuristics comprise shortcuts based on previous experience and intuition that may not be available through traditional analytical tools. Training and simulation techniques are among the tools that can improve heuristics—something that is imperative during emergency and crisis situations. The literature suggests the use of both analytical and heuristics mechanisms so as to provide the best emergence response.

Effective decision making and problem solving are critical for all emergency management practitioners, yet these outcomes may prove challenging to obtain. Clearly, the natural, social, and political environments play key roles in shaping the decision making of practitioners. In addition, impediments to making quality decisions under stress abound, including perceived or real time pressures and incomplete or erroneous information. Knowledge, skills, and tools have been developed that can mitigate such stressors and barriers to effective decision making and problem solving.

Review Questions

1. Why is decision making difficult in emergency and disaster response? What are some of the reasons why decision making is problematic during emergency and disaster response operations?
2. How can decision-making challenges be overcome when disaster strikes?
3. What is situational awareness?
4. What are the typical political problems that arise in conjunction with disasters? How can the political interests of various entities in disasters be used to the advantage of the emergency manager?
5. Why might conflicts arise between organizations during response operations?
6. Why may the emergency manager's career be in jeopardy after a disaster?
7. Why is it important to push for policy changes during and after a disaster?
8. How might the information you gained from this chapter affect you personally and professionally?

References

Aguirre, B. E. (1988). Feedback from the field: The lack of warnings before the Saragosa tornado. *International Journal of Mass Emergencies and Disasters, 6*(1), 65–74.

Allison, G. T., & Zelikow, P. (1999). *Essence of decision: Explaining the Cuban missile crisis.* New York: Longman.

Argenti, P. (2002, December). Crisis communication: Lesson from 9/11. *Harvard Business Review* 80 (12), 103–109, 134.

Boin, A. (2004). Lesson from crisis research. *International Studies Review, 6,* 165–174.

Carley, K. M., & Lin, Z. (1997). A theoretical study of organizational performance under information distortion. *Management Science, 43*(7), 976–999.

Cigler, B. (2007). "The big questions" of Katrina and the 2005 Great Flood of New Orleans. *Public Administration Review, 67*(1), 64–76.

Cosgrave, J. (1996). Decision-making in emergencies. *Disaster Prevention and Management, 5*(4), 28–35.

Crichton, M. T., Flin, R., & McGeorge, P. (2005). Decision-making by on-scene incident commanders in nuclear emergencies. *Cognition, Technology & Work, 7*(3), 156–166.

Crichton, M. T., Flin, R., & Rattray, W. A. (2000). Training decision makers: Tactical decision games. *Journal of Contingencies and Crisis Management, 8*(4), 208–217.

Danielsson, M., & Ohlsson, K. (1999). Decision-making in emergency management: A survey study. *International Journal of Cognitive Ergonomics, 3*(2), 91–99.

Dayton, B. W. (Ed.). (2004). Managing crises in the twenty first century. *International Studies Review, 6,* 165–194.

Dror, Y. (1988). Decision-making under disaster conditions. In L. Comfort (Ed.), *Managing disasters: Administrative and policy strategies* (pp. 255–273). Durham, NC: Duke University Press.

Federal Emergency Management Agency (FEMA) Emergency Management Institute (EMI). (2005). *IS-241: Decision-making and problem solving.* Emmitsburg, MD: Author. Retrieved October 16, 2009, from http://training.fema.gov/EMIWeb/downloads/IS241.pdf.

Fiore, S. M., Jentsch, F., Bowers, C. A., & Salas, E. (2003, October). *Shared mental models at the intra- and inter-team level: Applications to counter-terrorism and crisis response for homeland security.* Human Factors and Ergonomics Society 47th Annual Meeting. Santa Monica, CA, October.

Flin, R. (2001). Decision-making in crises: The Piper Alpha disaster. In U. Rosenthal, A. R. Boin, & L. Comfort (Eds.), *Managing crises: Threats, dilemmas, opportunities* (pp. 103–118). Springfield, IL: Charles C. Thomas.

Flin, R., Slaven, G., & Stewart, K. (1996). Emergency decision-making in the offshore oil and gas industry. *Human Factors, 38*(2), 262–277.

Flueler, T. (2006). *Decision-making for complex socio-technical systems: Robustness from lessons learned in long-term radioactive waste governance.* Dordrecht, Netherlands: Springer.

Forster, M. R. (1999). How do simple rules fit to reality in a complex world? *Minds and Machines, 9,* 543–564.

Gist, J. R. (1998). Decision-making in public administration. In J. Rabin, W. B. Hildreth, & G. J. Miller (Eds.), *Handbook of public administration* (pp. 265–291). New York: Marcel Dekker.

Godschalk, D. R., Brody, S., & Burby, R. (2003). Public participation in natural hazard mitigation policy formation: Challenges for comprehensive planning. *Journal of Environmental Planning and Management, 46*(5), 733–754.

Good, L., & Jolla, L. (2008). Ethical decision-making in disaster triage. *Journal of Emergency Nursing , 34*(2), 112–115.

Grabowski, M., & Roberts, K. H. (1999). Risk mitigation in virtual organizations. *Organization Science, 10*(6), 704–721.

Gregory, A. (2005). Communication dimensions of the UK foot and mouth disease crisis, 2001. *Journal of Public Affairs, 5,* 312–328.

Haggerty, R. (2007, December 6). Pandemic drill puts city, businesses to test. Retrieved January 10, 2008, from www.chicagotribune.com: www.chicagotribune.com/news/local/chi-pandemic_webdec07,0,1010807.story.

Henry L. Stimson Center. (2008). *New information and intelligence needs in the 21st century threat environment.* Washington, DC: Author.

Inzana, C. M., Driskell, J. E., Salas, E., & Johnston, J. H. (1996). The effects of preparatory information on enhancing performance under stress. *Journal of Applied Psychology,81*(4), 429–435.

Kapucu, N. (2006). Interagency communication networks during emergencies: Boundary spanners in multi-agency coordination. *American Review of Public Administration, 36*(2), 207–225.

Kapucu, N. & Garayev, G. (2011). Collaborative Decision-Making in Emergency and Crisis Management. *International Journal of Public Administration. 34*(6): 366–375.

Keinan, G. (1987). Decision-making under stress : Scanning of alternatives under controllable and uncontrollable threats. *Journal of Personality and Social Psychology, 52*(3), 639–644.

Kunreuther, H., Meyer, R., & Van den Bulte, C. (2004, October). Risk analysis for extreme events: Economic incentives for reducing future losses. Retrieved November 2007 from U.S. Department of Commerce: www.bfrl.nist.gov/oae/publications/gcrs/04871.pdf.

Larkin, G. L., & Arnold, J. (2003). Ethical considerations in emergency planning, preparedness, and response to acts of terrorism. *Prehospital Disaster Medicine, 18*(3), 170–178.

Lin, D.-Y. M., & Su, Y.-L. (1998). The effect of time pressure on expert system based training for emergency management. *Behaviour & Information Technology,* 17(4), 195–202.

Lindell, M. K., Prater, C. S., & Peacock, W. G. (February 2005). *Oganizational communication and decision-making in hurricane emergencies.* Pomona, CA: Hazard Reduction & Recovery Center.

McCarthy, F. (2009). *FEMA's disaster declaration process: A primer.* CRS Report for Congress.

Mendonca, D., & Fiedrich, D. (2004). Design for improvisation in computer-based emergency response systems. *Proceedings of the Eleventh Annual Conference of the International Emergency Management Society* (pp. 18–21). Melbourne, Australia.

Moynihan, D. P. (2008). Learning under uncertainty: Networks in crisis management. *Public Administration Review, 68*(2) 350–365.

Nice, D. C., & Grosse, A. (2001). Crisis policy making: Some implications for program management. In A. Farazmand (Ed.), *Handbook of crisis and emergency management* (pp. 55–68). New York: Marcel Dekker.

Olcer, A., & Majumder, J. (2006). A case-based decision support system for flooding crises onboard ships. *Quality and Reliability Engineering International, 22*(1), 59–78.

Parker, A., Nelson, C., Shelton, S., Dausey, D., Lewis, M., Pomeroy, A., et al. (2009). *Measuring crisis decision-making for public health emergencies.* Santa Monica, CA: RAND Corporation.

Paton, D., & Flin, R. (1999). Disaster stress: An emergency management perspective. *Disaster Prevention and Management, 8*(4), 261–267.

Pearce, L. (2003). *Disaster management and community planning, and public participation: How to achieve sustainable hazard mitigation. Natural Hazards,* 28(2–3), 211–228.

Perry, R. W. (1985). *Comprehensive emergency management: Evacuating threatened populations.* Greenwich, CT: JAI Press.

Pesik, N., Keim, M. E., & Iserson, K. V. (2001). Terrorism and the ethics of emergency medical care. *Annals of Emergency Medicine, 37*(6), 642–646.

Posner, E., & Vermeule, A. (2009). *Crisis governance in the administrative state: 9/11 and the financial meltdown of 2008. University of Chicago Law Review,* 76(4), 1613–1682.

Ritchie, B. W. (2005). Chaos, crises and disasters: A strategic approach to crisis management in the tourism industry. *Tourism Management, 25*(6), 669–683.

Rubin, C. B. (2007). *Emergency management: The American experience 1900–2005* (2nd ed.). Fairfax, VA: PERI.

Sacco, K., Galletto, V., & Blanzieri, E. (2003). How has the 9/11 terrorist attack influenced decision-making? *Applied Cognitive Psychology, 17*(9), 1113–1127.

Saunders, T., Driskell, J. E., Johnston, J. H., & Salas, E. (1996). The effect of stress inoculation training on anxiety and performance. *Journal of Occupational Health Psychology, 1*(2), 170–186.

Selves, M. D. (2003). The politics of disaster: Principles for local emergency managers and elected officials. *Journal of the American Society of Professional Emergency Planners, 10*, 77–82.

Smart, C., & Vertinsky, I. (1977). Designs for crisis decision units. *Administrative Science Quarterly, 22*, 640–659.

Stivers. C. (2007). "So poor and black": Hurricane Katrina, public administration, and the issue of race. *Public Administration Review, 67*(Supplement s1) 48–56.

Sylves, R. (2008). *Disaster policy and politics: Emergency management and homeland security.* Washington, DC: CQ Press.

Therrien, M.-C. (1995). Interorganizational networks and decision-making in technological disasters. *Safety Science, 20*, 101–113.

Thomas, J. C., MacDonald, P. D., & Wenink, E. (2009). Ethical decision-making in a crisis: A case study of ethics in public health emergencies. *Journal of Public Health Management Practice, 15*(2), E16–E21.

Tierney, K. J., Lindell, M. K., & Perry, R. W. (2001). *Facing the unexpected: Disaster preparedness and response in the United States.* Washington, DC: Joseph Henry Press.

Ulmer, R. R., Sellnow, T. L., & Seeger, M. W. (2007). *Effective crisis communication: Moving from crisis to opportunity.* Thousand Oaks, CA: Sage.

Vlek, C., & Stallen, P.-J. (1980). Rational and personal aspects of risk. *Acta Psychologica, 45*, 273–300.

Wallace, W. A., & De Balogh, F. (1985). Decision support systems for disaster management. *Public Administration Review, 45*(Special Issue) 134–146.

Chapter 8

Leadership in Managing Emergencies and Crises

Chapter Objectives

- Analyze management and leadership in disaster and crisis management.
- Understand trust and relationship building.
- Identify leadership characteristics in managing emergencies and crisis.
- Understand improvisation, creativity, and flexibility, and their importance in effective disaster response operations and management.
- Assess leadership performance in minimizing catastrophes.
- Discuss how weak leadership makes matters worse, compounding the damage from a disaster.

Introduction

Leadership and management require a different set of competencies depending on the situation. Fields such as leadership research, emergency management, and change management have proved useful in identifying styles, individual characteristics, and behaviors of successful leaders. These fields provide excellent heuristic frameworks for organizing the literature and informing practitioners about the concept. However, such leadership competency lists and associated models or frameworks are mostly either abstract or very detailed. Even so, competency models are not specific to context, and this is particularly true in leadership associated with crisis management.

There are many risks attached to ineffective leadership in crisis situations. During a crisis, information can be inaccurate, timely decisions must be made, and the stakes are high. In these hard times, the actions of leaders at all levels of government, nonprofit, and for-profit organizations are being monitored closely. Considering how leadership or the lack thereof can have devastating effects on a community, this chapter explores the risks of ineffective leadership during a disaster and identifies methods that can be employed to minimize them.

Effective Leadership

Officials and administrative managers in governments should have the leadership skills to address the challenges in dealing with superior authorities, partners, and subordinates. Several leadership skills for dealing with subordinates, those with higher authority, peers in partner organizations, volunteers, and the public have been developed to facilitate the emergence of effective leaders (Federal Emergency Management Agency [FEMA], 2005).

Leadership involves providing vision, direction, coordination, and motivation toward achieving emergency management goals. It is very important in emergency management, where its absence can result in increased losses, be they public trust, property, or lives. Effective leadership is the ability to create an environment that encourages self-discovery and the testing of assumptions that may nurture growth, change, and development of a shared vision. Effective leaders are often associated with the concept of a transformational leader—that is, a person who is able to determine an appropriate course for changes in the future, articulate a vision, and stimulate coworkers and self to challenge traditional ways of thinking. Organizations can foster such a leadership style by encouraging authentic feedback for self-improvement, nurturing an environment of shared learning by balancing inquiry and advocacy, adopting a leadership mindset about change, and facilitating acceptance of change within the organization (FEMA, 2005).

As argued by Boin and t'Hart (2003), crisis management is very much dependent on leadership. When a crisis ends and the response is perceived to have been successful, people tend to glorify the leader; conversely, if the outcome is negative, the leader is an obvious scapegoat. In a sense, the challenge to normalize the situation and the opportunity for a leader arising from a crisis situation often go hand in hand (Boin & t'Hart, 2003; Kunreuther & Useem, 2010). Boin and t'Hart (2003) argue that modern crisis leadership is especially challenging due to the processes of globalization, deregulation, developments in information and communication technology, other technological advances, and the emphasis on integration. Many scholars argue that newer types of leadership are more effective than the classic "control and command" style because they capitalize on the trend toward collaborative approaches (Kapucu & Van Wart, 2006; Kushma et al., 2008; McGuire & Silvia, 2009). According to McGuire and Silvia (2009), the new environment for leaders differs significantly from the classic bureaucratic structure. Network leadership represents a new leadership method, albeit one that has not yet been studied extensively; hence there is a need for evaluation of this approach.

Kushma et al. (2008) portray crisis leadership as a challenge of facilitating constructive processes for working together, including engaging a wide group of stakeholders in appropriate and meaningful ways. Moreover, these authors argue that emergency management leaders are simultaneously servants and transformational leaders; whichever model one prefers to follow, there are a lot of opportunities to demonstrate leadership. "By its very nature, emergency management leadership connotes leadership— safeguarding life and property by marshalling both the will and the required resources to respond to and recover from an emergency quickly" (FEMA, 2005, p. 1.2).

Trust and Relationship Building

Leaders within emergency management must build relationships of trust at multiple levels. "Your relationship with Local, State, and Federal officials, with other organizations, with media, and with public will affect your ability to manage a disaster successfully. Those relationships are built on a foundation of trust" (FEMA, 2005, p. 88). For example, during the September 11, 2001 terrorist attacks in the United States, the foundation of trust among the various responding agencies played an important part in the effective cooperative response efforts.

In addition to building trust and facilitating change, an effective leader must be able to influence others. Personal influence is critical in emergency management, and every one of the tasks that is outlined in the emergency manager's action plan requires some measure of personal influence. Using personal influence well and possessing political savvy can aid an organization in gaining visibility and obtaining resources. Effective leaders view and treat the people around them as partners or potential partners. Being an ally to others means using the principle of reciprocity; as we do things for others in the organization, they become more likely to help us in return (FEMA, 2005).

Successful leadership in networks occurs when the collaboration among network stakeholders is developed and cooperation information blockages are removed (Kapucu 2006; McGuire & Silvia, 2009). Activating external actors and combining networks with trust building, information sharing, and prioritizing the personal welfare of network members are the most important leadership behaviors in assessing network effectiveness (McGuire & Silvia, 2009).

Leadership Development and Characteristics

Disaster and emergency conditions require different leadership features than non-emergency situations. People expect their leaders to eliminate the adverse effects of the emergency conditions or take them out of harm's way urgently. In the context of managing emergencies and disasters, the question to ask is this: Which kind of competencies and characteristics must a public leader have to cope with the disaster conditions, meet the needs of the public, and minimize (if not totally eliminate) the damage?

Leaders and emergency managers are often in situations that are influenced by rumor, false information, panic, responsibility, and pressure. A successful emergency leader has the ability to make immediate decisions, forecast the consequences of those decisions made, follow ethical values and principles, maintain a vision of crisis resolution, care about people, face up to responsibility, be honest, communicate openly, and demonstrate a strong character and integrity.

Boin et al. (2005) underline the importance of the leadership role in the four phases of emergency management. Accordingly, they construct a framework for the tasks that public leaders must handle in coping with pre- and post-disaster conditions—specifically, sense making, decision making, meaning making, terminating, and learning. Briefly, Boin et al. (2005) explain these five tasks as follows:

- *Sense making* connotes the task of recognizing the extraordinary conditions from ambiguous and contradictory signs.
- *Decision making* in managing disasters covers prioritization of needs and use of resources as well as making effective decisions under stressful conditions.
- *Meaning making* refers to the process of reducing the uncertainty, communicating clearly with the public, and explaining to stakeholders what the current condition is, how the situation is managed, and what they are supposed to do to reduce the uncertainty.
- In the *terminating* task, leaders eliminate the disaster conditions and bring the routine life conditions back to life again.
- *Learning* involves recognizing lessons from the mistakes and building up experience to ensure that more accurate policies, procedures, and regulations are established going forward.

Van Wart and Kapucu (2011) identify several leadership competencies to deal with disasters (but only in the post-disaster phase) more effectively and promote change in the organization to turn it into a better-functioning mechanism. In their study, 51 emergency management officials across the United States were asked to highlight those competencies they viewed as most important by selecting from a list of 37 generic competencies. Based on these participants' responses, Van Wart and Kapucu (2011, p. 20) identify different competencies for three different leadership styles:

- "Competencies for managing disasters and organization change in [the] short term" include "flexibility, social skills, communication, motivation, mission and vision articulation, and decision making."
- For transformational leadership, competencies include "self-confidence, decisiveness, analytic ability, willingness to assume responsibility, and tendency to delegate.
- "Competencies for routine operations" include "operations planning, informing, team building, and networking and partnering."

According to Blythe (2008), during times of disasters, an essential leadership skill that must be exercised is the ability to communicate effectively. Citizens need to hear from a leader that actions are under way to provide assistance to those in need, and they need to receive reassurance that they will not be forgotten and that a rebuilding process will take place. It is vital that the citizenry maintain confidence in their leaders so that they can get through the trying times that lie before them. Additionally, in short-term emergency management or response to unexpected conditions of emergencies, leaders need to be able to assume responsibilities and fill the role of "person in charge" even if that function is not part of their formally defined duties or job description (Blythe, 2008; Peterson & Van Fleet, 2008; Van Wart 2011; Van Wart & Kapucu, 2011).

For long-term leadership, additional competencies are required. For instance, a hallmark of effective leaders in the long run is the ability to create an environment that encourages the development of future generations of leaders and fosters leadership qualities in every employee. A successful emergency response organization is known for maximizing the use of the "intellectual capital" found in the organization's members (FEMA, 2005).

Crisis leadership requires planning, training, exercises, and simulations, which in turn will help emergency managers to become emergency leaders. Blythe (2008, p. 2) emphasizes three main components of strategic crisis leadership: "Be, Know, Do." In other words, emergency leaders must know what their responsibilities are, which knowledge and skills they possess, and which actions they need to take in an emergency situation.

A favorable performance in dealing with disasters requires an ability to assess and adapt capacity rapidly, restore or enhance disrupted or inadequate communications, utilize a flexible decision-making process, and expand coordination and trust of emergency response agencies (Comfort, 1999; Kapucu, 2006; Kettl, 2007). High standards of responsiveness and ubiquitous media coverage compel political leaders and administrative heads alike to coordinate resources effectively. The massive numbers of public, nonprofit, and private organizations involved in disaster response and recovery operations mandate the effective use of horizontal and vertical communication and decision making, along with high-performing public leadership (Kapucu & Van Wart, 2006, 2008; Waugh & Tierney, 2007).

No single government agency or governmental jurisdiction possesses all of the resources and expertise required for a coordinated emergency management effort. Thus formation of a network that connects public agencies with private and nonprofit-sector organizations is critical. Emergency management requires the establishment of intergovernmental networks with federal, state, and local governmental units to share responsibilities, information, expertise, and communication. Specifically, the National Response Framework (NRF) requires the partnership of government, private, and nonprofit organizations as well as the citizenry. The success of the overall response effort will depend on the strength of the partnerships among federal, state, and local agencies, as well as private-sector organizations (Department of Homeland Security [DHS], 2010).

In most disaster management scenarios, local authorities are the first responders. When the mission is local in nature, federalizing or nationalizing emergency operations makes no sense. In most U.S. states, county governments are responsible for coordinating emergency response operations. In addition, some major cities have their own emergency operations centers. In reality, however, disasters tend to quickly overwhelm the resources and capabilities of local governments. Most of the time local governments rely on assistance from state governments, while larger-magnitude disasters might require the federal government's intervention as well.

The NRF establishes a comprehensive, all-hazards approach to enhance the ability of the United States to manage domestic crisis incidents. This plan places a strong emphasis on coordination and integration of capabilities among all levels of government, private organizations, nonprofit organizations, and individual citizens. Local governments play an important role in the NRF, as the plan calls for handling all incidents at the lowest possible organizational and jurisdictional level. To support this preference, a variety of coordination mechanisms that link local responses to federal capabilities for intelligence gathering and incidence response are needed. For example, joint field offices (JFO) are temporary federal facilities that are established locally to provide a central point of reference for the federal, state, local, and tribal representatives who have responsibility for incident support and coordination. The NRF includes several key concepts, all of which require sound attention to management: threat assessment strategies, incident reporting, vertical and horizontal communication and information sharing, training and exercising, mitigation strategies, organizing and planning to mobilize resources at different levels, response and recovery activities, and safety of personnel and the population, as well as hazard-specific components of these concepts.

Managing Routine and Catastrophic Disasters: Are They Different?

Without an understanding of what a catastrophic event is, the expectations of the public regarding the management of these events cannot be understood. Obviously, catastrophic disasters are unpredictable and can occur at any time and in any place. Routine emergencies are most often able to be predicted and "fit well into bureaucratized management protocols that increase the speed and quality of responses while minimizing expenses" (Kapucu & Van Wart, 2008, p. 12). A second difference between routine and catastrophic disasters is that catastrophic disasters cause disturbances in standard communication channels (i.e., telecommunications and information technology infrastructures); routine operations and data collection depend on a steady communication system for decision making (Kapucu & Van Wart, 2008). In addition, catastrophic events cause major disruptions to decision-making processes, which could ultimately affect the communication of management decisions that are necessary during extreme events. In contrast, in routine events, decision-making disruption is kept to a minimum and the ability for communication to flow is secure. Last, although "the scale of catastrophic disasters requires the intricate cooperation of hundreds of organizations just as communication and decision systems are severely damaged, coordination is either absent or simply overwhelmed initially" (Kapucu & Van Wart, 2008, p. 13). Routine events do not require cooperation and cross-sectoral relationships among a myriad of organizations.

With the differences between the two types defined, what must happen for catastrophic disaster management to progress effectively becomes clear. Kapucu and Van Wart (2008) identify several leadership competencies that are critical for managing catastrophes. The 2008 article by these authors focuses on two catastrophic events that took place in the United States in the past decade: the attacks on the World Trade Center on September 11, 2001, and the hurricanes that struck Florida in 2004. Although these events were different in nature, they occurred in a similar context when it came to public-sector involvement. On the one hand, the evolution of the public-sector involvement with catastrophic disasters depends on such tasks as contingency planning, training, interagency coordination, and the use of up-to-date technology. On the other hand, effective planning and coordination cannot be replaced by technology; when all of these capabilities are used in an integrated manner, however, they can be highly effective. Also, "capacity assessment and adaptation, special efforts to restore and enhance communication, flexible decision-making, and an expansion of coordination and goodwill among emergency agencies and personnel" (Kapucu & Van Wart, 2008, p. 24) are critical in managing both catastrophic and routine disasters.

For the governmental response to catastrophic disasters to be successful, four elements must exist: the need for an established plan and system; good communication and proper use of information technologies; prearranged decision protocols; and the existence of formalized cooperation agreements and effective boundary-spanning agencies. Because major disasters can create a chaotic environment, it is important for the emergency management team and responders to know how to react to large-scale events. Planning, exercises, and training can identify the gaps in the current system and suggest ways to bridge these gaps so as to prevent further potential chaos. All entities involved should understand who else is involved and how to connect with those entities if necessary. Additionally, it is important to know which technologies are in place and how to use them, as this knowledge can save lives. To make decisions quickly, Kapucu and Van Wart (2006) suggest decentralization of decision-making protocols and reliance on a formally stated chain of command. These procedures must be understood in advance by all key staff and personnel as well as other involved organizations if they are to operate efficiently and quickly during a catastrophic event. Other players can offer significant assistance, which means that there should be formalized relationships among them to ensure a better response during a crisis. Preparations that assure the ready availability of the four elements of a successful response to a catastrophic event can save lives, time, and energy, while ensuring efforts are not duplicated.

Successful response depends on key leadership to provide support and direction to all parties involved in the effort. The problems with leadership during the Katrina and Rita hurricanes, for example, resulted in mass casualties and approximately $81 billion in property damage (Kapucu & Van Wart, 2008). Due to the poor performance of leaders at all levels involved with the emergency response, Hurricane Katrina will forever be remembered as one of the worst-managed catastrophic disasters in U.S. history.

Understanding Disaster Policy Through Presidential Disaster Declarations

In the context of the United States, Sylves (2008) emphasizes the importance of the mutually integrated roles of the United States President, Congress, White House staff, DHS, FEMA, state governors, and other federal and local officials in the establishment and management of the emergency declaration process. In his work, this author explores the political issues, challenges, and causes that influence the presidential declaration process, policy determination, and decision-making process. Emergency management planners must understand the emergency powers of the president that are granted through the United States Constitution and have been strengthened over the years through laws and acts. Sylves (2008) goes into detail about the conception, historical markers, implications, and processes that make up a presidential declaration of disaster, emergency, catastrophic incident, or National Special Security Event. The events of September 11, 2001 ushered in a new era that "defined presidential disaster declaration authority as a national security instrument, thus drastically changing federal emergency management" (p. 79). They swiftly altered the federal role of emergency management to be one "predicated on terrorism as a paramount threat, whereas other types of disasters or emergencies occupy diminished positions within the federal EM [emergency management] and homeland security community" (p. 83).

Perhaps not surprisingly, given today's fractious political climate, politics can play a part in the approval or rejection of a governor's request for disaster declaration. Effective leadership is paramount not only during times of crisis, but also in the days leading up to an event, if prior warning is possible. Given that "presidents have always reserved this authority to declare a major disaster or emergency and have never delegated it" (p. 79), they must have a thorough understanding of the potential havoc the incident could wreak on a region. The decision to approve or decline a disaster declaration request can have far-reaching consequences, both financially and emotionally, for those in the affected areas.

While legislation has granted the president sole authority to declare a disaster, many other parties are involved in the information-gathering and recommendation process, including those from the local, state, and federal levels. The processes do not end with the approval or denial of the declaration. If the request for a declaration is denied, the spurned governor has the option of pursuing an appeal process. If the declaration is approved, it then becomes the job of FEMA to "determine how much money is to be allocated to the states, counties, and other eligible entities" (p. 102). Disaster expenditures are limited to $5 million of aid per declaration. Any expenses over that threshold require the president to notify Congress of the proposed expenditure.

Successful and effective leadership in one crisis does not always translate into the same outcome in another incident of different scope and sequence. President Jimmy Carter's handling of the Love Canal contamination was lauded, in contrast to his management of the Iran hostage situation, and President George W. Bush's handling of the September 11 terrorist attacks and Hurricane Katrina highlight how the complexities of a disaster can make or break leaders and their political careers. "[E]ach president's declaration decisions reveal something about that president as a person, as a public servant, and as a political leader" (p. 77). Additionally, the theory of congressional dominance suggests that nearly half of all disaster relief is motivated by political considerations rather than by need (p. 94). The political forces at times compete with need-based, subjective assessments, except in the cases of catastrophic disasters, which by their very nature necessitate a federal response.

It is very important for leaders to recognize that they are not alone in addressing crises. Often, scores of people are looking for direction in the same scenario, and the key to success in this setting for leaders is to make sure they are able to delegate responsibility accordingly and effectively. The federal government has provided some guidance in the NRF and National Incident Management System (NIMS). Although the NRF was largely developed based on the hard-learned lessons from Hurricane Katrina, it also incorporates concepts from the relevant literature that was available at the time of its inception.

The NRF and NIMS have been in place long enough that anyone working in government should be accustomed to their value. Leaders must not only lead after a disaster, but must also lead during pre-disaster times. Kapucu and Van Wart (2008) suggest that it is essential for the local communities to be involved in capacity building, especially at the lowest level, given that local communities are the primary parties responsible for dealing with catastrophes. Capacity building is a key element to preparedness and mitigation; it gets people thinking about what could happen and helps them to be prepared for when it does. For leaders, this endeavor requires many of the skills mentioned previously, such as personnel planning, scanning the environment, motivating, and informing.

It was not just the local governments that lacked the leadership competencies to be effective during Hurricane Katrina; rather, due to the size and scope of the disaster, the federal government had a hand in the failed response. One particular reality that hindered the federal response was the change in the focus and scope of FEMA that occurred following the September 11 attacks. Following the Bush administration's Cabinet shake-up, FEMA fell under the umbrella of DHS, which focused primarily on terrorist threats and human-made disasters. This arrangement marked a departure from the all-hazards scope of emergency management. In turn, the resulting loss of flexibility in approach made it very difficult for the federal government to offer assistance before, during, or after the 2005 storm (Kapucu & Van Wart, 2008).

Clear and consistent communication are always welcome, but are especially critical during times of disaster. Indeed, clear, concise, and consistent communications were key tenets of both NIMS and the NRP. Communication, however, was lacking in New Orleans from the onset of the storm and remained poor for weeks afterwards. The exact opposite was true in Florida's response to the wave of devastating hurricanes it endured in 2004 and in Mayor Giuliani's response in the wake of the September 11 attacks. In both of these situations, the public received a single message: to remain calm and be assured that life would continue as normal. It is amazing that even after these two very good responses to disaster it would be possible to witness a true lack of cohesive communication. The problem in Hurricane Katrina, however, stemmed from a lack of leadership. Kapucu and Van Wart (2008) note that coordination is critical, yet exceedingly difficult to achieve during disaster. They also stress there must be a high level of trust among the various agencies involved in the emergency response, as it takes more than one person to get a city through a disaster: "Networking and partnering, so critical in massive relief efforts, must largely be in place prior to catastrophes so that the actual team building is taking place over hours rather than days and weeks" (p. 25).

Case Studies

September 11, 2001 Terrorist Attacks

Primary communication in the World Trade Center (WTC) was lost during the September 11 attacks in New York after the Verizon network tower located in the World Trade Center failed. However, the resiliency of some systems in New York City let other subscribers communicate successfully.

It is important to enhance communication throughout disaster-prone areas so that communication is never lost. This goal can be accomplished through attention to certain critical details. First, the reduction of inefficiencies and redundancies is imperative among personnel to ensure that the emergency management process can run smoothly. Second, all personnel must have distinct tasks that are delegated to them with minimal overlap. Overlap in human resources assignments merely causes confusion and will make managing catastrophic disasters more difficult than need be. Third, given the growing demand for better public leadership, "preparedness for catastrophic disasters requires a much greater level of resources and training for events that may never occur" (Kapucu & Van Wart, 2008, p. 24). State and federal leadership is expected in catastrophic disasters; thus, instead of primarily financially funding routine disaster management, the public sector should invest in the training and resources necessary to prepare for a catastrophic disaster.

Cross-sectoral governance is needed across the public, nonprofit, and private organizations involved in catastrophic disasters. These organizations "require extensive ability to have horizontal and vertical communication and decision-making" (Kapucu & Van Wart, 2008, p. 24). Once an effective disaster management network is established across all sectors, the preparedness and response to catastrophic disasters will be efficient. Cross-sectoral relationships could effectively increase the amount of resources needed in catastrophic disaster management; for this reason, "state and federal leadership must be careful not to supplant the leadership of local governments and nonprofits that provide the bulk of relief and recovery efforts" (p. 25). To effectively manage these extreme events, effective leadership, communication, and cross-sectoral networking are necessary to help increase preparedness, which will in turn yield an effective response.

2002 German Floods

Floods are a destructive disaster that can paralyze all areas of human activity where they occur. "Floods can kill people, make them ill, leave them homeless, damage property, and/or pollute the environment, which is why taking a holistic view of flood awareness, prevention, and management is so important in today's world" (Schick-Richards, Fox, Juepner, Tzschirner, & Hundley, 2007, p. 2).

During August 2002, widespread heavy rainfall occurred all over central Europe. Ulbrich et al. (2003) argue that the reason for the heavy rain was an upper-tropospheric depression caused by surface low, which blew cool air from the Atlantic Ocean to Western Europe during this period (Ulbrich et al., 2003, p. 437). Ultimately, the floods of 2002 took the lives of 38 people and caused approximately $16.11 billion of property damage (Schick-Richards et al., 2007; Thieken, Kreibich, Muller, & Merz, 2007). The increased level of damage in some areas was directly related to the number of people living in those areas. Clearly, as this example demonstrates, "land use planning authorities play a significant role in the development of the damage potential and thus in flood risk management" (Petrow, Thieken, Kreibich, Bahlburg, & Merz, 2006, p. 718).

The 2002 floods in Germany were a test of leadership (Rohrschneider & Wolf, 2003). Moreover, the flooding occurred shortly before national elections, and the handling of them was expected to be a deciding factor in the public's voting decisions.

Then-Chancellor Gerhard Schröder announced assistance free of red tape and the postponement of tax cuts. "The chancellor and other officials quickly appeared at the flood sites, and later Schröder took a leadership role at emergency flood-related European Commission meetings" (Rohrschneider & Wolf, 2003, p. 10). It seems safe to say that Schröder's leadership in this crisis played an important role in his party gaining the majority seats in the German Bundestag in the ensuing election.

2004 Hurricanes in Florida (Charles, Frances, Ivan, and Jean)

It is almost exclusively in times of turmoil that we look toward leaders in government for guidance. Most people do not especially notice good leadership throughout their everyday activities, as the large bureaucracy of government generally seems to function successfully. Rather, it is when a strain is placed upon us or when it seems that order is no longer in hand that we expect leaders to step up and provide reassurance that all will be well.

It is interesting to contrast the performance of Florida Governor Jeb Bush in the 2004 hurricane season of Florida and the leadership of New Orleans Mayor Ray Nagin leading up to and throughout the Hurricane Katrina disaster. In Florida, we saw a calm governor speaking clearly and consistently to an entire state in two languages as necessary. In New Orleans, we saw what seemed to be an often disheveled and lost mayor who seemed to be more concerned about placing blame for his poor decision making and lack of a cohesive plan than about resolving the crisis.

Often the outcomes of extreme events are predicated on the quality of previous planning and the ability to act on those plans (Kapucu & Van Wart, 2008). But why is the focus almost always on the bad jobs and never on the good ones? Perhaps it is because "examples of especially good performance are less visible, at least to the public at large, because their very success reduces their visibility and newsworthiness" (Kapucu & Van Wart, 2008, p. 2). Although good leadership may not be a big rating grabber, it is the exact thing that allows us to muddle through our days even in times of extreme peril and fear.

London Bombings in 2005

The London bombings were a series of prepared suicide attacks on public transportation system that occurred early on the morning of July 7, 2005. Because London officials had predicted terrorist attacks in the aftermath of recent attacks in Istanbul and Madrid, London emergency management teams had previously engaged in large-scale disaster-response exercises that included the participation of several emergency services (Lockey et al., 2005). Consequently, the high levels of preparation by emergency managers and senior hospital staff reduced the number of deaths. "Rapid removal of the seriously injured with minimal medical intervention from potentially unsafe scenes is a priority and senior doctors are in a good position to direct and support ambulance and fire personnel in this difficult task" (Lockey et al., 2005, p. 11).

The year before the London bombings, the increasing number of human-made disasters and terrorist attacks had served as the inspiration for the U.K. Parliament's passage of the Civil Contingencies Act (CCA) of 2004 (Şahin, Kapucu, & Ünlü, 2008). After the 2005 bombings, the CCA underwent changes focused on adopting more proactive tactics for preventing damage and hazards (O'Brien & Read, 2005; Şahin et al., 2008). Over the years, U.K. emergency planning policies have undergone huge reforms in line with the changing emergency management trends in the world. One of the changes in the CCA, for example, was separation of management of emergencies into two separate wings: civil and terrorist. The head of civil contingency responders in the United Kingdom is the Civil Contingencies Committee, while the terrorist contingencies committee is headed by the Prime Minister and convenes in the Cabinet Office Briefing Rooms (COBR) in the Cabinet Office during such emergencies.

As Strom and Eyerman (2008) state, multiagency coordination is a huge challenge at all levels, especially during simultaneous attacks as was the case in the London bombings. They suggest encouraging participation of senior staff in different organizations in training programs to strengthen relationship building, communication, trust, and appreciation for others' roles. An emergency response can fail if any of the leaders of a critical partner agency is unwilling to participate and commit qualified staff. This is often a consequence of the way the agency might be unconvinced about the potential benefits of such an involvement. "Responding agencies faced challenges during and immediately after the attacks [the 2005 London bombings], but major problems in emergency coordination were minimized because London officials had established relationships with one another and had practiced agreed-upon procedures" (Strom & Eyerman, 2008, p. 8).

Hurricane Katrina

Does the U.S. President base his decision to approve or decline a declaration request strictly on the basis of the information presented to him? Although the average citizen would like to believe so, political factors do have a hand in this decision-making process. Some suggest that denials may come at the expense of the opposing party or "unfriendly" states, or approvals may be streamlined for "friends" within the party or states that may be crucial to presidential reelection. Waugh (2006) identifies the significance of administrative leadership and accountability, and the lack of government capacity, in this decision-making process, labeling it a traditional "blame game" among leaders. In the Hurricane Katrina disaster, the political issues that surrounded the response to this crisis contributed to the poor implementation of emergency plans, poor communication, and poor decision making. Although the Hurricane Pam exercise that took place between July 2004 and August 2005 provided practice for local and state leaders in dealing with massive casualties, extensive damage, existing vulnerabilities, and unpreparedness, little was done to address these problems. Little development regulation, investment, or attention was given by public officials and leaders to efforts to alleviate the future risk of disasters.

Even though warnings and aid requests for impending disaster were issued days before Katrina's landfall, there was a growing confusion and tension between the state and federal roles in the response. State and federal officials did not perfectly understand one another and were confused because of new regulations, federal procedures, and structures, leading to reluctance in taking the lead in the response actions because of fear of violating the other parties' authority (Cigler, 2007; Waugh, 2006). The shift in the focus of DHS to human-made disasters instead of all hazards had reduced funding and changed FEMA's role. Poor understanding of the NRP and deficiencies in the implementation of NIMS also demonstrated the confusion among state and federal officials, which in turn sparked the need for examination of the causes of this administrative and political chaos.

These same challenges were faced in relation to the September 11 attacks, when the "Government Accountability Office and the Congressional Research Service . . . also had difficulty extracting responses from DHS" (Waugh, 2006, p. 22). The experiences with Hurricanes Katrina and Rita should be a starting point for the federal government to give officials and leaders incentives to improve national emergency management system. As these incidents well illustrate, there can be political and economic costs to officials and communities that fail to address or respond to and mitigate disasters.

Any dialogue regarding risk should include the lessons learned from the hurricanes of 2005. In the aftermath of the Katrina and Rita disasters, numerous critics pointed out that local, state, and federal level governments failed miserably in their response to both incidents. The mounting body of evidence put forth against the responding entities revealed that both disasters were predicted in government reports, media stories, academic studies, and the simulation of Hurricane Pam one year previously. Local, state, and federal governments were well informed of the catastrophic risks, their capacity to respond, and the impending breach of the levees. The poor response and lack of congruency between government agencies clearly demonstrates the breakdown in leadership that may lead to additional consequences in the form of political costs for those responsible for the failures (Waugh, 2006).

By the nature of their positions, "[l]ocal and state officials have a political, legal, and ethical obligation to address the hazards that pose serious risk to their own communities, regardless of the priorities of the federal government" (Waugh, 2006, p. 22). Ineffective leadership permeated the response efforts to the 2005 hurricanes, resulting in high casualty counts, increased crime, long-term displacement of people, and overall lack of trust in government. Despite the poor leadership exhibited during Katrina and Rita, the expected political costs in the 2006 elections did not materialize as anticipated. In the end, the population that was most adversely affected and most likely to retaliate in the voting booth was the same population that was displaced and living outside of New Orleans and Louisiana and, therefore, unable to vote in the local and state elections in these areas (Logan, 2006).

During Hurricane Katrina, poor leadership between all parties resulted in the delay of response and recovery. No one seemed to be in control or aware of their specific responsibilities during the disaster. The leaders involved had failed to prepare and plan for such an event, they failed to communicate with other jurisdictions and partners, and they lacked the competencies needed to adapt, expand, restore, and troubleshoot in responding to the emergency (Kapucu & Van Wart, 2008). As this incident illustrates, it is important to build relationships and partnerships with surrounding jurisdictions and organizations in advance, so that in the event of a major disaster all stakeholders are able to work, share, and interact with one another successfully. The leadership described during Hurricane Katrina is a negative example—one to reference so as to avoid future mishaps in managing disasters. A great leader is one who takes charge and is able to coordinate plans, network with others, make decisions, problem solve, expand capacity, and adapt to changing environments (Kapucu & Van Wart, 2008). To minimize the effects of a major disaster, it is best if a leader follows the four leadership principles of managing catastrophic events.

Conclusion

In a crisis, the stakes are very high, the situation is extremely tense, and lives depend on leaders' quick thinking and decision-making skills. Leadership skills can be developed through various professional development seminars and courses. Individuals must understand the difference between a manager and a leader, however, and hone in on the skill set required to be an effective leader. Furthermore, leadership in routine events and in catastrophes requires different skills and competencies. Catastrophes cause more disruption in both technical and nontechnical emergency systems and put extra stress on individuals involved in the response, particularly the leaders. Catastrophic disasters draw attention to two major issues of emergency management "the general explanatory model of major disasters and . . . the problem of the integration of innumerable nonprofit, private, and public sector actors" (Kapucu & Van Wart, 2006, p. 14). Leaders need to have the various competencies addressed in this chapter to achieve success and take people out of harm's way during catastrophes.

Although emergency managers hold the key position in managing disasters, federal government and the president as representatives of the nation as a whole play an undeniable role in leading the U.S. emergency management system. The weight of the presidential office in emergency management has varied throughout American history because of the changing political environment (e.g., the change from a civil defense focus to a disaster management focus). The most direct and visible intervention tool for the executive branch of the federal government in emergency management is the presidential disaster declaration. Presidents' personal political initiatives also influence the government's ability to effectively manage the crises and emergencies.

Review Questions

1. What are the expected leadership competencies in managing catastrophic disasters (or extreme events)?
2. Where are the differences in various competencies the greatest?
3. Where does the nature of the competencies vary the most between emergency management and catastrophic management?
4. How do catastrophes and extreme events differ from routine emergencies and disasters?
5. What are the expectations of leadership for managing catastrophic disasters?
6. How different are the expectations of leadership for managing catastrophic disasters from those for managing routine disasters and emergencies?
7. How do intergovernmental and interorganizational systems function in response to catastrophic disasters and extreme events?
8. How might the information you gained from this chapter affect you personally and professionally?

References

Blythe, B. T. (2008). Strategic crisis leadership: Are you ready to lead in the midst of chaos? *Disaster Resource Guide Quarterly*. Retrieved May 27, 2011 from http://www.disaster-resource.com/articles/08exe_p10.shtml.

Boin, A., & 't Hart, P. (2003). Public leadership in times of crisis: mission impossible? *Public Administration Review, 63*(5), 544–553.

Boin, A., t' Hart, P., Stern, E., & Sundelius, B. (2005). *Politics of crisis management: Public leadership under pressure.* New York: Cambridge University Press.

Cigler, B. A. (2007). The "big questions" of Katrina and the 2005 Great Flood of New Orleans. *Public Administration Review, 67* (Supplement s1), 64–76.

Comfort, L. K. (1999). *Shared risk: Complex systems in seismic response.* New York: Pergamon Press.

Department of Homeland Security (DHS). (2010). Leadership and influence. *Independent Study Course IS-240a*, pp. 1–180. Retrieved May 27, 2011 from http://www.training.fema.gov/EMIWeb/IS/IS240A.pdf.

Federal Emergency Management Agency (FEMA). (2005). IS-204: Leadership and influence. Retrieved March 22, 2010 from http://training.fema.gov/EMIWeb/downloads/is240.pdf.

Kapucu, N. (2006). Interagency communication networks during emergencies: Boundary spanners in multi-agency coordination. *American Review of Public Administration, 36*(2), 207–225.

Kapucu, N., & Van Wart, M. (2006). The emerging role of the public sector in managing extreme events: Lessons learned. *Administration & Society, 38*(3), 279–308.

Kapucu, N., & Van Wart, M. (2008). Making matters worse: Anatomy of leadership failures in catastrophic events. *Administration & Society, 40*(7), 711–740.

Kettl, D. F. (2007). *System under stress: Homeland security and American politics.* Washington, DC: CQ Press.

Kunreuther, H., & Useem, M. (Eds.). (2010). *Learning from catastrophes: Strategies for reaction and response.* Upper Saddle River, NJ: Wharton School Publishing.

Kushma, J., Benini, J. K., and Holdeman E. (2008). Leadership Challenges in Emergency Management: A Moderated Panel Discussion. EIIP Virtual Forum Presentation—November 5, 2008. Available at http://www.emforum.org/vforum/lc081105.htm.

Lockey, D.J., MacKenzie, R., Redhead, J., Wise, D., Harris, T., Weaver, A., et al. (2005). London bombings July 2005: The immediate pre-hospital medical response. *Resuscitation, 66,* ix–xii.

Logan, J. R. (2006). *Population displacement and post-Katrina politics: The New Orleans mayoral race.* American Communities Project, Brown University.

McGuire, M., & Silvia, C. (2009). Does leadership in networks matter? Examining the effect of leadership behaviors on managers' perceptions of network effectiveness. *Public Performance and Management Review, 33(1),* 34–62.

O'Brien, G., & Read, P. (2005). Future UK emergency management: New wine, old skin? *Disaster Prevention and Management: An International Journal, 14*(3), 353–361.

Peterson, T. O., & Fleet, D. D. V. (2008). A Tale of two situations: An empirical study of behavior by nonprofit managerial leaders. *Public Performance and Management Review, 3*(14), 503–516.

Petrow, T., Thieken, A. H., Kreibich, H., Bahlburg, C. H., & Merz, B. (2006). Improvements on flood alleviation in Germany: Lessons learned from the Elbe flood in August 2002. *Environmental Management, 38,* 717–732.

Rohrschneider, R., & Wolf, M. R. (2003). The federal election of 2002. *German Politics and Society, 66*(21), 1–14.

Şahin, B., Kapucu, N., & Ünlü, A. (2008). Perspectives on crisis management in European Union countries: United Kingdom, Spain and Germany. *European Journal of Economic and Political Studies, 11,* 19–45.

Schick-Richards, L., Fox, P., Juepner, R., Tzschirner, M., & Hundley, A. (2007). *A comparison of flood management practices between Germany and the USA: An undergraduate research project on sustainable practices.* American Society for Engineering Education.

Strom, K. J., & Eyerman, J. (2008). Interagency coordination: A case study of the 2005 London train bombings. *National Institute of Justice Journal, 260,* 4–11.

Sylves, R. (2008). *Disaster policy and politics: Emergency management and homeland security.* Washington, DC: CQ Press.

Thieken, A. H., Kreibich, H., Muller, M., & Merz, B. (2007). Coping with floods: Preparedness, response and recovery of flood-affected residents in Germany in 2002. *Hydrological Sciences, 52*(5), 1016–1037.

Ulbrich, U., Brucher, T., Fink, A. H., Leckebusch, G. C., Kruger, A., & Pinto, J. G. (2003). The central European floods of August 2002: Part 2—Synoptic causes and considerations with respect to climatic change. *Weather, 8,* 434–442.

Van Wart, M. (2011). *Dynamics of leadership in public service: Theory and Practice.* second edition. Armonk, NY: M.E. Sharpe.

Van Wart, M., & Kapucu, N. (2011). Crisis management competencies: The case of emergency managers in the U.S. *Public Management Review, 13*(4) 489-511.

Waugh, W. L. Jr. (2006). The political costs of failure in the Katrina and Rita disasters. *Annals of the American Academy of Political and Social Science, 604*(1), 10–25.

Waugh, W. L. Jr., & Tierney, K. (Eds.). (2007). *Emergency management: Principles and practice for local government* (2nd ed.). Washington, DC: ICMA.

Chapter 9

Risk Perception and Risk Communication

Chapter Objectives

- Analyze strategic crisis management, risk, and risk assessment.
- Understand crisis management, risk-based decision making.
- Assess emergency information management and community-specific communication issues.
- Understand the use of technology as a communication tool.
- Learn about managing public complacency and working with the media.

Introduction

Effective communication is one of the hallmarks of successful disaster management. Throughout the disaster management cycle, the need for clear and consistent communication is a common theme. During the mitigation and preparedness phases, communication can help ensure the proper efforts are being put forth by the appropriate agencies. During the response and recovery cycle, it is often the only thing people have to help them get through very tough times. It can also make a difference in ensuring public safety and awareness. Choosing the right form of communication is the key to making people aware of what lies ahead of them so that they can plan accordingly.

Traditionally and historically, the responsibility for crisis communication has been placed squarely on the shoulders of public sector (Burnett, 1998). "Training spokespersons, developing guidelines/policies for notifying families, and determining general processes for dealing with the media, are just some of the areas that concern public relations professionals" (Burnett, 1998, p. 476). Consequently, it is very important to prepare communicative and responsible public relations managers who can inspire trust and stimulate dialogue among stakeholders (National Research Council of the National Academies [NRC], 2006; Özerdem & Jacoby, 2006; Paton, 2007).

This chapter explains how people perceive the risks of natural and human-made hazards and describes the actions they can take to protect themselves from those hazards. Addressing such perceptions is the most common way for emergency managers to change the behavior of those at risk from long-term threats or imminent impacts of disasters (Lindell, Prater, & Perry, 2007; Schneider, 1995). The chapter also focuses on risk communication during the continuing hazard phase, escalating crises, and emergency response.

Aakko (2004) defines risk communication as "a complex, multidimensional, evolving approach to communicating with the public about issues that pose a threat to health, safety, or the environment" (p. 25). He believes that risk communication differs from the traditional one-way communication model in that the former is a two-way process of communication that enhances participation from both the sender of the message and the audience. Furthermore, according to Aakko (2004), one of the main components of effective communication between spokespeople and audiences is trust—that is, building and maintaining trust between them. The other component affecting risk communication is risk perception, which differs among people for different reasons (Aakko, 2004; Auf der Heide, n.d.; Gibbons, 2007).

Effective communication enhances social capital which thrives on the bridges established through all types of communication, whether it be oral, written, or observed. The importance of effective communication has obviously not been lost on the Federal Emergency Management Agency (FEMA), which has developed an entire course to ensure that managers and responders are prepared to communicate their thoughts and actions to others so as to achieve the best possible outcome for largest possible population. During the hurricanes that struck Central Florida in 2004, for example, communication was a constant, and a key aspect of the area's ultimately successful response and recovery. At the time, Florida was fortunate to have a bilingual governor who was able to speak directly to the large Spanish-speaking population in the state. Not only did this help in getting out critical information, but it also may have been an effective tool to cross the cultural divide that often exists between government and its people.

Active listening is important for everyone who deals in disaster. However, it is probably most important for first responders. For those responders who are first on the scene, it is their job not only to help those who are in need, but also to gather information and report it back to the emergency operation centers (EOCs) so managers there can act on it. By listening emphatically and paraphrasing back to the speaker what they hear, first responders can ensure that they send back quality information for the EOC to act on.

Another focus of the FEMA course is the importance of keeping communication consistent, especially in times of disaster. Practicing consistent communication will allow all of those involved to be on the same page, which helps to both increase decision-making capability and cut down on confusion (Tierney, Lindell, & Perry, 2001; Ulmer, Sellnow, & Seeger, 2011). During times of crisis, people do not think everything through. Managing effectively in such a chaotic situation can be especially more difficult for those who do not speak the same language. Having the ability to cross cultural lines calms people down and lets them know they have not been forgotten.

Strategic Crisis Management, Risk, and Risk Assessment

Crisis management requires knowledge of a mixture of different areas, and achieving this breadth of knowledge can be a truly difficult task (Auf der Heide, n.d.; Coombs, 1999). Crisis management is often considered to comprise a set of dynamics necessary to fight crises and minimize the real damage. Ritchie (2005) suggests that the globalization process tends to make the world interdependent and connected, such that one part of the world is affected by the crises that occur in other parts of the world. "Political instability, or the outbreak of war in one part of the world can dramatically reduce tourist travel patterns to other parts of the world as experienced by the Gulf War of 1991 and the Iraq conflict in 2003" (Ritchie, 2005, p. 670). Consequently, crisis management is an important step to take over different crises and disasters at any level. Parsons (1996) defines crisis management as a combination of applied common sense, experience, and time.

Parsons (1996) argues that during disasters, organizations need to be in touch with all stakeholders and receive their support. Important strategies for the government to follow are to open all channels of communication, inform people by nominating an official spokesperson on the senior director level, establish a media source center to feed media with information, and build trust. According to Parsons (1996), "strong, positive, third-party endorsement not only helps to sell products, it also helps to calm down a crisis" (p. 27). In addition, Parsons (1996) highlights the need for a thorough evaluation of the crisis in its aftermath. Ritchie (2005) touches on other points regarding how strategies for dealing with crisis situations differ in terms of time pressure, the extent of control, and the scale of the incidents: "The threat, time pressure and intensity of these incidents can lead to the development of a crisis or disaster continuum to help classify and understand such incidents and, more importantly, illustrate to managers when an 'issue' or a 'problem' can develop into a 'crisis'" (p. 671).

Burnett (1998) believes that crisis management is first and foremost a strategic problem. He emphasizes six major tasks that he identifies as central to strategic management to resolve crises (**Figure 9-1**): (1) goal formulation; (2) environmental analysis; (3) strategy formulation; (4) strategy evaluation; (5) strategy implementation; and (6) strategic control. According to this author, the strategic management process entails proper identification of the crisis, active confrontation of organizations with the crisis, and reconfiguration of operations as necessary during implementation of strategies. "This consolidated view of the strategic management process—identification, confrontation, reconfiguration—is exacerbated during a crisis by time pressures, control issues, threat-level concerns, and response-option constraints" (p. 482).

In his study, Burnett (1998) proposes a classification matrix that utilizes four criteria: time pressure, degree of control, threat level, and response options. As shown in **Figure 9-2**, each of these criteria is related with crisis situations. For Burnett, classification is important because it simplifies complex structures, helps to organize the collection of information, provides diagnostic insights, and has the potential to facilitate improvements in strategic planning (p. 482). Burnett argues that use of this classification matrix can help organizations improve their strategies: "While the most challenging problems are found in the lone 'level four' cell where the time pressure is intense, the degree of control is low, the threat-level is high, and response-options are few in number, problems that would certainly be classified as

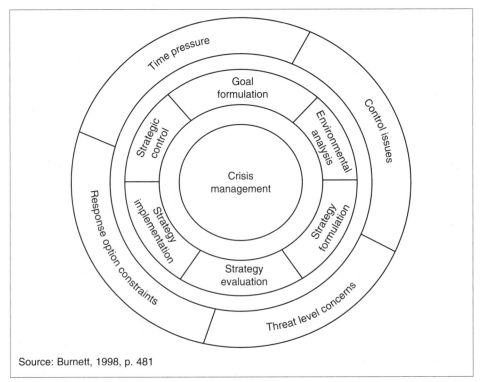

Source: Burnett, 1998, p. 481

Figure 9-1 *Crisis Management: Strategic Considerations*

Time pressure		Intense		Minimal	
Threat level	Degree of control Response options	Low	High	Low	High
Low	Many	(4) Level 2	(3) Level 1	(2) Level 1	(1) Level 0
	Few	(8) Level 3	(7) Level 2	(6) Level 2	(5) Level 1
High	Many	(12) Level 3	(11) Level 2	(10) Level 2	(9) Level 1
	Few	(16) Level 4	(15) Level 3	(14) Level 3	(13) Level 2

Source: Burnett, 1998, p. 483

Figure 9-2 *Crisis Classification Matrix*

crises can also be found in 'level two' and 'level three' cells" (p. 482). Levels one and two are not qualified as crises.

The Research and Special Programs Administration of the U.S. Department of Transportation (DOT, 1998) defines risk management as "the systematic application of policies, practices and resources to the assessment and control of risk affecting human health and safety and the environment." To promote awareness and knowledge, other essential elements of risk management are identified as outreach, training, and information dissemination (DOT, 1998). Coombs (1999) believes that crisis management has emerged from emergency preparedness: "Drawing from that base crisis management is a set of four interrelated factors: (1) prevention, (2) preparation, (3) response, and (4) revision" (p. 5).

Basic communication skills are simply the act of sending a message and having someone receive it. As FEMA (2005) points out, a point that is often overlooked is whether the message has been *effectively* received: "in the send–receive model, receiving or listening is as critical as sending the message; without listening, it is impossible to personalize and respond to the message" (p. 18). The best course of action for the listener is to become an active listener—that is, to empathize with the speaker and work to concentrate on the speaker's words and movements and the meaning of the message. It is also imperative that both the speaker and the listener confirm that their messages were sent correctly and received correctly. This can be done through signs of acknowledgment such as eye contact, and through asking questions, or making statements, that relay to the speaker that the listener is on point.

In an emergency, basic communication skills become even more important. When they are evident, people from different departments with different backgrounds and training are able to work together and communicate seamlessly and quickly to resolve issues (Lindell et al., 2007). Emergency managers have a variety of tools for this purpose at their disposal within the National Incident Management System (NIMS) and the National Response Plan (NRP), along with other government documents that help to provide frameworks and plans for emergencies. Unfortunately, roadblocks to effective communication may occur in any community and any area. One needs simply to think of a city like New York, which is home to people who come from diverse cultures and who speak many different languages, to understand the complexity of communication techniques for a community. The best practice for emergency managers is to get to know their community long before an emergency occurs. It is essential to know the traditions and cultures of the community as well as to create dialogues with cultural leaders of the community.

Crisis Management, Risk-Based Decision Making

It has been argued that uncertainty and risk are the major impediment of effective decision making. According to Lipshitz and Strauss (1997), "Conceptualizing the uncertainty that impacts decision-making as a sense of doubt that blocks or delays action has three essential features: (1) it is subjective (different individuals may experience different doubts in identical situations), (2) it is inclusive (no particular form of doubt, e.g., ignorance of future outcomes, is specified), and (3) it conceptualizes uncertainty in terms of its effects on action (hesitancy, indecisiveness, and procrastination)" (p. 150). Aakko (2004) notes that trust is another factor in the risk communication effort that significantly influences the transmission, reception, and perception of the information shared during an emergency situation. Consequently, risk communication could be summarized as a healthy distribution and sharing of information with all participants under crisis circumstances.

Much of the decision making in the real world is done in environments where the goals, constraints, and outcomes of actions are not set precisely (Bellman & Zadeh, 1970). "To deal quantitatively with imprecision, we usually employ the concepts and techniques of probability theory and, more particularly, the tools provided by decision theory, control theory and information theory" (Bellman & Zadeh, 1970, p. B-141). As March and Shapira (1987) note, risk-averse managers prefer low risks and are eager to sacrifice some expected return so as to reduce the variation in possible outcomes. Conversely, risk-seeking decision makers prefer to shoulder high risks.

In their study, Lipshitz and Strauss (1997) surveyed students in a course in decision making at the Israel Defense Forces Command and General Staff College. In their results, they identified three conceptualizations of uncertainty: as inadequate understanding, as undifferentiated alternatives, and as lack of information. Moreover, reduction, forestalling, assumption-based reasoning, weighing pro and cons, and suppression were identified as strategies for coping with uncertainty against those conceptualizations. "Inadequate understanding was primarily managed by reduction; incomplete information was primarily managed by assumption-based reasoning; and conflict among alternatives was primarily managed by weighing pros and cons" (p. 158).

March and Shapira (1987) conducted several studies on risk dealing and the ways that managers react to risk. To ensure that managers can handle risk appropriately, it is important to provide educational projects that seek to change managerial perspectives through direct training in theoretic decision-making approaches to risk and risk management.

Emergency Information Management and Community-Specific Communication Issues

Modern-day basic communication takes place through a variety of forms of technology, such as the telephone, fax, e-mail, and radio (FEMA, 2005). All of these technologies have at least some limitations, however, and one (or all) may fail during an emergency. The most basic—and still the best—practice is to use oral communication. Effective oral communication involves knowing who the audience will be and what the exact message that must be delivered, received, and understood. Although there is a large distinction between communicating one-on-one versus giving a media interview, both serve the same basic communication function. At all times and points of oral communication, it is essential to remember that posture, demeanor, and body language may either aid or hinder the message that is being delivered. It may not be necessary to be as formal when speaking to one colleague as when speaking to a large group, but understanding the time and importance of the conversation is critical.

Barriers to use of various communication techniques may include lack of training, equipment/software design, and monetary resources. For proficiency to be maintained and effective, training must be reoccurring and periodic. Equipment and software design barriers derive from these items' lack of customization. Specialized equipment and software that have been designed for particular users, situations, or functions are more efficient, but such customizations tend to be costly and have a major impact on the emergency management operating budget. These barriers to use demand that emergency managers practice resource management and have great policies on which they can rely. The policies of open access and privacy protection must be balanced to foster willingness to share. Nevertheless, the introduction of new communication technologies has helped emergency management personnel operate much more effectively in all four phases of the emergency management life cycle. As technology continues to evolve, emergency management's ability to operate successfully will likely grow in parallel.

The emergency information management process is expected to collect as much information as possible for productive decision making (Kapucu, Berman, & Wang, 2008). However, unprocessed raw information might be less useful for productive decision making; thus such data must be analyzed before being disseminated widely. The emergency information management process consists of three steps: information gathering, information processing, and processed information dissemination (Kapucu et al., 2008). As shown in **Figure 9-3**, in the first step information is identified and the availability of information is evaluated. At this point, it becomes important to control the accuracy of the information and eliminate any misconception, misinformation, or possible rumors. The second step, information processing, identifies useful information for appropriate decision making. The final step, dissemination of processed information, includes the exchange of information, modes of delivery, and timeliness and accuracy of delivery (Kapucu et al., 2008).

Kapucu et al. (2008) note that during the 2004 hurricane season in Florida, local governments engaged in intense communication practices to keep people up-to-date. Remarkable efforts were devoted to preparedness through location-specific outreaches that made extensive use of information technologies. At the same time, these authors argue, during the 2004 hurricane season there was a lack of adequate and accurate information. Although the local governments succeeded in gathering

EIM steps	Purposes	Examples of Actions in Response to Hurricanes
Information gathering	Gather sufficient and accurate information	• Gather information from a variety of sources such as weather services • Communicate with community leaders on community conditions • Create information hotlines • Assess truthfulness and integrity of initial information from first responders
Information processing	Create usable and presentable information methods	• Develop simple and easily understood languages for information presentation • Develop information messages that target different segments of community such as minority groups or the elderly • Develop visual images
Processed information dissemination	Effective decision making and coordination of information users	• Use timely information sharing among stakeholders during hurricanes • Provide frequent information updates to stakeholders during hurricanes • Use electronic roadway signs for hurricane information delivery

Source: Kapucu et al., 2008, p. 173

Figure 9-3 *Emergency Information Management Process*

information, assessing the accuracy of the information, and sharing it with other organizations, entities, and the public, there were issues with delivering the information in timely manner (Kapucu et al., 2008).

In regard to community-specific information, FEMA suggests that emergency managers use the tools that will maximize their messages' impact. It is also critical to recognize that high-tech messages are not always the best options; oftentimes, it is more important to speak in plain English to reduce confusion. No matter how they decide to communicate during disasters, FEMA asks its responders to take into consideration cultural concerns and be sure to use the right devices. Relationships should be developed before disasters occur, thereby ensuring that messages and communication will be well thought out and consistent during times of emergency.

Technology as a Communication Tool

Throughout the past decade, the cost of disaster events has drastically increased. For example, the most costly disaster in U.S. history was Hurricane Katrina in 2005, which led to more than $100 billion in estimated losses (Cutter, Emrich, Adams, Huyck, & Eguchi, 2007). Similarly, the flood of 2002 in Germany took lives of 38 people and cause approximately $16.11 billion of property damage (Schick-Richards, Fox, Juepner, Tzschirner, & Hundley, 2007). During the same decade, the world also witnessed the 2004 South Asian tsunami, which was among the deadliest of all natural disasters worldwide (Cutter et al., 2007). The increase in the devastation wrought by disasters has accentuated the need for ever more sophisticated emergency management tools, especially information technology (IT), which can alert us to what is happening around the world at any given moment. When disaster management does not have sufficient access to IT, the exacerbation of a disaster in the form of lack of resources, death, and money is sure to follow.

There is a thin line that emergency managers must be aware of when discussing IT. They must be able to take advantage of the information technologies available, which include advanced computing, geographic information systems, remote sensing, expert systems, the Internet, and wireless technology. Yet, they must not rely so much on IT that they and other citizens become overly dependent on the technology or complacent; doing so is also very dangerous.

Today, the technologies at the disposal of emergency management professionals are much more sophisticated than the tools available to practitioners in earlier eras. The advancements in IT have led to the emergence of a plethora of innovations, including better data collection and management, enhanced loss estimation techniques, and improved geographic information systems (GIS) technology (Cutter et al., 2007). Furthermore, we have been charged with improving our relationships with all stakeholders and responders so that more effective disaster management may be attainable.

According to Cutter et al. (2007), IT has had a major impact in helping manage emergencies since it was first implemented on a wide scale in emergency management. Programs such as Hazards U.S. Multi-Hazard (HAZUS-MH) run by FEMA and GIS technologies have been utilized in the mitigation and preparedness phases of emergency management. Remote sensing (RS) and the global positioning system (GPS) have also been used to assist in the response and recovery phases of emergency management. These new technologies have delivered major improvements in practitioners' ability to predict scenarios, which in turn has improved mitigation and preparedness efforts, and enhanced relief efforts during rapid response situations such as the 2004 hurricanes in Florida.

Advanced computing entails the use of computer-based modeling to simulate real-world phenomena; it confers major benefits in emergency management (Cutter et al., 2007). This technology allows forecasters and emergency managers to study the potential impact of natural disasters, such as the impact of a Category 5 hurricane. GIS has been used in emergency operation centers and disaster field offices across the United States for more than 10 years—hence its widespread popularity (Cutter et al., 2007). This technology utilizes geographic location to relate disparate data and provide ways for local governments to collect and manage location-based information. With remote sensing, "image sensors are flown by plane, helicopter, or satellite over an area of interest, collecting optical and radar-based imagery and transforming it into spatial information that can then be analyzed to gain an understanding of conditions at that moment in time" (p. 281). It is imperative in disaster situations such as hurricanes, earthquakes, and tornadoes to understand the conditions on the ground. Expert systems and the Internet allow available spatial data to be made available with only a few clicks of the mouse to emergency managers and decision makers; the major drawback of this technology is that the Internet is not a "universally embraced technology nor is it accessible everywhere" (p. 282). Lastly, wireless technology allows simple tasks, "such as talking to team members remotely rather than from a landline, as well as more complex tasks, such as collecting digital data with wireless tools" (p. 283), to be executed.

It is evident that there is a gap between having the information technologies and installing them. In 1989, Hurricane Hugo was a landmark for GIS and RS use in disaster response and recovery. Before 1989, GIS was not a component of disaster response and recovery policies (Cutter et al., 2007). Some technologies were already in hand, but it took a disaster to institutionalize them. Another example of this gap involved Hurricane Andrew in 1992. The United States had the technologies available to collect rapid and reliable geospatial information, but failure to institutionalize them before the hurricane struck meant that "real-time geographically referenced damage assessments and a systematic and consistent methodology for conducting them" were not available (Cutter et al., 2007, p. 291). Also, prior to the September 11, 2001 terrorist attacks, "mapping for emergency management purposes was such a low priority" (Cutter et al., 2007, p. 284) that a "makeshift"

EOC had to be set up on New York's Pier 92 which was devoted to the use of GIS and RS technologies in disaster rescue and recovery following the fall of the World Trade Center towers.

Garnett and Kouzmin (2007) discuss the use, misuse, and underuse of communication technology specific to Hurricane Katrina. Through a four-lens approach that follows a tradition of employing a multiperspective thinking mechanism to enable a variety of insights, they identify the following perspectives of crisis communication: interpersonal influence, media relations, technology showcase, and interorganizational networking. Each facet reinforces the significance of the previously mentioned themes of (1) the importance of using IT appropriately, which includes having staff and other key players knowledgeable enough to manage equipment and technologies, and (2) the use of social capital to prepare for and respond to disasters properly and adequately.

The first issue of crisis communication in relation to interpersonal influence focuses on the interpersonal dynamics of the key players involved in the actual crisis, specifically in the preparedness and response cycles of a disaster (Kapucu, 2006). For example, the failure of the working relationship between the Department of Homeland Security (DHS) and FEMA leadership serves as a tragic indicator of the failed response to the devastation caused by Hurricane Katrina. This case demonstrates how an untrusting, unworkable relationship between two chief stakeholders in response to crises and emergencies can wreck a response effort. Ultimately, it was the lack of social capital, the lack of cohesion, and the failure to engage in quick and effective teamwork that hindered the capabilities of each agency.

A second critical issue in crisis communication relates to media affairs. Officials' failure to disseminate proper, accurate, and timely information to the public proved devastating in the response to victims of Hurricane Katrina—not to mention the reputations of several individuals and agencies. The media represent a tool that, if used correctly, can heighten the information flow, inspire compassion in individuals not directly involved in the incident, and assist with the mitigation/prevention and recovery phases of emergency management. However, these areas are often less attractive to members of the media, who are less likely to interview people working in these phases because they are deemed "less newsworthy." It is these false notions that obstruct an all-encompassing and collaborative effort in disaster management.

Third, communication technology can be applied before, during, and after crises (Garnett & Kouzmin, 2007). This facet of response is vital to disaster efforts because technology has increased communications among first responders and other key stakeholders involved directly to such an extent that their capacity for response has grown dramatically. Nevertheless, certain vulnerabilities with communication technology, if not addressed prior to a crisis or disaster, can hamper relief efforts. These vulnerabilities may be environmental, but can also stem from the misuse of the technologies or the incompetence of the workers charged with deploying the technology. Thus adoption of technology without proper training is useless and possibly dangerous.

Garnett and Kouzmin (2007) discuss how Hurricane Katrina was a showcase for the challenges and opportunities inherent in crisis communication. Generally speaking, Hurricane Katrina is considered to exemplify a failure in crisis communication. The authors analyze this failure through four different lenses—namely, agency (the extent to which actors act reactively or proactively), transparency (the extent to which actors and their actions are visible to external stakeholders), technology (level of communication technology in each lens), and chronology (progression of scholarly emphasis on the four lenses over time).

The first lens focuses on crisis communication as interpersonal influence. This perspective deals mainly with how individuals interact with their environment and other individuals—whether they are decision makers, friends, neighbors, colleagues, or professionals—before, during, and after a crisis. The second lens addresses crisis communication as media relations, considering how the various media are used in crisis management. The third lens perceives crisis communication as a technology showcase, a view that primarily focuses on communication technologies used before, during, and after the crisis. The fourth lens emphasizes crisis communication's role as a form of interorganizational networking, focusing on written, oral, and electronic communication between various agencies and organizations from different sectors (public, private, or nonprofit).

Ideally, none of the lenses will predominate in the overall system, meaning that there should be a balance among these four dimensions. The four lenses are complementary and not necessarily mutually exclusive. However, some lenses, such as the media perspective, which rates high on transparency, technology, and chronology, overlap with other lenses, such that completely balanced attention to all of the lenses is not possible. To ensure successful crisis communication, other lenses should also be addressed. Moreover, the authors argue that viewing the world from only one perspective (i.e., through only one lens) would result in a biased and incomplete picture, focusing on only one dimension of a crisis. Such an approach, in turn, would result in a lack of transparency and accountability. In short, preoccupation with a certain lens is not a healthy approach to crisis communication and management.

Finally, Garnett and Kouzmin (2007) discuss crisis communication in relation to interorganizational networking, which includes governmental agencies, nonprofit organizations, individuals, first responders, and businesses. This aspect of crisis communication really encompasses the notion of collaboration and proper allocation of resources and materials (including human resources). With this perspective, we are once again confronted with the concept that emergency management is multifaceted, so that a wide-spectrum approach is the only way to ensure a comprehensive, all-encompassing recovery.

For example, in responding to floods in Europe, the use of technology is critical in terms of finding effective ways to minimize destruction. Blyth (1997) underscores that there is a need for a European Union (EU)-wide communication network "which will help with the coordination of requests for earth observation data for monitoring river and coastal floods" (p. 1359). Because of inadequate human resources availability and lack of information during these disasters, most EU authorities fail to respond effectively during European flooding scenarios (Blyth, 1997). The author proposes FLOODNET as a data sharing protocol, explaining its aim as a system created "to provide a communications and data distribution facility specifically designed to meet the demanding temporal requirements of flood monitoring within the European Union" (p. 1359). This network will encourage and facilitate cross-sectoral information exchange between emergency managers and experts (Blyth, 1997), highlighting the important role of information sharing and its analysis before dissemination in the emergency management life cycle.

Scholars such as Ge et al. (2009), Blyth (1997), and Liao et al. (2001) also focus on other communication-related issues in Europe. One of the important applications used during major disasters is a mobile ad hoc network (MANET). As emphasized by Ge et al. (2009), mounting cross-agency operations during disasters in those areas hit by a disaster requires some supporting communication system for command and control. "A MANET is one consisting of a set of mobile hosts which can communicate with one another and roam around at their will" (Liao et al., 2001, p. 37). A MANET management system is categorized into two groups: peer-to-peer key management and group key management that is used for secure group communication (Ge et al., 2009). Blyth (1997) notes that such a MANET network is a very reliable application for use in communications during disasters, especially during floods in Europe.

Managing Public Complacency

Complacency is a sense of confidence or self-satisfaction that is created by ignoring danger. Wang and Kapucu (2007) emphasize that public complacency is an important determinant of a society's level of preparedness. Focusing on this issue helps governments to understand and eliminate the reasons underlying the emergence of complacency. Thus the purpose of studying public complacency is to construct adequate communication policies for government officials that will enable them to improve emergency preparedness.

Wang and Kapucu (2007) believe that a truly accurate definition of public complacency "under repeated emergency threats" has not been developed yet. They define public complacency as "[the] public's propensity to believe a threat would not happen [so that] the public ignores the threat and is unwilling to prepare for the threat" (p. 58). Moreover, it is argued that public complacency includes construction of a threat by ignoring the existence of imminent threats. Even so, a well-aware public can be completely complacent. Public complacency may be just one of many reasons for poor public preparedness: "Other factors, such as lack of threat-dealing capability or poor awareness, may also cause poor public preparedness" (p. 58).

During the 2004 hurricane season, officials' repeated threat warnings might have been one of the main reasons that widespread public complacency developed in Florida. Wang and Kapucu (2007) argue that complacency might potentially increase after the public takes steps to prepare after the first warning; such measures might then give members of the public a feeling of confidence, and lead them to perceive there is no need to rush or to engage in additional preparation efforts with subsequent warnings. "They might have already known the location of hurricane shelters and evacuation routes, so there was no need to rush in until the last minute" (Wang p. 72). The other reason why public complacency might have increased in Florida was the weak effect of the hurricanes that struck first, which gave the public an impression of a less severe hurricane season. "The true lesson seems to be that after experiencing repeated threat warnings, the public becomes less alert even when a threat is imminent" (p. 72). Consequently, it is very important for government officials to take this kind of "danger fatigue" into account when disseminating warnings during disasters.

To circumvent public complacency, Wang and Kapucu (2007) suggest that it is key for decision makers to deliver specific information and in a timely manner. "The government plays a role in developing effective communication strategies to reduce public complacency; it may be able to deliver emergency information in a certain fashion to effectively reduce public complacency" (p. 73). The authors propose several effective communication strategies based on the results of their research:

- Monitoring public complacency in pre-disaster preparation is important for effective responses.
- There is a need to develop effective communication strategies to deliver the most accurate information in a timely manner to the public during emergencies.
- The styles of information delivery employed should include visual images and information tailored to specific residential groups such as elderly, children, and special-needs populations.
- Emergency managers should realize that the public response to warning is not a simple stimulus–response reaction.

Working with the Media

One of the most important instruments for spreading and receiving information and communication at all stages of a disaster is the media (Fischer, 1999; Tierney, Bevc, & Kuligowski, 2006; Vasterman, Yzermans, & Dirkzwager, 2005). It has been argued that the mass media create our perceptions of disasters. For instance, the images of what Chernobyl tragedy survivors experienced were widely disseminated by the television and print news media. Consequently, the accuracy of information spread by media is vital in forming the right perceptions among citizens and experts alike. "If the media accurately portrays how citizens and emergency personnel respond, then the viewer is more likely to gain an accurate perception and vice versa" (Fischer, 1999).

Nowadays, we can think of hundreds of types of media sources that are provided by the developed technology opportunities. For instance, Wang and Kapucu (2007), reporting on their study of public complacency, encourage government to use more electronic media in emergency information delivery. Moreover, it would be very productive to see the collaboration of or network information sharing between media and online social networks such as Facebook, Twitter, and others in an emergency setting. Parsons (1996) recommends constructing crisis news centers as soon as possible during disasters, so that a central source is available to feed information to the public and other stakeholders. Of course, providing accurate information without rumors is a very difficult task, and government monitoring of any information disseminated by official agencies is vital (Wang & Kapucu, 2007).

Establishing partnerships with both local and national media is important for providing accurate and timely information to the public (Bullock, Haddow, Coppola, Ergin, Westerman, & Yeletaysi, 2006; Kapucu et al., 2008; Parsons, 1996). One suggestion for how government should work with media during disasters comes from Parsons (1996); his advice is to be open and honest. According to Kapucu et al. (2008), having a prior relationship with media sources alters and improves the effectiveness of the response operations and public disaster preparedness; this relationship could take the form of "preseason coordination meetings with the media and community organizations [that] are designed to plan for effective coordination during emergencies" (p. 176). According to Fischer (1999), communities that establish an appropriate public information plan that anticipates media and community needs are more effective in maintaining good relationships with the media. At the same time, it is argued that organizational-level differences among the sources spreading information to the mass media play an important role in creating myths during an incident. For instance, during Hurricane Gilbert, differences between local and national media in spreading information occurred because they relied on different sources (Fischer, 1999).

Conclusion

Emergency management professionals should keep several important aspects in mind when communicating risks before, during, and after a crisis. First, knowing the audience for the message and understanding what their needs may be are important. Second, being an active speaker or listener—for example, by asking questions, remaining engaged, and providing feedback—is critical. Third, the emergency management professional should understand that various tools and assets for communication, such as technology, may not always be there; thus practicing effective communication is necessary, as it will be the bottom-line necessity in an emergency. Lastly, interorganizational relationships and networking as well as media and technology are effective tools for crisis communication.

Review Questions

1. What is a risk perception and why is it important? Which factors influence people's perception of risks?
2. Name the possible outcomes of communication action implementation.
3. What are the basic risk communication functions that emergency managers should address in the continuing hazard phase? What are the tasks of risk communication?
4. What are some important communication strategies that emergency managers must undertake to develop specific messages for different groups?
5. You have been asked by your city manager to evaluate the community's risk communication plan. The city council does not think it is necessary to spend money evaluating the program. How would you convince council members of the importance of evaluating the communication program?
6. How might the information you gained from this chapter affect you personally and professionally?

References

Aakko, E. (2004). Risk communication, risk perception and public health. *Wisconsin Medical Journal, 103*(1), 25–27.

Auf der Heide, E. (n.d.). Disaster response: Principles of preparation and coordination. Retrieved from http://orgmail2.coe-dmha.org/dr/static.htm.

Bazerman, M. H., & Watkins, M. D. (2004). *Predictable surprises: The disasters you should have seen coming and how to prevent them.* Boston: Harvard Business School Press.

Bellman, R. E., & Zadeh, L. A. (1970). Decision-making in a fuzzy environment. *Management Science, 17*(4), B141–B164.

Blyth, K. (1997). FLOODNET: A telenetwork for acquisition, processing and dissemination of earth observation data for monitoring and emergency management of floods. *Hydrological Processes, 11,* 1159–1375.

Bullock, J. A., Haddow, G. D., Coppola, D., Ergin, E., Westerman, L., & Yeletaysi, S. (2006). *Introduction to homeland security.* Burlington, MA: Elsevier.

Burnett, J. J. (1998). A strategic approach to managing crises. *Public Relations Review, 24*(4), 475–488.

Coombs, T. (1999). *Ongoing crisis communication: Planning, managing and responding.* Thousand Oaks, CA: Sage.

Cutter, S. L., Emrich, C. T., Adams, B. J., Huyck, C. K., & Eguchi, R. T. (2007). New information technologies in emergency management. In W. L. Waugh & K. Tierney (Eds.), *Emergency management: Principles and practice for local government* (pp. 274–297). Washington, DC: ICMA Press.

Department of Transportation (DOT). (1998). Risk based decision-making in the hazardous materials safety program. Retrieved March 27, 2010, from www.phmsa.dot.gov/staticfiles/PHMSA/.../Files/riskprog.pdf.

Federal Emergency Management Agency (FEMA). (December 2005). Effective communication. Retrieved September 20, 2009, from http://training.fema.gov/EMIWeb/IS/IS242lst.asp.

Fischer, H. W. III. (1999). Hurricane Georges: The experience of the media and emergency management of the Mississippi Gulf Coast. Quick Response Report #117. University of Colorado. Retrieved April 5, 2010, from http://www.colorado.edu/hazards/qr/qr117.html.

Garnett, J. L., & Kouzmin, A. (2007). Communicating throughout Katrina: Competing and complementary conceptual lenses on crisis communication. *Public Administration Review, 67*(S1), 171–188.

Ge, M., Lam, K. Y., Gollmann, G., Chung, S. L., Chang, C. C., & Li, J. B. (2009). A robust certification service for highly dynamic MANET in emergency tasks. *International Journal of Communication Systems, 22*(1),177–1197.

Gibbons, D. E. (Ed.). (2007). *Communicable crises: Prevention, response, and recovery in the global arena.* Charlotte. NC: Information Age Publishing.

Kapucu, N. (2006). Interagency communication networks during emergencies: Boundary spanners in multi-agency coordination. *American Review of Public Administration, 36*(2), 207–225.

Kapucu, N., Berman, E. M., & Wang, X. H. (2008). Emergency information management and public disaster preparedness: Lessons from the 2004 Florida hurricane season. *International Journal of Mass Emergencies and Disasters, 26*(3), 169–196.

Liao, W., Sheu, J., & Tseng, Y. (2001). GRID: A fully location-aware routing protocol for mobile ad hoc networks. *Telecommunication Systems, 18*(3), 37–60.

Lindell, M. K., Prater, C., & Perry, R. W. (2007). *Introduction to emergency management.* Hoboken, NJ: Wiley.

Lipshitz, R., & Strauss, O. (1997). Coping with uncertainty: A naturalistic decision-making analysis. *Organizational Behavior and Human Decision Processes, 69*(2), 149–163.

March, J. G., & Shapira, Z. (1987). Managerial perspectives on risk and risk taking. *Management Science, 33*(11), 1404–1418.

National Research Council of the National Academies (NRC). (2006). *Facing hazards and disasters: Understanding human dimensions.* Washington, DC: National Academies Press.

Özerdem, A., & Jacoby, T. (2006). *Disaster management and civil society: Earthquake relief in Japan, Turkey and India.* London: I. B. Tauris.

Parsons, W. (1996). Crisis management. *Career Development International, 1*(5), 26–28.

Paton, D. (2007). Preparing for natural hazards: The role of community trust. *Disaster Prevention and Management, 16*(3), 370–379.

Ritchie, B. W. (2005). Chaos, crises and disasters: A strategic approach to crisis management in the tourism industry. *Tourism Management, 25*(6), 669–683.

Schick-Richards, L., Fox, P., Juepner, R., Tzschirner, M., & Hundley, S. (2007). *A comparison of flood management practices between Germany and the USA: An undergraduate research project on sustainable practices.* American Society for Engineering Education.

Schneider, S. K. (1995). Flirting with disaster: Public management in crisis situations. Armonk, NY: M. E. Sharpe.

Tierney, K., Bevc, C., & Kuligowski, E. (2006). Metaphors matter: Disaster myths, media frames, and their consequences in Hurricane Katrina. *Annals of the American Academy of Political and Social Science, 604,* 57–81.

Tierney, K. J., Lindell, M. K., & Perry, R. W. (2001). *Facing the unexpected: Disaster preparedness and response in the United States.* Washington, DC: Joseph Henry Press.

Vasterman, P., Yzermans, C. J., & Dirkzwager, A. J. E. (2005). The role of the media and media hypes in the aftermath of disasters. (Second edition). *Epidemiologic Reviews, 27,* 107–114.

Wang, X. H., & Kapucu, N. (2007). Public complacency under repeated emergency threats: Some empirical evidence. *Journal of Public Administration Research and Theory, 18,* 57–78.

Chapter 10

Building an Effective Emergency Management Organization

Chapter Objectives

- Discuss individual and organizational outcomes.
- Discuss contingency planning.
- Analyze training and exercises.
- Examine the Incident Command System.
- Analyze crisis management team and crisis decision making.
- Describe ways of financing emergency management.

Introduction

Success in emergency management is directly related to the effectiveness of the emergency management organizations involved. This chapter describes the activities needed to build effective emergency management organizations, beginning with the fundamentals of running a local emergency management agency. An effective emergency management organization is defined as follows: "when applied during a disaster, [the organization] will provide the levels of protection for life and property, and recovery assistance, which are acceptable to citizens of the community" (Public Entity Risk Institute [PERI], 2001, p. 1). Such an objective is particularly important, because developing effective emergency management systems is equivalent to establishing reliable emergency response systems (Jackson, Faith, & Willis, 2010). Therefore, the main focus of this chapter is the development of a local emergency management agency or response team that is able to create high organizational and individual outcomes.

The chapter also discusses the necessity of establishing horizontal linkages among local government agencies. In addition, a local emergency management agency can provide vertical linkages downward to households and businesses and upward to state and central agencies. To build an effective emergency management organization, it is necessary to understand the various relationships among stakeholders, as described in Chapter 6.

The chapter continues by addressing issues related to finance and budgeting for an emergency management organization, including identifying the sources of funding and ways to utilize these sources. To conclude, it underlines the importance of regional and international structures in achieving effective results through the actions of emergency management organizations.

Individual and Organizational Outcomes

The first step in creating an emergency management organization is to develop a local emergency management agency (LEMA). The head of this organization is referred to as the local emergency manager, and will report to the chief administrative officer (CAO), who could be the mayor or city manager (Lindell, Prater, & Perry, 2007). It is the responsibility of the local emergency manager to develop a plan that describes the agency's annual goals, to organize a budget for the fiscal year, and to identify sources of funding for the agency (Lindell et al., 2007). To ensure efficiency, it is important for the organization to work both horizontally and vertically with all collaborating agencies and members.

The effectiveness of a LEMA is measured by assessing multiple determinants, including the following factors: organizational climate, individual outcomes, and organizational outcomes. An organizational climate is a pattern of collective beliefs, shared perceptions or experiences of policies, and behaviors or thoughts that are communicated to members through interaction and through their work environment (Lindell et al., 2007; Schneider, Ehrhart, & Ehrhart, 2010). Having a healthy, productive climate is extremely important, as emergency management depends on the motivation and effectiveness of all participants. LEMAs can motivate their members by establishing positive leadership, teamwork projects, job conditions, and reward schemes. Each component correlates with individual and organizational outcomes. Individuals' dedication and commitment to organizational goals, the satisfaction of their personal and social needs, and the satisfaction of their purposive needs (i.e., the feeling of doing something positive) will all affect individual outcomes (Lindell et al., 2007). Increasing job satisfaction by providing rewards, incentives, flexibility, and independence in the work environment for the members will result in positive outcomes for these individuals. With positive individual outcomes come organizational outcomes that will improve overall performance (Lindell et al., 2007; Perry & Lindell, 2007).

Two forms of staff dedication are affective and continuance commitment (Lindell et al., 2007; Perry & Lindell, 2007). Affective commitment is emotional in nature; for individual staff members, it is influenced by "organizational leadership, their perceptions of their own competence, role clarity, identification with organization's goals, [and] opportunity for reward" (Lindell et al., 2007, p. 63). Continuance commitment is related to material as well as emotional satisfaction of the employees. Although salary and other benefits are factors that keep people working for the organization, they do not guarantee high performance of the individuals (Lindell et al., 2007). Maiero (2002), for example, emphasizes the multifaceted nature of the relationship between successful outcomes and employee satisfaction. His study on emergency medical services (EMS) in Contra Costa County, California, revealed that leadership and quality management, better material conditions (i.e., higher pay), and quality teamwork and environment are the important factors that contribute to higher individual satisfaction. Pillai and Williams' (2004) study found a positive relationship between leadership and performance. Specifically, in their research transformational leadership had a direct relationship with commitment to organization and perceived unit performance.

In addition to individual outcomes, organizational outcomes play a role in determining the effectiveness of emergency management agencies. Emergency management programs, technical analysis such as vulnerabilities assessment, and public education and outreach efforts are important organizational outputs of emergency management agencies. The quality, effectiveness, and cost of such plans are important elements of organizational outcomes (Lindell et al., 2007). As Henstra (2010) notes, constant monitoring of emergency management programs ensures the quality and the effectiveness of work, bolsters citizen awareness of emergency management precepts, and strengthens the accountability of the organization. The four phases of emergency management constitute the backbone of the emergency management programs. At the local, state, or national level, the requirements of these phases may be fulfilled by organizations from the public, private, and nonprofit sectors. Despite this distribution of tasks, emergency management organizations bear overall responsibility for the achievements in each phase.

Henstra (2010) has developed a list of indicators for the effectiveness of the programs. For preparedness, his indicators include the "emergency manager, program committee, hazard identification and risk assessment, emergency response plan, plan review, emergency management bylaw, training and exercises, mutual aid agreement, critical infrastructure protection, planning for people with special needs, [and] engagement with [the] business community." For the mitigation phase, salient indicators are the "mitigation plan, warning system, public education, dangerous goods routing bylaw, [and] risk-based land use planning." For the response phase, the "emergency operations center, incident management system, evacuation plan, emergency shelter arrangements, volunteer management, community emergency response teams, search and rescue, [and] emergency public information" are the indicators of effectiveness. Finally, for the recovery phase, Henstra identifies "recovery plans, continuity of operations planning, damage assessment, debris management, [and] rehabilitation" as indicators (p. 241).

Table 10-1 *Characteristics for Effective Emergency Management Organizational Structure*

- Roles of elected officials defined
- Strong and definitive lines of command
- Similar routine and disaster organizational structures
- Emergency management procedures are as close to routine operational procedures as possible
- Good interpersonal relationships
- Emergency management planning is an ongoing activity
- All-hazards approach
- Disaster prevention and mitigation
- Motivation provided for involvement in the emergency management program
- Citizen involvement
- Strong coordination among participating agencies
- Public–private cooperation
- Multiple use of resources
- Public information function clearly defined
- Ongoing monitoring for potential disasters
- Internal alerting procedures
- Ability to alert the public maximized
- Active intergovernmental coordination
- Ability to maintain comprehensive records during a disaster
- Eligibility for state and federal subsidies considered

Source: PERI, 2001

The availability of well-thought-out plans and programs for emergencies and crises plays an important role in emergency management. Effective implementation of these plans and programs is the key factor in achieving success. PERI (2001), for example, has addressed the importance of organizational structure for effective emergency management by preparing a checklist of items that local emergency managers must consider when assessing their capacity (**Table 10-1**).

Emergency management requires the services of multiple agencies, which must learn to collaborate with one another if they are all to be effective. Like most traditional organizations, emergency management organizations do not engage in a top-down approach, as local officials are commonly those most immediately responsible for action. However, as Sylves (2008) discusses, this varied approach is often threatened by the "command and control strategies" that the Department of Homeland Security (DHS) or other central agency will often try to enforce.

Contingency Planning

Bloom and Menefee (1994) argue that traditional organizational planning efforts are vital, yet limit future possibilities. Scenario and contingency planning are designed to "prepare for dramatic and rapid changes in the environment" (Bloom & Menefee, 1994, p. 224). Scenario planning, which is widely used in emergency management planning, aims to preempt possible future events. Conventional plans describe the actions to be taken during emergencies, needs that may arise, and resources that might be required to support these actions (Perry, 2004). However, the unexpected and complex nature of disasters requires emergency management professionals to take additional precautions. Contingency planning attempts to fill the gaps, aiming to enhance preparedness for unexpected incidents.

A comprehensive discussion of contingency planning can be found in Bruins' (2000) study, which identifies the purpose of contingency planning as follows: "to develop risk and crisis management, as well as preparedness, mitigation and response options, in order to avert or minimize the impact of adverse development" (p. 69). Contingency planning includes planning for extreme but very low-probability cases, which might not be politically and economically viable because they can be impossible to handle (ten Brinke, Kolen, Dollee, van Waveren, & Wouters, 2010). Nevertheless, this form of planning forces managers to think more broadly about possible events (Clarke, 2006, as cited in ten Brinke et al., 2010). Contingency planning ought to include multiple scenarios and assess their potential impact on both a variety of sectors and individuals (Bruins, 2000).

Training and Exercises

Successful emergency management is very much about establishing a sequence of planning, training, and exercising efforts to prepare for risks (Perry, 2004). Training is a learning process that includes the education of emergency management professionals so as to build the necessary knowledge, skills, and abilities (KSAs) in these individuals that will enable them to reach the goals of an organization. This learning process helps individuals both to develop themselves and to enhance the team's overall expertise (Ford & Schmidt, 2000). Training focuses on the development of KSAs in three fields: technical, interpersonal, and system/process competencies. Technical competencies relate directly to the job of conducting emergency management activities. Development of interpersonal competencies aims to enhance the social capital between different actors of emergency management, thereby helping them overcome conflicts, communicate effectively, and promote the sharing of ideas. Lastly, building system competencies increases understanding of the work process of individuals (Ford & Schmidt, 2000).

In Canada, the United States, and Australia, exercises are referred to as drills; in Europe, they are called simulations (Perry, 2004). The three most common types of exercises are tabletop, functional, and full-scale (Perry, 2004; Peterson & Perry, 1999). Tabletop exercises are relatively simple; they usually include simulations in narrative form, and participants complete their role and tasks verbally. Functional exercises are more complex, testing the effectiveness of specific functions.

For instance, as Perry (2004) discusses, a functional exercise may aim to see the operational ability of an emergency medical system in the case of a "dirty bomb" attack. Full-scale exercises are the most extensive; Perry (2004) summarizes their purpose as "to test all or a major portion of the functions specified in an emergency response plan" (p. 67). The accomplishment of an emergency plan requires exercising several subfunctions. Full-scale exercises require the involvement of a full staff of evaluators and controllers, several individuals to fill roles that will be incorporated in the exercise scenario (e.g., victims and other people), and equipment to establish a realistic disaster scene (Peterson & Perry, 1999). Such exercises require extensive planning and costly resources, and they are largely being replaced with functional or tabletop exercises.

Perry (2004) and Peterson and Perry (1999) explicitly recognize the significant contributions made by exercises to both organizational and individual outcomes. From an organizational outcomes standpoint, exercises reveal the potential defects and weaknesses in plans and identify challenges in their implementation. They can also bring to light defective equipment and nonfunctional communication systems. Organizations strengthen their relationships through emergency drills, and strong interorganizational relationships in turn decrease the potential transaction costs of collaboration. Publicizing drills and simulations serves a public education function, creating an awareness that government is proactive in managing emergencies and crises. Lastly, exercises provide for a test of the viability and functionality of emergency management networks (Peterson & Perry, 1999).

Exercises can also influence individual outcomes. Peterson and Perry (1999) note that exercises frequently alter the perceptions of the individuals who participate in exercises. In their research on fire fighters, these researchers found that "exercises have the ability to change the participant perception of teamwork, response network effectiveness, training adequacy, equipment adequacy, and job risk" (p. 252).

Scott et al. (2006) found similar results regarding the impact of training on individual and team skills. In an examination of how training affected the individuals and teams involved in emergency medical response, these authors recognized that participating in exercises that include simulation enhances team mastery of specific skills. Moreover, their study indicated that individual skill acquisition occurred in certain areas.

Another study that reinforced the findings on the positive impact of training on emergency management personnel was conducted by Chi et al. (2001) in Taiwan. These authors observed that tabletop exercises helped to solidify disaster preparedness plans for emergency medical technicians, but argued that conducting fewer types of exercises limits the abilities of emergency management personnel to develop. For instance, the authors mentioned that in Taiwan, mostly field training and exercises—which focus on evacuation, rescue, and triage skills—were conducted. Based on the responses of the participants, their study suggests that tabletop exercises are effective in highlighting issues related to the necessity for coordination, communication, and preparedness of equipment and logistics (Chi et al., 2001).

Incident Command Systems Versus Horizontal Relationships

In the United States, the federal government has designated local and state authorities as the primary responders and funders for disasters occurring within their regions, and has removed itself as much as possible from providing "response" services. Using the National Response Framework (NRF) to identify its role in the structure of emergency management, the federal government has taken a bottom-up approach, rather than top-down directive, toward defining the roles and responsibilities of emergency managers. In this regard, the federal government's main responsibility is to coordinate and streamline the emergency management process through the National Incident Management System (NIMS), rather than to provide funding or direct services.

A second major theme that permeates the U.S. government's approach to emergency management is that a specific "process" exists that outlines the paths emergency managers must traverse to receive federal funding and support. This process necessitates the adoption of an all-inclusive approach to emergency management, in which partners from the nonprofit and private sectors must be a part of local and state government agendas. However, the lack of funding available to support this process has spurred a great deal of competition, which seems to have improved the emergency management system. Collaboration and forward-thinking budgeting can also provide stop-gap measures to counteract the lack of dedicated emergency management funds.

During his administration, President Bill Clinton sought to evaluate FEMA in effort to make it "work better, and cost less" (Sylves, 2007, p. 136). Prior to the creation of DHS, FEMA was responsible for providing much of the emergency management support to local and state officials. Currently, "FEMA's job is to plan, prepare, and respond to disasters in a way that functionally coordinates, or helps to coordinate, the provision of federal resources, human-power, and equipment possessed by 'other' federal departments, agencies, or offices" (Sylves, 2008, p. 137). In addition to the establishment of DHS, several other changes have been made to the federal emergency management system in recent years: the establishment of the NRF, the shift from the Federal Response Plan to the National Response Plan (NRP), and the development of NIMS and the Incident Command Systems (ICS), a component of NIMS. The NRP sought to create a national approach that would advance coordination and implementation of existing plans, while enforcing a consistent approach to managing an incident. Additionally, NIMS was established to incorporate "best practices" into a national approach to incident management across all levels of jurisdiction (Sylves, 2008, p. 150). Some critics, however, have questioned the value of these processes.

Sylves (2008) has examined the role of intergovernmental relationships in coordinating emergency management processes. The core functions and agencies responsible for emergency management in the United States clearly overlap, resulting to some degree in a grab for power by the major players. Despite this fact, the current system does have some advantages. Specifically, emergency management is dynamic, especially as it relates to terrorism responses, and needs a unified approach. Since the terrorist attacks on September 11, 2001, the United States has sought to be proactive in approaches to preempt any attack on the nation and its allies; however, such action requires a great deal of information collection, sharing, processing, and managing—a broad endeavor that requires the services of multiple agencies. To streamline these efforts, DHS has required all states to adopt NIMS as a condition of receiving federal funding for emergency management. DHS has also made it easier for emergency managers to familiarize themselves with the new structures and terminology associated with NIMS and the NRF through FEMA's Emergency Management Institute (EMI).

NIMS is designed to be a "core set of doctrines, principles, terminology, and organizational processes" (Sylves, 2008, p. 151) that facilities a standardized approach to emergency management. However, this standardization requires the outlay of large amounts of (typically scarce) federal funds, which has created competition among stakeholders for the necessary financial resources; such jousting for money is often perceived as counterproductive to the goal of establishing an effective system. Of course, pursuing these scarce funds may also lead to a more unified approach among emergency players as local and state governments and agencies recognize that sharing of information, equipment, and other resources can reduce redundancy and costs of the emergency process, among other benefits.

Leveraging resources from the plethora of volunteer organizations (VOLOGs) that participate in different aspects of the disaster cycle is one source of funding that NIMS encourages. These funding sources do not require state or federal reimbursement after disaster recovery is complete. VOLOGs are key players that have ongoing roles in emergency management regardless of the crisis or stage in the cycle. Experience has shown that the first responders to any disaster are usually those who are located nearby, and at the time of an incident nonprofit organizations such as the Red Cross and the Salvation Army are typically the quickest to mobilize and provide assistance to victims. This "growing trend of cooperation and coordination of volunteer organizations that participates in disaster relief" (Sylves, 2008, p. 159) is exemplified by the establishment of National Volunteer Organizations Active in Disaster (NVOAD), which plays a critical role in emergency management. Including these organizations in local, state, and federal disaster planning is crucial in achieving the best response and recovery possible after an emergency. However, when the nonprofit and public sectors fall short in these endeavors, the federal government has turned to the private sector in times of crisis.

Hiring private contractors to perform specific jobs is an emerging trend in the United States' emergency management design. The reason for doing so is simple: Often "contractors have more flexibility and freedom to complete work" at a lesser cost than government agencies (Sylves, 2008, p. 164). The disadvantage of involving the private sector in the emergency response derives from the lack of regulation via internal controls applied to such organizations. During a disaster, it is often necessary for the government to award a contract to private contractors without a competitive bidding process, unintentionally creating an opportunity for unethical practices by those involved. Nevertheless, DHS and FEMA continue to rely on the services of these kinds of private contractors during an emergency. This trend certainly raises the question of whether a common code of conduct or ethics should be applied to all parties who work in the emergency management field, whether they belong to the private sector or not.

While most disasters, including some terrorist attacks, can be handled by civilian emergency managers, some prolonged and major disasters can prove overwhelming for civilian, nonprofit, private, and governmental agencies, requiring the assistance of the military to provide an adequate response. Throughout history, the National Guard has been used to respond to domestic as well as international crises. The role of the National Guard and the creation of the Northern Command (NORTHCOM) in 2002 have facilitated the use of the military in the past decade to complement emergency management in the United States. However, merging of military with civilian personnel can end up "undermining or supplanting the authority of mayors and governors [which] in a moment of national crises would be a mistake" (Sylves, 2008, p. 191). It could be considered counterintuitive for the federal government to usurp power from state and local governments after it has defined the U.S. emergency management system based on bottom-up administration.

Sylves (2008) also discusses the important role of voluntary agencies— including nonprofit organizations, church groups, and community service groups— in coordination of resources during an incident. These voluntary groups often provide a coordinated effort under NVOAD, which include 49 national organizations in its members.

Sylves (2008) concludes by discussing the vital role of contracts and negotiations within intergovernmental relationships. As this author notes, "Those who seek to understand the intergovernmental relations of disaster management need to understand the world of government contracting" (p. 168).

Crisis Management Teams

The importance of collaboration and teamwork has been repeatedly emphasized throughout this book. Team building establishes a common task force of different actors to act in collaborative actions, a method widely used in handling disasters.

Schaafstal, Johnston, and Oser (2001) describe emergency management as requiring a "team of teams." Teams from different backgrounds come together to solve problems stemming from the adverse effects of emergencies. As mentioned in earlier chapters, formations such as Community Emergency Response Teams (CERT) and Business Emergency Response Teams (BERT) work together with emergency management officials and formal crisis management teams to enhance the effectiveness of the emergency management efforts.

A variety of KSAs are needed both for teams and for individual team members to ensure effectiveness of the overall response (Crichton & Flin, 2004). Team skills include coordination, communication, synchronization, and adaptation of behaviors and actions (Salas & Cannon-Bowers, 1997, as cited in Crichton & Flin, 2004). In addition, Crichton and Flin (2004) identify several other skills that are sought in teams: teamwork, stress management, decision making, leadership, and situational awareness. Training interventions and exercises can be used to strengthen the skills needed for teamwork. Such training should not only seek to enhance team capacity and communication, but also bolster interteam coordination and communication capacity (Schaafstal et al., 2001).

The effectiveness of emergency management organizations is also related to the success of the decision-making mechanism in each organization. Some scholars consider crisis decision making from an individual perspective (Allison & Zelikov, 1999; Bigley & Roberts, 2001; Flin, Slaven, & Stewart, 1996; Flueler, 2006); others examine it from a teamwork approach (Driskell & Salas, 1991; Salas, Burke, & Samman, 2001; Takada, 2004) or organizational standpoint (Quarantelli, 1997; Rosenthal & Kouzmin, 1997). Regardless of the unit of decision making, decisions need to be made in a rapid, smooth, and effective manner.

The interorganizational nature of emergency management requires a collaborative approach in decision-making mechanisms, and the interdependency of partners is directly associated with this collaboration. Communication and information sharing are two vital constituents of collaborative decision making. First, strong communication leads to better connectivity between organizations, and technological tools can be deployed to facilitate such interactions. Second, the quality of information plays a role in determining its impact, which is influenced by information reliability, availability, relevance, flow, and volume (Carley & Lin, 1997). In addition, environmental factors such as situational stress, time pressure, uncertainty, and complexity of situations influence the decision-making process, and failure to manage these factors effectively often leads to negative outcomes in decision making.

The seamlessness of collaboration between emergency management actors reflects the structure of organizations and their goals. Organizational structure, culture, and habits may determine willingness to collaborate, to establish means of communication, and to share information with others. Clashes between organizational cultures can diminish the effectiveness of the collaboration and, therefore, of the organizations itself. Schaafstal et al. (2001) describe this challenging condition as failure of the "team of teams" (p. 617).

Training for emergency management organizations that includes team building, teamwork, and decision-making exercises could improve the effectiveness of these organizations. Schaafstal et al. (2001) point out the benefits of having cross-trained teams in which team members are trained in the duties of colleagues so they can anticipate one another's needs, learn about their tasks, and better appreciate the ultimate goal of the team.

Financing Emergency Management

To provide the necessary services to their community members, emergency management offices across the globe must work together with other agencies to secure support and resources for their operations. Because some of these resources come from national-level agencies, emergency managers must understand how the national allocation system operates so that they can obtain the most resources possible. Emergency managers are continuously seeking additional stakeholders and funding sources to complete their mission of creating an agency that effectively protects its community members and property.

The decentralized approach to emergency management in the United States has placed the burden of emergency management funding squarely on the shoulders of local and state governments. As a consequence, these governments must allocate specific funding for emergency management in their budgets. Using federal and state grants and tax collection as tools of income, local emergency managers have been able to increase funding streams to their departments. The disadvantages associated with these sources include the risks of grant-regulated policy revision, budgeting cutbacks, and the counterproductive politics involved in obtaining a portion of local tax income. Communities, for their part, stand to gain more than they lose from funding emergency management initiatives.

Redirecting taxes toward supporting emergency management departments could have a positive effect on a community as a whole. First, getting local government involved in planning the budgets for emergency management agencies via local taxes and fees may serve to increase awareness of the importance of emergency management. Second, local fees and taxes go toward improving many different entities, including public schools and nonprofit organizations. Therefore, linking emergency management to other community objectives through voting on tax division and breakdowns may stimulate more citizen participation in these programs. Third, emergency management funding may benefit the city by supporting disaster mitigation efforts such as building parks or river walks.

Some emergency managers may have access to sources of funding other local income and property taxes. Payments in lieu of taxes (PILOT)—that is, voluntary payments made by otherwise tax-exempt organizations such as churches, hospitals, and colleges—are viable sources of income because tax-exempt organizations enjoy many of the benefits of emergency management services. Business improvement districts (BIDs) are another means through which emergency managers can fund mitigation efforts and have other societal benefits as well, much like the creation of parks and river walks discussed previously. Nevertheless, tax exemptions and abatements remain the most commonly used method to have individuals and businesses contribute to mitigation measures. Local governments may also issue bonds to finance emergency management activities whose costs exceed their budgetary limits. This form of capital budgeting allows local governments to decrease disaster vulnerability and is frequently used to finance infrastructure expenditures on a post-disaster basis.

FEMA often provides financial assistance in the form of pre-disaster planning grants and post-disaster grants to cover the cost of recovery. Pertinent to local disaster management is the Public Assistance Grant Program. Managers may also receive grant funding from one of six major sources: the State Homeland Security Grant Program, the Urban Area Security Initiative, the Law Enforcement Terrorism Program, the Emergency Management Performance Grant Program, the Assistance to Firefighters Grant Program, and the Metropolitan Medical Response System. Another cost-efficient way for emergency agencies to function is through coproduction or by leveraging the support of citizens, nonprofit organizations, and the private sector to support disaster mitigation. Citizen Corps is one of the most well-known examples of coproduction, in which "safe construction" initiatives are used to create better-built homes whose construction decreases post-disaster costs.

In the United States, local municipalities and counties have historically allocated a larger portion of their revenues to emergency management than state and federal governments. Over the last decade, however, there has been a significant increase in federal funding in the form of both categorical and block grants. Block grants are funding sources that are provided to state and local governments with general supervision. They allow grantees flexibility in implementing local strategies for reaching goals designated by the federal government through grants (Government Accounting Office [GAO], 2003). By comparison, categorical grants are designed to address specific activities or issues such as flood mitigation assistance, hazard mitigation, and state fire training systems; they do not provide as much flexibility as block grants (Sylves, 2007). These grants help emergency managers meet the increasing budget gaps that are emerging as federal government funding decreases.

The U.S. democratic system has constrained funding through the "pass-through approach" of state governments (Sylves, 2007, p. 303). With this approach, funds provided to local governments by the federal government are distributed through state governments. According to Waugh and Tierney (2007), only one-third of the total funding of local governments comes from outside local municipalities. Even though emergency management provides indirect benefits to all community stakeholders, the funding process filters out its resources. The funding remaining for local governments in some instances is significantly reduced due to administrative fees charged on the grant.

Once the money is obtained and incorporated into the budgets of local municipalities, there are considerations for further allocation that emergency managers must understand. Entitlements are mandatory allocations that local governments must pay first; they include pension plans, outstanding debt, and contract payments. The public's predilection also guides political aspects of funding, which will be redirected toward other initiatives if the public does not perceive emergency management to be a priority. Taxes and fees can provide additional funding, with property tax being one of the largest sources of support for local emergency management programs. In Tulsa's Mooser Creek area, residents were educated and given the opportunity to add a sales tax to fund both quality of living and disaster mitigation upgrades to their community (Sylves, 2007). Ultimately, a 2.9 percent sales tax was levied, with the proceeds going toward improving the creek and protecting residents from possible flooding.

Some strategic public–private and community partnerships, specialized privatization initiatives, and smart capital budgeting strategies used by local governments have shown that it is possible to implement practical solutions to increase emergency management funding. Whether federal funding is provided on a pre-disaster or post-disaster basis, it is clear that officials must aggressively research all available options to supplement their income, especially through assistance programs such as the Public Assistance Grant Program, Individual and Family Grant Program, and Mitigation Grant Program, to help their communities and local economies recover as quickly from a disaster as possible (Sylves, 2007).

Regional and International Structures

International stakeholders in emergency management are covered in Chapter 12 of this book, but this section addresses the role of regional and supranational organizations in supporting emergency management organizations. Both regional and supranational organizations often make substantial contributions to relief efforts in disaster-stricken areas.

In the United States, local governments and states may sign regional agreements that promise to provide interjurisdictional aid in case of a disaster. The Emergency Management Assistance Compact (EMAC) is the most well-established and effective agreement among states for responding disasters. EMAC was first introduced by the state of Florida after Hurricane Andrew in 1993 and initially covered cooperation among southern states. It was approved by Congress in 1996 as Public Law 104-321, with states subsequently required to incorporate EMAC into their own laws for membership purposes. Today the 50 states, the District of Columbia, Puerto Rico, and the U.S. Virgin Islands are the members of the EMAC (Kapucu, Augustin, & Garayev, 2009). Regional assistance agreements such as EMAC function as interorganizational collaboration mechanisms, with EMAC committee and executive positions being filled by the officials from the member states. The effectiveness of these mechanisms and, therefore, the participating organizations can be maintained by strong communication in an interagency context. Trust and interdependence are the lifeblood of the continuity of the interagency relationship. Partnering states and organizations have to be committed to maintaining the relationship and fulfilling their responsibilities (Kapucu et al., 2009).

The international disaster aid system has been formed through a series of nonbinding agreements between institutions. The effectiveness of this system and the actions of the relief organizations can be scrutinized both in the context of their interorganizational relations and in terms of their relations with victim countries. Thus international relief efforts have two sides—relations with disaster-stricken countries and relations with other international organizations—in an environment where there is no legally binding structure. International organizations may provide help via direct contact with victims, by working with governments of disaster-stricken areas, or by providing support and funding to other local response and relief organizations. In an interorganizational coordination context, interpersonal relationships, informal networks, and a common organizational culture are vital to ensure the effectiveness of the network. Unfortunately, many factors have the potential to impede effective action of international actors in providing disaster response. Because there is no single authority in international disaster relief, uniting different organizations around a single goal or structure can prove challenging. Competition for scarce resources, direct and administrative costs, and cultural and language barriers among the organizations also have the potential to undermine the success of the coordination necessary for effectiveness (see Chapter 12 for more on international emergency and crisis management structure).

In an international community and victim country relations context, the conditions are slightly different. As with interorganizational relations, coordination and collaboration between disaster-stricken governments and the international community are imperative. Additionally, administrative know-how and a legal infrastructure capable of admitting international aid are necessary for effectively managing incoming relief aid. A government that has not established any procedures for using international relief might turn down aid or might not be able to utilize it efficiently.

In the United States, some questions were raised about why the country did not accept international aid following Hurricane Katrina. Because the United States had always been the provider of such aid before this disaster struck on its home turf, perhaps the governmental system and emergency managers did not know how to best integrate international aid with local efforts (Kapucu & Yuldashev, 2009).

Conclusion

Effective disaster management involves all sectors, including every level of government and all of a country's citizens. Collaboration is the most effective means not only to effectively mitigate the disaster cycle and increase budgeting, but also to provide better services while reducing duplication of efforts. Certain practices can be followed by emergency management organizations to bolster organizational and individual outcomes. Proper planning for disasters, including contingencies, requires training of emergency management participants; conducting exercises will also dramatically improve the effectiveness of such organizations.

Financing of emergency management encompasses the issues of how to obtain resources for activities of organizations and how these resources have been used in the past and will be used in the future. Careful management of funds will satisfy individuals working in the organization as well as promote disaster preparedness.

In regional and international contexts, the need for coordination and collaboration during emergency management is even more apparent than in a local context. Because relationships are built upon mutual trust and interdependency, and there is no single authority in the international disaster relief community, collaboration and relationship building become indispensible when a large-scale disaster occurs. Administrative knowledge regarding how to best integrate international relief efforts with local efforts is a key aspect of effectiveness in such scenarios.

Review Questions

1. Discuss trends and policy changes involved in federal–state agreements and top-down command and control systems (versus bottom-up/local systems).

2. During the response to Hurricane Andrew, the military—specifically, the U.S. Army and the U.S. Coast Guard—performed outstanding emergency search and rescue work, much of it well ahead of civilian government agencies at the local, state, and federal levels. After the hurricane, some lawmakers proposed folding up FEMA and moving its duties to the Pentagon. Should domestic emergency management be assigned to the military rather than to civil authorities? Explain why or why not, and defend your answer. What advantages does the military have in providing emergency relief to disaster victims? Given that we count on the military to provide aid in foreign disasters, why might officials not want them to assume a similar role at home?

3. The European Union has developed standards that are applied to a variety of fields, including administrative systems, health, agriculture, and energy policies. How can EU members achieve integration of disaster relief efforts from other EU members with their own disaster management systems?

4. What were the successes achieved by the National Guard in dealing with the Hurricane Katrina devastation in 2005? What problems resulted from the National Guard operations during the same disaster?

5. How might the information you gained from this chapter affect you personally and professionally?

References

Allison, G. T., & Zelikov, P. (1999). *Essence of decision: Explaining the Cuban missile crisis* (2nd ed.). New York: Longman.

Bigley, G. A., & Roberts, K. H. (2001). The Incident Command System: High reliability organizations for complex and volatile task environments. *Academy of Management Journal, 44*(6), 1281–1299.

Bloom, M. J., & Menefee, M. K. (1994). Scenario planning and contingency planning. *Public Productivity and Management Review, 17*(3), 223–230.

Bruins, H. J. (2000). Proactive contingency planning vis-á-vis declining water security in the 21st century. *Journal of Contingencies and Crisis Management, 8*(2), 63–72.

Carley, K. M., & Lin, Z. (1997). A theoretical study of organizational performance under information distortion. *Management Science, 43*(7), 976–999.

Chi, C-H, Chao, W-H., Chuang, C-C., Tsai, M-C., & Tsai, L-M. (2001). Emergency medical technicians' disaster training by tabletop exercise. *American Journal of Emergency Medicine, 19*(5), 433–436.

Crichton, M., & Flin, R. (2004). Identifying and training non-technical skills of nuclear emergency response teams. *Annals of Nuclear Energy, 31*(12), 1317–1330.

Driskell, J. E., & Salas, E. (1991). Group decision-making under stress. *Journal of Applied Psychology, 76*(3), 473–478.

Flin, R., Slaven, G., & Stewart, K. (1996). Emergency decision-making in the offshore oil and gas industry. *Human Factors, 38*(2), 262–277.

Flueler, T. (2006). *Decision-making for complex socio-technical systems: Robustness from lessons learned in long-term radioactive waste governance.* Dordrecht, Netherlands: Springer.

Ford, J. K., & Schmidt, A. M. (2000). Emergency response training: Strategies for enhancing real-world performance. *Journal of Hazardous Materials, 75*(2–3), 195–215.

Government Accountability Office (GAO). (2003). *Federal assistance: Grant system continues to be highly fragmented.* GAO-03-718T.

Henstra, D. (2010). Evaluating local government emergency management programs: What framework should public managers adopt? *Public Administration Review, 70*(2), 236–246.

Jackson, B. A., Faith, K. S., & Willis, H. H. (2010). *Evaluating the reliability of emergency response systems for large-scale incident operations.* Santa Monica, CA: RAND Corporation.

Kapucu, N., Augustin, M. E., & Garayev, V. (2009). Interstate partnerships in emergency management: Emergency Management Assistance Compact in responding to catastrophic disasters. *Public Administration Review, 69*(2), 297–313.

Kapucu, N., & Yuldashev, F. (2009). *International partnerships in emergency management.* Paper presented at the American Society for Public Administration (ASPA) 70th Annual Conference, Miami, FL.

Lindell, M. K., Prater, C., & Perry, R. W. (2007). *Introduction to emergency management.* Hoboken, NJ: Wiley.

Maiero, S. (2002). Factors leading to better satisfaction and performance in the EMS Division of Contra Costa County Fire Protection District. Retrieved from http://www.usfa.dhs.gov/pdf/efop/efo34049.pdf.

Perry, R. W. (2004). Disaster exercise outcomes for professional emergency personnel and citizen volunteers. *Journal of Contingencies and Crises Management, 12*(2), 64–75.

Perry, R. W., & Lindell, M. K. (2007). *Emergency planning.* Hoboken. NJ: Wiley.

Peterson, D. M., & Perry, R. W. (1999). The Impacts of disaster exercises on participants. *Disaster Prevention and Management, 8*(4), 251–255.

Pillai, R., & Williams, E. A. (2004). Transformational leadership, self-efficacy, group cohesiveness, commitment and performance. *Journal of Organizational Change Management, 17*(2), 144–159.

Public Entity Risk Institute (PERI). (2001). *Characteristics of effective emergency management organizational structures.* Fairfax, VA: Author.

Quarantelli, E. L. (1997). Ten criteria for evaluating the management of community disasters. *Disasters, 21*(1), 39–56.

Rosenthal, U., & Kouzmin, A. (1997). Crises and crisis management: Toward comprehensive government decision-making. *Journal of Public Administration Research & Theory, 7*(2), 277–305.

Salas, E., Burke, S. C., & Samman, S. N. (2001). Understanding command and control teams operating in complex environments. *Information Knowledge Systems Management, 2*(4) 311–324.

Schaafstal, A. M., Johnston, J. H., & Oser, R. L. (2001). Training teams for emergency management. *Computers in Human Behavior, 17*(5–6), 615–626.

Schneider, B., Ehrhart, K. H., & Ehrhart, M. G. (2010). Organizational climate. In C. L. Cooper (Ed.), *The Blackwell encyclopedia of management.* Blackwell Publishing. Blackwell Reference Online. Retrieved from http://www.blackwellreference.com/public/tocnode?id=g9780631233176_chunk_g978063123536119_ss2-8#citation.

Scott, J. A., Miller, G. T., Issenberg, B., Brotons, A. A., Gordon, D. L., Gordon, M. S., et al. (2006). Skill improvement during emergency response to terrorism training. *Prehospital Emergency Care, 10,* 507–514.

Sylves, R. T. (2007). Budgeting for emergency management. In W. L. Waugh, Jr., & K. Tierney (Eds.), *Emergency management: Principles and practice for local government* (2nd ed., pp. 299–318), Washington, DC: ICMA.

Sylves, R. T. (2008). *Disaster policy and politics: Emergency management and homeland security.* Washington, DC: CQ Press.

Takada, A. (2004). The role of team efficacy in crisis management. *International Journal of Emergency Management, 2,* 35–46.

ten Brinke, W. B. M., Kolen, B., Dollee, A., van Waveren, H., & Wouters, K. (2010). Contingency planning for large scale floods in the Netherlands. *Journal of Contingencies and Crisis Management, 18*(1), 55–69.

Waugh, W. L., & Tierney, K. (2007). Future directions in emergency management. In W. L. Waugh, Jr., & K. Tierney (Eds.), *Emergency management: Principles and practice for local government* (2nd ed., pp. 319–333). Washington, DC: ICMA.

Chapter 11

Evaluation and Professional Accountability in Managing Disasters

Chapter Objectives

- Understand the trend toward professionalization of emergency and crisis management.
- Appreciate the role of accountability in emergency management.
- Analyze the performance of emergency management.
- Understand ethical issues in emergency management and emergency management misconduct.
- Discuss the IAEM Emergency Management Code of Ethics.

Introduction

Just as the practice of emergency management has undergone many changes over the past half-century, so has the concept of an emergency manager. An emerging profession, emergency management needs to establish standards and evaluate compliance with those standards. This chapter begins by examining the concept of a profession and then identifies the process by which emergency management is moving toward professionalization. It next turns to procedures for periodic evaluation of the local emergency management agency and local emergency management committee. This section describes general principles for organizational evaluation and then examines the U.S. National Fire Protection Association Standard 1600 and Emergency Management Accreditation Program. The chapter describes procedures for evaluating drills, exercises, and incidents; organizational training; and community risk communication programs. It also discusses accountability issues and ethical standards pertaining to the emergency management field.

Emergency management has changed dramatically over the last 50 years (Lindell, Prater, & Perry, 2007). From the 1980s onward, the occupational field was termed "civil defense," which transformed the idea of emergency management by emphasizing not only preparedness, response, and recovery, but also mitigation. During this time, emergency management's role in the United States was exemplified by the civil defense director, who had a nontraditional educational background, which did not include the suggested military experience, college education, or previous local government position. Today, an emergency manager needs not only experience, but a college education with exemplary skills in communication, organizational skills, technical fundamentals, and interpersonal networking capabilities (Lindell et al., 2007). Although many might argue that emergency management is still a young profession, a strong emphasis is placed on the continuation of personal development via involvement in associations and education through specialized training and certifications, as this arena operates on a proactive (versus reactive) approach to management.

Professionalization and Features of Emergency Management

Lindell, Prater, and Perry (2006) identify professions based on six criteria. First, there must be a professional society of practitioners, which serves to accomplish their goals. Second, there must be a consensus on members' duties. Third, members of a profession must define the standard knowledge, skills, and abilities that constitute the necessary body of knowledge for the profession. Fourth, ethical standards must be identified in the profession; they will serve as the guideline for assessing the performance of an agency or individual. Fifth, members of a profession must prepare minimum standards in their practice regarding the body of knowledge. These standards should be applied to both current and prospective members of the profession. Sixth, the body of knowledge of a profession should be revised based on new methods and developments in the field (Lindell et al., 2006).

Members of the professional society identify and implement methods so as to improve their skills. "For example, a professional society might establish a committee that evaluates a new theory or procedure for handling a specific type of problem. If the new theory or procedure is judged to be better than the one(s) in current use, it is incorporated into a professional standard that is binding for all members of the profession" (Lindell et al., 2007, p. 346).

Another important aspect of the emergency management profession is its legitimacy. According to Lindell et al. (2007), the actions of a professional society "promote public recognition of its existence as an organized group with specialized expertise" (p. 346). As a result of this legitimacy, the professional society protects itself from encroachment by unauthorized nonprofessionals who do not meet the standards of task performance and ethics (Lindell et al., 2007). Professional affiliation and membership also serve to establish legitimacy, as the "competence of prospective members is evaluated by some combination of education, specific training, testing, and duration of professional experience" (p. 347).

Identifying the Emergency Management Profession

Emergency management practitioners and scholars accept that the occupation of emergency management is professionalizing and becoming more collaborative in nature (Wilson & Oyola-Yemaiel, 2001). One important indicator of the evolving perception of emergency management as a profession is the Federal Response Plan (FRP) of 1992 (Wilson & Oyola-Yemaiel, 2001). The FRP served as a basis for standardization of the knowledge, skills, and abilities necessary for the emergency management profession. It identified many agencies and organizations as a part of disaster response and emphasized the need for more skilled and trained specialists to enter this field (Wilson & Oyola-Yemaiel, 2001).

Professionalization in emergency management "occurs through sponsoring, development, and execution of training by organizations in order to certify individuals as professional emergency managers" (Wilson & Oyola-Yemaiel, 2001, p. 123). The increasing opportunities for professionals to obtain a specialized education and certification in disaster management are notable indicators of standardization of emergency management. As Wilson and Oyola-Yemaiel (2001) state, the International Association of Emergency Managers (IAEM) is an exemplary organization that ensures future professionals go through the processes of appropriate selection, training, and socialization, with their successful passage through this pathway being confirmed by certification.

Marincioni (2007) defines emergency managers in the United States as professionals focusing on education and emphasizing training to overcome community apathy toward hazard and disaster prevention. In his study, Marincioni noted that most of the emergency managers in the United States are male, middle aged, with a military or law enforcement background. Moreover, he recognized that majority of the older emergency managers lack "formal academic training in disaster management, although many [have] attended a wealth of short-term specialized courses in emergency management" (p. 464). In contrast, professionals younger than the age of 40 have academic training and degrees in emergency management, and there is a higher proportion of females among this younger generation of professionals.

Performance in Managing Disasters and Crises

Professionalism in emergency management emerges from the development of best practices that shape the outcomes of emergencies uniformly and favorably. As groups evaluate what works, they document this knowledge and distribute it through constant development and training. These standardized actions are then compiled so that they become part of the standard operating instructions in emergency situations. Over time, best practices work their way up from practitioners to departmental heads, and eventually reach the state and federal levels.

The National Fire Protection Agency (NFPA) and the National Incident Management System (NIMS) in the United States are examples of what can result from the growth of standards and best practices. The NFPA and NIMS can trace their roots back to Firescope, a wildfire firefighting management system that was developed in California during the 1970s. The NFPA has a more advisory role than NIMS, which chiefly deals with operational issues. NIMS has become the guiding force for emergency management in the United States and provides the regulation, knowledge base, and associations needed to form the professional guidance in operational situations through the National Response Framework (NRF). The NRF is only a guiding force like the NFPA, however; although compliance is not mandatory, failure to comply results in exclusion from the professionalism imparted by compliance.

NFPA 1600 is considered to be an excellent benchmark for planners in both the public and private sectors, and was recommended to be a national preparedness standard by the American National Standards Institute (ANSI). The formal name of the NFPA 1600 standard is "National Fire Protection Association's Standard on Disaster/Emergency Management and Business Continuity Programs" (Nicholson, 2007, p. 243). This standard provides numerous methodologies for defining and identifying risk and vulnerabilities within a community or business/service organization, as well as thorough planning guidelines. Its provisions address stabilizing the restoration of the physical infrastructure of the community or business organization, protecting the health and life safety of personnel housed in those communities or businesses, and crisis communications procedures and management structure for both short-term recovery and ongoing long-term continuity of operations within that community or business/service organization. In addition, NFPA 1600 identifies methodologies for exercising those plans and provides a listing of numerous resource organizations within and for the fields of disaster recovery, emergency management, and business continuity planning. In the wake of the September 11, 2001 terrorist attacks, ANSI recommended that the 9/11 Commission report that NFPA 1600 should become the standard guiding emergency management across the United States.

Professions are identified by a specific skill set or regulation. Professionals in the field are expected to possess highly specialized skills or advanced education that suits the demands they might encounter in that field. This education may be identified through degrees, certificates, and licensing, all of which help maintain the knowledge, skills, and abilities (KSAs) set by the preexisting standards. Those familiar with emergency management through public safety organizations will recognize this component as a blend of academic education, institutional training such as that provided by police and fire academies, and Federal Emergency Management Agency (FEMA) certifications. These skill levels allow professionals to work autonomously, make independent decisions, and operate without the need for direct instruction or supervision. During emergencies, the ability to make decisions quickly and independently could mean the difference between life and death and is an effective resource management tool. This autonomy separates professionals from tradespeople, who may also possess a very specialized skill set, but require direction or input from outside sources to guide their actions (Lindell et al., 2007).

The required competencies for emergency managers include the following KSAs:

- Knowledge of a large range of natural and technological hazards
- Knowledge of various ways to assess communities and their vulnerabilities
- Skill in managing and implementing emergency procedures in many different situations during various phases of emergencies such as mitigation, preparedness, and response
- Knowledge of how different disciplines and agencies can contribute to emergency programs
- Knowledge of the policy process, so that emergency managers are able to navigate and create new policies
- Ability to organize, lead, and coordinate an emergency management organization

In his 2007 study, Marincioni compared the United States and Italy in terms of perception and exchange of disaster knowledge of professionals, arguing that new technologies such as "computer networks, virtual reality, remote sensing, GIS, and decision support systems" (p. 461) have the potential to improve the performance of these professionals. Nevertheless, faster and more efficient technology does not increase the level of knowledge transfer. To be effective in ensuring fast knowledge transfer, technical innovations must be supported by an organizational and professional culture that will allow knowledge diffusion (Marincioni, 2007). According to Marincioni (2007), three main conditions must be present for effective disaster knowledge exchange to take place: "(a) technological systems must be perceived capable of increasing interpersonal interaction; (b) emergency managers must be willing to accept and share new disaster knowledge; and, most of all, (c) disaster knowledge must be perceived to be transferable between people" (p. 468). As noted by this author, communication technologies can support long-distance communication, interaction, and networking among emergency managers, with knowledge sharing representing a major contribution to the overall emergency management profession.

Besides the skills and knowledge of emergency professionals in the information-sharing process, other factors may play a role in improving performance in a disaster scenario, such as professional culture, the context of information, technology, and interaction (Marincioni, 2007). However, these factors vary from case to case. As for professional culture, it "encompasses the beliefs, traditions, perceptions, objectives, language, communication style, dynamics between colleagues, and aggregate understanding and technical knowledge of a professional group of emergency managers" (p. 469). In his comparative study, Marincioni highlighted the most important filters for culture: "(a) the educational and professional background of the emergency managers; (b) the perceived purpose of emergency management; and (c) the definition of disaster knowledge" (p. 469).

According to Marincioni (2007), the other conceptual category influencing emergency management professionals' knowledge exchange is its context. "Context [comprises] economic and technological resources, the social organization of the community, and the environmental setting in which the emergency manager operates" (p. 470). The sequence of disasters in the local area and the importance of disaster-related issues to public opinion are the most important determinants of the scenario's ability to attract emergency management resources.

Information technology has emerged as one of the important factors facilitating disaster knowledge exchange among professionals. Marincioni (2007) argues that the successful integration of a certain technology in emergency management practice depends on characteristics perceived as necessary to advance knowledge sharing.

Finally, the last conceptual category mentioned by Marincioni (2007) is interaction, which comprises a bundle of activities targeted to improve interpersonal communications within the emergency management community.

Hutchins et al. (2008) mention planning as one of the key factors in determining performance when managing crises and emergencies. Including stakeholders in the planning process is likely to increase the success of the planning phase as well as its implementation. Brody (2003) argues that the quality of local planning is usually perceived as an isolated event taking place in public decision making. To demonstrate this point, this author compares the jurisdictions of Florida and Washington, where planning is fostered by different factors. Plans in Florida were improved in terms of emergency preparedness and sheltering capability. In contrast, "[j]urisdictions in Washington strengthened their policies to protect areas subject to flooding through permitted land uses, setbacks, and locating public facilities outside of hazard-prone areas" (Brody, 2003, p. 198).

In particular, performance improvement professionals can demonstrate their value in crisis planning by (1) informing stakeholders of crisis planning research, resources, and processes; (2) using performance improvement tools (such as the HPT [*human performance technology*] model) to assess crisis vulnerabilities in individuals and systems; and

(3) designing performance interventions that align with organizational goals to enhance individual, team, and organizational crisis preparedness. (Hutchins et al., 2008, p. 47)(italics added).

Emergency Management Standards and Evaluations

Professional standards and compliance with those standards are the foundation for a profession. A profession is a group of practitioners whose specialized education and training gives them the KSAs needed to perform the tasks within a specified work domain. In describing the difference between an emergency responder and an emergency manager, Lindell et al. (2007) state that the former deals with a narrower field and hands-on experience with the emergency situation, while the latter focuses on a broader range of expertise and may involve knowledge and experience of several emergency response fields. Lindell et al. (2007) also distinguish between public and private emergency managers, suggesting that public emergency managers deal with a broader resource base and are more accountable, while private managers deal with a specific audience and have limited accountability.

Ideally, emergency management should be an interdisciplinary field with an improved sphere of certification and scholarly programs offered by science-based practitioners. Emergency management practitioners need not try to analyze and understand everything through one fixed lens, but rather should embrace this multidisciplinary approach and perspective. The ideal situation is to successfully implement the plan intended for emergency situations.

Measurement is an indispensible component of management. As Behn (2003) explains, performance measures can be used for many purposes. Just because the private sector measures performance and is managed better, that does not mean that the public sector should be transformed to exactly match it (Behn, 2003). As Alexander (2003) emphasizes, there is no standard in emergency management training and education. To date, this lack of standards in the field has impeded efforts to measure performance accurately. Before standards are promulgated, however, a dialogue among stakeholders is required. In the end, it is important to construct a consultative document with clear scope and objectives.

Accreditation is another important feature of emergency management professionals. It may be defined as "a form of self-regulation which implies less regulation from outsiders and thus greater autonomy for the emergency management practitioners" (Wilson & Oyola-Yemaiel, 2006, p. 124). According to the Emergency Management Accreditation Program (EMAP), accreditation is a way of indicating, by self-assessment, documentation, and peer review, that a program meets national standards for emergency management programs. EMAP is a voluntary standard assessment and accreditation process for state and local government disaster preparedness programs that seeks to foster excellence and accountability in emergency management and homeland security programs by establishing credible standards applied in a peer review accreditation process (EMAP, 2010). Wilson and Oyola-Yemaiel (2001) argue that many emergency managers at the federal, state, and local levels of government have not yet reached a consensus on the definition of a professional emergency manager and the emergency management profession. Consequently, it is not possible to ensure an overall framework of agreed professional qualities by accreditation of all government agencies and organizations. According to these authors, certifying and accrediting the government emergency professionals will ensure that "the emergency management profession [has] a greater degree of intergovernmental consistency" (p. 124).

Although it is challenging, evaluating response and relief efforts is important for confirming the appropriateness of emergency assistance. Without proper evaluation of these efforts, funders, providers, and decision makers cannot determine whether the services and assistance were delivered efficiently, nor can they learn lessons from mistakes made and prepare better for future emergencies (Henstra, 2010; Ritchie & MacDonald, 2010b). Ritchie and MacDonald (2010a, 2010b) underscore the role of evaluation in emergency management in preventing any harm and doing better for the public. Evaluation findings can guide policy makers in eliminating deficiencies in current policies so as to minimize, if not totally prevent, loss of life and property.

Ritchie and MacDonald (2010a) have developed a framework for evaluating emergency management actions (preparedness, response, and recovery). Their framework focuses on evaluation of emergency preparedness, response, and recovery efforts in intraorganizational, interorganizational, and system-wide contexts. The intraorganizational evaluation focuses on procedures conducted within an organization for reaching designated goals. The interorganizational evaluation focuses on the functionality of network and collaboration among partnering agencies. The system-wide evaluation examines, for example, a response system such as the nonprofit sector. The Tsunami Evaluation Coalition, for example, brought together a number of nongovernmental organizations to conduct a joint evaluation of the response and recovery efforts after the December 2004 tsunami in Southeast Asia (Ritchie & MacDonald, 2010a).

In regard to intra-agency evaluation, Henstra (2010) suggests that program evaluation is an important factor in determining the local government's performance. In emergency and crisis management, "program evaluation is a means by which local public managers can raise the profile of emergency management, demonstrate the value of efforts in this area, and buttress requests for additional resources when they are needed" (p. 243). Evaluation or emergency management activities might find that local resources are being allocated primarily to preparedness, while comparatively little effort has been devoted to recovery and mitigation (Henstra, 2010).

When the information is measured systematically through such evaluations, it becomes possible to create standards that might improve future programs. Henstra (2010) suggests that program evaluation and performance measurement might be used to promote an assessment of services provided by local emergency managers.

There is a clear movement toward interagency and system-wide evaluation efforts among emergency management professionals today (Ritchie & MacDonald, 2010b). The complex and collaborative nature of emergency management systems have naturally drawn substantial attention to interagency evaluation; nevertheless, it does not simply take the place of intra-agency evaluation (Bornemisza, Griekspoor, Ezard, & Sondorp, 2010; Ritchie & MacDonald, 2010b).

As an example of interagency evaluation, Janis, Stiefel, and Carbullido (2010) discuss about the Katrina Aid Today (KAT) organization, which was established for monitoring and evaluating the disaster recovery aid for Hurricane Katrina victims as provided by the United Methodist Committee of Relief (UMCOR). UMCOR has established a consortium of agencies for providing disaster recovery case management services. The authors identified five key aspects of their monitoring and evaluation of the UMCOR efforts:

- The need for flexibility in program design
- The need to implement and adapt an interagency monitoring and evaluation system
- Interagency data collection
- The need to develop outcome measures
- An emphasis on program evaluation in disaster recovery

KAT was the first disaster case management program that was funded by the U.S. federal government. According to Janis et al. (2010), "KAT was an opportunity to reflect on best practice and lessons learned. It was successful in designing and implementing a monitoring and evaluation system that may serve as a model for emergency response efforts" (p. 77).

Bornemisza et al. (2010) mention the Interagency Health and Nutrition (IHE) initiative as an international institute that shows promise as a vehicle for evaluating the effectiveness of emergency relief efforts in a system-wide perspective. The aim of IHE is "to assess international performance in the health and nutrition sector during [the] emergency response and recovery phase" (p. 23). Its work is also complementary to individual organization assessments because system performance is related with organizational performance. IHE conducted six health and nutrition evaluations between 2003 and 2006 in six different countries. One of its major contributions was to the interagency process. As Bornemisza et al. (2010) explain, the IHE initiative enhanced trust and collaboration between those organizations that participated in the evaluation process. IHE staff further helped policy processes that were in transition at the time of the evaluation to replace the emergency response with a post-emergency response. They provided critical recommendations to aid providers and local authorities so as to ensure better integration of efforts. IHE advisors shared their results with the key stakeholders in each case and conducted follow-up visits to observe whether their recommendations were used by the countries to make further progress in improving the health and nutrition of their populations (Bornemisza et al., 2010).

In addition to pointing out the necessity for taking an interagency approach in evaluation, Ritchie and McDonald (2010b) underline the significance of digestion of international and domestic evaluation best practices. As discussed earlier in this chapter, there is an ongoing lack of standards in the emergency management profession, with a relatively less dense set of events taking place at the local or national level. As a consequence, local-level experience and capacity may remain insufficient to handle a disaster of an unexpected scope. Ritchie and MacDonald (2010b) note that international evaluators are more experienced when compared to agents working only at the national level. Because they have likely encountered numerous methodological challenges, they are better able to avoid potential pitfalls owing to their prior lessons learned.

Accountability in Emergency Management

Every disaster comes with consequences for all of the stakeholders affected by it. While ordinary citizens might be affected by the very tangible impacts of the disasters, the public administrators or key officials and decision makers responsible for managing emergency situations and disasters might face intangible consequences related to the way they make decisions, respond to disasters, or inform the public. In this sense, disasters are the events that test the overall resilience of societies and their leaders (Boin, McConnell, & t'Hart, 2008). During disasters, decision makers are in a position to provide the response in the most effective and efficient way. This aspect of the situation, however, is in tension with the requirement to provide effective control and accountability mechanisms (Government Accountability Office [GAO], 2006). While the former consideration presses responsible officials to provide the best response to the people in need, the latter aims to ensure that the resources and capital are used in an appropriate way for correct, meaningful, and valid purposes. Because disasters require an expeditious response and quick decision making, it might sometimes be difficult to make decisions with all possible consequences in mind, which might lead to failures in accountability. Boin et al. (2008) argue that disasters always have a political side, which is mainly related to the political agendas of the incumbent government and key officials. Such political agendas, they say, are always in tension with the demands to make reforms during or after the disasters. In a sense, the tension is between being accountable for what happened and taking responsibility to implement necessary changes. This tension, in turn, may lead to a "blaming game," in which all parties maneuver and manipulate the conditions and the situation to avoid accountability.

According to Humanitarian Practice Network (1995), one of the most effective tools to guarantee accountable practices is to assess the impact and effectiveness of the disaster-related actions and operations. While this strategy is important to provide post-disaster accountability control mechanisms, actions and operations during disasters are often difficult to control and account for. It is also important to distinguish between the parties to whom the key officials are responsible. While mechanisms controlling accountability for financial resources are relatively more developed, sophisticated, and easy to handle, accountability for actions affecting the general public in direct or indirect ways is more complex and prone to ambiguities and uncertainties. In other words, it is easier to monitor financial inputs and expenditures and find the officials who were responsible for their procurement and use than to identify the key individuals who were responsible for the impact of the response operations on the population being served. Hurricane Katrina is a good example of why it is important to analyze response and recovery efforts in terms of the accountability concept (Koliba, Mills, & Zia, 2011). According to the GAO (2006) report that investigated the case of Hurricane Katrina, several problems with accountability occurred, some of which were related to contracting, accounting for, and managing the assistance offered by international organizations; management of food and water resources; and screening of fraudulent applications for assistance.

According to GAO (2006), the need to provide an effective response must be balanced with the need to ensure accountability in emergency management. Boin et al. (2008) similarly suggest that politicians and public administrators who are responsible for preparing, responding to, and recovering from disasters should, to their greatest ability, avoid the dilemma that pushes them to defend their political stakes rather than admit responsibility and proceed with necessary reforms and actions. The Humanitarian Practice Network (1995) indicates that appropriate criteria and methods to evaluate during- and post-disaster actions and to measure success need to be developed to provide better accountability control mechanisms. What is more, the same importance assigned to accountability in financial issues should be assigned to accountability in services provided to the general population.

Creating an accountability culture is another tool to ensure that the officials responsible for providing effective emergency response and recovery act in line with accountability principles. Such a culture is expected to embrace issues like setting performance standards and monitoring, evaluating performance against standards of ethics and conduct, and incorporating critical issues such as minorities, gender, and other topics in the organization's agenda (International Federation of Red Cross and Red Crescent Societies [IFRC], 2010).

Generally speaking, emergency and disaster management practices differ from regular management practices in that the nature of the disaster situation itself imposes different conditions and demands. While some of those demands can be met with experience-based, quality decision making, others are likely to receive less attention, especially in a relatively unstable and uncertain situation where managers are under intense time pressure. Such circumstances may lead to unaddressed issues and gaps in the response provided to the population, thereby creating accountability problems for the responsible officials. It is for this reason that emergency management should adopt proper accountability standards as well as compliance monitoring. Furthermore, to obtain the most effective results, emergency management should be politics-blind and demand-oriented, with proper and due attention being given to every constituency of the society. This tenet is especially critical due to the ever-increasing use of participatory and democratic governance tools by today's public.

International Standards and Emergency Management

To resolve a crisis situation through the process of collaboration and coordination on an international level, standards and regulations are needed. Standards are qualitative in nature, universal, and applicable in any operating environment. To help emergency management organizations deal with the unexpected and to safeguard the interests of stakeholders, as well as their reputation, brand, and value-creating activities, the International Organization for Standardization (ISO) has offered to develop standards that specify how to successfully mitigate risks and be prepared to respond to crises. Alexander (2003) notes that compliance with such international standards could promote learning from others' experiences, exchange of professionals, and transfer of knowledge. At present, however, international educational standards are not available; in fact, anyone can purport to offer a training course for emergency managers.

As Alexander (2003) points out, numerous countries have developed their own national emergency standards, such as the U.K. National Civil Protection Requirements, the NFPA's "Standard on Disaster/Emergency Management and Business Continuity Programs," the European Humanitarian Charter and Minimum Standards in Disaster, and the Australia/New Zealand Risk Management Standard. According to Alexander, none of these national or regional emergency standards is an appropriate model for an international standard because of their heterogeneity, lack of important details, and concentration on only specific areas.

As part of the ISO's efforts to develop standards for managing crises, the organization created ISO/TC 223, a standard whose focus was formerly identified as "societal security" (ISO, 2006). "The mission of ISO/TC 223 is to develop International Standards or other ISO deliverables that will improve preparedness before a crisis, coordination during a crisis and reconstruction and remedial action afterwards" (ISO, 2006). Ambassador and Senior Adviser to the Swedish Emergency Management Agency Krister Kumlin states that "Standardized channels save time and simplify cooperation in crisis management and are therefore of vital importance" (ISO, 2006). He also believes that in the future, standardization will allow all information to be interpreted and shared among national and international emergency management organizations. So far, 22 countries are participating members in the ISO/TC 223 effort, while another 21 countries have observer status (ISO, 2006).

The other important international ISO standard for information technology is ISO/IEC 24762:2008 (ISO 2008). Also known as the guideline for information and communication technology disaster recovery services, this standard aims "to offer guidance on the information and communications technologies and services necessary for disaster recovery (ICT DR) as part of business continuity management" (ISO, 2008).

The ISO/IEC 24762:2008 project editor, Philip Sy, has commented that this advanced, new-generation standard reflects recent technological developments, which focus on minimization of damage in crisis situations in terms of information security and communication standpoint (ISO, 2008). "The fallback arrangements included in the standard will help out both during periods of minor outages and, more importantly, will play an essential role in ensuring information and service availability during a disaster or failure, and for a long-term complete recovery of activities" (ISO, 2008).

Sphere Project also offers standards for international humanitarian assistance. Its aim is to improve the quality of humanitarian assistance to disaster-stricken areas and enhance accountability of the organizations partnering in the humanitarian assistance efforts (Sphere Project, 2004). As part of the project, various nongovernmental organizations created the Humanitarian Charter and addressed minimum standards for humanitarian assistance. The Humanitarian Charter is based on the principles and provisions of international humanitarian law, international human rights law, refugee law, and the Code of Conduct for the International Red Cross and Red Crescent Movement and Non-governmental Organizations (NGOs) in Disaster Relief (Sphere Project, 2004). The charter addresses emergency management organizations' commitment to minimum standards identified for humanitarian assistance, and it raises standards related to participation, initial assessment, response, targeting, monitoring, evaluation, aid worker competencies and responsibilities, and supervision of management and support for personnel. At the same time, the charter specifies minimum standards developed by obtaining feedback from wide networks of practitioners and experts in different sectors from 80 countries. "Most of the standards, and the indicators that accompany them, are not new, but consolidate and adapt existing knowledge and practice" (p. 6).

Ethical Issues

Professions oblige their members to act in ways that meet professional norms and standards. The values that those norms represent are held in high regard and are often evidenced in ethical codes. A profession requires compliance with this code, and can administer punishment for noncompliance, such as the loss of accreditation or expulsion. In terms of legal liability, the emergency management profession has two major concerns: damage to people and property that occurs while professionals are responding to an emergency, and failure of government to plan for a response (Lindell et al., 2007). Certification ensures that emergency managers have sufficient education, knowledge, training, and experience to perform their vital duties.

Ethics has been described as a decision of right and wrong (Ulmer, Sellnow, & Seeger, 2007). Ulmer et al. (2007) suggest that we make ethical judgments every day in our lives and we cannot avoid them: "In evaluating or judging behaviors as 'wrong' or 'unethical,' we are applying some set of standards or values regarding what we think to be appropriate behavior" (p. 168). Furthermore, Ulmer et al. (2007) believe that ethical judgments inform our behaviors and choices. For instance, an organization with a good reputation may receive greater support from its public and stakeholders than one judged as bad or unethical.

An ethical perspective and ideology are one of the important defining features of professionals. As Lindell et al. (2007) note, "in addition to substantive knowledge, professions socialize members to act in terms of professional norms and perspectives (the 'lens' mentioned by Mosher) that might differ from the views of either the public or the management of organizations in which the professional is employed" (p. 348). In the last two decades, professional ideologies have been frequently embodied in ethical codes. "Ethical codes not only encourage compliance as proof of professionalism, but typically describe the punishments for those who fail to comply" (p. 348).

Common problems seen in today's organizational management are noted in the writings of Jurkiewicz (2007) and Stivers (2007), who examine these issues in the context of Louisiana and the Hurricane Katrina disaster. Jurkiewicz (2007) notes that corruption has become part of life in Louisiana, and Louisianans are proud of it. Behaviors that contradict Louisiana cultural traditions are shunned by citizens, and attempts to change "the way things are" have been met with staunch resistance and accusations of "Northern" interference (Jurkiewicz, 2007). Social norms identify wordplay, situational manipulation, and personal reward as favorable traits; in this light, the state government's mishandling of funds and the neglect of the lower ninth ward during Hurricane Katrina is seen as something that should have been expected (Jurkiewicz, 2007).

Moreover, repeated abuse of Louisiana minorities, who are disproportionably black, and unfavorable living conditions at the lowest elevation (below sea level) have led to the belief among the poorest people in Louisiana (and in the United States in general) that fate controls the future and that individuals have no control over events and very little opportunity for betterment (Stivers, 2007). Underlying racism can be seen not only in the form of physical actions, but also in administrative policies that have led to much loss and suffering among the poor. The problem with the system is that such policies are not viewed as a failure of the administrators, but rather seen as acceptable behavior (Stivers, 2007). In Louisiana, values such as family, inclusion, food, and cultural endeavors are rated as having a much higher importance than education, organization, networking, and policy processes, which ultimately leaves those individuals who most need help the least able to engage the system and make a difference (Jurkiewicz, 2007).

Would the aftermath of Hurricane Katrina be different if the disaster had occurred in a state such as California or New York instead of Louisiana? This is the concluding question that Jurkiewicz (2007) responds to in her article. The rationale for the failure in emergency management response in the 2005 disaster is that Louisiana has a brash and seedy political landscape that is rife with corruption and unethical practices. Hurricane Katrina hit a state whose politics prevented it from responding directly and effectively to the crisis. Louisianans, seeing no help forthcoming from their elected officials, used their own skiff boats, row boats, and other means to help their neighbors. Such behavior was touted as an act of heroism, but it also underscored the gross negligence of the elected officials in the area, from the parish level to the governor's office.

Even after the initial crisis was averted and discussions on rebuilding had begun, Louisiana's elected state officials were slow to move, possibly deliberately, toward rebuilding efforts. Jurkiewicz (2007) observes that elected officials and those in powerful positions have a different set of needs and wants, as can be seen in the perception of food: Those who are at lower economic levels view food as a necessity that they must have to survive, whereas those at higher economic levels view food as a function of "quality and presentability." This distinction lies at the heart of Louisiana politics.

In Louisiana, the ethical political culture has allowed itself to become separated from the rest of the country, such that embezzlement and scandal are accepted as norms. Using Michal Foucault's observations on ethical behaviors, Jurkiewicz (2007) finds that the natural order of Louisiana is based on the ability to beguile and outsmart others.

IAEM Code of Ethics

The International Association of Emergency Managers (IAEM) has created a code of ethics, which professionals who choose to work in the field must embrace and uphold. This code of ethics specifies that in emergency management, the key criteria in saving lives and protecting property are mitigation, preparedness, response, and recovery. The three values stated by the code of ethics—respect, commitment, and professionalism—are specifically geared toward individuals who are recognized as Certified Emergency Managers (CEMs) or Associate Emergency Managers (AEMs).

The IAEM provides a formal ethical code divided into three parts: the first focuses on respect of people, laws, and regulations; the second addresses gaining trust, acting fairly, and being effective with resources; and the third concerns embracing professionalism through education, safety, and protection of life and property (Lindell et al., 2007). Emergency managers employed by the government are required to comply with formal ethical codes in their jurisdiction as well. Given that emergency management is an interdisciplinary endeavor, a number of codes of ethics from different associations may come into play as well. Thus emergency managers have to comply with multiple codes of ethics, which usually do not contradict one another.

Each of the three values identified by the IAEM in its code of ethics has a purpose that goes further than just requiring effective work in the workplace; it holds these professionals, whose decisions can affect the whole community, accountable for their decisions. The first value, respect, refers not only to respecting superiors and colleagues in the workplace, but more importantly to respecting those whom the organization serves. One aspect of showing respect for those served is being fiscally responsible without a reduction in quality of services. The second value, commitment, ensures that members make decisions that improve the quality of life for those served. As stated in the code, emergency management professionals "commit themselves to promoting decisions that engender trust and those we serve" and are focused on "enhancing the caliber of service [they] deliver while striving to improve the quality of life in the community" (IAEM, 2010). The final value stated in the code of ethics is professionalism, with those who work in the field being held to the highest level of professionalism during all duties. The professionalism of emergency managers is founded on their mission of education, safety, and protection of life and property.

To determine whether emergency management is a profession, one must look at the code of ethics observed by all recognized emergency managers. These codes hold emergency management professionals to the same level that many other professions such as law enforcement, teaching, and medicine must also meet. Although 15 to 20 years ago people who worked in emergency management may not have been recognized as members of a particular profession, since then all signs point toward an evolution of emergency management from being "just a job" to full-blown recognition as "a profession."

Conclusion

The degree of education and autonomy possessed by professionals in the emergency management field requires a level of supervision provided by associations and regulatory agencies through licensing and certification. Managers may delve into various areas of public life to gain experience from different organizations and in different settings. Emergency management requires education and training, mandates familiarity with a certain body of knowledge, and sets a minimum standard of knowledge, which managers can then pass on to newcomers to the field (Lindell et al., 2007). Another requirement of emergency managers is that those in the profession must be accountable to their peers and can be punished for noncompliance with the overall professional standards. Collectively, these attributes satisfy the three criteria of a profession: membership certification, organized body of knowledge, and ethical standards. Moreover, evaluations of emergency management efforts have been embraced as a valid way to reveal potential deficiencies in intraorganizational, interorganizational, and system-wide contexts.

The practice of emergency management has undergone many changes in recent decades, but as a group emergency managers need to continue their professional development. Emergency management needs to continue to meet the challenges that will inevitably arise in the future, improve standards, and maintain high expectations. In addition, the experiences in Hurricane Katrina and other disasters should be recognized as opportunities to build upon failures by establishing and enforcing ethical standards. As the saying goes, those who do not learn from their past are condemned to repeat it.

Review Questions

1. How has professionalism emerged in emergency management?
2. Is emergency management a true profession?
3. What are some of the standards and accepted accountability measures in emergency and crisis management?
4. The 9/11 Commission recommends in its report that NFPA 1600 become the standard governing emergency management professionals in the United States. What does NFPA 1600 require an emergency management organization to have?
5. What are the required competencies for emergency managers?
6. How might the information you gained from this chapter affect you personally and professionally?

References

Alexander, D. (2003). Towards the development of standards in emergency management training and education. *Disaster Prevention and Management, 12*(2), 113–123.

Behn, R. D. (2003). Why measure performance? Different purposes require different measures. *Public Administration Review, 63*(5), 586–606.

Boin, A., McConnell., A., & t'Hart, P. (2008). Governing after crisis. In A. Boin, A. McConnell, & P. t'Hart (Eds.), *Governing after crisis: The politics of investigation, accountability and learning,* pp. 3–32. Cambridge, UK: Cambridge University Press.

Bornemisza, O., Griekspoor, A., Ezard, N., & Sondorp, E. (2010). The Interagency Health and Nutrition Evaluation initiative in humanitarian crises: Moving from single-agency to joint, sector wide evaluations. In L. A. Ritchie & W. MacDonald (Eds.), *Enhancing disaster* and emergency preparedness, response, and recovery through evaluation: New directions for evaluation (pp. 21–35). San Francisco: Wiley/Jossey Bass.

Brody, S. D. (2003). Are we learning to make better plans? A longitudinal analysis of plan quality associated with natural hazards. *Journal of Planning Education and Research, 23*(2), 191–201.

Emergency Management Accreditation Program (EMAP). (2010). What is EMAP? Retrieved April, 15, 2010, from http://www.emaponline.org/index.php?option=com_content&view=article&id=25&Itemid=28.

Government Accountability Office (GAO). (2006). *Enhanced leadership, capabilities, and accountability controls will improve the effectiveness of the nation's preparedness, response, and recovery system*. Washington, DC: Author.

Henstra, D. (2010). Evaluating local government emergency management programs: What framework should public managers adopt? *Public Administration Review, 70*(2), 236–246.

Humanitarian Practice Network (HPN). (1995). Accountability in disaster response: Assessing the impact and effectiveness of relief assistance. Retrieved July 10, 2010, from Humanitarian Practice Network: http://www.odihpn.org/report.asp?id=1166.

Hutchins, H. M., Annulis, A., & Gaudet, C. (2008). Crisis planning: Survey results from Hurricane Katrina and implications for performance improvement professionals. *Performance Improvement Quarterly, 20*(3–4), 27–51.

International Association of Emergency Managers (IAEM). (2010). Emergency management code of ethics. Retrieved November 5, 2008, from http://www.iaem.com/about/IAEMCodeofEthics.htm.

International Federation of Red Cross and Red Crescent Societies (IFRC). (2010). *Annual report: Disaster management: Operations technical advice*.

International Organization for Standardization (ISO). (2006). ISO considers development of standards for improving crisis management. Retrieved April 10, 2010, from http://www.iso.org/iso/pressrelease?refid=Ref1011.

International Organization for Standardization (ISO). (2008). Managing crises with new ISO/IEC standard for IT disaster recovery. Retrieved April 10, 2010, from http://www.iso.org/iso/pressrelease.htm?refid=Ref1118.

Janis, A., Stiefel, K. M., & Carbullido, C. C. (2010). Evaluation of a Monitoring and evaluation system in disaster recovery: Learning from the Katrina Aid Today National Case Management Consortium. *New directions for evaluation 126*, 65–77.

Jurkiewicz, C. L. (2007). Louisiana's ethical culture and its effect on the administrative failures following Katrina. *Public Administration Review, 67*(1), 57–63.

Koliba, C., Mills, R. and Zia, A. (2011). Accountability in Governance Networks: Implications Drawn from Studies of Response and Recovery Efforts Following Hurricane Katrina. *Public Administration Review. 71*(2): 210–220.

Lindell, M. K., Prater, C., & Perry, R. W. (2006). Fundamentals of emergency management. FEMA. Retrieved from http://training.fema.gov/EMIWeb/edu/fem.asp.

Lindell, M. K., Prater, C., & Perry, R. W. (2007). *Introduction to emergency management*. Hoboken, NJ: Wiley.

Marincioni, F. (2007). Information technologies and the sharing of disaster knowledge: The critical role of professional culture. *Disasters, 31*(4), 459–476.

Nicholson, W. C. (2007). Legal issues. In W. L. Waugh, Jr., & K. Tierney (Eds.), *Emergency management: Principles and practice for local government* (2nd ed., pp. 237–255). Washington, DC: ICMA.

Ritchie, L. A., & MacDonald, W. (2010a). Enhancing disaster and emergency preparedness, response, and recovery through evaluation. In L. A. Ritchie & W. MacDonald (Eds.), *Enhancing disaster and emergency preparedness, response, and recovery through evaluation: New directions for evaluation* (pp. 3–7). San Francisco, Wiley/Jossey Bass.

Ritchie, L. A., & MacDonald, W. (2010b). Evaluation of disaster and emergency management: Do no harm, but do better. In L. A. Ritchie & W. MacDonald (Eds.), *Enhancing disaster and emergency preparedness, response, and recovery through evaluation: New directions for evaluation* (pp. 107–111), San Francisco: Wiley/Jossey Bass.

Sphere Project. (2004). The Humanitarian Charter and minimum standards in disaster response. In *Sphere Project handbook*. Geneva, Switzerland: Author. Retrieved April 27, 2010, from http://ocw.jhsph.edu/courses/RefugeeHealthCare/PDFs/SphereProjectHandbook.pdf.

Stivers, C. (2007). "So poor and so black": Hurricane Katrina, public administration, and the issue of race. *Public Administration Review, 67*(1), 48–55.

Ulmer, R. R., Sellnow, T. L., & Seeger, M. W. (2007). *Effective crisis communication: Moving from crisis to opportunity.* Thousand Oaks, CA: Sage.

Wilson, J., & Oyola-Yemaiel, A. (2001). The evolution of emergency management and the advancement towards a profession in the United States and Florida. *Safety Science, 39,* 117–131.

Chapter 12

International Actors and Perspectives

Chapter Objectives

- Analyze the international emergency and crisis management system.
- Identify key international actors in emergency and crisis management.
- Study international disaster management actors from a network perspective.
- Describe the role of nongovernmental organizations in managing emergencies and crises.
- Apply the international emergency and crisis management framework to three cases.

Introduction

Countries across the globe have experienced a number of major disasters, both human-made and natural, over the past decade. Whether they involve terrorism, earthquakes, fires, tsunamis, or hurricanes, disasters have increasingly become an international concern, in terms of both their scope and their consequences. As a result, there is an increasing need for advancement in mitigation and response operations as well as international coordination and collaboration in such environments. In an attempt to contribute to the knowledge base and improve the governance of response operations, this chapter identifies the current structure of international disaster management with regard to coordination, collaboration, and networking capacities. It closely studies the major actors and describes the activities of international organizations such as the United Nations (UN) and its specialized agencies, the International Federation of Red Cross and Red Crescent Societies (IFRC), and international and regional economic and security organizations such as the North Atlantic Treaty Organization (NATO) and the Association of Southeast Asian Nations (ASEAN). Studying three cases of disaster response in detail, this chapter seeks to identify problems in the system in terms of coordination and collaboration, and explores ways of effectively resolving them.

Students of emergency and crisis management are exposed to a great deal of information on what is being done in the United States and, to a lesser degree, the English-speaking world. However, they are often unaware of the approaches to emergency management used in other regions. This chapter identifies some of the ways in which countries differ systematically in their hazard vulnerability, economic resources, government organization, built environments, civil society, role of the military, and role of international organizations.

The way in which international agencies respond to disasters is important when it comes to saving lives in those communities. Nevertheless, although international response agencies offer help to affected countries, delivery of such assistance is not as simple as just arriving on site. Organizations must take into account what their roles will be and how they will coordinate their efforts with those undertaken by the country in need. Even more importantly, they must wait for a request before they can respond.

Resource coordination represents one of the central tenets of emergency management. Without a coordinated response to disasters, it is difficult to meet the needs of those affected. The majority of past problems in coordinating international aid have been related to the lack of communication and policy. Emergency management needs to develop an effective means to request assistance from and integrate these international agencies into response frameworks.

The UN can play a unique role in helping countries, including providing assistance to countries so as to enable them to properly prepare for disaster. Many affected countries do not have the financial ability to prepare for a disaster. The UN has already begun the process of using a collaborative effort to assist other countries through its International Strategy for Disaster Reduction (UNISDR). In addition, because the UN represents the viewpoints of numerous countries, the sheer diversity of its membership can ease tensions, alleviating concerns about ulterior motives in offering aid.

This chapter includes a literature review of the coordinative mechanisms of international emergency and crisis management. The case studies presented here analyze the responses to the Myanmar cyclone, Sichuan earthquake, and 2010 Pakistan flooding in detail from network theory perspectives. After giving brief background information on each disaster and the host government's attempts to respond and coordinate the relief operations, the chapter concentrates on the coordinative mechanisms employed at the international level during the crisis. Identifying problems with coordination in international disaster management operations, the chapter highlights ways in which those issues can effectively be resolved. Finally, international organizations with responsibilities in managing disasters and their regional and local/host coordinating agencies are discussed.

International Disaster Management Systems

Coordination and communication are significant factors that affect the success or failure of a relief operation undertaken by the international community (Kapucu, 2011; Sylves, 2008; White, 1999). The scope of this issue can best be captured by the analytical tools provided by network theory and network analysis (Comfort & Haase, 2006; Kapucu, 2006; Stephenson, 2006), as the structure of coordination shapes the rules of engagement and coordination of partnerships during relief operations (Byman, Lesser, Pirnie, Benard, & Waxman, 2003). This section describes the current elements of the international emergency management system using a network theory perspective to analyze the structure.

The international disaster relief arena comprises many independent actors who respond to natural and humanitarian crises in their own ways. For the overall governance of disaster relief operations to be effective, however, those organizations need to coordinate their activities by sharing information, logistics, staff, and goods with one another. Given the importance of coordinative mechanisms for the effectiveness of the disaster relief operations, there is a strong need to assess the system-wide structure of interorganizational coordination. An effective evaluation of the coordination system necessitates situating disaster relief operations within an interorganizational network framework, as individual coordination and collaboration mechanisms are a product of the interorganizational structure in which those organizations operate. It is, therefore, important to address how the disaster relief network puts certain organizations in better or worse positions to collaborate with other organizations, how an organization's position in the network influences its and other organizations' functions and outcomes, and which kinds of organizations occupy or play key mediating roles during disaster relief operations. Understanding the influence of the network structure on interorganizational coordination and disaster relief outcomes can help emergency managers to identify key organizations for specific types of relief or recovery activities (Moore, Trujillo, Stearns, Basurto-Davila, & Evans, 2007).

Kent (1987) defines the international disaster relief network as "an amalgam of non-binding contacts, sustained by various channels of communication and by an awareness of who is around" (p. 69). Yet, such informal network arrangements, which include diverse groups of actors that are tenuously connected by scores of informal contacts and temporary commitments, do not have a long life span and merely create short-term interdependencies (Kent, 1987). In managing complex emergencies and disasters that often involve a multiplicity of actors with diverse interests and that have the potential for technical and organizational failures, informal networks play more important roles than formally established hierarchical structures in ensuring effective system-wide coordination (Chisholm, 1989). The high level of uncertainty associated with complex emergencies and disasters actually permits the development of networks, thereby enhancing effective coordination. Powell (1990) describes the network perspective as follows: "Reciprocity and mutually supportive actions rather than administrative fiat and resource dependence and [a] win-win situation rather than paternalistic hierarchy are the defining characteristics of networks" (p. 303).

Informal networks also play an important role in terms of information exchange and dissemination at time when a crisis breaks out. For instance, the international community and World Health Organization (WHO) officials did not know about the severe acute respiratory syndrome (SARS) outbreak in China until an e-mail was received through informal channels from a physician in China. As this example demonstrates, informal networks can overcome barriers of political expediency, lack of scientific diagnosis, and delays in reporting (Bryant, Vertinsky, & Smart, 2007).

In his research on international peacekeeping in Bosnia, Lipson (2005) demonstrated that network theory provides a rich menu of conceptual tools and frameworks for understanding interorganizational coordination in complex events. He also found that interorganizational coordination mostly develops through networks and informal arrangements on an ad hoc basis, some of which become institutionalized. According to Lipson, formal coordination comprises the rearrangement of organizational charts, hierarchy of authority, and responsibility and explicitly prescribed procedures. In contrast, "informal coordination develops spontaneously through social networks and ad hoc responses to interdependence" (p. 14).

Barriers to effective coordination among the various disaster relief organizations include the environment and structures in which the operational relationships of these organizations are embedded—specifically, competition for scarce resources; efforts to attract donors through the excessive use of media; autonomous actors and organizations; and direct and administrative costs of coordination (Stephenson, 2005). Effective communication is crucial to ensure effective coordination of response actions to pandemic diseases such as SARS. For example, Singapore responded effectively to the outbreak of SARS thanks to its centrally coordinated response system. By comparison, Canada experienced serious problems in the same pandemic because of interorganizational coordination problems as well as interjurisdictional conflicts (Bryant et al., 2007).

To improve the coordination of disaster response operations among a multiplicity of international actors, Stephenson (2005) suggests that actors in the disaster relief network develop organizational cultures that actively promote interorganizational trust. He proposes the adoption of a collective rationality by the organizations with respect to their missions and personnel training and development. During the disaster relief in Rostaq, Afghanistan, after a devastating earthquake struck the region, Benini (1999) observed the dissolution of organizational boundaries of the collaborating disaster relief agencies, whereby identity and internal configuration of organizations blurred and became meaningless by way of sharing authority and a flexible exchange of resources. More notably, he observed that decision-making patterns did not necessarily centralize under crisis situations. On the contrary, "the networked organizations remained without a clearly recognizable center" (p. 45) and this type of network design provided a greater scope for learning than a centralized arrangement would have (Benini, 1999).

In his crisis case study, Moynihan (2008) recognized the need to take into account the factors contingent upon each crisis in identifying better systems of governance for managing disasters. This author studied the U.S. Incident Command System, in which a diverse network of actors is governed by a hierarchy; he suggests this structure could be adopted as a "best practice" model for international emergency management, as it offers a solution for interorganizational coordination problems without abandoning the spirit of the network perspective. Eberlein and Newman (2008) advocate a similar idea—namely, combining emergent transnational networks with formal institutions in the European Union (EU). In their works, these authors found that the incorporation of transgovernmental networks into authoritative rule-making processes provides a better framework for EU governance. Extending this example into international disaster relief, blending the networks of diverse actors with the more centralized UN governance system could yield a better framework for the governance of international disaster response operations (**Figure 12-1**).

The intensity and scope of disasters determine the level of international involvement and disaster assistance. Disaster relief coordination is then set up based on the number of lost lives and the extent of property damage. The capacity of the host governmental and nongovernmental bodies in terms of experience, policy, and planning is also crucial in determining the level of international involvement and disaster relief coordination. Local and international media are also considered influential actors, as they are able to relay the impact of a disaster more broadly, thereby affecting the level of international public and private donations, and publicize the disaster relief activities of international organizations, thereby driving competition for funding and visibility among the diverse actors in the response.

International disaster relief coordination is also shaped by the extent of institutionalization and the operational capacity of organizations already active in the affected communities. The level of trust between development organizations and the host government, the extent of authority granted to organizations, and the level of coordination and collaboration among preexisting development organizations are all crucial factors that influence the functioning of international disaster relief coordination. This relationship arises primarily because most disaster response organizations arrive with one item on their agendas—disaster response. Preexisting facilities of coordination and practices of collaboration catalyze the institutionalization process for emergent networks of disaster responders.

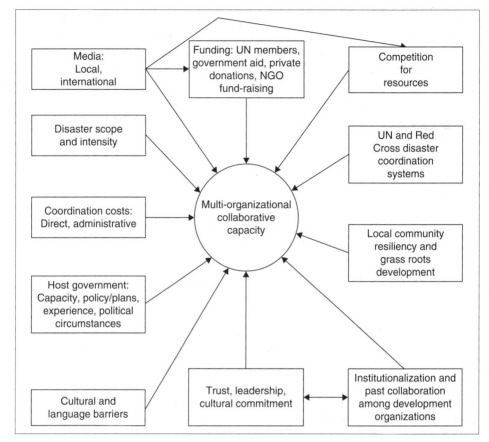

Figure 12-1 *Capacity for Collaborative Governance in International Disaster Relief*

The cultivation of interpersonal relationships and trust among disaster relief partners, development of standards and norms among partners, pre-established coordination mechanisms due to strong donor requirements, a dominant lead agency, and use of best practices facilitate the governance of multiorganizational disaster relief. Of equal importance in shaping effective collaboration is the resilience of communities and grassroots development in affected countries.

In contrast, competition for scarce resources, direct and administrative costs of coordination, and cultural and language barriers impede the attainment of successful coordination. Some crucial concerns and issues embedded within the UN disaster coordination system and International Red Cross networks may also obstruct successful partnerships in international disaster response. The UN system is embroiled in perennial problems related to institutional survival (Kent, 2004; UN Office for the Coordination of Humanitarian Affairs [UNOCHA], 2002), interagency rivalries (Natsios, 1995); UNOCHA's lack of controlling authority over other UN agencies

(Byman et al., 2003; Stephenson, 2006); the nonexistence of a secure UN budget (Stephenson, 2006); dependence of the UN on solicitation of help from host nations; and unequal UN–international nongovernmental organization (INGO) relationships, in which the subcontracting aspect is a stressed relationship rather than a partnership of equals (Natsios, 1995). Likewise, the International Red Cross network and its coordinative system are not in a position to become an all-inclusive coordinative body of global disaster relief policy because of many factors, but especially because of its strict political neutrality, a stance that restricts its ability to form partnerships with political organizations such as the UN.

The United States also has specialized departments dedicated to helping developing countries following a disaster once an official request for assistance is received. The U.S. Agency for International Development (USAID) assists developing countries with economic growth, agriculture, trade, and economic development, albeit while advancing U.S. foreign policy. The U.S. Office of Foreign Disaster Assistance, which is housed within USAID, coordinates all U.S. response to international incidents and provides relief in all types of disasters. Finally, the United States makes its military available to assist with international disaster response through the Department of Defense. The military's role in foreign disaster response comes with many stipulations; however, these forces' main role is to provide security and assistance through logistical, physical, and communications support as well as the delivery of food and medical relief (Sylves, 2008).

Although the United States clearly has many resources for assisting foreign nations, the fact that it is the world's major superpower may lead countries to view U.S. support through a skeptical lens. The fear is that the United States may help them recover, but in so doing may look out for only its own interests. Sylves (2008) mentions territorial sovereignty—the desire for governments to maintain jurisdiction and control—as a factor that must be taken into account when deciding to request or refuse the help of other countries. This was the case in May 2008 following a cyclone in Myanmar that killed hundreds of thousands of people. Owing to a multitude of fears concerning the intentions of the United States as well as pride (the government wanted to prove it could handle the situation on its own), the government of Myanmar refused the help of the United States, the UN, and many other countries.

Although the UN's offer of assistance following the Myanmar disaster was denied, this organization is generally seen as a neutral international emergency responder. The UN can deliver relief to countries while at the same time providing comfort because it is seen as a unifier of nations. Made up of more than 192 countries, the UN is clearly not a single governmental body and, therefore, may be seen as not having a political agenda in aiding a country. The UN is dedicated to improving emergency management practices through its International Strategy for Disaster Reduction (Lindell, Prater, & Perry, 2007).

In 2002, the UN collaborated with the government of Japan, the World Meteorological Association, and the Asian Disaster Reduction Center to publish *Living with*

Risk: A Global Review of Disaster Reduction Initiatives (Lindell et al., 2007), an international strategy for disaster reduction. The main objectives of the initiative were to increase public awareness of risk, vulnerability, and disaster reduction globally; to obtain commitment from public authorities to implement disaster reduction policies and actions; to stimulate interdisciplinary and intersectoral partnerships (including the expansion of risk reduction networks); and to improve scientific knowledge about disaster reduction.

International Actors in Emergency and Crisis Management

This section reviews the key organizations that play a role in international emergency management. Network analysis of the Myanmar cyclone, Sichuan earthquake, and 2010 Pakistan floods cases provides an opportunity to compare and contrast the emergency management system with the actual practice in these three incidents.

United Nations and Its Specialized Agencies

When an emergency occurs, the UN responds immediately and on a continuing basis by supplying aid in the form of food, shelter, medical assistance, and logistical support. The UN Emergency Relief Coordinator heads the international UN response to crises, which acts through a committee of several humanitarian bodies including the UN Children's Fund (UNICEF), the UN Development Program (UNDP), the World Food Programme (WFP), the UN High Commissioner for Refugees (UNHCR), the World Health Organization (WHO), the UN Food and Agriculture Organization (FAO), and other specialized agencies as deemed necessary depending on the problems specific to the event (Coppola & Haddow, 2007; UNOCHA, 2002; White, 1999).

The World Food Programme (WFP) is a UN specialized agency that has a key role in coordinating the provision of food aid by conducting crop production calculations, developing food aid requirements, and planning the logistics of disaster relief operations (Natsios, 1995). It works closely with the FAO in helping disaster victims, especially those in rural areas (Sylves, 2008).

UNICEF targets women and children in providing disaster relief and development operations, but also collaborates with other disaster relief organizations to restore food distribution as well as water and sanitation services fundamental to restoring normal living conditions. Primary activities of this agency include emergency medical interventions, mass vaccination campaigns for children, water and sanitation programs, and therapeutic aid for severely malnourished children in emergencies (Natsios, 1995; Sylves, 2008).

The UNDP not only has a development mission, but also is the resident coordinator of the agency in each country and acts as the UN's resident coordinator with preeminent executive authority to coordinate other UN agencies under the guidelines established by the UN General Assembly (Natsios, 1995). The UNDP ties its response and recovery efforts to long-term and sustainable development and has two operant programs: (1) the Emergency Response Division and (2) the Disaster Reduction and Recovery Program. Moreover, the UNDP runs the UN's International Strategy for Disaster Reduction Working Group on Risk, Vulnerability, and Disaster Impact Assessment, which promotes the standardization of guidelines for increasing awareness and sensitivity of emergency responders to the social consequences of a disaster (Sylves, 2008).

The WHO is another UN specialized agency—an organization with a bureaucratic nature that reflects the interests of its members. As of 2007, 72% of the agency's resources came from voluntary contributions of member states and other partnering agencies (WHO, 2007). Dominated by a single profession (medicine), this organization is vulnerable to "competency traps," which are difficult to unlearn. In particular, Bryant et al. (2007) note that professional organizations tend to define problems unidimensionally, which in turn may cause new crises. In an epidemic such as the SARS pandemic, for instance, medical authorities prefer to limit travel-purpose circulation of people. Initially, that measure may be perceived as a positive attempt to limit communication of the disease, but it may trigger other problems such as economic crises if the scope and period of limitations are not balanced rationally. The WHO has its own agenda and standard operating procedures to deal with crises, but it needs to consult multiple parties before it issues travel advisories (Bryant et al., 2007).

The Office for the Coordination of Humanitarian Affairs in the UN was established in 1998 by the UN General Assembly under the chairmanship of the Emergency Relief Coordinator to build consensus and share best practices among all UN partner organizations involved in disaster relief. For each disaster case, UNOCHA collaborates with multiple organizations to formulate a joint and coordinated course of action. In addition, this agency collects and disseminates information monitoring ongoing disasters and conducts post-disaster assessments through its Disaster Response System unit. UNOCHA also coordinates the field missions of a variety of UN agencies in the assessment of needs, mobilization of resources, management of donations, and issuance of follow-up reports. Moreover, the agency lends money to disaster-affected communities from its cash reserve fund, known as the Central Emergency Revolving Fund (Selves, 2008).

International Red Cross and Red Crescent Movement

The International Red Cross movement is composed of the International Committee of the Red Cross (ICRC) and the International Federation of Red Cross and Red Crescent Societies (IFRC). When a disaster strikes and the local capacity is overwhelmed, an appeal by the affected country's national Red Cross chapter is made to the IFRC's Secretariat. As the coordinating body, the Secretariat initiates an international appeal for support to the IFRC and many other outside sources, and provides personnel and humanitarian aid supplies from its own stocks. These supplies, which can be shipped if they are not locally available, are intended to meet needs in the areas of health, logistics and water specialists, aid personnel, and relief management (Coppola & Haddow, 2007).

The ICRC was established after the horrific events of the Solferino battle in 1859, with a mission to lessen the suffering during armed conflicts; it now has a mandate to do so under international law (the Geneva Conventions and Additional Protocols). Its work is funded by block grants from donor governments as well as by fundraising activities undertaken by the national chapters. One of the most important principles for the Red Cross is its political neutrality. According to Natsios (1995), "The age, doctrine, funding mechanism and mandates of the ICRC set it apart from both the UN system and the NGO community" (p. 412).

North Atlantic Treaty Organization

The North Atlantic Treaty Organization (NATO) was once an important actor only in military operations, including conflicts and wars among the nation-states that make up its membership. Toward the end of the Cold War, however, NATO transformed its mission by incorporating the provision of humanitarian aid, peacekeeping, and natural disaster response as well as civil crises and emergencies response into its scope of concern (NATO, 2004). NATO's assistance in disaster relief during the earthquake in 2005 in Pakistan was an important factor in the success of the overall disaster response operations. It also delivered disaster relief assistance to the United States following Hurricane Katrina in response to an official request for aid (NATO, 2006). NATO has extensive logistical capacity and expertise in dealing with emergency relief under the aegis of the UN (Hanning, 1978).

Association of Southeast Asian Nations

The Association of Southeast Asian Nations (ASEAN) has set up a disaster assistance agency as the organization has evolved and its economic and political influence has grown. ASEAN's resources and collaborative initiatives have helped its disaster relief agency to assist its members, many of which are vulnerable to natural disasters, and developed its logistic capacity and experience in dealing with disasters.

International Nongovernmental Organizations

Not all INGOs get involved in international disaster relief. Most of them arrive at the affected region and transfer resources (e.g., gifts, donations) to the relatively few operating organizations and then leave the disaster scene. INGOs that have a development mission in addition to disaster relief have certain advantages in providing an effective response to crises because of their familiarity with local staff and their social and cultural understanding gained before the onset of the disaster (Natsios, 1995).

International Development Agencies

It is important for the entire global community to react or respond to a disaster, not just because it is the humanitarian thing to do, but because natural disasters have an increasing potential to affect everyone (Sylves, 2008). These ramifications could be realized through the displacement of people, infectious diseases, economic upheaval, or security risks.

Under the guidance of the U.S. State Department, USAID has been involved in disaster response and recovery operations since the Marshall Plan was developed to reconstruct Europe after World War II. Within USAID, the Office of Foreign Disaster Assistance (OFDA) facilitates and coordinates U.S. emergency response and mitigation to natural and human-made disasters overseas (Sylves, 2008). USAID is "officially obligated to further U.S. foreign policy interests in expanding democracy and free markets while improving the lives of the citizens in developing countries" (Sylves, 2008, p. 197). Another important U.S.-based entity in dealing with international disasters is the Department of Defense (DOD), which houses the Office of Peacekeeping and Humanitarian Affairs.

The European Commission's Humanitarian Aid Office (ECHO), Japan International Cooperation Agency (JICA), German Federal Agency for Technical Relief (THW), Russian Ministry of Emergency Situations (MES), and British Foreign and Commonwealth Office (FCO) deliver considerable funding and services in international disaster relief as well.

The European Union (EU) has entities established for disaster preparedness and relief efforts both for EU member and nonmember countries. The EU's Environmental Department emphasizes regional cooperation for civil protection inside and outside of the EU (Coppola, 2007). One of the EU's major disaster management efforts is the Solidarity Fund, which was established in 2002 to provide financial assistance grants to help EU member and candidate countries. Two other mechanisms are designed to maintain civil protection: the Community Action Programme and the Community Civil Protection Mechanisms (Coppola, 2007).

The Community Action Programme supports national, regional, and local efforts for civil protection within EU member countries. It aims to foster cooperation, exchange, and mutual assistance between member countries via workshops, projects, and training courses (Coppola, 2007).

The Community Civil Protection Mechanisms have two functions: providing assistance to disaster-stricken countries and fostering preparedness (Coppola, 2007). The Monitoring and Information Centre (MIC) serves as a common platform for mutual aid and assistance in response to disasters. In case of a disaster, member and nonmember countries can seek assistance from the MIC. In such a case, the MIC contacts EU members and affiliates and asks whether they are willing to provide assistance to the disaster-stricken country. Additionally, the Community Civil Protection Mechanism provides disaster preparedness programs that include courses, exercises, and expert exchange programs (Coppola, 2007; ECHO, 2010).

The European Commission Humanitarian Aid Department (ECHO) within the EU deals with humanitarian affairs outside of Europe. The aim of this department is to provide emergency assistance and relief to victims of natural disasters and armed conflicts. Moreover, ECHO provides technical assistance, training, and financing for disaster-stricken countries and seeks to enhance public awareness about humanitarian affairs (Coppola, 2007).

A government's failure to respond and govern effectively during a time of crisis or emergency could lead to a loss of legitimacy and allow for the governing system to break down, which can result in chaos and extreme consequences with uncontrollable outcomes (Farazmand, 2007). As the world becomes much more interdependent, there is a necessity to change how governments prepare for and respond to emergencies. All emergencies are similar in their urgency; therefore, an important aspect of responding to all emergencies is to have a sharp and timely recognition of the situation as an emergency. Through the failures of the Hurricane Katrina disaster, the global community has realized the need to change its current emergency management processes so as to be adequately prepared for the future. To do so, the world needs to engage in preventive planning and preparation, and to develop an institutionalized response system with "a strong central command structure, a well-coordinated network of response and recovery systems, a specialized crisis management team along with decentralized field commands armed with flexibility, and the presence of a functioning expertise in distinct areas of crisis situations" (Farazmand, 2007, p. 153). Two hard lessons were learned from Katrina's failures: (1) The sense of futility in the face of such disasters is a hindrance to emergency management and (2) resilience and solidarity against this sentiment are key to mounting an effective response (Farazmand, 2007).

Networks of International Emergency and Crisis Management Actors

The current structure of international disaster relief coordination is made up of the UN coordinative mechanism and International Red Cross relief system, both of which incorporate activities of other major actors such as INGOs and regional economic and security organizations. The UN and its specialized agencies play a vital role in disaster relief operations; however, none of those agencies has been granted a controlling authority by the General Assembly to manage or oversee the efforts of its peers (Byman et al., 2003; Stephenson, 2006). In addressing humanitarian crises, the UN is divided organizationally along functional lines (Borton, 1993; Kent, 1987), and UNOCHA does not have any authority over the actions and behaviors of any other UN entity dealing with a crisis (Reindorp, 2002; Reindorp & Wiles, 2001). In addition, UN agencies do not have secure budgets with which to fund emergency management efforts, as they depend on contributions from member states and their citizens (Stephenson, 2006). The UN coordination mechanism has been criticized by several authors who claim that the UN has wasted its energy on alleviating its interagency rivalries and supporting its own institutional survival instead of running effective coordination and leadership as tasked by the General Assembly (Kent, 2004).

It is also important to note that many UN agencies are not operating entities, meaning that they do not directly deliver services to disaster-affected communities. Usually UN agencies need to work with international and local NGOs in providing disaster relief (Kent, 1987; Stephenson, 2006). This kind of pluralistic organizational structure characterized by no single entity commanding authority over the others, and made up of somewhat interdependent, quasi-autonomous participants (Stephenson, 2006), may lead to operational chaos, lengthy delays in delivering aid to those who need it most, and ultimately failure in disaster response (Natsios, 1995).

Given the infeasibility, both politically and administratively, of a complete overhaul of the international disaster response structure, Natsios (1995) proposes that the focus should be on incremental reform of the existing system. This kind of reform would include "aggregating relief actors within each organizational sector" (p. 417), such that the UN centralizes its decision-making authority within one entity (Department of Humanitarian Affairs). NGOs similarly would organize themselves under the umbrella of InterAction (American NGO Partnership Association) and ICVA (International Council of Voluntary Agencies). After such changes were implemented, representatives from each of these groups as well as from the International Red Cross, international financial institutions, NATO, and military establishments (if necessary) could meet to design a unified strategy to international emergency management. Unfortunately, reform at the top may not also trickle down to the bottom, and coordination at the headquarters level may not lead to field-level cooperation (Natsios, 1995).

In the complex and dynamic environments of catastrophic disasters, UN field offices provide "a natural coordination mechanism for nongovernmental organizations and UN organizations that has at least improved the exchange of information among the response agencies" (Natsios, 1995, p. 413). "The defining element for immediate response from the UN or INGOs [is] physical presence prior to the disaster and resultant local knowledge that [enables] their staff to respond quickly" (Tsunami Evaluation Coalition [TEC], n.d.).

In the UN, there is a notable lack of coordination among its agencies at the headquarters, regional, and host country office levels (Benini, 1999; TEC, n.d.). Managerial problems also affect coordination: The UN staff need to be "adequately supported, equipped and trained" (TEC, n.d.). To tackle these problems and increase the effectiveness of its coordination activities, UNOCHA recently initiated some reforms. These measures aim to strengthen the role of the Humanitarian Coordinator to better support the field coordination and focus on "strengthening of the response capacity through a system of lead clusters in activity areas where there are clearly defined gaps" (Hicks & Pappas, 2006). Unfortunately, even this new approach has some problems, one of which is that lessons learned from previous disasters have not been incorporated into the reforms (Hicks & Pappas, 2006). Moreover, a lead agency may give a priority to its own interests and goals at the expense of an overall effort (Byman et al., 2003).

Partnerships are seen as a key element in response to disasters internationally. For example, the WHO cannot operate without the assistance of other partner agencies in the provision of necessary logistics, equipment, supplies, transport, human resources, and knowledge of the cultures and languages of the local area (Ritson & Youssef, 2006). "Collegiality, rather than command and control, [and] coordination [have] characterized the relationships between the governments, the WHO, and other agencies" (Oyegbite, 2005, p. 472). If organizations insist on working independently, the fragmented response typically results in redundancy and wasted time, resources, and energy. To improve partnerships, interpersonal relationships should be fostered in addition to better chemistry among organizations. Development of standards and norms among partners is crucial; the WHO, for example, might take the lead and establish "best practices" (Oyegbite, 2005).

Among the major actors in the international emergency management scene, the UN family of organizations has a formal arrangement for operational-level coordination without successful implementation. The ICRC is fully operational and controls operations through its Delegates General. NGOs have no formal arrangements to ensure operational coordination (Byman et al., 2003), but do engage in informal webs that promote coordination. For example, USAID expects that U.S.-funded NGOs will consult among themselves (Byman et al., 2003). "Pre-established INGO coordination structures with coherent systems for collaboration" and "capacity mapping in high risk regions" help enhance INGO coordination (Völz, 2005, p. 27). Although the International Red Cross has a well-institutionalized disaster coordination system among its national chapters, international bodies, Western NGOs, and grassroots initiatives in disaster-affected communities, the Red Cross coordinative mechanism is not in a position to serve as a worldwide disaster relief coordination body, nor it is in good standing in terms of coordinating its disaster relief activities with those of the UN.

Effective international disaster response requires that actors in the system develop relationships with other members through boundary-spanning networks (through their staff members) before working together in disaster response. Coordination and relationship building cannot be accomplished without the intentions of and encouragement from institutional leadership (Kapucu, 2006; Stephenson & Schnitzer, 2006). Moreover, good relationships cannot be developed without trust (Scott & Davis, 2007). "Building these shared understandings among actors at multiple levels of organization among network players can elicit a broader and deeper dialogue on the nature of operations and missions and how best to realize them" (Stephenson & Schnitzer, 2006, p. 53).

Nonprofit Organizations and International Nongovernmental Organizations

In addition to the UN, several INGOs participate in international emergency management. Many local and national governments are ill prepared to coordinate their own operations effectively with these agencies' efforts. INGOs, however, are well practiced in providing assistance to poor and developing nations. Most INGOs have policies and protocols dictating when and how aid will be rendered in the wake of such disasters, which streamline the coordination process. Unfortunately, when operating in developing countries, certain difficulties may arise for a variety of reasons. Notably, differences in governmental structure, inadequate or nonexistent disaster relief policies, and a lack of basic resources to handle such events can often hinder relief efforts.

Recent research has shown that INGOs encountered incredible difficulty in providing aid to the United States in the wake of Hurricanes Katrina and Rita (Eikenberry, Arroyave, & Cooper, 2007). Because the United States was largely known as an aid-rendering nation, the U.S. government was unaccustomed to requiring or receiving aid from international agencies. Insufficient communication was the initial problem that these agencies faced. Agencies reported being unable to contact the Federal Emergency Management Agency (FEMA) or government representatives to determine what was truly needed (Eikenberry et al., 2007), and several agencies reported relying heavily on news media when making the decision to respond. The perceived inadequacy of the response was so severe that some agencies went outside of their missions and jurisdictions to provide aid. A disconnect between what was being reported by FEMA and what was actually needed on the ground was also observed. Agencies found it difficult to garner the necessary donations because donors were hearing that these needs were already met when, in fact, they were not. Insufficient policy regarding international aid was also an area of difficulty in the Hurricane Katrina response. International agencies found that once they decided to respond, there was no preexisting framework within which they could operate. Although most agencies had assumed they would be rendering support and resources to existing operations, they found themselves largely on their own. Local and faith-based organizations were effectively rendering aid in the area; however, there was a perceived reluctance to work with international organizations.

Confusion as to what role international organizations should play in the Katrina disaster response was readily apparent when these organizations worked with FEMA or the local government. Representatives of these agencies were unable to provide INGO officials with adequate information about resources, policies, or need. This lack of information stemmed from the gaping policy shortcomings both in the overall response and in dealing with international aid agencies. The apparent administrative failures of the national response to Hurricane Katrina brought a new wave of disaster response organizations into the U.S. emergency management framework—INGOs. These perceived administrative failures included not only the lack of initial response to the disaster, but also the lack of planning for the response by such "outsider" organizations, which proved detrimental to relief efforts. Even so, many international organizations that had typically limited their responses to underdeveloped and developing countries in the past, as a result of pressures from donors and victim requests, worked toward trying to assist in the Katrina response and relief efforts. Many of these agencies went against their own charters to provide humanitarian relief to those affected by the hurricane, including providing medicine, school supplies, medical and mental health assistance, and other necessities to assist in the short-term and long-term recovery efforts (Eikenberry et al., 2007).

The collaborative efforts of such groups sparked new relief and response questions that governmental agencies, such as FEMA, should identify and resolve to smooth over future emergency management efforts. Most of the INGOs interviewed by Eikenberry and her colleagues suggested that they met with a number of barriers that prevented them from assisting in relief efforts following Hurricane Katrina; in many cases, they were more successful if they bypassed FEMA altogether because the lack of communication and coordination on FEMA's end prevented an accurate response on the part of the INGOs (Eikenberry et al., 2007). FEMA's lack of control of the situation proved to be a particular hindrance to these organizations: When they contacted FEMA with questions about resources, they were told that they were not needed, even though the INGOs were getting requests for help from victims on the ground (Eikenberry et al., 2007). The nonstop media coverage of the catastrophe exacerbated the situation further, as the images of survivors in need proved that governmental agencies had minimal control over the situation, and over time these agencies' relationship with the NGOs active in the region continued to unravel.

As the Hurricane Katrina failures amply demonstrate, emergency managers must provide a method for the integration of new organizations into existing frameworks. This blending of operations must be done under the aegis of a suitable regulatory system that realizes the potential of such organizations but reduces any negative risks associated with them. It is perhaps most important to acknowledge that these organizations can assist in many ways that governmental organizations cannot, and that they have a superior level of experience and can serve as a valuable resource to all responders (Eikenberry et al., 2007). Since the Katrina response, many organizations have adjusted their "organizational mandates to include the United States in their list of countries to assist in future disasters" (Eikenberry et al., 2007, p. 166). It is in this spirit that emergency managers must acknowledge one of their most important planning decisions: how to integrate these agencies into their response framework.

Case Study Analysis of the International Emergency Management Network

Myanmar: Cyclone Nargis

On May 2, 2008, the devastating Cyclone Nargis struck the Ayeyarwady Delta and Yangon in Myanmar, leading to the deaths of more than 84,530 people, with 53,836 still reported missing. The impact of the disaster was as devastating as the 2004 tsunami in South Asia, especially in terms of its community and household impact, and was the worst disaster in Myanmar's history. The cyclone destroyed approximately 450,000 homes and damaged 350,000 others. Nearly 75% of health facilities and 4000 schools in the affected areas were destroyed or severely damaged. The cyclone swept away the livelihoods of people, inundating more than 600,000 hectares of agricultural land, killing 50% of draught animals, and destroying fishing boats, agricultural stocks, and plants (ASEAN, 2008).

The disaster came at an untimely political moment, hitting Myanmar a few days prior to a scheduled referendum. The governmental regime had been under pressure from Western governments and pro-democratic Buddhist opposition forces to open up the country and democratize the election process. With the onset of disaster, the ruling junta was not only ineffective at organizing a response, but also distrustful about the motives of Western governments and institutions, which prevented the expedient delivery of aid and relief workers.

The technical information regarding the intensity and direction of the cyclone could not be clarified until the last moments, and the lack of communication and preparedness of the government led to massive loss of life and property in Myanmar. However resilient the dwellers of the area were at an individual level, the local community and government entities lacked the capacity to effectively manage the disaster. The political situation and inefficiency exacerbated the already high-intensity disaster outcome.

UN interventions to disaster relief efforts are possible through an assistance request from a disaster-stricken country. Even though there were local branches of UN agencies in Myanmar, along with the Red Cross and some other INGOs, the capacity of these organizations was overwhelmed by the huge impact of the disaster.

Making matter worse, the Myanmar government did not allow international experts and cargo ships with aid into its territory for several weeks. The international Anglophone media did nothing more than denounce the oppressive regime, portraying a negative image of Myanmar that likely diminished international donations for relief efforts.

At a time when UN members pressed for military intervention based on the need to protect peoples' lives in Myanmar, neighboring countries that were trusted by the Myanmar government were delivering disaster response assistance. Chinese, Japanese, Russian, Indonesian, and Singaporean disaster relief teams were approved by the regime to help in search and rescue, medical, and other operations. Singaporean government leaders led the effective intervention by ASEAN, setting up a tripartite ASEAN–UN–Myanmar government joint task force to coordinate, facilitate, and monitor international disaster relief assistance (ASEAN, 2008). For a regional organization like ASEAN, the joint coordination of international disaster relief assistance with the UN and Myanmar government was a novel role, and brought about a new approach to emergency management. Ultimately, the strong trust and positive relationships among the neighboring nations and institutions led to more effective coordination in the disaster relief operations (Holmes, 2008).

The UN is a complex bureaucracy whose span encompasses many specialized agencies and coordination mechanisms. Clusters are a way of coordinating different agencies functioning under the UN umbrella. In response to Cyclone Nargis, the UN agencies used the lead cluster approach. On May 7, eight clusters were established under the leadership of UN Emergency Relief Coordinator, John Holmes, at UNOCHA. These clusters consisted of Water, Sanitation, and Hygiene (WASH); Nutrition; Education; Protection of Children and Women; Emergency Shelter; Food; Logistics; and Emergency Telecommunications. The clusters of Health, Early Recovery, and Agriculture were added to this initial list. With this approach, each cluster is headed by the relevant UN agency, which leads the rest of the agencies and other NGOs as partners. For example, the lead agency of the Food cluster is the WFP. There are also subgroups in clusters, such as Infant Feeding in Emergencies in the Nutrition cluster; these subgroups consist of partners such as the WHO, UNICEF, and Save the Children (UNOCHA, 2008). One organization might also be involved in multiple clusters. For instance, the UN Population Fund (UNFPA) is involved in the Health, Logistics, and Protection of Children and Women clusters.

Within the health cluster network, various NGOs, UN agencies, and the U.S. Institute of Medicine (IOM) held meetings to minimize overlap and compose a draft for a joint UN Flash Appeal as the disaster relief progressed. The WHO's South East Asia regional office started to coordinate the response with the media. Its regional surveillance officers (RSOs) coordinated the flow of information in the health cluster at the township level, with information being received through both formal and informal channels. The role of the RSOs is vital because communicable disease generally spreads faster than human and organizational communication.

Effective communication, exchange, and coordination (collection, analysis, and dissemination) of information are crucial for the success of disaster relief. The UN Disaster Assessment and Coordination (UNDAC) team was deployed from a regional office in Thailand. The WHO has developed protocols with various organizations in the medical response sector to establish standard operational procedures and to coordinate drug donations. The Interagency Emergency Health Kit 2006 (IEHK, 2006) is designed to meet the initial primary healthcare needs of a displaced population without medical facilities during an emergency (WHO, 2006).

Intercluster collaboration is vital to the success of the cluster model. The Health cluster collaborated with the Logistics, Shelter, Nutrition, and WASH clusters both in Myanmar and Thailand after Cyclone Nargis struck the region. The longstanding presence of international NGOs in the affected areas, such as Merlin, an NGO located in the UK dealing with health issues, allowed for close collaboration between the health cluster and local and national health officials.

The UN also provides help through other structures in disaster relief apart from clusters. For example, the WHO participates in and leads the health cluster network, but also has a Health Action in Crises program through which a WHO emergency public health specialist is sent to the field to help implement and coordinate disaster health operations.

In the Cyclone Nargis response, a Civil Society Information Resource Centre was opened on May 15 for local self-help groups upon the recommendation of an INGO forum. Initially, the health cluster network included approximately 20 INGOs, UN agencies, and the IOM. A week later, the number of NGOs reached 30, and after another week 40. By the fourth week of the disaster relief, 50 NGOs had responded, indicating a rapid growth in the number of health cluster participant organizations. Nevertheless, the number of core groups within the cluster network remained stable. The WHO, UNICEF, IOM, Merlin, and Doctors Without Borders (Médecins Sans Frontières [MSF]) were core service providers with their own logistics, staff, and funding. Red Cross Myanmar undertook an important role in disaster response and recovery. Burmese expatriates throughout the world actively organized fundraising activities and donated to the Red Cross and other charity foundations involved in disaster relief in Myanmar. Because many of these expatriates are pro-democratic groups that oppose the current regime, they were not allowed into the country to personally provide assistance.

The Cyclone Nargis disaster demonstrated once again that international partnerships and effective coordination mechanisms for delivering disaster aid are important for saving lives and property throughout the world. It also showed the importance of engaging with the host government, employing diplomacy, and remembering that Western humanitarian agencies are not the only relief actors (Katoch, 2008). Moreover, the disaster highlighted the reality that capacity building at the local level to organize effective prevention and risk reduction and preparedness activities are important for protecting both lives and property (UN, 2008).

Sichuan Earthquake in China

On May 12, 2008, a major earthquake measuring 7.9 on the Richter scale struck Wenchuan County, Aba Prefecture, in China's Sichuan Province at 2:28 P.M. Nearly 70,000 people died and 375,000 others were injured, according to official government figures. Immediately after the earthquake struck, Chinese Prime Minister Wen Jiabao arrived at the disaster scene to lead the coordination of an all-out emergency response as ordered by President Hu Jintao. The Chinese PM set up a National Disaster Relief Headquarters in the disaster-affected areas, and the National Committee for Disaster Reduction activated the highest level of emergency response according to the National Plan on Emergency Response for Disaster Relief. The army, armed police and paramilitary forces, rescue and medical teams, and relief supplies were sent to the region (UNOCHA, 2008).

As summarized in **Table 12-1**, 15 million people were displaced and 5 million became homeless as a result of the earthquake. An appeal for assistance from the international community ensued, and the public, private, and NGO communities responded generously with both cash and in-kind donations. The international media portrayed a positive image of the successful and vigorous, centrally-coordinated emergency response. Although China turned down disaster assistance teams from the United States, Canada, and Australia, it accepted the disaster relief teams from Russia, Germany, Japan, Taiwan, and Singapore.

The UN Resident Coordinator conveyed his condolences to the Chinese government on behalf of the UN community, readied the UN Country Team (UNCT), and

Table 12-1 *Estimated Death and Destruction as a Result of the Sichuan Earthquake in China, May 2008*

	Estimate	Source
Total dead	69,222	Government of China: August 7, 2008
Total injured	374,638	Government of China: August 7, 2008
Total missing	18,176	Government of China: August 7, 2008
Total homeless (estimated)	5 million	International Federation of Red Cross and Red Crescent Societies: June 11, 2008 and July 29, 2008
Total displaced (estimated)	15 million	International Federation of Red Cross and Red Crescent Societies: June 11, 2008 and July 29, 2008
Total affected (estimated)	46 million	United Nations: July 16, 2008

Source: USAID, 2009.

set up the UN Disaster Management Team (UNDMT) to coordinate the UN agencies' disaster relief operations. The UN Central Emergency Response Fund (CERF) provided monetary help for its agencies to undertake, under the coordination of the UNCT, important shelter and mass-care disaster relief operations.

The UN effort was coordinated by the UNDMT and chaired by the UNICEF director. As central government was effective in its response and coordination, there was no need for organizing the UN response by lead cluster, as was the case in the Myanmar disaster. The Ministry of Foreign Affairs coordinated the international assistance, and the Ministry of Civil Affairs coordinated the logistics and emergency management.

With its considerable experience, the Chinese Red Cross was one of the most active participants in the Sichuan earthquake. Using its capacity in conjunction with the regional and national coordinating networks of IFRC, the Red Cross Society of China was effective in garnering donations from around the world. The Chinese government also granted the Chinese Red Cross the authority to bring in international doctors when necessary.

A grassroots movement of Chinese volunteers established informal networks to deliver aid to the earthquake victims in several ways. Amateur radio clubs played an important role in providing communication facilities following the collapse of telecommunications in Sichuan. Taxi drivers and their hub played an important role in reaching severely hit areas and delivering aid. The economic interests of states and private businesses throughout the world, as well as the spirit of preparation for the Olympic Games to be held in Beijing later that year, influenced the successful organization of the emergency response by the central government. The generous donations from private companies, NGOs, UN agencies, the Chinese Red Cross and its sister societies, and Chinese people as volunteers contributed to a great extent to the successful response and recovery operations in Sichuan.

2010 Pakistan Floods

Pakistan is a country prone to natural disasters such as flooding, landslides, earthquakes, droughts, and cyclones (Asian Development Bank [ADB], 2010). In 2010, Pakistan experienced the worst flooding since the country had become an independent state. Heavy monsoon rains began on July 22, 2010, and resulted in flash floods in the northwest and east regions of Pakistan. The rain continued until August, when the runoff resulted in breached levees and water flowed and gushed to floodplains in mostly rural areas. Some intentional levee breaks were also created to protect urban regions of the country (Kronstadt, Sheikh, & Vaughn, 2010).

The National Disaster Management Authority (NDMA) reported that the floods affected more than 78 districts that cover approximately 100,000 square kilometers (ADB, 2010). At one point, one-fifth of the country was inundated with water (Oxfam, 2011). This flood resulted in a huge humanitarian disaster, affecting

20 million people and leading to widespread displacement. Many individuals lost access to clean drinking water, their shelter and housing, their land, their livestock, and their livelihoods. Out of the 20 million people affected, approximately 14 million required immediate assistance (Independent Evaluation Group [IEG], 2010; Kronstadt et al., 2010). Even six months later, the homeless and affected population, especially children, were at risk of catching water and vector-borne diseases. Cases of malnutrition, diarrhea, skin infections, cholera, malaria, and hepatitis have been reported. The floods fully or partially destroyed 1.9 million houses, forcing their former occupants into makeshift tents and sites including school and college buildings (Kronstadt et al., 2010).

The worst-hit areas were rural areas, where many farmers lost their livelihoods because standing water in their fields hindered the planting of seasonal crops; fewer crops translated into a reduced food supply in Pakistan. Along with the agricultural land destruction, the death livestock also resulted in food price hikes (Kronstadt et al., 2010).

Disaster management in Pakistan is divided into federal, provincial, and district levels. The NDMA in Pakistan, which is the equivalent of FEMA in the United States, is responsible for coordination of disaster response efforts by all disaster response and relief organizations (both national and international players). The Economic Affairs Division (EAD) coordinates donor funds and sources, while the NDMA provides leadership and works closely with the various government departments, the military, international agencies, and international donors to ensure effective relief operations such as relief goods distribution (Kronstadt et al., 2010).

After the 2005 Kashmir earthquake, the government of Pakistan passed National Disaster Management Ordinance 2006 and developed its National Disaster Risk Management Framework (NDRMF), which is a strategic policy document that guides disaster risk management activities within the country's borders. Under the 2006 ordinance, the NDMA was created as the leading federal-level organization for disaster management, under the leadership of the Prime Minister; in addition, the National Disaster Management Commission (NDMC) was developed as the policy creation entity for disaster and risk management. At the provincial level, Provincial Disaster Management Authorities (PDMAs) handles emergency management; at the district/local level, District Disaster Management Authorities (DDMAs) serve the same purpose. Although PDMAs have been created in all provinces, DDMAs have yet to be established in all districts across Pakistan. The DDMAs that have been established within some districts currently have restricted capacity (ADB, 2010).

Specific to flood management, the Federal Flood Commission (FFC) handles flood coordination, management, and mitigation in Pakistan. This agency is responsible for creating and implementing the National Flood Protection Plan. In addition, the Ministry of Environment (MOE) is responsible for developing climate change policies and plans, and coordinating work on climate change (ADB, 2010).

Immediate challenges faced during the response to the 2010 floods included difficulties in accessing victims due to the destruction of infrastructure such as roads, bridges, and electricity plants; lack of capacity for response; and security concerns in some northern geographical areas (Kronstadt et al., 2010). The major relief effort was coordinated by the Pakistani government with the help of UN organizations and NGOs. By November 2010, approximately 1.5 million people had been rescued by the 20,000 military troops deployed by the government and other relief teams. Despite the challenges, excellent search and rescue operations helped to save many lives. Also, the timely distribution of food and medical assistance helped in averting disease outbreaks (Oxfam, 2011). To ensure that organizations were not involved in petty corruption regarding delivery and distribution of relief goods, the government of Pakistan developed a National Oversight Disaster Management Council (Kronstadt et al., 2010), whose membership consists of highly reputed and honest officials from the civil society (ADB, 2010).

Government cash-based assistance in the form of the Watan cash transfer scheme which incorporated a card registered to each family head to obtain cash from ATM machines has proved to be largely successful, although incidents of petty corruption have been reported. The scheme needs to be further improved to ensure that this cash-based system is free from corruption of any sort and that deserving people get the cash equitably (Oxfam, 2011). Currently, the infrastructure to deliver such assistance is weak within the country. For example, in a district in the Sindh province, only three ATMs were available within a 2500-kilometer to serve the flood-affected population (Oxfam, 2011).

Overall, the civilian government's response to the 2010 flooding was fairly weak, as it does not really have the capacity, or the capabilities, to respond to a disaster of this magnitude effectively. Ultimately, the military and armed forces played a more prominent role in the national response by providing equipment for evacuation and by carrying out search and rescue operations (Kronstadt et al., 2010).

The United States has been actively involved in providing response and relief goods and operations and is currently the largest donor to Pakistani relief efforts. USAID led the U.S. response in Pakistan. Initially, 30 U.S. military helicopters along with C-130 planes were used to supply relief goods. In addition, 26 U.S. mobile medical teams provided first aid and healthcare services, as approximately 450 health centers and facilities in Pakistan were destroyed by the floods. While the most notable reason for providing relief operations is humanitarian, the U.S. government is clearly motivated to improve its perception among the Pakistani citizens so as to strengthen its diplomatic ties with the country (Kronstadt et al., 2010).

The UN agencies have also played a very important role in coordinating relief efforts and providing support to the government of Pakistan. Notably, they have helped in preventing potentially devastating disease outbreaks by providing crucial health care (Oxfam, 2011). The UN outlined an initial response plan for Pakistan in August 2010 for relief and recovery needs. This plan, which follows a cluster approach, continues to seek money to fund relief and recovery within 12 sectors: water and sanitation, health, shelter, agriculture, food, community restoration, protection, education, nutrition, logistics, coordination, and camp management. Each cluster is led by a designated agency that coordinates relief and recovery operations pertaining to the specific cluster. For example, WFP is heading the food cluster and is responsible for coordinating efforts to provide food to affected populations in the flood-ravaged regions. WFP is coordinating and working with more than 30 NGOs to provide food to approximately 150,000 people per day (Kronstadt et al., 2010).

In September 2010, the UN initiated its biggest humanitarian appeal ever, asking for $2 billion to provide relief goods to the Pakistani population for 12 months (ADB, 2010). Unfortunately, the response from international donors was patchy and slow. **Figure 12-2** shows recent disasters and their corresponding UN appeals for funding per person within the first 10 days of the disaster. Only $3.20 was provided per flood-affected person in the 10 days following the Pakistani disaster. Despite the low rate, some countries have been truly generous in providing funds, such as the United States, the United Kingdom, Saudi Arabia, Japan, the EU, Australia, Norway, and Turkey (Oxfam, 2011).

Although the earthquake in Haiti and the floods in Pakistan both took place in 2010, the international response to both events has been quite different. The floods in Pakistan affected 20 million people, while the earthquake in Haiti affected 3 million people. In terms of displacements and number of citizens killed, however,

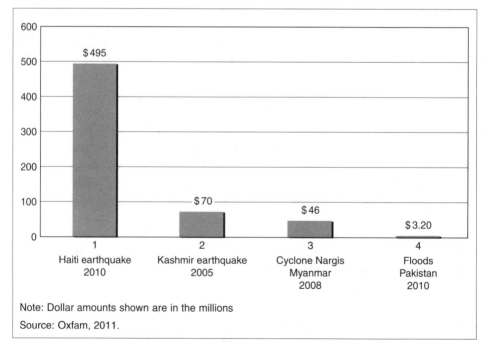

Note: Dollar amounts shown are in the millions

Source: Oxfam, 2011.

Figure 12-2 *UN appeal funding per person 10 days into the disaster.*

Haiti experienced a greater impact compared to Pakistan. Reports show that after two weeks of appeals for funds and aid, approximately $157 were raised per affected person in Haiti compared to $15 per affected person in Pakistan. The main reasons that led to such a stark difference between the humanitarian relief and funding in these two situations are as follows:

- Flooding in Pakistan occurred relatively slowly, while the Haiti earthquake was a single high-impact and a visibly tragic event.
- There was more media coverage in Haiti compared to the Pakistan floods.
- The high death rate in Haiti compared to Pakistan helped to increase donations.
- Pakistan's association with militancy and terrorist threats, along with the perceived level of corruption of the country, negatively affected attempts to obtain donations and other funding.
- The United States' closer proximity to Haiti put Haiti in a better fund-receiving position compared to Pakistan (Kronstadt et al., 2010).

For long-term success in response and recovery from the 2010 floods, efforts and plans for resilient development in Pakistan have to be supported. The initial reports pertaining to needs assessments for the country that were carried out by the UN, World Bank, and Asian Development Bank show that the costs for recovery and reconstruction may total as much as $9.7 billion. Many believe that Pakistan's government institutions do not have the capacity to coordinate response agencies effectively, and that there is an underlying risk of corruption and nepotism where large donor and relief funds are concerned. Allaying these fears will require proper monitoring and evaluation systems (IEG, 2010).

The Pakistan disaster is not over: Approximately 1 million internally displaced persons (IDPs) do not have anywhere to go (Oxfam, 2011). In mid-November 2010, 10,000 flood victims were discovered in a region that had been completely ignored by relief operations. Apart from astonishing incidents of failure to attend to certain populations out of neglect, cases of impartiality in aid distribution to religious and ethnic minorities have been noted (Oxfam, 2011). These shortcomings in the relief effort need to be addressed by the current government. Moreover, given that Pakistan is a disaster-prone country, it clearly needs to invest in developing a "country catastrophe risk financing strategy which could rely on reserves to finance frequent but not severe hazards, contingent credit facilities to finance the mezzanine layer of risk and insurance and/or catastrophe bonds to finance the upper layer of risk" (p. 45). This strategy will ultimately lead to development of a proper catastrophe insurance market in Pakistan. Currently, Pakistan relies heavily on ex-post donor funds for relief and recovery operations—an unsustainable and insufficient source for managing disasters (ADB, 2010). The country also has a good network of microfinancing institutions and agencies that needs to be utilized for recovery and reconstruction funding (Kronstadt et al., 2010).

Many believe that the recent floods and natural disasters are the result of the predicted climatic changes taking place around the globe. The Pakistan floods of 2010, which started with monsoon rains that then turned into flash floods, are consistent with climate change forecasts for the area, but their causality may not be proved easily. Thus new developments and reconstruction practices in the wake of this disaster have to take into account factors related to climate change (Kronstadt et al., 2010).

The areas flooded form "the world's largest contiguous irrigation network" (IEG, 2010, p. 1)—albeit a network that lacks investment and has not been maintained, improved, or modernized. Restoring rural livelihoods (IEG, 2010) is one of the main targets of the flood recovery and reconstruction phase. This effort is crucial because most of the affected population lived in rural areas and lost their agricultural and irrigational jobs. Reviving the agricultural sector is important for restoring not only the livelihoods of these victims but also the overall economy of the country. Moreover, nonfarm income opportunities for those who have lost their farm-related jobs are being emphasized as part of recovery plans. As mentioned earlier, the livestock sector also experienced a major blow from the floods, and a breeding import strategy would be well advised as part of efforts to revive this sector in the country (IEG, 2010).

While agricultural lands were destroyed in the 2010 disaster, land rights documents were also often lost in the floods. In some regions, the floods even altered the topology. As a consequence, land rights disputes have emerged and threatened recovery efforts in some areas. Community resolution plans and processes need to be developed to resolve these outstanding land rights issues, which requires a lot of community engagement and consultation (IEG, 2010).

Overall, the successful implementation of recovery and reconstruction plans in Pakistan depends on monitoring, evaluation, and comprehensive auditing, which should be accompanied with a redress and grievance system. Local and community involvement is essential to build resilient systems, create opportunities for nonfarm income for younger generations, alter existing land rights with the help of political will, invest in irrigation development, ensure the recovery livestock and milk production, and develop monitoring and evaluation systems that attract donors and gain their unswerving support (Kronstadt et al., 2010). Oxfam (2011) believes that this disaster can be a transformative moment for the country. Rebuilding and reconstruction, if intelligently done, should lead to sustainable development and growth for this often-challenged country.

Comparing the Three Cases from an International Emergency and Crisis Management Perspective

The Myanmar cyclone and Sichuan earthquake cases are characterized by very different response patterns within each country and between the international system and the affected nations. Both disasters involved a high intensity of need, scope, impact, and uncertainty, and both occurred in densely populated areas. However, whereas the delicate political situation and harsh media reports had negative effects on the disaster relief coordination process in the Nargis cyclone case, a healthy political climate and positive media depictions made positive contributions to the Sichuan earthquake relief coordination process.

Bureaucratic inertia and lack of governmental capacity in the Myanmar case obstructed the disaster response operations, and the regime failed to save many lives and properties. During the first two weeks of the disaster response, there was a distressed and distrustful environment that negatively affected the coordination process. With the involvement of ASEAN, inter-actor trust increased because of the positive past experience of the Myanmar government with ASEAN and the Singaporean government, which was chairing the ASEAN organization at the time. With the involvement of ASEAN, a tripartite committee was established between Myanmar, the UN, and ASEAN to oversee, monitor, and coordinate disaster relief operations. Due to the lack of host government capacity, massive international involvement in disaster relief was necessary, and its level increased even further after the involvement of ASEAN. A strong international presence meant that the UN's and its partners' responses were coordinated in clusters. The disaster relief agencies of major countries also increased their presence, although Western agencies remained absent except for the German team, primarily due to the Myanmar government's distrust of Western nations.

In comparison to the Myanmar case, the Sichuan earthquake included less international involvement in disaster relief primarily because of the prompt response of the centralized Chinese government and its strong capacity to act. The successful response by China explains why direct involvement by international organizations and their role in coordination was reduced in this incident. In addition, the UN coordinated its disaster relief operations and those of its partners via the UN Disaster Management Team, in contrast to the cluster approach used in the Myanmar case. In China, international disaster assistance was mostly received in the form of donations of supplies and money, with the Chinese government actually delivering the services.

The Chinese national Red Cross chapter had a strong capacity and experience with disasters of many kinds. It also had legal authority granted by the Chinese government to hire international doctors. In addition, the Red Cross housed its East Asian regional headquarter in Beijing, which facilitated the coordination of the international Red Cross response. In the Nargis cyclone, the UN and Red Cross used regional headquarters in Bangkok, Thailand, to facilitate their international coordination and delivery of logistics and services to Myanmar.

The increasing commitment of Chinese citizens to help their fellow citizens and improving grassroots development in China were other positive factors influencing the international disaster relief coordination process in the Sichuan earthquake. In the Myanmar cyclone, the strong moral and financial support of Burmese expatriates throughout the world contributed positively to the grassroots involvement in international disaster relief coordination.

In both cases, WHO proved strikingly effective in filling the role of lead agency in health, primarily because of its strong, preestablished relationships with its partners and its well-developed norms, standards, and protocols of information communication and reporting. Both cases once again demonstrate the need for international partnership in disaster relief due to the increasingly global effects of disasters, and they show the urgent necessity of strengthening local capacity and building resilient communities so as to reduce disaster risks and vulnerabilities.

Meanwhile, the disaster management system in Pakistan shows that there are plenty of organizations involved in flood management, but highlights the need for better coordination of and cooperation between these diverse entities to ensure effective flood and disaster management. The roles and responsibilities of each organization have not been delineated categorically, which injects a great deal of ambiguity into their interactions during response. Although Pakistan's NDRMF aims to provide a framework for defining roles and responsibilities for response, "actual reporting lines and controlling ministries and departments determine the tasking of response agencies" (ADB, 2010, p. 44). Thus there is a dire need to assimilate roles, address overlap in the roles and responsibilities of organizations, and invest in coordination mechanisms and systems (ADB, 2010). This duplication is a particularly striking difference from the clarity evident in the Sichuan earthquake response. Although theoretically the cluster approach in Pakistan made a lot of sense, it has been plagued with some inherent problems. As the 2010 flooding response revealed, cluster coordinators lacked experience, intercluster coordination was weak, and some mismanagement and duplication of sources and delays hindered the relief operation's effectiveness. According to Oxfam (2011), cluster effectiveness will improve if interagency coordination becomes strong and there is proper mapping of needs.

Conclusion

Because emergencies themselves know no borders, management of emergencies should have an equally democratic reach. In many countries, coordination mechanisms need to be expanded to allow for assistance from overseas. Identifying the main actors operating at international disaster scenes was one of the aims of this chapter; these actors, though they have laudable aims, require better integration of their operations to improve their effectiveness on a global scale.

To explore the topic of network governance, this chapter examined three recent disaster cases. The three cases—the Myanmar cyclone, the Sichuan earthquake, and the 2010 Pakistan floods—are characterized by very different response patterns from the international community. A major factor in response from the international system is the dependence of the UN system on the request of the affected nations for assistance. In addition, the response of the international community to UN calls for funding. This fundamental weakness in the UN system for disaster assistance affected the response in all three events profiled here. Additionally, coordination issues within and among UN agencies have the potential to hinder response. Working with different international entities, INGOs, and local partners in a context characterized by a lack of coordination is a challenge, and one that must be addressed to improve disaster relief efforts.

Review Questions

1. What is the structure of international disaster relief coordination?
2. What are the key international actors involved in disaster response and recovery operations?
3. What are the major problems associated with disaster relief coordination at the international level?
4. How is the United Nations trying to promote improved emergency and crisis management practices?
5. What is the role of civil society in response to global crises and disasters?
6. Compare and contrast the three cases presented in the chapter from the international disaster response perspective. How did the international community engage with the three countries? How did the political and administrative system play a role in coordinating the national response and the international community in each disaster? What role did culture play in the response?
7. How might the information you gained from this chapter affect you personally and professionally?

References

Asian Development Bank (ADB). (2010). Pakistan 2010 floods: Preliminary damage and needs assessment. Retrieved February 2, 2010, from http://www.adb.org/Documents/RRPs/PAK/44372/44372-01-pak-oth-02.pdf.

Association of South East Asian Nations (ASEAN). (2008). The joint ASEAN–UN Press release. Retrieved August 21, 2008, from http://www.aseansec.org/21765.htm.

Benini, A. A. (1999). Network without center? A case study of an organizational network responding to an earthquake. *Journal of Contingencies and Crisis Management, 7*(1), 38–47.

Borton, J. (1993). Recent trends in the international relief system. *Disasters:* The Journal of Disaster Studies, Policy, and Management, *17*(3), 187–201.

Bryant, J., Vertinsky, I., & Smart. C. (2007). Globalization and international communicable crises: A case of SARS. In D. E. Gibbons (Ed.), *Communicable crises: Prevention, response, and recovery in the global arena* (pp. 265–300). Charlotte, NC: Information Age Publishing.

Byman, D., Lesser, I. O., Pirnie, B. R., Benard, C., & Waxman, M. C. (2003). *Strengthening the partnership: Improving military coordination with relief agencies and allies in humanitarian operations.* Pittsburgh, PA: RAND Corporation.

Central Emergency Response Fund (CERF). (2008). CERF Around the world: China. Retrieved September 20, 2008, from http://ochaonline.un.org/Default.aspx?tabid=4602.

Chisholm, D. (1989). *Coordination without hierarchy: Informal structures in multiorganizational systems.* Berkeley, CA: University of California Press.

Comfort, L. K., & Haase, T. W. (2006). Communication, coherence, and collective action: The impact of Hurricane Katrina on communications infrastructure. *Public Works Management and Policy, 10*(3), 328–343.

Coppola, D. (2007). *Introduction to international disaster management.* Burlington, MA: Butterworth-Heinnemann.

Coppola, D., & Haddow, G. (2007). International disaster management. In *Emergency and risk management case studies textbook.* FEMA Online Book. Retrieved April 6, 2008, from http://training.fema.gov/EMIWeb/edu/emoutline.asp.

Eberlein, B., & Newman, A. L. (2008). Escaping the international governance dilemma? Incorporated transgovernmental networks in the European Union. *Governance: An International Journal of Policy, Administration, and Institutions, 21*(1), 25–52.

Eikenberry, A. M., Arroyave, V., & Cooper, T. (2007). Administrative failure and the international NGO response to Hurricane Katrina. *Public Administration Review, 67,* 160–170.

European Commission Humanitarian Aid and Civil Protection (ECHO). (2010). European civil protection. Retrieved April 25, 2010, from http://ec.europa.eu/echo/civil_protection/civil/prote/mechanism.htm.

Farazmand, A. (2007). Learning from the Katrina crisis: A global and international perspective with implications for future crisis management. *Public Administration Review, 67,* 149–160.

Hicks, E. K., & Pappas, G. (2006). Coordinating disaster relief after the South Asia earthquake. *Society, 43*(5), 42–50.

Holmes, J. (2008, August 6). Disaster lessons. *Washington Post.* Retrieved August 10, 2008, from http://www.washingtonpost.com/wp-dyn/content/article/2008/08/05/AR2008080502924.html.

Independent Evaluation Group (IEG). (2010). Response to Pakistan's floods: Evaluative lessons and opportunities. The World Bank Group. Retrieved February 2, 2010, from http://siteresources.worldbank.org/EXTDIRGEN/Resources/ieg_pakistan_note.pdf.

Kapucu, N. (2006). Interagency communication networks during emergencies: Boundary spanners in multi-agency coordination. *American Review of Public Administration, 36*(2), 207–225.

Kapucu, N. (2011). Collaborative governance in international disasters: Nargis Cyclone in Myanmar and Sichuan earthquake in China cases. *International Journal of Emergency Management, 8*(1): 1-25.

Katoch, A. (2008). Myanmar: The response. *Crisis Response, 4*(4), 12–16.

Kent, R. C. (1987). *Anatomy of disaster relief: The international network in action.* London: Printer Publishers.

Kent, R. C. (2004). International humanitarian crises: Two decades before and two decades beyond. *International Affairs, 80*(5), 851–869.

Kronstadt, K. A., Sheikh, P. A., &Vaughn, B. (2010). *Flooding in Pakistan: Overview and issues for Congress.* CRS Report for Congress.

Lindell, M. K., Prater, C., & Perry, R. W. (2007). *Introduction to emergency management.* Hoboken, NJ: Wiley.

Lipson, M. (2005). *Interorganizational coordination in complex peacekeeping.* Paper presented at the annual meeting of the International Studies Association, March 1–5, 2005, Hawaii.

Moore, M., Trujillo, H. R., Stearns, B. K., Basurto-Davila, R., & Evans, D. (2007). *Models of relief: Learning from exemplary practices in international disaster management.* RAND Corporation, WR-514, Available at http://www.rand.org/content/dam/rand/pubs/working _papers/2007/RAND_WR514.pdf.

Moynihan, D. P. (2008). Combining structural forms in the search for policy tools: Incident command systems in U.S. crisis management. *Governance: An International Journal of Policy, Administration, and Institutions, 21*(2), 205–229.

Natsios, A. S. (1995). NGOs and the UN system in complex humanitarian emergencies: Conflict or cooperation? *Third World Quarterly, 16*(3), 405–419.

North Atlantic Treaty Organization (NATO). (2004). *NATO transformed.* Brussels, Belgium: Author. Retrieved October 17, 2008, from http://www.nato.int/docu/nato-trans/nato-trans-eng.pdf.

North Atlantic Treaty Organization (NATO). (2006). *NATO's role in civil emergency planning.* Brussels, Belgium: Author. Retrieved August 10, 2008, from http://www.nato.int/docu/ cep/cep-e.pdf.

Oxfam. (2011). Six months into the flood: Resetting Pakistan's priorities through reconstruction. 144 Oxfam Briefing Paper. Retrieved February 2, 2010, from http://www.oxfam.org.uk/ oxfam_in_action/emergencies/downloads/oxfam_pakistan_6mth_briefing_note.pdf.

Oyegbite, K. (2005). What have we learned? Coordination. *Prehospital and Disaster Medicine, 20*(6), 471–474.

Powell, W. W. (1990). Neither market nor hierarchy: Network forms of organization. *Research in Organizational Behavior, 12*, 295–336.

Reindorp, N. (2002). Trends and challenges in the UN humanitarian system. In J. Macrae (Ed.), *The new humanitarianisms: A review of trends in global humanitarian action.* Humanitarian Policy Group Report 11.pp. 29-38 London: Overseas Development Group.

Reindorp, N., & Wiles, P. (2001). *Humanitarian coordination: Lessons from recent field experience.* Study Commissioned by the Office for the Coordination of Humanitarian Affairs. London: Overseas Development Institute.

Ritson, R., & Youssef, M. (2006). Global partnerships in humanitarian crises: World Health Organization's response and the South Asian earthquake of October 2005. *Refugee Survey Quarterly, 25*(4), 96–99.

Scott, R. W., & Davis, G. F. (2007). *Organizations and organizing: Rational, natural, and open system perspectives.* Upper Saddle River, NJ: Prentice Hall.

Stephenson, M. Jr. (2005). Making humanitarian relief networks more effective operational coordination. *Disasters, 29*(4), 337–350.

Stephenson, M. Jr. (2006). Toward a descriptive model of humanitarian assistance coordination. *Voluntas: International Journal of Voluntary and Nonprofit Organizations, 171*, 41–57.

Stephenson, M. Jr., & Schnitzer, H. H. (2006). Interorganizational trust and boundary spanning behavior in humanitarian assistance coordination. *Nonprofit Management and Leadership, 17*(2), 211–233.

Sylves, R. T. (2008). *Disaster policy and politics: Emergency management and homeland security.* Washington, DC: CQ Press.

Tsunami Evaluation Coalition (TEC). (n.d.). *Coordination of international humanitarian assistance in tsunami-affected countries.* Sri Lanka: Evaluation Findings.

United Nations (UN). (2008). *Towards national resilience: Good practices of national platform for disaster risk reduction.* Geneva, Switzerland: United Nations Secretariat of the International Strategy for Disaster Reduction.

United Nations Office for the Coordination of Humanitarian Affairs (UNOCHA). (2002). Orientation handbook on complex emergencies. Retrieved September 21, 2009, from http://reliefweb.int/rw/lib.nsf/db900sid/LGEL-5R8DWY/$file/ocha-orient-2002.pdf?openelement.

United Nations Office for the Coordination of Humanitarian Affairs (UNOCHA). (2008). Cyclone Nargis Myanmar: OCHA Situation Report No. 21. Retrieved August 21, 2008, from www.ochaonline.un.org/OchaLinkClick.aspx?link=ocha&docId=1089978.

United Nations Office for the Coordination of Humanitarian Affairs (UNOCHA). (2009). About OCHA. Retrieved November 17, 2009, from http://ochaonline.un.org/AboutOCHA/tabid/1076/Default.aspx.

Völz, C. (2005). Humanitarian coordination in Indonesia: An NGO viewpoint. *Forced Migration Review, 16*, 26–27.

White, P. (1999). The role of UN specialized agencies in complex emergencies: A case study of FAO. *Third World Quarterly, 20*(1), 223–238.

World Health Organization (WHO) (2006). *The Interagency Emergency Health Kit 2006, An Interagency Document: Medicines and Medical Devices for 10,000 for approximately 3 Months.* Geneva, Switzerland. Available at http://whqlibdoc.who.int/hq/2006/WHO_PSM_PAR_2006.4_eng.pdf.

World Health Organization (WHO). (2007). *Working for Health: An Introduction to the World Health Organization.* Geneva, Switzerland. Available at http://www.who.int/about/brochure_en.pdf.

Chapter 13

Future Directions in Emergency and Crisis Management

Chapter Objectives

- Evaluate development in the field of emergency and crises management.
- Summarize national and global challenges, professional challenges and opportunities, pedagogical needs of the profession, and research gaps related to emergency and crisis management.

Introduction

This final chapter discusses future directions in emergency and crisis management, which can be classified based on whether they reflect challenges or opportunities at the global, national, and professional levels. Many of the trends identified by emergency management scholars in the early 1990s continue to dominate emergency management today: increasing exposure to environmental hazards, increased capabilities offered by advanced emergency management information technology, increasing recognition of the need for pre-impact action (hazard mitigation, emergency preparedness, and recovery preparedness), and increased professionalization of emergency management. Nonetheless, some new issues will affect the field in coming years, including the ever-changing nature and scope of environmental hazards and the increased salience of global terrorism.

Evolution of Emergency and Crisis Management

Our ancestors faced similar risks that we are experiencing in the modern era (Coppola, 2007). Evidence indicates ancient peoples took measures to mitigate and reduce the effects of disasters, such as the organized response in Rome when Pompeii's leaders undertook a mass evacuation before the eruption of the Mount Vesuvius volcano. Incas from the thirteenth to the fifteenth centuries are known to "have practiced a form of urban planning that focused on their need to defend themselves from enemy attack" (Coppola, 2007, p. 3). The difference between the past and today lies in the way these practices are organized. Emergency management is a field that requires deliberate planning and actions to eliminate or minimize the risk to human life and property. There has been much change in the understanding of this emergency management concept over centuries.

When the United States is considered, substantial changes have occurred in emergency management since the country's early days, but especially since the nineteenth century. In the early 1800s, emergency management was mostly provided at a local level by communities, neighborhoods, relatives, and religious organizations (Sylves, 2008). Structures were also created to manage hazards and control their impacts on the lives and property (Wilson & Oyola-Yemaiel, 2001). Events in the early twentieth century, however, showed that local and state governments as well as charities and social institutions were far away from providing an effective response to all types of disasters (Rubin, 2007). According to Petak (1985), before the federal take-over of emergency management in the United States in the twentieth century, emergency management was provided by law enforcement and fire departments with the assistance of public health and civil defense organizations. The period 1927–1950 saw an increase in response by the federal government (Sylves, 2008). Rubin (2007) argues that over most of the twentieth century, the federal government's role in emergency management continued to increase. Nevertheless, there was no national policy to deal with disasters before 1950 (Haddow, Bullock, & Coppola, 2008).

A new era in emergency management began with the Cold War. As Coppola (2007) observes, this period, which could be characterized as the "civil defense era," was the only period in history when the great powers across the world moved toward a centralized safeguarding of citizens. In the United States, the Civil Defense Act of 1950 and the Disaster Act of 1950 founded modern emergency management at the federal level (Sylves, 2008). With the establishment of the Federal Emergency Management Agency (FEMA) in 1979, a notion of unified mission to manage disasters and emergencies was embraced at the national level. In contrast, from the 1950s until the end of Cold War, the focus of federal emergency management was mainly civil defense (Wilson & Oyola-Yemaiel, 2001), and federal requirements and funding played a vital role in shaping governments' and organizations' preparation and response to disasters (Rubin, 2007).

The founding of FEMA signaled the adoption of a new approach in emergency response, consisting of a comprehensive all-hazards concept (Wilson & Oyola-Yemaiel, 2001) that sought to provide more inclusive and responsive emergency management dealing with both natural disasters and civil defense issues. This shift in policies proved ineffective when several disasters occurred during the 1990s, forcing the government to pay more attention to pre-disaster mitigation and more proactive measures.

The September 11, 2001 terrorist attacks launched a new period in emergency management that, in case of the United States, focused more on the concept of homeland security. With creation of the Department of Homeland Security (DHS) in 2003, FEMA's role in emergency management became limited, for the most part, to dealing with natural disasters. This shrinking of the agency's scope concerned many experts, who worried how the focus on countering terrorism might erode the degree of attention, level of expertise, and retention of scientific and operational knowledge related to disasters (Rubin, 2007). Sylves (2008) confirms the validity of this concern: "Federal emergency management today is suffused with a homeland security ethos, and this applies throughout the federal system" (p. 218). All too soon, the Hurricane Katrina disaster and several other incidents proved that emergency management under DHS was ineffective.

Europe also has wide-ranging experience in dealing with natural and human-made disasters throughout its history. As an example, one can consider the evolution of disaster management in the United Kingdom. Considered to have begun during World War II in response to the London Blitz, the UK national approach to emergencies was adapted quickly to the Cold War context. In 1948, the Civil Defense Act was enacted with the purpose of preserving civilian lives against the perceived Soviet threat (Kapucu, 2009). Over this period, local organizations and agencies were encouraged to apply for resources from central government funds, but were under no obligation to coordinate their efforts under a national plan.

As the world emerged from the throes of the Cold War, the United Kingdom enacted the Civil Defense in Peacetime Act of 1986, which was intended to legislate a central and local government responsibility approach. Despite its existence, the country continued to be plagued by a spate of failures in safety protocols and disaster mitigation, as it experienced a number of natural and human-made incidents (Kapucu, 2009).

The U.K. government had begun development of a national strategy for emergencies prior to 2001, in response to the poor management of flooding, fuel protests, and a foot and mouth disease outbreak (Coaffee & Wood, 2006). When the government faced increased pressure following the September 11, 2001 terrorist attacks, however, it responded by enacting the Civil Contingencies Act (CCA) in 2004. This policy was in effect during the London bombings of 2005, the avian influenza pandemic of 2006, and several incidents of large-scale flooding. As discussed earlier, the CCA is split into two parts, addressing local arrangements for civil protection and emergency powers. The legislation establishes the action required in mitigation, preparation, response, and recovery, by addressing three core groups: the vulnerable, victims, and responders (Cabinet Office, 2009). The CCA represents a significant development in U.K. disaster policy, eliminating antiquated legislation, revising priorities in modern crises, and laying a foundation for responders and government (O'Brien & Read, 2005).

Today citizens, state agencies, and local organizations expect the national government to be involved in disaster preparation and response more than ever before (Rubin, 2007). The emergency management field has experienced dramatic changes and drastic reforms over the last century. Most modern-day emergency management systems are designed in a top-down manner, which should not be the case when emergency management is considered (Mileti, 2005). Given that the number of disasters is on the rise and such incidents will likely be more devastating in the future (Quarantelli, 1993), there is a need for systematic and structural changes in emergency management (McEntire, 2005). In light of the recent disasters experienced by different nations around the world, there is widespread agreement that change is needed; the disagreement arises in terms of the nature of the changes proposed. McEntire (2005) argues that there are two frontiers in this regard—one advocating a revolutionary transformation, the other proposing evolutionary change.

Proponents of a revolutionary transformation suggest that today's systems are ineffective and need to be replaced with a system focusing on pre-disaster mitigation and planning. In contrast, advocates of evolutionary change argue that whatever the change, it should be based on the practices of the past. Mileti (1999) is a vocal advocate of the revolutionary change position, asserting that there is a need for change in values, norms, and practices as well as adjustment in political, social, and economic issues with specific focus on a preemptive, preventive, and proactive approach to disaster management. McEntire (2005), in contrast, favors evolutionary change in emergency management, suggesting that changes should focus on creating a proactive, all-hazards, and interdisciplinary approach toward emergency management. Whichever position one takes, the changes more or less envision a reimaging of our understanding of natural and human-made disasters and the way we manage them today. It is only the extent to which the proposed reforms undermine today's approach that makes those changes revolutionary versus evolutionary.

Various propositions have been put forth in terms of the specificity of the changes the scholars and practitioners advocate for. While some envision rebuilding emergency management based on the relationship concepts of collaboration, partnership, coordination, and networks (Agranoff & McGuire, 2003; Drabek, 2003; Kapucu, 2006; Mitchell, 2006), others focus on the necessity to improve leadership and decision making (Boin, t'Hart, Stern, & Sundelius, 2005; Kapucu & Van Wart, 2006; Waugh & Streib, 2006). Still others focus on the structural tenets of emergency management (Mileti, 1999). Despite the differences in the approach taken, all parties agree that the change in and evolution of emergency and crisis management is and should be directed toward a proactive, rational, more flexible, holistic, and leadership-oriented approach to be undertaken by an interdisciplinary, well-trained, and well-organized team of decision makers and practitioners.

Networks and Horizontal Relationships

One of the most pronounced yet hotly debated propositions in regard to reform of emergency management is the proposal to replace vertical relationships with horizontal ones. Rubin (2007) argues that response to and resolution of any type of public and safety issue are made easier by participative approaches that are not based on a central and hierarchical system. To effectively respond to disasters, all agencies participating in emergency management operations require partnerships and trust between them at all levels (Kapucu 2009; Kapucu, Augustin, & Garayev, 2009). To meet the needs of twenty-first-century governance, emergency management agencies should work more collaboratively, becoming less hierarchical and process oriented under a networked structure (McEntire, Fuller, Johnson, & Weber, 2002).

Networks include a variety of individuals and organizations that are linked by formal and informal relationships. They serve as a tool "to devise policy and to implement programs that will reduce vulnerability, limit the loss of life and property, protect the environment, and improve multi-organizational coordination in disasters" (Waugh & Tierney, 2007, p. 60). Such constructs are products of collaborative practices intertwined with highly interdependent relationships (Kamensky, Burlin, & Mark, 2004). Successful collaboration, however, depends on a clear understanding of roles and responsibilities on the part of the network participants. In the wake of a disaster, most collaborative networks are formed spontaneously and automatically. To work productively within these networks, emergency managers must be in continuous contact with stakeholders and must sharpen their administrative skills so they are ready to improvise in cooperation with others (Waugh & Tierney, 2007).

Given that disaster management is becoming more complex over time, it requires the participation of a multitude of agencies (Coppola, 2007). For instance, in response to the December 2004 tsunami in Asia, more than 200 organizations were involved in determining the quality of water in affected areas, and thousands more provided food aid, shelter, medicine, medical assistance, and other rehabilitation activities. Individual attempts of agencies to deal with issues translated into unnecessary delays and inefficiencies in distribution of assistance (Coppola, 2007).

As Lindell et al. (2007) state, regional collaboration is an important solution for many types of disasters, especially when local capacity is limited and becomes overwhelmed by the scope of an incident. Intergovernmental and interjurisdictional collaboration allows local jurisdictions and communities to access services that none of them could afford by themselves (Kapucu et al., 2009). Increased coordination among participants reduces the time between the occurrence of a disaster and relief provision, and helps to increase the area covered by assistance, reduce costs, and standardize the quality of relief. It is for this reason that effectively coordinated disaster response "is the foundation on which increased international disaster response capacity will be built" (Coppola, 2007, p. 527). Of course, such approach requires a degree of organizational standardization, which should be taken into account when designing appropriate disaster response policies.

Among the most important players in a disaster response network are the mass media, which can provide more effective communication, serve as the best alert system, and easily act as a member of the emergency management team (Coppola, 2007). Media's role in crisis communication is indispensible, because media messages constitute an effective tool for letting stakeholders know how to prepare, where to get related information, and how the response will be performed (Mileti & Darlington, 1995).

In the United States, the collaborative approach as a major concept in emergency management was fostered by FEMA during the Carter administration, with the agency pulling together the components of federal emergency response into a "one-stop shop" (Rubin, 2007). The United States has a national network of public agencies, nonprofit organizations, and private firms that provide services in emergency management. This network comprises "FEMA and its state and local counterparts, emergency response agencies (e.g., fire departments, emergency medical services agencies, and search and rescue units), American Red Cross [ARC] and other general purpose nonprofit organizations, regional and local charities and civic organizations, and firms that provide services ranging from emergency planning to debris removal to psychological counseling" (Waugh, 2003, p. 376). Before, during, and after disasters, Americans rely on hundreds of organizations. Nevertheless, it is not the quantity of collaborating entities that matters, but rather the nature of collaboration and the quality of coordination that determines the success of any disaster response network.

Despite being one of the key management tools that emergency managers use to develop priorities, set goals, and agree on implementation strategies (Waugh & Tierney, 2007), networks remain to be tested across several settings, systems, and disasters. There is much to be added along the networked emergency management structure. Nevertheless, one caveat is clear: Networks are a temporary panacea to overcome today's administrative and management problems when disasters are concerned. Although they allow for flexibility in relationships, additional resources, and streamlined disaster response, networks are still problematic in terms of trust and accountability issues (Ward & Wamsley, 2007). Clearly defined roles and responsibilities are a must to solve this problem (Rhodes, 1996).

Challenges

National and Global

Many scientists suggest that the consequences of climate change are likely to be tremendous, although the debate over this theory remains fierce. Statistical analyses show clear warnings of this phenomenon, with the Earth's temperature exceeding norms by 2 degrees Celsius per decade (Coppola, 2007). Climate change will increase the number of extreme events taking place across the globe, including the number of severe storms and floods. Bissell (2005) argues that climate change will surely be related to the disasters we will observe in the future: Heat emergencies, wildfires, floods, and more severe storms are some of these predicted events. UN specialists believe that many of the natural disasters that have occurred since 2005, such as Hurricane Wilma and flooding in Europe during the summer of 2005, are the result of the climate change (Coppola, 2007). Other environmental problems that may be faced in the future include rising ocean levels, water pollution, air pollution, ecological degradation, and collapse of petroleum-based economies.

Another challenge in emergency management derives from the process of globalization. Even though public health facilities and capacities in the world have improved, the ease and speed of modern air, ground, and sea transportation have the potential to lead to more disease-related fatalities in a very short amount of time (Coppola, 2007). Bissell (2005) argues as the world is being globalized, so are the hazards, which should prompt a search for solutions beyond local borders. In addition, this author suggests that there has been a shift in the concept of warfare, which has moved away from targeting soldiers and toward targeting civilians. Although the strategy of targeting civilians is not completely new, it is increasing in popularity, with terrorists in particular favoring this tactic.

Population growth poses another challenge for emergency managers. Today, human settlement is spreading across uninhabited areas that were previously identified as hazardous (Bissell, 2005). In the United States, for example, the country's population is projected to grow over the next 50 years, with vulnerability increasing as the population density increases. In addition, aging of the general population means that there will be an increase in those persons older than age 65 who require special assistance during emergencies.

Another important aspect of emergency management that must be addressed is the language barriers in nations with diverse populations. To overcome this challenge, emergency information must be translated into all major languages used by citizens.

Lindell, Prater, and Perry (2007) underline that although emergency managers have learned to reduce causalities in terms of human losses by using improved forecasts and warning systems, property losses will remain an issue.

Professional

While emergency management is a well-developed field, especially in terms of its practices, whether it is a profession remains a topic of scholarly debate. It is clear that emergency management experienced dramatic professionalization across the twentieth century, with specific focus on identifying the boundaries and the responsibilities of the field. Britton and Lindsay (2005) argue that the emergency management profession today is very much shaped by the background of the respective practitioners. While the majority of practitioners in the past were military men, fire fighters, and health practitioners, it is imperative today to create an autonomous field of emergency management that emphasizes theory, a code of ethics, social values, commitment, and training as requirements for membership in the profession (Britton & Lindsay, 2005). For emergency management to be recognized as a profession, "it is necessary to highlight how the application of this special body of knowledge must be restricted to those who have the judgment to apply it" (p. 50). Recently, many institutions in the United States have begun to offer programs that culminate in graduate-level certificates and degrees in emergency and disaster management. As a result, the field has experienced an increase in educational and academic programs, which satisfy one of the major criteria of a profession—namely, a unified body of knowledge.

Another challenge mentioned by Lindell et al. (2007) is the need to link emergency management with new professions. For many years, emergency managers have worked with different agencies whose tasks are related to emergency response. As a consequence of new projects and emerging threats, managers must now work with a variety of new agencies and organizations. Bissell (2005) argues that for this specific reason, the emergency management professions should be interdisciplinary. Being interdisciplinary, in turn, means engaging in continuous collaboration with multiple professions. The success of such an approach, however, is highly dependent on network sustainability as well as on the existence (or not) of an ongoing issue to be addressed (Lindell et al., 2007). In other words, the linkage of emergency management with other professions is based on the ongoing presence of specific issues.

Another challenge for the profession involves the relationship between practitioners and scholars (Lindell et al., 2007). Cooperation among them is not always easy to achieve, with each sometimes blaming the other for failing to understand problems. This conflict partly arises because the representatives on each side "are employed by organizations that have very different culture" (Lindell et al., 2007, p. 488). However, this situation appears to be changing for the better, owing to more extensive contact between both parties, participation in a greater number of common projects, and an increasing number of emergency management programs that incorporate both perspectives. Mileti (2005) likewise argues that there is a gap between the scholarly world and real-world practitioners, which should be bridged by teaching people how to use the knowledge and skills they possess.

Teaching of the Profession

Britton and Lindsay (2005) argue that the first step toward development of a profession of emergency management is university-based education. Creation of such academic programs is not without costs, but investment should be made in the teaching of a profession that would establish a cognitive and knowledge base for emergency management practitioners in applying their skills and expertise to disaster settings. The discipline of emergency management, therefore, is expected to turn out graduates who are equipped with knowledge and skills solely directed at the emergency management field (Mileti, 2005). The teaching of the profession, in addition, should be interdisciplinary in nature (Kiltz, 2009).

It is also important to establish a culture of research in the field. Research funding remains a key challenge to be overcome along these lines (Rubin, 2007). Compared to the beginning of 1990s, a small but viable disaster research structure has emerged in recent years. Nevertheless, academic studies and proposals have little or no influence over emergency management policies, procedures, or practices (Rubin, 2007). A better connection should be established between the research environment and actual practice—a challenge that affects not only emergency management, but almost all disciplines.

Britton and Lindsay (2005) argue that emergency management of the future should be grounded in five areas:

1) Assisting in the creation and management of community resilience, development and growth by being able to recognise resources and risks, and help communities choose a level of risk appropriate to their circumstances;

2) Helping to manage communities as sustainable entities, with the understanding that reducing losses from disasters alone is too narrow a goal;

3) Assisting with linking emergency management concepts and practices with sustainability through long-term hazard and loss reduction and through employing risk management processes;

4) Helping to reduce community losses and enhance the long-term equilibrium between human and natural environmental interactions; and

5) Helping to ensure appropriate emergency management mechanisms are in place, are operable, and are capable of responding to the overall risk environment. (p. 55)

These authors assert that emergency management education should ultimately be about individual and system-wide capacity building that invests in the development of skills and capabilities necessary to deal with nontraditional disaster settings.

Conclusion

Emergency management is a dynamic field that needs continuous improvements, developments, and adjustments. The premise underlying these demands is that there is no hazard-free place on Earth despite our efforts to avoid disasters by relocation or implementation of safety measures (McEntire, 2005). This fact unavoidably pushes us toward designing structures and systems that take into consideration a myriad of social, technical, administrative, political, legal, and economic factors (Petak, 1985). The changes and reforms required to improve emergency management are mostly contextual, although several general tenets can be gleaned from the scholarly research in this field as well as experience from the past.

The first issue emergency managers need to tackle is clarification of the concepts of hazard and vulnerability. These definitions should be a cornerstone of emergency management planning and operations. Practitioners should have a clear understanding of which actions need to be undertaken under which circumstances.

In addition, the emergency management cycle should be redesigned in a proactive way, so that disaster mitigation and planning are emphasized. This approach should complement—not replace—the other cycles of emergency management (i.e., preparedness, response, and recovery).

In doing so, various stakeholders should be integrated into the picture to implement a bottom-up, rather than a top-down, perspective. The roles of the stakeholders at the local level should be accounted for in community-based and contextual disaster response plans, which, if needed, should be supplemented by central government assistance. It is important to keep in mind that disaster management is mostly a local concept, rather than a national one.

While local capacity is certainly critical to the success of emergency management, the leaders and key decision makers in emergency and crisis management efforts will also affect—if not determine outright— the consequences of the disasters. While effective decision making depends on a variety of contextual and leadership factors, it is the community-based, inclusive, representative, flexible, knowledge-based, and experience-oriented decision-making style that will be most successful in managing future disasters. The most important supporting tool of effective leaders, however, is a well-equipped and well-organized emergency management organization that invests in capacity building, training, exercises, and team building. Accountability and ethical considerations are also indispensable in terms of guiding and directing the practice of emergency management.

Lastly, emergency management professionals should be aware of regional and global developments, and understand how they may be required to shape and adjust their local practices based on what is happening beyond their local area. The failure to grasp the general picture may at best lead to temporary and incomplete solutions.

While the field of emergency management is maturing, it is clear that the traditional ways of dealing with disasters are ineffective and must be cast aside in favor of a more collective perspective. The most prominent approach, at least in the context of today's conditions, is reliance on holistic, all-hazards, networks/collaboration-based, representative, proactive, knowledge-based, experience- and research-oriented emergency management.

References

Agranoff, R., & McGuire, M. (2003). *Collaborative public management: New strategies for local government.* Washington, DC: Georgetown University Press.

Bissell, R. (2005). Future challenges to human survival in the 21st century. In W. L. Waugh & A. Young (Eds.), *The future of emergency management: Papers from the 2005 Higher Education Conference* (pp. 3–6). Emmitsburg, MD.

Boin, A., t'Hart, P. E., Stern, E., & Sundelius, B. (2005). *The politics of crisis management: Public leadership under pressure.* New York: Cambridge University Press.

Britton, N. R., & Lindsay, J. (2005). Designing educational opportunities for the emergency management professional of the 21st century: Formulating an approach for a higher education curriculum. In W. L. Waugh & A. Young (Eds.), *The future of emergency management: Papers from the 2005 Higher Education Conference* (pp. 47–61). Emmitsburg, MD.

Cabinet Office. (2009). Emergency planning. Retrieved March 24, 2010, from http://www.cabinetoffice.gov.uk/ukresilience/preparedness/emergencyplanning.aspx.

Coaffee, J., & Wood, D. M. (2006). Security is coming home: Rethinking scale and constructing resilience in the global urban response to terrorist risk. *International Relations, 20*(4), 503–517.

Coppola, D. P. (2007). *Introduction to international disaster management.* Burlington, MA: Elsevier.

Drabek , T. E. (2003). *Strategies for coordinating disaster responses.* Boulder, CO: University of Colorado, Natural Research and Applications Information Center.

Haddow, G. D., Bullock, J. A., & Coppola, D. P. (2008). *Introduction to emergency management* (3rd ed.). Burlington, MA: Elsevier.

Kamensky, J., Burlin, T., & Mark, A. (2004). Networks and partnerships: Collaborating to achieve results no one can achieve alone. In J. Kamensky & T. Burlin (Eds.), *Collaboration using partnerships and networks* (pp. 3–20). New York: Rowman and Littlefield.

Kapucu, N. (2006). Public–nonprofit partnerships for collective action in dynamic contexts of emergencies. *Public Administration, 84*(1), 205–220.

Kapucu, N. (2009). Interorganizational coordination in complex environments of disasters: The evolution of intergovernmental disaster response systems. *Journal of Homeland Security and Emergency Management, 6*(1), 1–26.

Kapucu, N., Augustin, M. E., & Garayev, V. (2009). Interstate partnerships in emergency management: Emergency Management Assistance Compact in response to catastrophic disasters. *Public Administration Review, 69*(2), 297–313.

Kapucu, N., & Van Wart, M. (2006). The emerging role of the public sector in managing extreme events: Lessons learned. *Administration & Society, 38*(3), 279–308.

Kiltz, L. (2009). Developing critical thinking skills in homeland security and emergency management courses. *Journal of Homeland Security and Emergency Management, 6*(1), 1–21.

Lindell, M. K., Prater, C., & Perry, R. W. (2007). *Introduction to emergency management.* Hoboken, NJ: Wiley.

McEntire, D. A. (2005). Revolutionary and evolutionary change in emergency management: Assessing paradigm shifts, barriers, and recommendations for the profession. In W. L. Waugh & A. Young (Eds.), *The future of emergency management: Papers from the 2005 Higher Education Conference* (pp. 29–46). Emmitsburg, MD.

McEntire, D. A., Fuller, C., Johnson, C., & Weber, R. (2002). A comparison of disaster paradigms: The search for a holistic policy guide. *Public Administration Review, 62*(3), 267–281.

Mileti, D. S. (1999). *Disasters by design: A reassessment of natural hazards in the United States.* Washington, DC: Joseph Henry Press.

Mileti, D. S. (2005). The evolution of U.S. emergency management. In W. L. Waugh & A. Young (Eds.), *The future of emergency management: Papers from the 2005 Higher Education Conference* (pp. 7–10). Emmitsburg, MD.

Mileti, D. S., & Darlington, J. (1995). Societal response to revised earthquake probabilities in the San Francisco Bay Area. *International Journal of Mass Emergencies and Disasters, 13*(2), 119–145.

Mitchell, J. K. (2006). The primacy of partnership: Scoping a new national disaster recovery policy. In W. L. Waugh, Jr. (Ed.), *Shelter from the storm: Repairing the national emergency management system after Hurricane Katrina: Annals of the American Academy of Political and Social Science, 604,* 228–255.

O'Brien, G., & Read, P. (2005). Future UK emergency management: New wine, old skin? *Disaster Prevention and Management, 14*(3), 353–361.

Petak, W. J. (1985). Emergency management: A challenge for public administration. *Public Administration Review, Special Issue, 45*(special issues), 3–7.

Quarantelli, E. L. (1993). The environmental disasters of the future will be more and worse but the prospect is not hopeless. *Disaster Prevention and Management, 2*(1), 11–25.

Rhodes, R.A.W. (1996). The New Governance: Governing without Government. *Political Studies, 44*(4), 652–667. Rubin, C. B. (2007). *Emergency management: The American experience 1900–2005* (2nd ed.). Fairfax, VA: PERI.

Sylves, R. (2008). *Disaster policy and politics: Emergency management and homeland security.* Washington, DC: CQ Press.

Ward, R., & Wamsley, G. (2007). From a painful past to an uncertain future. In C. B. Rubin (Ed.), *Emergency management: The American experience 1900-2005.* Fairfax, VA: Public Entirety Risk Institute.

Waugh, W. L. Jr. (2003). Terrorism, homeland security and the national emergency management network. *Public Organization Review, 3*(4), 373–385.

Waugh, W. L. Jr., & Streib, G. (2006). Collaboration and leadership for effective emergency management. *Public Administration Review, 66*(suppl), 131–140.

Waugh, W. L. Jr., & Tierney, K. (2007). Future directions in emergency management. In W. L. Waugh, Jr., & K. Tierney (Eds.), *Emergency management: Principles and practice for local government* (2nd ed., pp. 319–333). Washington, DC: ICMA.

Wilson, J., & Oyola-Yemaiel, A. (2001). The evolution of emergency management and the advancement towards a profession in the United States and Florida. *Safety Science, 39,* 117–131.

Index

Figure and Table Credits

Chapter 1

1-1 Reprinted from Tourism Management, Vol 22, Faulkner B, Towards a Framework for Tourism Disaster Management, pp. 135–147., Copyright (2001), with permission from Elsevier.

Chapter 2

2-Table 1 U.S. Geological Survey, Department of the Interior/USGS; **2-Table 2** Courtesy of NOAA.

Chapter 4

4-1 Harrald J.R., Agility and Discipline: Critical Success Factors for Disaster Response. pp. 17, copyright © 2006 by Sage Publications. Reprinted by Permission of SAGE Publications.; **4-2** U.S. Geological Survey, Department of the Interior/USGS; **4-3** © Nigel Roddis/ Thomson Reuters; **4-4** Reproduced from Pitt, M. 2008. Learning Lessons from 2007 Floods. Cabinet Office. Available at http://webarchive.nationalarchives.gov.uk/20100807034701/ http://archive.cabinetoffice.gov.uk/pittreview/_/media/assets/www.cabinetoffice.gov.uk/ flooding_review/pitt_review_full%20pdf.pdf. Accessed August 23, 2011.; **4-5** Courtesy of Photographer's Mate 1st Class Jon Gesch/U.S. Navy.; **4-Table 1** Courtesy of International Bank for Reconstruction and Development/The World Bank: Turkey: Marmara Earthquake Assessment, 1999.; **4-Table 2** Courtesy of International Bank for Reconstruction and Development/The World Bank: Turkey: Marmara Earthquake Assessment, 1999.; **4-Table 3** Reproduced from Pitt, M. 2008. Learning Lessons from 2007 Floods. Cabinet Office. Available at http://webarchive.nationalarchives.gov.uk/20100807034701/ http://archive.cabinetoffice.gov.uk/pittreview/_/media/assets/www.cabinetoffice.gov.uk/ flooding_review/pitt_review_full%20pdf.pdf. Accessed August 23, 2011.

Chapter 5

5-1 Map © Olinchuk/ShutterStock, Inc.; **5-2** © STR New/Thomson Reuters; **5-3** © Jason Reed/Thomson Reuters; **5-4** Courtesy of Debbie Larson, NWS, International Activities/ NOAA.

Chapter 6

6-1 Her Majesty's (HM) Government. (2010). Emergency Response and Recovery: Non Statutory Guidance Accompanying The Civil Contingencies Act 2004. Available at http:// www.cabinetoffice.gov.uk/sites/default/files/resources/emergency-response-recovery_0 .pdf.; **6-2** Her Majesty's Government. (n.d.). Emergency preparedness: Guidance on Part I of the Civil Contingencies Act 2004, its Associated regulations and non-statutory arrangements. Retrieved from http://www.cabinetoffice.gov.uk/media/131903/emergprepfinal .pdf.; **6-3** © Dylan Martinez/Reuters/Landov; **6-4** Kapucu N. 2011. Collaborative Response to Act of Terrorism: A Comparative Network Analysis in Dynamic Environment. Forthcoming.; **6-5** Kapucu N. 2011. Collaborative Response to Act of Terrorism: A Comparative Network Analysis in Dynamic Environment. Forthcoming.; **6-Table 1** Kapucu N. 2011. Collaborative Response to Act of Terrorism: A Comparative Network Analysis in Dynamic Environment. Forthcoming.

Chapter 9

9-1 Reprinted from Public Relations Review, Vol 24, Burnett JJ, A Strategic Approach to Managing Crises, pp. 475–488., Copyright (1998) with permission from Elsevier.; **9-2** Reprinted from Public Relations Review, Vol 24, Burnett JJ, A Strategic Approach to Managing Crises, pp. 475–488., Copyright (1998) with permission from Elsevier.; **9-3** Kapucu, N., E.M. Berman, and X.H. Wang. 2008. Emergency Information Management and Public Disaster Preparedness: Lessons from the 2004 Florida Hurricane Season. International Journal of Mass Emergencies and Disasters. 26 3, 173.

Chapter 10

10-Table 1 Public Entity Risk Institute (PERI). 2001. Characteristics of Effective Emergency Management Organizational Structures. Fairfax: PERI.

Chapter 12

12-2 This material, from Six Months Into the Floods: Resetting Pakistan's priorities through reconstruction, 2011, is reproduced with the permission of Oxfam GB, Oxfam House, John Smith Drive, Crowley, Oxford OX4 2JY, UK www.oxfam.org.uk. Oxfam GB does not necessarily endorse any text or activities that accompany the materials.; **12-Table 1** Source: USAID, 2009.

Unless otherwise indicated, all photographs and illustrations are under copyright of Jones & Bartlett Learning or the author.

Some images in this book feature models. These models do not necessarily endorse, represent, or participate in the activities represented in the images.

Use of released U.S. Navy imagery does not constitute product or organizational endorsement of any kind by the U.S. Navy.